International Law in Asia

Series Editor

Eric Yong Joong Lee, #402 Taejin Bd, YIJUN Institute of International Law, Seoul, Korea (Republic of)

This series aims to provide the latest perspectives on international law in this ever changing region of Asia. Each book of this series will address specific aspect of highly contemporary global issues such as armed conflict, maritime disputes, human rights and refugee crises, sustainable development/climate change, outer space, finance and economy, trade (WTO and FTA), investment, development, technology, intellectual property, international crime, global health, regional questions, etc.

This book series invites leading international law scholars and practitioners in Asia to contribute their expertise in interpreting a wide range of legal questions that arise in relation to the above topics through an Asian lens. This series will serve as useful guide for international lawyers, diplomats, businessmen and students to understand current and future trends of international law in Asia.

Mohammad Zulfikar Ali

Worker Injustices in the South Asian Shipbreaking Industry

Developing a Framework for International Legal Accountability

Springer

Mohammad Zulfikar Ali
Curtin Law School
Curtin University
Perth, WA, Australia

ISSN 2731-8044 ISSN 2731-8052 (electronic)
International Law in Asia
ISBN 978-981-95-8324-9 ISBN 978-981-95-8325-6 (eBook)
https://doi.org/10.1007/978-981-95-8325-6

This Springer imprint is published by the registered company Springer Nature Singapore Pte Ltd.
The registered company address is: 152 Beach Road, #21-01/04 Gateway East, Singapore 189721, Singapore

Preface

The book examines the gaps in the international and national legal instruments of shipbreaking and argues for an international liability framework to address the worker injustices.

Shipbreaking is the process of breaking up old ships mainly for their steel. International shipping companies own and use ships for their trade and finally sell them predominantly to Bangladesh, India, and Pakistan for breaking up. As these South Asian countries have no iron ore deposits to support their growing steel demand, they need irons from ships and shipbreaking companies usually offer attractive prices to shipowners. The shipbreaking businesses in South Asian countries break ships on open beaches using dangerous manual methods that pollute the environment and cause deaths, injuries and diseases to workers in the shipbreaking industry, for which workers generally receive no compensation. Despite making good profits and knowing the problems, shipowners have not taken any responsibility for compensating shipbreaking workers. The book explores that these problems are likely to continue unless shipowners take responsibility for shipbreaking workers' deaths, injuries, and diseases by subscribing to a civil liability and compensation framework.

Considering the importance of rectificatory justice, international human rights law, and international maritime law—the book offers a unique approach to issues surrounding the global shipbreaking business. Drawing on the case studies of international civil liability frameworks introduced in international maritime sector and waste trade, the author introduces the debate to implement a rectificatory global justice framework examining the need for an international civil liability framework in the business of shipbreaking. The analysis is based on the relationship between sustainability in the workplace and human rights protection. The aspect of third world countries in relation to rectificatory global justice will also be highlighted through a discussion and criticism of shifting liability on South Asian countries for the expensive implementation of the Hong Kong Convention.

The book will be of great interest to scholars in the area of justice and international law, international human rights law and international liability law. Lawyers interested in international claim of compensation will also find the arguments useful placed in the book.

Bentley, Australia Mohammad Zulfikar Ali

Acknowledgements and Dedications I am extremely grateful to my examiner of Master's thesis, Professor Rosemary Rayfuse, for introducing me the topic of injustice in the shipbreaking industry in 2013. In her comments to my Master's thesis, she raised the question whether it was crucial to look into the issue of shipbreaking workers from a global perspective and propose a regulatory reform. As I researched more into the topic, I realised that I had to do something more to make a difference and that a civil liability framework that aims at changing the industry practice by a remedy system could be the answer.

My greatest debts are to Associate Professor Prafula Pearce, Edith Cowan University; Dr. Sharmin Tania, Curtin University; and Dr. Hugh Finn, Curtin University. They were my PhD supervisors and without their support, encouragement and advice nothing would have been possible. Prafula read a primary draft of the thesis. Her sharp comments and criticisms, reflecting her industry experience, have always been very useful in writing the thesis. Later, as I embarked on revising the research for the book, Sharmin and Hugh made valuable suggestions and read, commented on, and corrected various drafts of the chapters. I would like to extend my deepest gratitude to them for being a source of my inspiration and guidance and supporting me until the very end of the journey.

I am indebted to faculty members of Curtin Law School. I especially thank Professor Robert Cunningham, Professor Helen Hodgson, Dr. Anna Bunn, and anonymous reviewers at Curtin Law School, who all made helpful, acute, and provocative suggestions and criticisms. Many of their suggestions and criticisms have been taken into account in the final product.

At a personal level, I am deeply indebted to an endless list of people. Shahin, regional coordinator of the NGO Shipbreaking Platform walked with me through this journey. He shared his knowledge and resources. Bob, my engineer friend, has always listened with patience and kindness and shared his practical knowledge in industry regulation. I received similar support and encouragement from my friend and faculty member at Curtin Law School, Dr. Mostofa Haider. I am also grateful to my father-in-law for his kindness and affection. I also acknowledge Lynn's time and advice for providing me her editing assistance.

Last but not the least, I acknowledge my father and late mother who taught me to advocate for the disadvantaged segments of society. If not for this strong foundation rooted in making social change, I could not have recognised the need to pursue this journey to make a difference in the lives of the shipbreaking workers. I also thank my wife, Nahida and my two daughters, Rifah and Aakifa, for their sacrifices while I undertook this arduous journey.

I dedicate this book to the workers who faced deaths, injuries, or work-related diseases in the shipbreaking industry.

This book is also dedicated to my late mother for her endless love and wisdom that have made me who I am.

Competing Interests The author has no competing interests to declare that are relevant to the content of this manuscript.

Contents

Abbreviations

AD	Appellate Division
BAN	Basel Action Network
BC	Basel Convention
BDA	Balochistan Development Authority (Pakistan)
BELA	Bangladesh Environmental Lawyers' Association
BIMCO	Baltic and International Maritime Council. Trade Organisation representing shipowners, brokers, agents, and others
BMTF	Baia Mare Task Force
BSBA	Bangladesh Shipbreakers Association
CFC	Chlorofluorocarbon
Civ	Civil
Class NK	Nippon Kaiji Kyokai (Japanese Classification Society)
COP	Conference of Parties
CRISAL	Contract Regarding a Supplement to Tanker Liability for Oil Pollution
CSME	Centaurus Special Maritime Enterprise, a Liberian shipping company
CSR	Corporate Social Responsibility
DEFRA	Department of Environment, Food and Rural Affairs
DNV	Det Norske Veritas
DoE	Department of Environment (Bangladesh)
DWT	Deadweight tonnage—the carrying capacity of a ship when fully loaded, including cargo, bunkers, water (boilers, ballast and portable), stores, passengers, and crew
EC	European Community
ECA	Environmental Conversation Act (Bangladesh)
ECHR	European Court of Human Rights
EMSA	European Maritime Safety Agency
EU	European Union
EWCA	The Court of Appeal of England and Wales
EWHC	The High Court of Justice
FIDH	International Federation of Human Rights

FNV	Federati Nederlands Vakbeveging—a federation of Netherlands Trades Union
GMB	Gujarat Maritime Board
GMS	Global Marketing Systems (cash buyer)
GPCB	Gujarat Pollution Control Board
GT	Gross tonnage—the nonlinear measure of a ship's internal volume
HCD	High Court Division
HCFC	Hydrofluorocarbons
HKC	Hong Kong Convention
HRC	Human Rights Committee (UN)
IA	Intervention Application
ICHM	International Certificate on Inventory of Hazardous Materials
IEE	Initial Environmental Examination
IHM	Inventory of Hazardous Materials
ILC	International Law Commission
ILO	International Labour Organisation
ILO	International Labour Organization
ILPI	International Law and Policy Institute
IMCO	Inter-governmental Maritime Consultative Organisation
IMF	International Metal Workers' Federation
IMO	International Maritime Organization (UN)
IRRC	International Ready for Recycling Certificate
ISRA	International Ship Recyclers Association
ITOPF	International Tanker Owners Pollution Fund
LDT	Light displacement tonnage—the actual weight of the ship, excluding cargo, stores, fuel, ballast passengers and crew and used to calculate steel value of a ship
LNG	Liquefied Natural Gas
MARPOL	International Convention for the Prevention of Pollution from Ships 1973 as modified by the 1978 Protocol (MARPOL 73/78)
MEA	Multilateral Environmental Agreement
MEPC	Marine Environment Protection Committee
MoEF	Ministry of Environment and Forest (Bangladesh)
MoU	Memorandum of Understanding
MTS	Maran Tankers Ship holdings Limited
NGO	Non-Government Organisation
NOC	No Objection Certificate
OCIMF	Oil Companies International Marine Forum
OECD	Organisation of Economic Co-operation and Development
OEWG	Open-ended Working Group
PAHs	Polycyclic Aromatic Hydrocarbons
PCBs	Polychlorinated Biphenyls
PIC	Prior Informed Consent
PIL	Public Interest Litigation
PLD	Pakistan Legal Decision

PPE	Personal Protective Equipments
QB	Queen's Bench
RINA	Royal Institute of Naval Architects. Also Registro Italiane Navale Classification Society
RMG	Readymade Garments
SC	Supreme Court
SDPI	Sustainable Development and Policy Institute
SDR	Special Drawing Rights (Currency defined by the International Monetary Fund)
SLC	Shipbreaking Liability Certificate
SPCB	State Pollution Control Board
SRF	Ship Recycling Facility
SRO	Statutory Regulatory Order (Bangladesh)
SRP	Ship Recycling Plan
SRR	Ship Recycling Regulation
STOPIA	Small Tanker Oil Pollution Indemnification Agreement
TBT	Tributyltin
TBTO	Tributyltin Oxide
TOPIA	Tanker Oil Pollution Indemnification Agreement
TOVALOP	Tanker Owners Voluntary Agreement Concerning Liability for Oil Pollution
UKHL	The United Kingdom House of Lords
ULCC	Ultra Large Crude Carrier, Tanker of 320,000 DWT and above
UN	United Nations
UNCLOS	United Nations Convention on the Law of the Sea 1982
UNCTAD	United Nations Conference on Trade and Development
UNECE	United Nations Economic Commission for Europe
UNEP	United Nations Environmental Program
UNGA	United Nations General Assembly
UNGP	United Nations Guiding Principles
VLCC	Very Large Crude Carrier, Tanker of 200,000 to 320,000 DWT
WSR	Waste Shipment Regulation
WTO	World Trade Organisation
YPSA	Young Power in Social Action

List of Figures

List of Tables

Chapter 1
Introduction

Abstract The introductory chapter provides an overview of human rights issues and highlights the importance of a civil liability framework for the shipbreaking industry. Shipbreaking is an essential industry practice for the global maritime industry because it involves resolving its overcapacity problem in merchant fleets. However, workplace deaths, injuries, and diseases are the main downsides of the shipbreaking industry. The reason is that international shipowners earn millions of dollars from selling ships to South Asia. But they can escape responsibility for both paying compensation and ensuring safe working conditions through an opaque transfer process, by which a ship is taken out of service and sold for breaking without exposing the chain of ownership from cradle to grave. The involvement of shipowners in the transfer process but the absence of an international mechanism to address the issue of providing adequate compensation to harmed workers signifies flaws and injustices in the governance structure of the shipbreaking and maritime industries.

Keywords Human rights · Workplace · Compensation · Shipbreaking · Shipowners · Chain of ownership · Injustice · Governance structure · Maritime industry · Civil liability framework · Overcapacity problems

Prologue

Shipbreaking industry poses high risk to both workers and the environment. International Labour Organisation (ILO) has identified shipbreaking as one of the most hazardous occupations, frequently resulting in fatalities, especially within South

Note: Part of this chapter has been published in two journals. The references are mentioned below:

1. 'Shipbreaking Industry- Responsibility of the Maritime Industry' (November 2020) 19 *Perspective Australian New Zealand Society of International Law* 20–26.
2. 'The South Asian Shipbreaking Industry and its Unsafe Mining Practices' (2020) *Aspects of Mining and Mineral Science* 565–568.

M. Z. Ali, *Worker Injustices in the South Asian Shipbreaking Industry*, International Law in Asia, https://doi.org/10.1007/978-981-95-8325-6_1

Asian shipbreaking operations.[1] Countries in South Asia—including Bangladesh, India, and Pakistan—are responsible for dismantling approximately 90% of the world's end-of-life ships, as they provide attractive purchase prices to global shipowners.[2] In 2023, Human Rights Watch, an international organisation expressed concern over shipbreaking practices in South Asia, describing them as a major international human rights issue that negatively impacts several fundamental rights, such as the right to life, the right to maintain sound physical and mental health and the right to safe working conditions.[3]

While shipbreaking is an issue of human rights violations, it is beneficial to global shipping industry addressing merchant fleets' overcapacity issue. Shipowners only decide to dispose of their end-of-life ships when their commercial operational life becomes less profitable.[4] But in limited cases, the global shipping industry considers the concerns with the shipbreaking process in South Asia, where accidents, fatalities, and occupational diseases are prevalent.[5] More than one hundred workers die and many face serious physical injuries every year.[6]

Shipbreaking workers are exposed to hazardous substances such as mutagens, carcinogens, and asbestos-containing materials that is responsible for various health risks, including short-term and long-term diseases. Because of the dangerous and labour-intensive nature of shipbreaking, they also suffer traumatic and other injuries. Regardless of these significant occupational health and safety concerns,[7] there is no dedicated international or regional legal framework that focuses on providing adequate compensation for workers affected by fatal accidents, injuries, or work-related illness.

Shipowners profit substantially from selling their vessels to South Asian shipbreaking yards,[8] but they often evade accountability for ensuring safe labour conditions or offering compensation. This is made possible through a complex transfer

---

[1] International Labour Organisation, *Shipbreaking: A Hazardous Work* (Webpage) https://www.ilo.org/resource/ship-breaking-hazardous-work-0 ; Greenpeace, YPSA and FIDH, '*End-of-Life Ships: The Human Cost of Breaking Ships*' (online 2005) https://www.fidh.org/IMG/pdf/shipbreaking/2005a.pdf

[2] Lin et al., 'Hazardous Waste from the Global Shipbreaking Industry: Historical Inventory and Future Pathways' (2022) 76 *Global Environmental Challenge* 1, 2–6.

[3] Human Rights Watch, *Trading Lives for Profit: How the Shipping Industry Circumvents Regulations to Scrap Toxic Ships on Bangladesh's Beaches* (28 September 2023). *(Human Rights Watch on Shipbreaking).*

[4] Md Shakhaoat Hossain et al., 'Impact of Shipbreaking activities on the coastal Environment of Bangladesh and a Management System for its Sustainability' (2016) 60 *Environmental Science and Policy* 84–94.

[5] Hasan Ruhan Rabbi and Aevelina Rahman, Shipbreaking and Recycling Industry of Bangladesh: Issues and Challenges (2017) 194 *Procedia Engineering* 254–259.

[6] See Chapter 3 for detailed statistics on this.

[7] Anand M. Hiremath, Sachin Kumar Panday, and Shyam R. Asolekar, 'Development of Ship-specific Recycling Plan to Improve Health Safety and Environment in Ship Recycling Yards' (2016) *Journal of Cleaner Production* 279, 280.

[8] See Chapter 3 that explains that yearly income of the maritime industry is around 2400 million USD from selling ships to South Asia; also see Ozan Sahiner, *Ship Breaking – Is It the Answer to*

process that removes ships from operation and sells them for breaking without revealing the full ownership chain (discussed in section "Background" below).

Want of responsibility of shipowners in paying adequate compensation brings into the question of accountability for the human consequences that occur within South Asia's shipbreaking industry. This raises the question of whether they ought to bear responsibility for deaths, injuries, and work-related diseases under a new international civil liability framework.[9]

The book is a response to the above inquiry and the legal gap that follows a proposal for introducing an international framework, which is to impose civil liability on shipowners. A key contribution of the book is its proposal for a mandatory shipbreaking liability certificate (SLC) and shipbreaking liability insurance for all shipowners under the international civil liability framework, requiring them to take financial responsibility for the consequences of an end-of-life ship and to actively work towards safer shipbreaking practices. While the proposed SLC framework does not directly address environmental concerns, it could contribute to minimising them by promoting sound shipbreaking practices. The extent of this impact depends on the effectiveness of the international civil liability framework, which is examined in Chap. 9 of the book.

Background

Responsibility for adequate compensation payments and changes in industry practices must lie primarily with international shipowners. However, the regulatory approach introduced under the *Hong Kong International Convention for the Safe and Environmentally Sound Recycling* (*Hong Kong Convention*) is weak on the issue of responsibility of international shipowners.[10] A reason for this is that the *Hong Kong Convention* does little to impose liability on shipowners for the uncontrolled health and safety issues of shipbreaking workers. It is silent about how shipowners can support shipbreaking facilities based in Bangladesh, India, and Pakistan (South Asian shipbreaking industry) who contribute 90% to the total capacity of global shipbreaking activity but lack the financial capacity to create safe working and environmental protection arrangements in their yards.[11]

The Shipping Industry's Overcapacity Problem?(Blog Post, 24 February 2017) https://www.morethanshipping.com/ship-breaking-answer-shipping-industrys-overcapacity-problem/

[9] Mohammad Zulfikar Ali, 'Injustice to Workers in the Shipbreaking Industry in South Asia: A Quest for a Civil Liability Framework in International Law' (PhD Thesis, Curtin University, 2022) 2–3.

[10] *The Hong Kong International Convention for the Safe and Environmentally Sound Recycling of Ships*, opened for Signature 1 September 2009, IMO Doc. SR/CONF45 (entered into force 26 June 2025).

[11] Mohammad Zulfikar Ali and Prafula Pearce, Effectiveness of the Hong Kong Convention on Ship Recycling in India, Bangladesh, and Pakistan 2019 (6) *Curtin Law and Taxation Review* 69, 80–81.

The question to pay compensation or support shipbreaking facilities should mainly be the responsibility of the South Asian shipbreaking industry, but the business model promoted by the maritime industry is the principal reason why shipbreaking industries face difficulties to protect their workers from these extreme consequences and to pay adequate compensation. The problem with the business model is explained in Chapter 3 of the book, which suggests that the South Asian shipbreaking facilities must offer high purchase price to shipowners of end-of-life ships—which accounts for 82% of the total shipbreaking cost. Consequently, after spending the large amount for purchasing ships, their ability to improve workplace health and safety, or to pay an adequate amount of compensation becomes limited.[12] Problems identified below in sections "Problems with the Inter-State Transfer Process of Ships" to "Weaknesses in the Application of International Legal Frameworks" have also created a situation for Bangladesh, India, and Pakistan to run the dangerous shipbreaking industry as it is, without imposing any liability on shipowners.[13]

Problems with the Inter-State Transfer Process of Ships

A problematic transfer process makes it hard to impose liability on shipowners for the human consequences that occur at the end of life of a ship. The final journey of a ship begins once a sale agreement is reached between the shipowner and a temporary buyer, commonly referred to as a cash buyer. A cash buyer's role in the inter-State transfer process of a ship is simply to purchase a ship with cash and resell it—usually to a shipbreaking facility in South Asia—using a letter of credit (L/C) as the mode of transaction.

Typically, the procedure starts with the cash buyer paying 10% of the ship's value as a booking deposit to the shipowner. Shipowners generally favour the involvement of a cash buyer as it eliminates the potential for price renegotiations, locking in the sale price from the outset. Given the volatility of steel prices, shipbreaking facilities may attempt to lower the purchase price if market conditions shift unfavourably. Cash buyers absorb the financial risk and ensure the agreed payment to shipowners. This is the reason why 90% of the world's old ships travel to shipbreaking facilities through this dominant brokerage service.[14] This means that the transfer process, which ultimately leads to the ship being broken at a shipbreaking facility, involves multiple stakeholders and established industry practices.[15] In *Hamida Begum v Maran (UK) Limited*, for instance, the Court of Appeal of England and Wales observed that

---

[12] Ali, 'Injustice to Workers in the Shipbreaking Industry in South Asia (n 9).

[13] Wei-Te Wu et al., 'Cancer Attributable to Asbestos Exposure in Shipbreaking Workers: A Matched-Cohort Study' (2015) 10(7) *Plos One* 6, 6.

[14] Tony George Puthurcherril, *From Shipbreaking to Sustainable Ship Recycling: Evolution of a Legal Regime* (Matinus Nijhoff Publishers, 2010) 32.

[15] Cash buyers or brokers who purchase ships from the original owners and negotiate the sale with shipbreaking yards also fall into the category of short-term shipowners.

Maran (UK) Limited (Maran)—a company incorporated under the laws of Cayman Islands—acted in the capacity of demolition broker for the vessel known as the Maran Centaurus. Maran arranged for the vessel's sale to the Zuma shipbreaking facility in Bangladesh through the intermediary services of Hsejar Maritime Inc., a cash buying entity registered in Nevis.[16] Facts of *Hamida Begum* suggest that Maran undertook inquiries, obtained quotes for selling the vessel, and facilitated the negotiation process through the engagement of the cash buyer, Hsejar Maritime Inc. The cash buyer also assumed the credit risk associated with the transaction—estimated at approximately USD 16 million.[17] On 5 September 2017, Hsejar Maritime Inc. reflagged the ship from Greece to Palau and renamed it EKTA. Departing from Singapore with a very low quantity of fuel reserves on 22 September 2017, the ship arrived at a shipbreaking facility in Bangladesh on 30 September 2017,[18] where it was subsequently dismantled (A more detailed analysis of this case is provided in Chap. 2).[19]

Besides taking credit risk, the principal benefit of involving a cash buyer is to conceal the national identity of a shipowner. This eventually allows a shipowner to circumvent costly regulatory restrictions of precleaning. Using cash buyers, an example of regulation that is circumvented by the shipowners is the European Union (EU) *Waste Shipment Regulation* that does not allow a ship transfer beyond the EU jurisdiction for breaking unless the exporting State or the owner precleans the toxic materials found in the body of a ship.[20] The requirement of precleaning is also crucial under relevant international legal frameworks. The *Basel Convention on the Control of the Transboundary Movement of Hazardous Wastes and their Disposal (Basel Convention)* (discussed in Chap. 5) is a key international instrument addressing this issue.[21] Importantly, an amendment to the *Basel Convention* that is effective from December 2019 restricts the export of waste from the member countries of the Organisation of the Economic Cooperation and Development (OECD) non-OECD

---

[16] *Hamida Begum (on behalf of MD Khalil Mollah) v Maran (UK) Limited* [2021] EWCA Civ 326. (10 March 2021) *(Maran Shipping)* [8]*;* See also Jamie Curle, Sarah Ellington and Daniel D'Ambrosio, *Shipping Agent Potentially Responsible for Alleged Negligent Disposal of Ship in Bangladesh* (Web Page, 3 August 2020), https://www.lexology.com/library/detail.aspx?g=84ba8284-3468-4d9b-82ec-6103bf4051cc.

[17] Ibid [8].

[18] Ibid [13].

[19] Ibid.

[20] *Regulation No 1013/2006 of the European Parliament and of the Council on the Shipment of Wastes* [2006] OJL 190/1. *(Waste Shipment Regulation)*; David Azoulay and Nathaniel Eisen, 'Legality of the EU Commission Proposal on Ship Recycling' (Research Report No 1101, Centre of International Environmental Law, December 2012) 3 https://www.shipbreakingplatform.org/wp-content/uploads/2020/09/CIEL-Legality-EU-Proposals-on-Ship-Recycling-2020.pdf.

[21] *The Basel Convention on the Control of Trans-boundary Movements of Hazardous Wastes and their Disposal*, opened for signature 22 March 1989, 1673 UNTS 126 (entered into force 5 May 1992) (*The Basel Convention*) United Nations Environment Program, *Basel Convention Controlling Transboundary Movements of Hazardous Wastes and Their Disposal* (Web Page, Overview) http://www.basel.int/TheConvention/Overview/tabid/1271/Default.aspx

countries.[22] These legal constraints are circumvented by shipowners from developed countries engaging cash buyers as intermediary owners. Cash buyers obscure the original ownership by altering a ship's name and national registry—commonly known as reflagging or change of ownership. As a ship cannot sail on international water without flying flag of a State, reflagging is used to change a ship's original flag State to a new flag State for a temporary period. Reflagging, which may take as little as 24 to 48 h through online platforms, can occur multiple times before a vessel arrives at a shipbreaking facility.[23]

The NGO Shipbreaking Platform, an international organisation that investigates the legal and factual matters of shipbreaking practices characterises reflagging practice as a deliberate process of severing the 'genuine link between a country that operates the ship for international trade and its flag of a country (with which it sails before arriving a shipbreaking facility)'.[24] Breaking the link enables the shipowners to sell ships without transparency regarding onboard hazardous materials. Such nondisclosure of waste stored in a ship's body has led to severe consequences, particularly in South Asian countries, which often lack the infrastructure to detect and handle these hazardous substances responsibly.

Considering the issues related to cash buyers' involvement, a proper legal approach is to apply international law principles, mitigate risky waste disposal practices, and compel responsible entities to provide an adequate remedy to shipbreaking workers (see Chap. 2). In regulating a business, remedy follows an enquiry of adequate safety and prevention in the workplace. Supporting the claim of an adequate remedy framework, the next section is used to examine the extent to which preventive measures can be effectively implemented under current practices in South Asian shipbreaking sector.

Problems with Shipbreaking Methods in South Asia

South Asian shipbreaking industry uses three problematic methods leading to poor prevention system.[25] First, international shipowners send their old ships to South Asian shipbreaking facilities without following the process of precleaning.[26] Because

---

[22] United Nations Environment Program, *Decision III/1: Amendment to the Basel Convention on the Control of Transboundary Movement of Hazardous Wastes and Their Disposal*, 22 September 1995, UN Doc UNEP/CHW.3/35 (entered into force 5 December 2019).

[23] Puthurcherril (n 12) 32.

[24] Flag State is the country where a ship is registered. It may be different from its original country of registration where a ship is primarily registered for commercial operation: at NGO Shipbreaking Platform, *Flag of Convenience* (Web Page) https://www.shipbreakingplatform.org/issues-of-interest/focs/

[25] Shafat Hosen et al., 'Impact of Shipbreaking Industries on the Sitakunda Coastal Environment, Chattogram by Analysing Water Quality Parameters' 2025 (211) *Marine Pollution Bulletin* 1, 1–3.

[26] Precleaning refers to the procedure which aims at the shipping companies to remove all hazardous substances stored in the body of a ship before a ship is delivered to a shipbreaking facility for

of this, ships remain highly contaminated with hazardous materials, such as asbestos, heavy metals, mineral oil, bilge and ballast water, Polycyclic Aromatic Hydrocarbons (PAHs), Polychlorinated Biphenyls (PCBs), Tributyltin (TBT), lead paints, mercury, fuel deposits, and other harmful substances (inbuilt waste or internal waste) at their arrival for breaking in South Asia.[27] Exposure of these inbuilt wastes harms water, air, and soil quality in the surrounding environment in absence of their proper identification, removal, and disposal.[28] Lack of expertise in handling these inbuilt wastes is also responsible for work-related diseases or explosions and the death of dozens of workers.

Second, beaching is the common method used to break ships in South Asia; thus, rather than using a platform, shipbreaking facilities clean the ships on shallow open beaches, which is not generally far away from coastal mangrove forests. The only thing which is required for beaching is to anchor ships on sandy beaches and to make sure that the ships are brought as close as possible to the intertidal zones of coastal areas. The principal reason for using the beaching method is to save cost and break ships without the use of expensive safety structures. Although beaching method saves cost of shipbreaking in South Asia, problems arise when the South Asian shipbreaking industry releases the harmful substances into the sea directly. Such uncontrolled discharge of ships' hazardous materials causes widespread environmental damage, including air pollution, degradation and contamination of soil, water pollution, harm to coastal ecosystems, and a significant decline in biodiversity.[29] Particularly, the release of ships' hazardous materials is not only a cause of damaging the mangrove forests but it is also harmful for critical habitats.[30] Examples of the impact of pollution from the shipbreaking industry include 'toxic hotspots' or 'sacrifice zones' in Alang, India, Sitakunda, Bangladesh and Gadani, Pakistan.[31]

Third, in South Asia, workers use dangerous manual methods to break ships. Examples of the manual methods include cutting ships with blowtorches or transporting heavy metal plates on shoulder—practices that regularly lead to worker injuries and fatalities. Common incidents include explosions from undetected gases within ship chambers that accounts for forty-nine per cent of the total accidents.

---

breaking. Ensuring the precleaning is the key issue since the shipbreaking sector in South Asia negates this process due to technical and physical incapacity that create the environmental and safety issues. Kit Chapman, 'The Toxic Tide of Ship Breaking' *Chemistry World* (Blog Post, 21 February 2022) https://www.chemistryworld.com/features/the-toxic-tide-of-ship-breaking/4015158.article.

[27] Sakhawat Sajjat Sejan et al., 'A Critical Analysis of Legal Regime of Shipbreaking and Ship Recycling in Bangladesh' (2024) 4 (1) *Journal of Environmental Law and Policy* 54, 56–60.

[28] Hosen et al. (n 25).

[29] Ibid 6–7.

[30] Camelia Dewan and Elizabeth A. Silbia, 'Global Containments and Local Linkages: Structural Violence and the Toxic Flows of Shipbreaking' (2024) 42(1) *Environmental and Planning C: Politics and Space* 80, 84-90.

[31] International Metalworkers Federation, 'Special Report: Cleaning up shipbreaking the world's most dangerous job' (Research Report, 15 December, 2015) 10 http://www.industriall-union.org/cleaning-up-ship-breaking-the-worlds-most-dangerous-job.

Twenty per cent of the accidents occur for plates and parts of ships falling on the workers during a shipbreaking process. Further, inhalation of harmful chemicals contributes to sixteen per cent of the total fatalities and workers falling from significant heights results in eight per cent accident rates in the shipbreaking industry.[32] Study in relation to long-term exposure to hazardous materials from end-of-life ships found that thirty-five per cent of workers have asbestos-related diseases from long term.[33]

Building on the issues explained above, the next section explores whether an injured or sick worker or the family members of a deceased worker can seek an adequate amount of compensation under the current workplace environment in the South Asian shipbreaking industry.

Lack of Transparency in the Employment System and Limited Scope to Claim Financial Remedies

Claiming an adequate amount of compensation is challenging for injured workers or the families of those who have lost their lives while working in the shipbreaking sector.[34] A family member of a dead worker may receive compensation between USD 341 and USD 2273,[35] from the owners of a shipbreaking facility. However, such payments are generally made on a discretionary basis and often only when incidents receive public attention through national newspapers or electronic media, making them difficult to ignore. Media coverage generally does not focus on an incident unless the number of casualties is high, meaning that smaller-scale incidents go unreported. This suggests that a substantial number of workplace injuries and fatalities may neither be acknowledged nor compensated. Evidence from Bangladesh also indicates that, in order to receive such a small amount of compensation injured workers or the family members of a deceased worker often compel to sign a no-claim agreement.[36] The no-claim agreement effectively absolves shipbreaking facility owners of any future legal accountability, demonstrating that the compensation payment is no more than a discretionary power of the shipbreaking facility owners. This exploitative arrangement is closely linked to the industry's opaque appointment system, which

[32] Hosen et al. (n 25) 7.

[33] Venkiteswaran Muralidhar, Md Faizul Ahasan, and Ahad Mahmud Khan, 'Parenchymal Asbestosis Due to Primary Asbestos Exposure Among Ship-breaking Workers: Report of the First Cases from Bangladesh' (2017) *BMJ Case Report* 1, 4.

[34] International Metalworkers Federation, 'Metal World' (2011) 2 *The Biannual Magazine*, 16.

[35] Puthurcherril (n 14) 36.

[36] Saiful Karim, *Shipbreaking in Developing Countries: A Requiem for Environmental Justice from the Perspectives of Bangladesh* (Taylor and Francis Group, 2018) 105–106; Taqbir Huda, 'Justice in Practice: Why is the Price of Killing a Worker only Tk 2 Lakh' *The Daily Star e-paper* (online 11 July 2021) E-paper http://epaper.thedailystar.net .

lacks transparency and enables employers to avoid responsibility for paying compensation to affected workers. Sections "Opaque Appointment System" and "No Job Contract, Appointment Letter or Identity Card" will further examine the inequities of this system.

Opaque Appointment System

Shipbreaking is a labour-intensive job that requires a significant number of workers, but there is no direct employment relationship between employers and workers. Workers cut ships with bare hands and carry heavy steel plates on their shoulders—two of the commonly used conventional practices in the shipbreaking industry. Workers mostly perform these tasks with no personal protective equipment that create significant workplace risks.[37] Owners of the shipbreaking facilities avoid the liability of the risks by an indirect appointment system. Their appointment is outsourced to contractors who work as managers in the shipbreaking facilities.[38] Accordingly, workers remain directly in touch with the contractors in the workplace instead of the facility owners. Workers consider their accountability to the contractors for their total employment period. The orders and decisions of the managers are final for them.[39] The involvement of managers thus breaks the direct legal link between employers and workers.[40]

No Job Contract, Appointment Letter or Identity Card

Workers are not generally provided with a job contract, appointment letter or an identity card in the shipbreaking industry. Absence of any of these documents leads to the deprivation of their workplace rights since they join. Contractors who work as managers do not issue a letter of appointment or any identification (ID) card or enrol them as workers.[41] Worker's particulars are not also maintained in a record book.[42] A worker's legal status eventually remains weak in a shipbreaking facility. Such weak status of workers is beneficial to both long and short-term shipowners who can deny the employment status of workers. This allows the owners to escape liability as employer and provide compensation to workers.

---

[37] Hosen et al. (n 25).

[38] International Metal Workers Foundation (n 34) 12.

[39] Antoine Bernard (ed) '*Where Do the Floating Dustbins End Up? Labour Rights in Ship Breaking Yards in South Asia: the Cases of Chittagong (Bangladesh) and Alang (India)*' (International Federation for Human Rights, December 2002) 1–10.

[40] Ibid 19–21.

[41] Karim (n 36) 126.

[42] Ibid.

The above three sections ("Problems with the Inter-State Transfer Process of Ships" to "Lack of Transparency in the Employment System and Limited Scope to Claim Financial Remedies") demonstrate the business model of the shipbreaking industry, which creates regulatory imbalances through transboundary movement of ships, risky shipbreaking practices, and non-transparent labour practices. The shipbreaking business model supports the global maritime sector and boosts economies in South Asian through employment and recycled steel, but these benefits often overshadow the severe risks faced by workers.[43] The benefits of the industry are crucial for economic development of the South Asian shipbreaking industry, but the benefits must not come at the expense of uncompensated deaths, injuries, and exposure to the diseases of shipbreaking workers. Existing legal and regulatory mechanisms prioritise economic gains over human welfare, revealing significant gaps in governance and academic discourse. These shortcomings raise two pressing concerns about how the shipbreaking industry is regulated, discussed in the following sections.

Limited Possibilities for Domestic Reforms in South Asian Countries

In the context of national law, individual State mechanisms to comply with worker safety and environmental standards in South Asian nations have so far been unsuccessful without required support from the international shipowners.[44] Some shipbreaking countries have implemented stricter regulatory frameworks, but shipping companies have not supported these countries. They have rather shifted their business to jurisdictions with more lenient regulatory oversight. For example, between 2005 and 2006, when India implemented stricter regulations, the shipbreaking industry in Bangladesh benefitted, with a sharp rise in the number of ships being taken there for breaking. This trend highlights the challenge faced by States attempting regulatory reforms. It is therefore doubtful to have significant domestic legislative reforms to better safeguard worker health and safety. Reasons for the doubt include concerns that greater compliance costs (and consequent reductions in the prices offered for ships) will cause businesses to go to other competing shipbreaking locations within

[43] International Maritime Organisation introduced the *Hong Kong Convention* specifically to regulate the shipbreaking industry considering that shipbreaking industry is a part of the maritime sector. See Md Saiful Karim, 'Recycling of Ships' in *Prevention of Pollution of the Maritime Environment from Vessels: The Potential Limit and Limits of the International Maritime Organisation* (Springer, 2016) 85–90.

[44] Although ships operate on international waters and shipbreaking occurs within national jurisdictions, this jurisdictional division does not disapprove the application of international law. Application of international law is compelling where there exists a commercial nexus between international actors—such as shipping companies or private owners—and domestic shipbreaking facilities: at Tony George Puthurcherril 'Limitations of a National Response to Regulate Global Shipbreaking Industry - A Study of the Indian Experience' in David Freestone (ed), *From Shipbreaking to Sustainable Ship Recycling: Evolution of a Legal Regime* (Matinus Nijhoff Publishers, 2010) 53.

South Asia (and possibly elsewhere). The competition of regime creates a 'race to the bottom' situation for workers.[45] The book thus proposes an international mechanism that addresses the root of this problem.

Weaknesses in the Application of International Legal Frameworks

Until 2009, the only international regulatory mechanism for the shipbreaking industry was the *Basel Convention*. The *Basel Convention*'s objective is to reduce the generation of waste and restrict the movement of waste, through measures aimed at keeping waste closest to the place of production. However, shipowners circumvent the *Basel Convention* by arguing that the Convention only applies to the transfer of wastes, not ships. Since a ship is not waste, the central argument has been that the transfer of ships for breaking is beyond the scope of the *Basel Convention*. The core problem for the application of the *Basel Convention* to the shipbreaking industry is definitional, namely, whether ships are 'wastes'. Art 2(1) of the *Basel Convention* is relevant as it defines 'wastes' as 'substances or objects, which are disposed of, or are intended to be disposed of, or are required to be disposed of by the provisions of national law'.[46] Therefore, the legal transformation of a ship to waste depends on whether the owner or the management company 'intends' the ship to be 'wastes'. This approach means that the *Basel Convention* only applies to the shipbreaking industry if it can be inferred—whether expressly, such as by a declaration of intent, or by the conduct of the shipowner—that the owner or the management company intends that the ship is on its last journey for dismantling. The intention must be deduced from the express or implied activities of the immediate owner; if the immediate owner does not evince such an intention (whether expressly or by their conduct), then the *Basel Convention* cannot be applied.

In response to the difficulty of applying the *Basel Convention* to older ships, the International Maritime Organisation (IMO) adopted the *Hong Kong Convention*. The *Hong Kong Convention* has introduced a 'cradle-to-grave approach' for ensuring occupational safety and health. According to this approach, flag States must prepare an inventory of hazardous materials (IHMs) for each ship before starting their commercial operation. The IHM requires that detailed information about the toxic substances contained in the ship be prepared and maintained as a written record. Regulation 5(4) of *the Regulation for Safe and Environmentally Sound Recycling of Ships, 2009* (adopted under the *Hong Kong Convention*) provides that at the completion of the lifecycle of a ship,[47] flag States are required to supply the IHM to the

---

[45] Ali (n 9) 11.

[46] In general, the *Basel Convention* regulates the inter-State movement of wastes.

[47] *The Hong Kong International Convention for the Safe and Environmentally Sound Recycling of Ships*, opened for Signature 1 September 2009, IMO Doc. SR/CONF45 (entered into force 26 June 2025) Annex ('*Regulation for Safe and Environmentally Sound Recycling of Ships)* provides that

shipbreaking industry or the recycler. Every shipbreaking industry must then prepare a ship-specific plan ('the plan') for breaking with respect to a ship's IHM. Under reg 16 of *the Regulation for Safe and Environmentally Sound Recycling of Ships, 2009*, the plan is required to include all the information regarding the management of hazardous materials identified by the IHM. Therefore, under the *Hong Kong Convention*, the shipbreaking industry is required to meet certain standards in 'the area of planning' and 'training to workers' in cases of emergency operation, preparedness for accidents and spills, and other matters.[48]

With these new approaches, the *Hong Kong Convention* has entered into force on 26 June in 2025.[49] The principal argument against the effectiveness of the *Hong Kong Convention* is that the *Hong Kong Convention* does not include a mandatory obligation on shipping companies for 'precleaning' toxic ships before sending them to developing countries. Instead, the *Regulation for Safe and Environmentally Sound Recycling of Ships* merely provides that 'ships destined to be recycled shall conduct operations in the period prior to entering into the ship recycling yard to minimise the amount of cargo residues, fuel oil, and wastes remaining on board'.[50] This means that shipowners have no liability to preclean their ships before the ships start their last journey. The *Hong Kong Convention* also does not question the issues of tightening ownership from cradle to grave, precleaning, beaching, and conventional shipbreaking practices (see Chap. 5).

Despite these major weaknesses as an international legal instrument for regulating the shipbreaking industry, the maritime industry argues that the *Hong Kong Convention* is appropriate and is capable of resolving any problems; therefore, it is unnecessary to consider the question of liability for work-related deaths, injuries, and diseases

---

every ship is required to keep a certificate on Inventory of Hazardous Materials (IHM) to provide notice about existing toxic materials of a running ship: at reg 5(4). ('*Regulation on International Ship Recycling*').

48 *Regulation on International Ship Recycling*, regs 18(1) and 18(4).

49 There are three requirements to entry into force of the *Hong Kong Convention*. First, the *Hong Kong Convention* requires 15 States, second, it requires the States that have acceded to it or have ratified it represent not less than 40 per cent of the world's merchant shipping fleets. The critical part for the *Hong Kong Convention*'s entry into force is its third condition, which provides that the combined maximum annual ship recycling volume of the States that have acceded to it or have ratified it must constitute not less than 3% of their combined merchant shipping tonnage. Data on shipbreaking between 2007 and 2018 shows that the States acceded into the Convention have capacity of 1714,973 GT only, which is much less than the required 16,003,720 gross tonnage (i.e. 3% of the tonnage condition of 533,457, 349 gross tonnage of their combined fleets) to meet the 3% capacity. After Liberia and Bangladesh acceded into the *Hong Kong Convention* on 23 June 2023, the capacity has increased to meet the required level. After two years of cooling off period, the Hong Kong Convention entered into force in 26 June 2025: See generally Nikos Mikelis, 'The Recycling of Ships' (2018) April, *Future of the Ship Recycling Sector* 27; Nikos Mikelis, 'The Recycling of Ships' (2nd ed, *Global Marketing System*, October 2019) 36–38; International Maritime Organisation, *Recycling of Ships and the Hong Kong Convention* (Webpage) https://www.imo.org/en/MediaCentre/HotTopics/Pages/Recycling-of-ships-and-Hong-Kong-Convention.aspx#:~:text=The%20Hong%20Kong%20International%20Convention,force%20on%2026%20June%202025 .

50 *Regulation on International Ship Recycling*, regs 5(1), 17.

suffered by workers or to tighten the change in ownership from cradle to grave.[51] The question of liability can still be raised because a treaty-based civil liability mechanism can address the liability of both long-term and short-term shipowners for work-related deaths, injuries, and diseases while breaking their end-of-life ships.[52] Moreover, a civil liability mechanism with financial liability of all shipowners,[53] across the life span of a ship, will enhance workplace protection and change industry practices.

The question of global injustice and its remedy by applying the theory of rectificatory justice is raised as a theoretical basis for the civil liability mechanism proposed in the book. The question of injustice is relevant with respect to the imbalance between the profit earned by international shipowners based in developed countries and the economic loss of workers in the shipbreaking industry in South Asia. The question of global injustice is also relevant to shipbreaking industries in South Asia because shipowners promote the industry in South Asia for their profit only besides having knowledge about South Asia's poor shipbreaking practices and employment standards.

Remedying Injustices in the Shipbreaking Industry: Rectificatory Justice Approach

Rectificatory justice is a theoretical framework aimed specifically at addressing an injustice caused by an imbalance between two parties. The philosophical approach for this book is thus the rectificatory global justice approach,[54] with a focus on remedying an injustice.[55] The proposition that 'a regulatory system is required when an injustice is globally constructed' underpins the theoretical framework.[56]

The theoretical framework is adopted with the aim of remedying future injustice rather than rectifying past injustices.[57] It acknowledges that the current problems, such as beaching, transferring ships to developing countries for breaking without

---

[51] Maersk, 'Breaking the Stalemate' *Case Studies* (Web Page, 25 October 2019) https://www.maersk.com/news/articles/2017/01/03/breaking-the-stalemate.

[52] Maersk, 'Maersk Tightens Its Ship Recycling Procedures', *Case Studies* (Web page, 04 April 2019) https://www.maersk.com/news/articles/2019/04/04/maersk-tightens-its-ship-recycling-procedures.

[53] *The Basel Convention on the Control of Transboundary Movements of Hazardous Wastes and their Disposal*, opened for signature 22 March 1989, 1673 UNTS 126 (entered into force 5 May 1992), art 12. *(Basel Convention).*

[54] See Goran Collste, *Global Rectificatory Justice* (Palgrave McMillan, 1st ed, 2015) 17.

[55] Ibid.

[56] Gregory Ticehurst and Anthony Veal, *Business Research Methods: A Managerial Approach* (Pearson Education, 2000).

[57] Goran Collste referred some to historical injustice issues to apply the theory of rectificatory justice. His study acknowledges the past abuse of human rights in the context of shipbreaking, but it proposes to use it for regulating future injustice instead of the past abuses: at Collste (n 54) 76–77.

precleaning, and the manual labour and workplace hazards inherent to traditional shipbreaking methods, as unfortunate necessities, may not be phased out soon.[58]

Before establishing a case to use the rectificatory justice theory it is important to establish whether shipbreaking is an injustice to the developing countries. The injustice argument in the current research stems from two reasons. The first is that an international instrument in place, namely the *Hong Kong Convention,* provides neither a mechanism for funding the developing countries to support them in meeting the prescribed standards, nor a provision so that shipowners undertake responsibility for the work-related deaths, injuries, and diseases. The second is that the maritime and shipbreaking industries jointly perpetuate a system whereby the shipowners send off their waste to poor developing countries for breaking, and in so doing violate the principles of duty of care, good faith, preventing the abuse of others' rights, and due diligence (see Chap. 3 that discusses the annual profit of shipowners and how it attracts the application of these international principles).

On the other hand, Hadjiyianni and Kloni argue that shipbreaking is not an injustice to developing countries. Rather shipbreaking is an example of a circular economy approach because the business is deeply rooted within the society and economy of developing counties.[59] The industry minimises the wastes of ships and contributes to the economic development of shipbreaking countries. The European Commission defines circular economy as a 'transition where the value of products, materials and resources is maintained in the economy for as long as possible and the generation of waste minimised'.[60]

According to the circular economy approach, exporting ships to developing countries for steel is not illegal or unjust.[61] The legality of the industry using the circular economy approach makes it nearly impossible to impose liability on shipowners for selling the hazardous ships.[62] This book, however, discounts the circular economy approach, contending that the circular economy approach has a limit, and that developed countries should not use it to justify clear risks to human lives. Application of the rectificatory justice approach is to argue that in order to rectify the injustice, any industry that causes such work-related deaths, injuries, and diseases must have a remedy system.

---

[58] Michael Galley, *Shipbreaking: Hazards and Liabilities* (Springer International Publishing, 2014) 230.

[59] Ioanna Hadjiyianni and Anna Kloni, Regulating Shipbreaking As a Global Activity: Issues of Fragmentation and Injustice (2021) *Journal of Environmental Law* 211, 215; see more generally Gordon Walker, *Environmental Justice, Concepts, Evidence and Politics* (Routledge, 2012) 98.

[60] European Commission, *Communication from the Commission to the European Parliament, the Council, the European Economic and Social Committee and the Committee of the Regions: Closing the Loop – A EU Action Plan for the Circular Economy*, COM (2015) 614/2, EU Commission: Brussels, Belgium, 2015 cited in Christian Jageuken et al., 'The EU Circular Economy and Its Relevance to Metal Recycling' (Special Issue 2016) 1(2) *Public Policy Directions for Directions for Recycling, Waste Management, Resource Recovery and Circular Economy* 242, 243–250.

[61] Hadjiyianni and Kloni (n 59) 215.

[62] Ibid.

Aristotle and Sen's concepts of corrective and remediable justice have also been used in the book, particularly focusing on the idea of 'balance between business profit and human consequences'. Aristotle, who is widely regarded to be the first to state this kind of justice,[63] finds a similarity between rectificatory and corrective justice, and argues that corrective justice is important to benefit the victims and balance things by means of a penalty or take-away from the gain of the accused.[64] Amartya Sen's approach with respect to justice is also persuasive. According to Sen, the goal of justice is to identify an injustice, which is curable.[65] If not in full, a society should at least try to eliminate remediable injustice.[66]

To date, research on shipbreaking has not used the concept of rectifying the injustice as proposed by Aristotle and Sen since the existing research has not identified the causes of injustice in the shipbreaking industry.[67] Shipbreaking industry represents a clear example of injustice by its failure to recognise and account for the interests of the workers.[68] In this context, Hadjiyianni and Kloni note that the *Hong Kong Convention* encourages inter-State technical assistance and technology transfer, but the Convention does not provide for the generation or supply of funds by maritime nations so that developing countries can invest in meeting the *Hong Kong Convention*'s standards of safe ship recycling (see Chap. 5). The current research corroborates this argument and applies the concept of rectificatory justice, examining these weaknesses in the *Hong Kong Convention* (see Chap. 3).[69]

Weeramanty's notion of the postcolonial theoretical framework is instrumental to form the basis of the global injustice argument in the shipbreaking industry. He argues that the international laws adopted after the end of colonialism have provided enormous authority without responsibility to western nations.[70] Use of this theoretical framework is crucial to conceptualise that shipbreaking is a matter of global injustice

---

[63] G. Stanley Whitby, 'Justice' (1942) 52 (4) *Ethics* 399, 400.

[64] Peter Singer, 'Famine, Affluence and Morality' (1972) 1 *Philosophy and Public Affairs* 229, 229–233.

[65] Amartya Sen, 'Rawls versus Bentham: An Axiomatic Examination of the Pure Distribution Problem' (1974) 4 *Theory and Decision* 301, 302–309 https://doi-org.dbgw.lis.curtin.edu.au/10.1007/BF00136651;.

[66] Amartya Sen, *The Idea of Justice* (Allen Lane, 2009) 7.

[67] See Hadjiyianni and Kloni (n 59) 220; Pogge argues that inter-State businesses are designed in a way to serve the interest of Western States. Poor countries do not have the resources to pursue their interests at the negotiating tables where international agreements are agreed: at Thomas Pogge, *World Poverty and Human Rights, 2008* (Cambridge: Polity Press, 2nd ed, 2008), 17–18, cited in Kasper Lippert-Rasmussen, 'Global Injustice and Redistributive Wars, Law' (2013) 1 *Ethics and Philosophy*, 69–71.

[68] Corinna Mieth, 'Global Injustice: Individual Duties and Non-Ideal Institutional Circumstances' (2012) 12(1) *Civitas-Revista de Ciencias Sociais* 47, 47–50.

[69] Ensuring human rights is a global issue: at the United Nations, *Global Issues Overview* (Web page) https://www.un.org/en/sections/issues-depth/global-issues-overview/; Brooke Ackerly, *The Hardest Cases of Global Injustices: The Responsibility to Inquire in Justice, Sustainability, and Security: Global Ethics for the 21st Century* (Palgrave McMillan, 2013) 27–30.

[70] Christopher George Weeramanty, *Universalising International Law* (Martinus Nijhoff Publishers, 2004) 85.

because the international laws that apply (or ought to apply) to the shipbreaking industry provide no liability and remedy system for work-related deaths, injuries, and diseases.

The proposition of injustice is developed on the ground that the shipbreaking industry, as one component of the global maritime industry, does not impose any liability for work-related deaths, injuries, diseases, and environmental problems on the international shipowners, who are the parties that benefit most from the industry.[71] Further, drawing on Pogge's claim that global institutions have established an economic order that is inherently biased in favour of developed nations,[72] the book posits that this bias is evident in the design of the *Hong Kong Convention*, which mainly favours the shipping nations. The reason being that the *Hong Kong Convention* is to enable a business model that allows international shipowners to profit from the sale of end-of-life ships into a competitive South Asian shipbreaking market (which reflects the high demand for recycled material in the three South Asian nations, who lack the mineral resources to make steel), and to escape financial responsibility for cleaning hazardous substances from the ships and for compensating shipbreaking workers (see Chap. 5).[73]

International shipowners are well aware of the dangers involved in breaking the unclean ships, but nonetheless are content to keep earning a significant profit by selling ships to developing countries for breaking.[74] The ultimate burden of the shipbreaking accidents is borne by poor workers.[75] This is a clear derogation from three liability principles—namely, duty of care, good faith and prevention of abuse of rights, and due diligence.[76] According to these principles, a party to a business transaction has fiduciary duties to provide a minimum standard of protection to the other party and ensure that the other party does not face any foreseeable harm. It means, a concerned party to a business transaction must not intend to abuse the rights of others and if a party fails to protect the interest of others in a business relationship, the parties in control of the business have legal responsibility. These international law principles provide a strong legal and normative foundation to argue that shipowners should have liability for compensating the workers who face deaths,

[71] Stephen M. Gardiner, 'Ethics and Global Climate Change' (April 2004) 114(4) *University of Chicago Press Journals* 580, 555–600; Alpana Roy, 'Postcolonial Theory and Law: A Critical Introduction' (2008) 29 *Adelaide Law Review* 315, 317.

[72] Thomas Pogge, 'World Poverty and Human Rights' (2005) 19(1) *Ethics and International Affairs* 1–7.

[73] Md Saiful Karim, 'Recycling of Ships' in *Prevention of Pollution of the Maritime Environment from Vessels: Potential Limit of the International Maritime Organisation*' (Springer, 2015) 98–100.

[74] Ingvild Jenssem et al., 'Impact Report 2018–2019' (Research Report, NGO Shipbreaking Platform, 2020) 4 https://shipbreakingplatform.org/wp-content/uploads/2020/06/NGOSBP-Bi-Annual-Report-18-19.pdf.

[75] George Cairns, 'A Critical Scenario Analysis of end-of-life Ship Disposal: The Bottom of the Pyramid as Opportunity and Graveyard' (2014) 10(3) *Journal of Critical Perspectives on International Business* 172, 172–175.

[76] Karim (n 73).

or injuries, or diseases from the exposure to hazardous substances in the shipbreaking industry.

The theories and the principles discussed above, guide the book to explore the social and economic realities of the workers in the shipbreaking industry[77] and develops a regulatory mechanism—the shipbreaking liability certificate (SLC) and insurance—to remedy and control the work-related deaths, injuries, and diseases.[78]

Defining the Key Terms

The term 'shipbreaking industry' in the book refers broadly to businesses engaged in breaking ships along the coastlines of India, Bangladesh, and Pakistan—countries located in South Asia.[79] In South Asia, shipbreaking is a process that involves break entire ship and remove reusable materials, such as steel scraps, iron, aluminium, furniture, and electronic materials found in an end-of-life ship. While the International Maritime Organisation (IMO), prefers the term 'ship recycling' because of the potential for repurposing much of a ship's material,[80] the book opts for 'shipbreaking'. This is because the process used in South Asian shipbreaking industry's lies in the physical process of beaching, decontaminating, and cutting ships to retrieve valuable materials, rather than the subsequent manufacturing of products like iron rods from the recyclable materials, which falls outside the book's scope.

The term 'shipbreaking workers' refers to individuals employed in the industry that breaks old ships. 'Shipbreaking nations' is a term used to refer to India, Bangladesh, and Pakistan, all of which are developing countries in South Asia. Importantly, the phrase 'shipbreaking yards or facilities' is used to refer to shipbreaking companies who purchase ships for the purpose of breaking on the beaches of South Asia.

The phrase 'international shipowners' is used in the book to highlight the inherently cross-border nature of ship ownership and operations—even when such companies are legally based in a single country. These shipowners manage ships for global trade and eventually sell them off for breaking. The term 'shipowners' as applied in

---

[77] Ishtiaque Ahmed, 'Unravelling Socio-Economic and Ecological Distribution Conflicts in Shipbreaking in Bangladesh for Addressing Negative Externalities in Law and Policy Making,' 2020 (29) 2, *Minnesota Journal of International Law* 159, 187.

[78] Cairns (n 75).

[79] South Asia is a subregion of Asia. 'South Asian shipbreaking countries' is a term that the book refers to the shipbreaking industry established in India, Bangladesh, and Pakista: at Shawkat Alam and Abdulla Faruque, 'Legal Regulation of the Shipbreaking Industry in Bangladesh: The International Regulatory Framework and Domestic Implementation Challenges' (2014) 47 *Marine Policy* 46; see also Chap. 3.

[80] Under art 2(10) of *the Hong Kong International Convention for the Safe and Environmentally Sound Recycling*, the term 'ship recycling' is used instead of shipbreaking: at *The International Convention for the Safe and Environmentally Sound Disposal of Ships*, opened for signature 1 September 2009, IMO Doc. SR/CONF/45 (19 May 2009) (not yet in force). (*The Hong Kong Convention*).

the book, encompasses both those who own ships for extended durations and those who become owners for a short term such as cash buyers.

In the book, references to 'shipping industry', 'maritime industry', and 'shipping companies' are intended to include both long-term or original and short-term shipowners. Long-term or original shipowners are individuals or entities that typically operate a ship from the point of its initial registration for commercial use. On the other hand, short-term shipowners acquire ships for limited durations, often with the intention of reselling them—particularly for shipbreaking operations.

With reference to responsibility of shipowners, the book uses the term 'civil liability' and 'shipbreaking liability'—these terms are intended to argue for legal responsibility of shipowners for paying compensation to the shipbreaking workers (who face deaths, injuries, or work-related diseases). Civil liability as used in this study is different from criminal liability in that the book does not argue for imposing criminal fines or sentences on shipowners. It also differs from State liability in that the civil liability argues for the liability of private shipowners rather than major shipping nations for failing to protect workers from deaths, injuries, or work-related diseases in the shipbreaking industry. The book also uses the term 'civil liability framework' that generally refers to the 'shipbreaking liability certificate (SLC) framework' discussed in Chap. 9.

Overview of the Book

The book consists of ten chapters including an introduction (Chapter 1) and a conclusion (Chap. 10). The discussion below provides a summary of the remaining eight chapters of the book.

Chapter 2 presents the theoretical framework underpinning the proposed treaty-based civil liability mechanism. It critically engages with the question of which legal theory should inform the development of an international regulatory structure governing the shipbreaking industry. The chapter lays a theoretical foundation for later discussions by exploring the principles of rectificatory global justice and positions shipbreaking being a typical instance of structural injustice on a global scale. It highlights the disproportionate advantages accrued by shipowners from developed nations at the significant cost of lives and well-being of shipbreaking workers in South Asia. This chapter thereby advances a preliminary justification for invoking rectificatory justice as a normative basis for reforming the shipbreaking regime.

Through the lens of global injustice, Chaps. 3, 4, and 5 describe the shipbreaking industry in South Asia and domestic and international legal frameworks relevant to shipbreaking in South Asia.

Chapter 3 examines the financial benefits that the international maritime industry receives through its engagement with the South Asian shipbreaking industry. Despite generating substantial annual revenue from the sale of old ships to this region, the industry has largely abstained from initiating or supporting any formal mechanism aimed at compensating workers who suffer fatalities, injuries, or occupational illnesses for their economic loss. The chapter frames these adverse outcomes as manifestations of global injustice and asserts that maritime sector bears both an ethical and financial obligation to address the harms endured by shipbreaking workers in South Asia. The chapter accordingly advocates for the establishment of an international legal framework designed to provide redress for work-related deaths, injuries, and diseases.

Chapter 4 critically examines the principal factual and legal shortcomings prevalent within the shipbreaking sector. Among the factual issues, it highlights the widespread use of the beaching method, the lack of mandatory precleaning protocols, and the hazardous manual breaking of ships, all of which exacerbate the unsafe and exploitative working conditions faced by workers in the shipbreaking industry. In relation to legal issues, the chapter undertakes a detailed analysis of the constitutional provisions, legislative instruments, and judicial directives in India, Bangladesh, and Pakistan. The comparative legal analysis demonstrates that while these jurisdictions are formally obligated to uphold workers' rights to life and health, their existing legal frameworks fall short in effectively addressing the associated risks and violations. One of the underlying causes of injustice identified in this chapter is the absence of legal mechanisms that impose direct or indirect liability on the buyers and sellers of ships for work-related deaths, injuries, and diseases. The chapter contends that current national regimes do not compel these parties to provide adequate compensation to workers affected occupational fatalities, injuries, and illnesses, thereby perpetuating a critical accountability gap.

Chapter 5 critically evaluates the international regulatory mechanisms governing shipbreaking, with a particular focus on the *Hong Kong Convention*. It undertakes a detailed analysis of the *Hong Kong Convention*'s preventive and remedial provisions, arguing that the *Hong Kong Convention* fails to establish mechanisms for holding the global maritime industry financially accountable for work-related deaths, injuries, and diseases that occur in shipbreaking facilities in developing countries.[81] Because it shifts the burden of regulation and recycling of toxic ships to developing host countries without recognising their technical and financial incapacity and the vulnerability of workers, the chapter concludes that the *Hong Kong Convention* maintains the domination of shipowners.

Using the rectificatory global justice theory, Chaps. 6, 7, and 8 present case studies in which industry reform measures have applied financial mechanisms to better regulate global problems for an industry.

Chapter 6 presents the European Union's (EU) regulatory approaches as the first case study. The EU contains several large shipping nations and is therefore responsible for a significant proportion of the ships entering the global shipbreaking market. The chapter examines the regulatory measures that the EU has implemented for regulating inter-State transfer of EU ships. The literature review in the chapter examines the *EU Ship Recycling Regulation, 2013*. It also explores the financial mechanisms

[81] K.P Jain, J.F.J. Pruyn and J.J. Hopman, 'Critical Analysis of the Hong Kong International Convention on Ship Recycling' 2013 (7) 10 *International Journal of Environmental, Ecological, Geological and Mining Engineering* 683, 689.

that are under review by the European Commission to address several issues that this book also addresses, such as the lack of regulatory standards to impose liability on EU shipowners for selling ships to substandard shipbreaking yards. The underlying aim of these mechanisms is to impose financial liability on the ships registered in EU countries. After these approaches are examined, this chapter argues for introducing a financial mechanism to impose financial liability on global shipowners to compensate for the injured or ill workers or the family members of deceased workers within the shipbreaking industry.

Chapter 7 presents case studies of regulatory approaches and reforms related to international oil transport, offshore oil rigs, and appropriate loading of merchant ships. The chapter draws analogies between incidents that occurred in these three global industries and the hazards inherent in shipbreaking and explores the advantages of the liability systems introduced after some incidents to support the proposal of a similar civil liability framework for the shipbreaking industry.

Chapter 8 presents the Koko incident in relation to the international waste trade and the Baia Mare incident that occurred in 2000 in relation to the mining industry and the subsequent liability protocols.

The Protocols adopted after the Koko and Baia Mare incidents supplemented their pre-existing Conventions within their respective industries, as the frameworks of those Conventions did not previously address the liability of inter-State parties involved in the industry.[82] By using these case studies, the chapter argues for an additional mechanism to supplement the *Hong Kong Convention* and, further, to rectify future injustice a new inter-State mechanism to regulate the shipbreaking industry. The chapter develops criteria for shipbreaking liability and insurance frameworks and for designing the shipbreaking liability certificate (SLC) proposed in Chap. 9.

Chapter 9 draws on the propositions discussed in Chaps. 2 to 8 and proposes a compulsory SLC and shipbreaking liability insurance for all ships sailing in international waters. It also proposes that before a shipbreaking facility can purchase a ship for breaking, that facility must also obtain a certificate and insurance. The IMO would monitor the two SLCs (one for a ship seller and another for a ship buyer), whereas global maritime insurance industries would administer the insurances. This chapter also evaluates the SLC framework using the balance between 'loss and profit' or righting the injustice theory discussed in the theoretical framework chapter (Chap. 2).

Chapter 10 provides conclusions, identifies problems associated with the introduction of the proposed SLC framework, and suggests areas for further research.

[82] The *Basel Convention*; *The Convention on the Protection and Use of Transboundary Watercourses, and International Lakes*, signed 17 March 1992, 1936 UNTS 269 (entered into force 6 October 1996); *the Convention on the Transboundary Effects of Industrial Accidents*, signed 18 March 1992, 2105 UNTS 457 (entered into force 18 April 2000). *(The 1992 Helsinki Conventions)*.

Bibliography

Articles/Books/Reports

Adekola, Olalekan and Md Jahir Rizvi, 'How to Recycle a Huge Ship- Safely and Sustainably' *The Conversation* (e-article, 24 August 2020) https://theconversation.com/how-to-recycle-a-huge-ship-safely-and-sustainably-143519#:~:text=Shipbreaking%20itself%20is%20important%20and,aluminium%20and%20plastics%20for%20recycling

Ahmed, Ishtiaque, 'Unravelling Socio-Economic and Ecological Distribution Conflicts in Shipbreaking in Bangladesh for Addressing Negative Externalities in Law and Policy Making,' 2020 (29) 2, *Minnesota Journal of International Law* 159

Alam, Shawkat and Abdulla Faruque, 'Legal Regulation of the Shipbreaking Industry in Bangladesh: The International Regulatory Framework and Domestic Implementation Challenges' (2014) 47 *Marine Policy* 46.

Alcadia, Juan Ignacio, Francisco Piniella and Emilio Rodriguez-Diaz, '"The Mirror Flags": Ship Registration in Globalised Ship Breaking Industry' (2016) 48 *Transportation Research Part D*, 378

Cairns, Georgez, 'A Critical Scenario Analysis of end-of-life Ship Disposal: The Bottom of the Pyramid as Opportunity and Graveyard' (2014) 10(3) *Journal of Critical Perspectives on International Business* 172

Demaria, Federico, 'Shipbreaking at Alang-Sosiya (India): An Ecological Distribution Conflict' (2010) 70 *Ecological Economics* 250

Gardiner, Stephen M., 'Ethics and Global Climate Change' (April 2004) 114(4) *University of Chicago Press Journals* 580

Grant, Dylan, 'Aristotelian Justice in The Illiad' (2015) 24(6) *Agora ejournal* (University of Lynchburg, 2015) https://digitalshowcase.lynchburg.edu/cgi/viewcontent.cgi?article=1188&context=agora

Hadjiyianni, Ioanna and Anna Kloni, Regulating Shipbreaking As a Global Activity: Issues of Fragmentation and Injustice (2021) *Journal of Environmental Law* 211

Handl, G., 'International Liability of States for Marine Pollution' (1983) 21 *Canadian Yearbook of International Law* 85

Hiremath, Anand M., Sachin Kumar Panday, and Shyam R. Asolekar, 'Development of Ship-specific Recycling Plan to Improve Health Safety and Environment in Ship Recycling Yards' (2016) *Journal of Cleaner Production* 279

Hossain, Md. Shakhaoat et al, 'Impact of Ship-breaking Activities on the Coastal Environment of Bangladesh and a Management System for Its Sustainability' (2016) 60 *Environmental Science and Policy* 84

Jageuken, Christian et al, 'The EU Circular Economy and Its Relevance to Metal Recycling' (Special Issue 2016) 1(2) *Public Policy Directions for Directions for Recycling, Waste Management, Resource Recovery and Circular Economy* 242

Jain, J.F.J. Pruyn and J.J. Hopman, 'Critical Analysis of the Hong Kong International Convention on Ship Recycling' 2013 (7) 10 *International Journal of Environmental, Ecological, Geological and Mining Engineering* 683

Lippert-Rasmussen, Kasper, 'Global Injustice and Redistributive Wars, Law' (2013) 1 *Ethics and Philosophy*, 69

Mieth, Corinna, 'Global Injustice: Individual Duties and Non-Ideal Institutional Circumstances' (2012) 12(1) *Civitas-Revista de Ciencias Sociais* 47

Mikelis, Nikos, 'The Recycling of Ships' (2018) April, *Future of the Ship Recycling Sector* 27

Muralidhar, Venkiteswaran. Md Faizul Ahasan, and Ahad Mahmud Khan, 'Parenchymal Asbestosis Due to Primary Asbestos Exposure Among Ship-breaking Workers: Report of the First Cases From Bangladesh' (2017) *BMJ Case Report* 1

Pogge, Thomas, 'World Poverty and Human Rights' (2005) 19(1) *Ethics and International Affairs* 1
Roy, Alpana, 'Postcolonial Theory and Law: A Critical Introduction' (2008) 29 *Adelaide Law Review* 315
Sen, Amartya, 'Rawls versus Bentham: An Axiomatic Examination of the Pure Distribution Problem' (1974) 4 *Theory and Decision* 301, 302–309 https://doi-org.dbgw.lis.curtin.edu.au/10.1007/BF00136651
Singer, Peter, 'Famine, Affluence and Morality' (1972) 1 *Philosophy and Public Affairs* 229, 229–233
Whitby, G. Stanley, 'Justice' (1942) 52 (4) *Ethics* 399, 400.
Wu, Wei-Te et al, 'Cancer Attributable to Asbestos Exposure in Shipbreaking Workers: A Matched-Cohort Study' (2015) 10(7) *PLoS One* 6
Zakaria, N. M. Golam, Mir Tareque Ali and Khandakar Akhter Hossain, 'Underlying Problems of Ship Recycling Industries in Bangladesh and Way Forward' (2012) 9(2) *Journal of Naval Architecture and Marine Engineering* 91
Ackerly, Brooke, *The Hardest Cases of Global Injustices: The Responsibility to Inquire in Justice, Sustainability, and Security: Global Ethics for the 21 st Century* (Palgrave MacMillan, 2013)
Aristotle, *Aristotle: Nicomachean Ethics*, ed Roger Crisp (Cambridge University Press, 2000) vol 5
Bernard, Antoine (ed), 'Where Do the Floating Dustbins End Up? Labour Rights in Ship Breaking Yards in South Asia: the Cases of Chittagong (Bangladesh) and Alang (India)' (Report No. 348/2, Dec 2002, International Federation for Human Rights)
Galley, Michael, *Shipbreaking: Hazards and Liabilities* (Springer International Publishing, 2014)
Karim, Saiful, *Shipbreaking in Developing Countries: A Requiem for Environmental Justice from the Perspectives of Bangladesh* (Taylor and Francis Group, 2018)
Karim, Md Saiful, 'Recycling of Ships' in *Prevention of Pollution of the Maritime Environment from Vessels: The Potential Limit and Limits of the International Maritime Organisation* (Springer, 2016) 85
Mikelis, Nikos, 'The Recycling of Ships' (2nd ed, *Global Marketing System*, October 2019)
Pogge, Thomas, *World Poverty and Human Rights, 2008* (Cambridge: Polity Press, 2nd ed, 2008)
Puthurcherril, Tony George, 'Limitations of a National Response to Regulate Global Shipbreaking Industry - A Study of the Indian Experience' in David Freestone (ed), *From Shipbreaking to Sustainable Ship Recycling: Evolution of a Legal Regime* (Matinus Nijhoff Publishers, 2010)
Sen, Amartya, *The Idea of Justice* (Allen Lane, 2009)
Smith, B. D., *State Responsibility and the Marine Environment: The Rules of Decision* (Oxford: Clarendon Press, 1988)
Ticehurst, Gregory and Anthony Veal, *Business Research Methods: A Managerial Approach* (Pearson Education, 2000)
Walker, Gordon, *Environmental Justice, Concepts, Evidence and Politics* (Routledge, 2012) 98
Collste, Goran, *Global Rectificatory Justice* (Palgrave MacMillan, 1st ed, 2015)
Weeramanty, Christopher George, *Universalising International Law* (Martinus Nijhoff Publishers, 2004)
Azoulay, David and Nathaniel Eisen, 'Legality of the EU Commission Proposal on Ship Recycling' (Research Report No 1101, Centre of International Environmental Law, December 2012) 3 https://www.shipbreakingplatform.org/wp-content/uploads/2020/09/CIEL-Legality-EU-Proposals-on-Ship-Recycling-2020.pdf
Hussain, Mohammad Maruf and Mohamamad Mahmudul Islam, 'Ship Breaking Activities and Its Impact on the Coastal Zone of Chittagong, Bangladesh: Towards Sustainable Development' (Research Report, Young Power in Social Action, Chittagong, Bangladesh, 2006)
Ibeanu, Okechukwu, 'Adverse Effects of the Movement and Dumping of Toxic and Dangerous Products and Wastes on the Enjoyment of Human Rights', UN Doc. A/HRC/12/26 (15 July 2009)

International Metalworkers Federation, 'Special Report: Cleaning up shipbreaking the world's most dangerous job' (Research Report, 15 December, 2015) 10 http://www.industriall-union.org/cleaning-up-ship-breaking-the-worlds-most-dangerous-job
International Metalworkers Federation, 'Status of Shipbreaking Workers In India - A Survey' (Special Report, IMF-FNV Project in India, 2007)
NGO Shipbreaking Platform, 'Annual Report 2016' (Research Report, NGO Shipbreaking Platform, 2017) 4 https://shipbreakingplatform.org/wp-content/uploads/2018/02/NGO_Shipbreaking_Platform_Annual_Report_2016_05-web-page.pdf.
Sarraf, Maria et al, 'Ship Breaking and Recycling Industry in Bangladesh and Pakistan,' (Report No. 58275-SAS, World Bank, 2010)
Jenssem, Ingvild et al, 'Impact Report 2018–2019' (Research Report, NGO Shipbreaking Platform, 2020) 4 https://shipbreakingplatform.org/wp-content/uploads/2020/06/NGOSBP-Bi-Annual-Report-18-19.pdf.

Cases

Hamida Begum (on behalf of MD Khalil Mollah) v Maran (UK) Limited [2021] EWCA Civ 326. (10 March 2021)

Treaties

The Convention on the Transboundary Effects of Industrial Accidents signed 18 March 1992, 2105 UNTS 457 (entered into force 18 April 2000). *(The 1992 Helsinki Conventions)*
The International Convention for the Safe and Environmentally Sound Disposal of Ships, opened for signature 1 September 2009, IMO Doc. SR/CONF/45 (19 May 2009) (not yet in force). (*The Hong Kong Convention)*
The Basel Convention on the Control of Trans-boundary Movements of Hazardous Wastes and their Disposal, opened for signature 22 March 1989, 1673 UNTS 126 (entered into force 5 May 1992) (The *Basel Convention*)
Regulation No 1013/2006 of the European Parliament and of the Council on the Shipment of Wastes [2006] OJL 190/1. *(Waste Shipment Regulation)*
United Nations Environment Program, *Decision III/1: Amendment to the Basel Convention on the Control of Transboundary Movement of Hazardous Wastes and Their Disposal*, 22 September 1995, UN Doc UNEP/CHW.3/35 (entered into force 5 December 2019)
The Hong Kong International Convention for the Safe and Environmentally Sound Recycling of Ships, opened for Signature 1 September 2009, IMO Doc. SR/CONF45 (not yet in force) Annex (*'Regulation for Safe and Environmentally Sound Recycling of Ships)*
European Commission, *Communication from the Commission to the European Parliament, the Council, the European Economic and Social Committee and the Committee of the Regions: Closing the Loop – A EU Action Plan for the Circular Economy*, COM (2015) 614/2, EU Commission: Brussels, Belgium, 2015

Other

Curle, Jamie, Sarah Ellington, and Daniel D'Ambrosio, *Shipping Agent Potentially Responsible for Alleged Negligent Disposal of Ship in Bangladesh* (Web Page, 3 August 2020) , https://www.lexology.com/library/detail.aspx?g=84ba8284-3468-4d9b-82ec-6103bf4051cc

International Labour Organisation, *Shipbreaking: A Hazardous Work* (Webpage) https://www.ilo.org/safework/areasofwork/hazardous-work/WCMS_110335/lang--en/index.htm#:~:text=In%20addition%20to%20taking%20a,the%20soil%20and%20coastal%20waters.

International Maritime Organisation, *Recycling of Ships and the Hong Kong Convention* (Webpage) https://www.imo.org/en/MediaCentre/HotTopics/Pages/Recycling-of-ships-and-Hong-Kong-Convention.aspx#:~:text=The%20Hong%20Kong%20International%20Convention,force%20on%2026%20June%202025

Krishna, Gopal, 'High on Hazard, Alang Poses Big Threat to Environment and Health of Local Communities, Migrant Workers', *Financial Chronicle* (online at 21 December 2012) http://www.mydigitalfc.com/industry/high-hazard-463

Maersk, 'Breaking the Stalemate' *Case Studies* (Web Page, 25 October 2019) https://www.maersk.com/news/articles/2017/01/03/breaking-the-stalemate

Maersk, 'Maersk Tightens Its Ship Recycling Procedures', *Case Studies* (Web page, 04 April 2019) https://www.maersk.com/news/articles/2019/04/04/maersk-tightens-its-ship-recycling-procedures

NGO Shipbreaking Platform, *Flag of Convenience* (Web Page) https://www.shipbreakingplatform.org/issues-of-interest/focs/

Sahiner, Ozan, *Ship Breaking – Is It the Answer to The Shipping Industry's Overcapacity Problem?*(Blog Post, 24 February 2017) https://www.morethanshipping.com/ship-breaking-answer-shipping-industrys-overcapacity-problem/

Schuler, Mike, 'NGO Shipbreaking Platform: Use of Polluting South Asia Scrap Yards Accelerating' *gcaptain News* (online at 1 February 2017) https://gcaptain.com/ngo-shipbreaking-platform-use-of-polluting-south-asia-scrap-yards-accelerating/ .

Shipbreaking Platform, Why Ships are Toxic? *Issues of Interest* (Webpage) https://shipbreakingplatform.org/issues-of-interest/why-ships-are-toxic/

Taqbir Huda, 'Justice in Practice: Why is the Price of Killing a Worker only Tk 2 Lakh' *The Daily Star e-paper* (online 11 July 2021) E-paper(http://epaper.thedailystar.net

United Nations Environment Program, *Basel Convention Controlling Transboundary Movements of Hazardous Wastes and Their Disposal* (Web Page, Overview) http://www.basel.int/TheConvention/Overview/tabid/1271/Default.aspx

Chapter 2
Conceptualising the Theory of Rectificatory Global Justice for Civil Liability in Shipbreaking Industry

Abstract Rectificatory justice is a theoretical concept that focuses on remedying the unequal distribution of profit and harm between two opposite parties. This chapter uses rectificatory justice and contends that shipowners should be held accountable for the fatalities, injuries, and occupational illnesses occurring in shipbreaking nations. The central aim of this justice framework with its philosophical underpinning of remedying worker injustices in the shipbreaking industry is to align between the business of shipowners and right of shipbreaking workers to claim remedy.

Keywords Rectificatory justice · Multinational corporation · Inequality · Distribution of profit · International cooperation · Postcolonialism · Hong Kong Convention · Due diligence · Corporate responsibility · Financial mechanism · Remedy system

Introduction

The international regulatory framework governing shipbreaking operations continues to neglect the issue of liability for fatalities, injuries, and occupational diseases endemic to the industry. As these adverse outcomes to workers typically occur within the domestic jurisdictions of shipbreaking States, shipowners frequently evade responsibility, protected by geographic and legal distance. This evasion of liability underscores the pressing need to articulate a legal and moral foundation for holding shipowners accountable. In this regard, rectificatory global justice provides a compelling theoretical basis. Rooted in the principle of addressing transnational harm, this framework justifies the imposition of responsibility across borders, especially where systemic injustices cross a single jurisdiction.[1]

Rectificatory justice generally refers to a principle of remedy to address imbalances in benefits and burdens between individual parties by seeking to restore

[1] Mohammad Zulfikar Ali, 'Injustice to Workers in the Shipbreaking Industry in South Asia: A Quest for a Civil Liability Framework in International Law' (PhD Thesis, Curtin University, 2022) 2–3.

M. Z. Ali, *Worker Injustices in the South Asian Shipbreaking Industry*, International Law in Asia, https://doi.org/10.1007/978-981-95-8325-6_2

fairness. Extending this concept to the international sphere, rectificatory global justice aims at a systematic framework through which equitable redress can be pursued, aiming to rectify disparities in profits and losses resulting from transnational interactions or agreements.[2]

In developing a theoretical basis of the rectificatory global justice theory, a relevant inquiry is to see whether shipbreaking in South Asia is a case of global injustice. According to Cara Nine, an issue is a concern of global justice if it affects agents or residents of more than one State jurisdictions or cannot be resolved without cooperation of international parties.[3] Shipbreaking in South Asia is an issue of global injustice because unless shipowners undertake responsibility for the deaths, injuries, and work-related diseases that occur elsewhere from shipowners' State jurisdiction, workers' suffering is unlikely to be reduced.[4] Another reason why shipbreaking is a matter of global injustice is because the workplace problems faced by shipbreaking workers are not reasonably resolvable to their betterment without international cooperation.[5] In alignment with these arguments, an international framework of civil liability, namely shipbreaking liability certificate (SLC) is proposed in Chap. 9 of the book.[6]

A key justification to propose the civil liability framework lies in three objectives. First objective is to articulate and address the injustices prevalent in the shipbreaking sector in South Asia. This is based on the ground that the current legal regime has failed to introduce responsibility to international shipowners for the fatalities, workplace injuries, and diseases experienced by shipbreaking workers.[7]

The second objective is to establish the link between the shipbreaking and shipping industries positioning that shipbreaking is practically a value chain of old ships. The reason to construct shipbreaking as value chain of shipping industry is because shipbreaking is part of maritime supply chain, where old ships are broken and recycled into commercially valuable steel commodities. This process involves a series of operations designed to transform old ships—otherwise regarded as liabilities by their owners—into profitable material assets.

The final aim is to lay the theoretical foundation for implementing a civil liability (a treaty-based strict liability). The framework is to incorporate both a financial

---

[2] Ibid.

[3] Cara Nine, *Global Justice and Territory* (Oxford University, 2012) 135.

[4] Ali (n 1).

[5] Shannen Trout, 'First World Problems, Developing World Impacts: An Assessment of the Adequacy of the Law on Shipbreaking'(2018) 10 *Plymouth Law and Criminal Justice Review* 43–66, 46.

[6] The primary framework for accountability under international law is State responsibility, which holds nations liable for violation of legal obligations. However, this mechanism proves insufficient for addressing breaches arising within the context of intergovernmental commercial activities. On the other hand, civil liability—assigning direct accountability to specific entities such as operators or facilities—is a more effective regulatory tool, particularly in hazardous industries: See Panova A.S., 'Difference between the Concepts of State Responsibility and State Liability for the Nuclear Damage' (2023) 19 (2) *Economic Problems and Legal Practice* 157–163, 160.

[7] Ali (n 1) 28.

instrument—referred to as the shipbreaking liability certificate—and a mandatory insurance scheme (shipbreaking liability insurance). Together, these mechanisms are introduced in the book to ensure timely compensation for affected workers while equitably distributing the financial responsibility for such compensation across all entities engaged in the shipbreaking industry's business chain.

Building upon the above objectives, section "The Argument of Injustice in South Asian Shipbreaking Industry" of this chapter advances the thesis that the shipbreaking laws embody a continuation of colonial legacy meeting the interest of the agents of developed countries.[8] Employing postcolonial legal analysis, it examines the structural inequalities that render shipbreaking a manifestation of global injustice. Section "Philosophical Basis for Rectificatory Global Justice and Responsibility of Shipowners" explores the application of rectificatory justice within this industry, advocating for the accountability of shipowners based on the duty of care, due diligence obligations, and principles underpinning corporate liability. Section "Argument for a Treaty-Based Civil Responsibility Approach for the Shipbreaking Industry" introduces the proposed civil liability framework, emphasising the necessity of a binding treaty-based approach.[9] Finally, section "Conclusion" underscores the pivotal role of the shipbreaking liability certificate (SLC) as a corrective mechanism that aimed at delivering redress to affected workers and addressing the broader injustices embedded in the shipbreaking sector.

The Argument of Injustice in South Asian Shipbreaking Industry

Injustice occurs in the shipbreaking industry in the absence of a system to address responsibility for deaths, injuries, or work-related diseases while breaking ships. There are two reasons to argue that the shipbreaking industry is South Asia is a case of injustice. First, shipowners know that the South Asia's shipbreaking yards do not maintain safety standards for workers, buy the knowledge does not prohibit them to transfer their end-of-life ships to South Asian countries—India, Bangladesh, and Pakistan. Second, although it is well-known that shipbreaking is a dangerous industry, international community has not developed a responsibility and compensatory system. The following sections discuss these points in detail.

Absence of a Responsibility System to Compensate Victims

Shipowners face limited problems for their decision to send their hazardous ships to developing countries. Because shipbreaking is a legal business under the *Hong Kong*

[8] See Chap. 5 for detailed analysis of the international frameworks.

[9] Ali (n 1) 28.

International Convention for the Safe and Environmentally Sound Recycling of Ships (*Hong Kong Convention*), it has created increased problem to impose liability.[10] This leaves no scope to argue against sending off ships for breaking even though it leads to risk for workers and environment. But through the lens of post colonialism,[11]externalisation of such human and environmental risk from developed countries to shipbreaking countries is a matter of debate. This is since industrialised nations expanded their influence globally through colonisation, primarily driven by profit motivation. The profit motive continues even after the formal end of colonialism, demonstrated in international legal systems that continuously served the rich nations.[12]The relocation of the shipbreaking industry to developing countries in South Asia reflects a modern extension of continuing colonialism, based on the continuation of economic dominance of wealthier States over developing nations.

Post-Colonialism, Economic Dependency, and the Shipbreaking Industry

The economic priorities of colonial powers have shaped the architecture of the international legal order, with little regard for the welfare of the long-term consequences for developing nations.[13] This legacy persists in contemporary legal systems, where multinational corporations (MNCs) headquartered in developed countries often operate with impunity in the Global South. These corporations frequently engage in practices that harm both human communities and the environment, yet because of the structural biases embedded in international law they face minimal legal accountability. A pertinent example of that is the *Hong Kong Convention.*

While ostensibly designed to regulate the shipbreaking industry, the *Hong Kong Convention* fails to impose meaningful obligations on shipowners from affluent nations, effectively shielding them from liability. This legal asymmetry reflects what postcolonial theorists term 'postcolonial'—a continuation of colonial hierarchies through legal mechanisms that favour former colonisers and their economic interests. Scholars like Weeramanty argued that postcolonialism is not merely a historical condition but an ongoing process in which international law serves as a vehicle for

---

[10] *The Hong Kong International Convention for the Safe and Environmentally Sound Recycling of Ships*, opened for Signature 1 September 2009, IMO Doc. SR/CONF45 (entered into force 26 June 2025).

[11] Shipbreaking law refers to a world-system that does not limit transferring hazards or environmental harms on jurisdictions beyond the border of a country. For detailed discussion see Wictoria Wenneberg, 'Responsible Ship Recycling and Corporate Responsibility: Regulatory Aspects and Legal Challenges' (Master Thesis, Lund University, 2025)7–10. ttps://lup.lub.lu.se/luur/download?func = downloadFile&recordOId = 9,189,279&fileOId = 9,194,529 .

[12] Frank Aragbonfoh Abumere, 'Migration, Colonial Historical Injustice and Postcolonial Rectificatory Justice', (2025) 15 (1) *Ubuntu and Migration: Reflections from African Perspective* 62–81, 65–66.

[13] Ibid.

neocolonial control.[14] Under the paradigm, developed countries and their corporations propagate a dominant legal logic that legitimises exploitative business practices while marginalising the voices and rights of developing nations. This 'single logic of rule' reinforces global inequalities and undermines the pursuit of justice in international legal discourse.[15]

The enduring injustices rooted in colonialism cannot be fully understood without examining the historical trajectories of India, Bangladesh, and Pakistan. Although these nations gained independence in the mid-twentieth century, their developmental paths remain closely tied to their former colonies. This dependency is not only economic but also legal, as many of the laws and institutional frameworks established during colonial rule continue to shape governance today.[16] These legal systems were originally crafted to solve the commercial interests of colonial powers, not the welfare of local populations. Environmental and natural resource governance offers striking example of this legacy. With few exceptions, the legal and institutional structures in these countries still reflect a colonial mindset—prioritising the exploitation of natural resources over their conservation.[17] Rather than safeguarding ecosystems or ensuring equitable access, these 'use-oriented' laws were designed to facilitate the extraction of raw materials from Indian subcontinent to fuel industrial growth in Europe.

As a result, the legal frameworks often disregarded the rights and needs of local communities who rely on these resources for their livelihoods, perpetuating a system that privileges external economic interests over human and environmental rights of developing nations.[18]

The legal frameworks governing shipbreaking, as explored in Chap. 4, demonstrate the continuation of postcolonial priorities in modern regulatory systems. Instead of safeguarding rights of workers and the environment, these laws permit hazardous shipbreaking practices—particularly the 'beaching' method—on vulnerable shorelines. This technique involves grounding old ships directly onto beaches, where they are broken with minimal oversight. The consequences are severe: widespread marine pollution, frequent worker fatalities, chronic injuries, and occupational diseases are common outcomes of this unregulated industry. Crucially, the permissiveness of beaching serves the financial interests of shipowners based in developed nations. By externalising the environmental and human costs to developing nations, these laws enable shipowners to minimise shipbreaking expenses while

[14] Christopher George Weeramanty, *Universalising International Law* (Brill Publications, 2004) vol 48, 20.

[15] Lavanya Rajamani, *Differential Treatment in International Environmental Law* (Oxford University Press, 2006) 5.

[16] Ibid 17.

[17] D. Parthasarathy, 'Law-breakers and Law-makers: Critical Legal Pluralism, Normative Subjects and Ecological Regimes in India' in Maarten Bavinck and Amalendu Jyotishi (eds), *Conflict, Negotiations and Natural Resource Management: A Legal Pluralism Perspective from India* (Routledge 2014).

[18] Zheng Wan et al., 'Ship Scrappage Records Reveal Disturbing Environmental Justice' (2021) 130 *Marine Policy* 1–6, 1–2.

maximising profits through inflated resale value of their unwanted ships. In essence, the legal acceptance of beaching shifts the burden of risk and harm onto marginalised coastal communities, reinforcing a global economic structure that privileges capital over environmental and human rights.[19]

Pogge is critical about postcolonial laws that perpetuate economic priorities of colonisers. He contended that constructing a global economic order primarily to serve the interests of developed nations and their corporate actors constitutes a profound moral failing.[20] Similarly, Weeramanty highlighted the absence of accountability and remedial mechanisms in international legal frameworks as a manifestation of systemic global injustice.[21] Pogge and Weeramanty's propositions are particularly pertinent to regulation of the shipbreaking industry. This is because the *Hong Kong Convention*—the sole international treaty addressing shipbreaking—fails to establish any legal obligation for shipowners to bear responsibility for the occupational hazards faced by workers. As detailed in Chap. 5, the *Hong Kong Convention* does not provide avenues for redress in cases of death, injury, or illness resulting from shipbreaking activities. The regulatory gap underscores the ethical concerns raised by Pogge and Weeramanty, revealing how international law can continue to privilege powerful economic actors while neglecting the rights and safety of vulnerable labour forces in the Global South.[22]

The critiques advanced by Pogge and Weeramanty also underscore a broader ethical concern: the persistent dominance of develop nations in shaping international legal norms that disproportionately shift burdens onto developing countries.[23] This imbalance is particularly evident in legal regimes that fail to equitably distribute the social, environmental, and economic costs of global industries. The growing trend of exporting end-of-life ships to developing nations—where they are broken under hazardous conditions—illustrates how international law continues facilitate asymmetrical cost-sharing. The *Hong Kong Convention*, while positioned as a regulatory milestone, does not impose meaningful accountability on shipowners for the human toll of shipbreaking, including fatalities, injuries, and occupational diseases. This legal void reflects a broader pattern in which international frameworks function less as tools of justice, and more as mechanisms for preserving economic advantage. In this context, the shipbreaking industry exemplifies how postcolonial legal structures remain complicit in perpetuating global inequalities under the guise of regulatory legitimacy.[24] However, a critical question arises: why do workers in South Asian developing nations continue to engage in such perilous shipbreaking activities?

---

[19] See Chap. 3.

[20] Thomas Pogge, 'World Poverty and Human Rights' (2005) 19 (1) *Ethics and International Affairs* 1–7.

[21] Weeramanty (n 14) 20.

[22] Kristina Siig, 'Private Law Responses to Imperfect Regulation in International Public Law – the Case of Vessel Recycling' in *Routledge Handbook of Private Law and Sustainability* (Routledge, 2024) 224, 225–226.

[23] Lea Ypi, 'What's Wrong with Colonialism' (2013) 41 (2) *Philosophy and Public Affairs* 158–191.

[24] Alpana Roy, 'Postcolonial Theory and Law: A Critical Introduction' (2008) 29 *Adelaide Law Review* 315, 319.

The answer lies in a complex interplay of structural economic factors. High levels of unemployment, widespread poverty, and a scarcity of domestic iron ore—essential for meeting regional steel demands—create strong incentives for labour participation in this hazardous industry. These socio-economic vulnerabilities have arguably been exploited by shipping industries based in developed countries, which have strategically relocated shipbreaking operations to South Asia to capitalise on lower costs and weaker regulatory enforcement.[25] However, the narrative of injustice in the shipbreaking sector is complicated by the economic interdependence between shipbreaking nations and global shipping powers. While the industry undeniably benefits shipowners by externalising waste management costs, it plays a significant role in the economies of countries like India, Bangladesh, and Pakistan. Shipbreaking is deeply embedded in local economic structures and is often framed within the logic of the circular economy—a model that emphasises the prolonged use of materials and resources within the production cycle while minimising waste generation.[26]

From this perspective, the breaking of end-of-life ships is not inherently exploitative but rather a form of resource recovery that supports industrial development in the Global South. Proponents of the circular economy argue that the reuse of steel from the unwanted ships contributes to sustainability goals and economic resilience.[27] Application of the circular economy approach on shipbreaking complicates efforts to hold shipowners accountable under international law, as the practice of exporting toxic ships is not easily classified as illegal or unjust within this paradigm. The circular economy lens thus presents a significant challenge to advancing legal responsibility and environmental justice in the global shipbreaking industry.[28]

While the circular economy framework offers a compelling rationale for resource efficiency, its application to inherently hazardous industries such as shipbreaking is ethically and practically limited. Development, at its core, must prioritise human well-being; therefore, invoking circularity to justify the continuation of unsafe labour practices and environmental degradation is fundamentally flawed. The circular economy should not serve as a shield for corporate irresponsibility or to absolve powerful actors from the consequences of their actions.

---

[25] Camelia Dewan and Elizabeth A. Sibilla, 'Global Containments and Local Leakages: Structural Violence and the Toxic Flows of Shipbreaking' (2023) 42 (1) *Environment and Planning C: Politics and Space* 80–101.

[26] Federic Demaria, 'Shipbreaking in Alang: A Conflict against Capital Accumulation by Contamination' in *The Political Ecology of Informal Waste Recyclers in India: Circular Economy, Green Jobs, and Poverty* (Oxford, online edn, May 2023) https://doi.org/10.1093/oso/9780192869050.003.0003 .

[27] European Commission, *Communication from the Commission to the European Parliament, the Council, the European Economic and Social Committee and the Committee of the Regions: Closing the Loop – A EU Action Plan for the Circular Economy*, COM (2015) 614/2; EU Commission: Brussels, Belgium, 2015 cited in Christian Jageuken et al., 'The EU Circular Economy and Its Relevance to Metal Recycling' (Special Issue 2016) 1(2) *Public Policy Directions for Directions for Recycling, Waste Management, Resource Recovery and Circular Economy* 242, 243–248.

[28] Ioanna Hadjiyianni and Anna Kloni, 'Regulating Shipbreaking as a Global Activity: Issues of Fragmentation and Injustice' (2021) *Journal of Environmental Law* 211, 214.

A more ethically sound and sustainable alternatives lies in the establishment of a civil liability regime that ensures redress for future harms—specifically, deaths, injuries, and occupational diseases arising from shipbreaking activities. Central to this framework is the principle that shipowners, particularly those based in developed countries, must bear primary responsibility for the risks their ships impose on workers and communities in shipbreaking nations.[29]

Moreover, major shipping nations bear a broader moral obligation to confront the enduring legacies of colonial exploitation embedded in global shipping practices. Addressing these historical injustices requires not only legal reform but also a commitment to equitable development that places human dignity and environmental integrity at the forefront of international maritime governance.[30]

Philosophical Basis for Rectificatory Global Justice and Responsibility of Shipowners

The shipbreaking industry is an example of a sector where casualties occur regularly.[31] Given the history of fatalities and severe injuries in South Asian shipbreaking yards, there is a *prima facie* case for applying the concept of rectificatory global justice to adequately compensate victims by shipowners under an international legal framework. One of the grounds to argue for an international system to rectify the injustice is 'profit motive' of shipowners who earn USD 2.35 billion annually.[32] Moreover, as ships generate wastes in foreign waters and shipowners finally externalise the wastes on top of earning millions of dollars by selling ships, according to the theory of rectificatory global justice, shipowners have a special duty to compensate victims.

Rectificatory Justice to Rectify Injustice in Shipbreaking Businesses

Justice serves as the foundation for addressing and remedying historical and ongoing injustices. Within this broader concept, rectificatory justice plays a distinct and

[29] Daksha Gupta and Patrick Schroder, 'Towards a Just and Circular Shipbreaking Industry in South Asia', *Circular Economy Watch* (Webpage, 16 January 2025) https://circulareconomy.earth/publications/towards-a-just-and-circular-shipbreaking-industry-in-south-asia .

[30] Martin Siecker and Richard Adams, *Report on the Shipbreaking and the Recycling* Society, CCMI/145-EESC (19 October 2016).

[31] NGO Shipbreaking Platform, *Impact Report 2022–2023* (Webpage) https://shipbreakingplatform.org/wp-content/uploads/2025/02/ImpactReport2223.pdf .

[32] Annual income of the shipping industry is approximately 2350 million USD: at Table 5, Chap. 3.

critical role to transform a relationship from unjust to just.[33]Unlike distributive justice—which focuses on the equitable allocation of resources and opportunities across society—rectificatory justice is concerned with correcting specific wrongs and restoring fairness in relationships marked by imbalance or harm.[34] In this context, rectificatory justice seeks to establish moral and legal equilibrium by acknowledging past injustices and implementing mechanisms for redress. It emphasises the need to repair the asymmetry between the powerful and the marginalised, often through compensation, restitution, or other forms of remedy. This approach is particularly relevant to postcolonial and transnational contexts, where systemic inequalities persist and where justice must involve not only recognition of harm but also tangible efforts to correct it.[35]

According to Aristotle, rectificatory justice is a mechanism that operates between 'loss and profit' and aims at restoring a balance when one party has been wronged by another. This form of justice seeks to justify an act through the imposition of penalties or by deducting unjust gains from the responsible party to compensate the victim. In modern terms, this principle underscores the necessity of a remedial system that not only acknowledges harm but also provides timely and adequate relief to those affected.[36] The idea of 'between loss and profit' also implies a moral obligation to accept liability when one's actions result in harm to others. Rectification, in this sense, involves repairing the damage caused by wrongful conduct, particularly when it infringes upon the rights of another. Compensation becomes essential in cases where such transgressions occur, serving both as a corrective measure and as a deterrent against future harm. In the context of commercial relationships, the entitlement to profit must be tempered by considerations of justice. Profit derived from activities that cause harm or violate the rights of others cannot be deemed legitimate unless accompanied by mechanisms that ensure fairness and accountability. Thus, rectificatory justice demands that economic gain be aligned with ethical responsibility, particularly in industries where power imbalances and externalised harms are prevalent.[37]

In other words, profit, which results from injustice in a business relationship necessitates the payment of adequate compensation to set the relationship right. This must also lead to improving the economic condition of the 'neediest'. In that sense, consistent with SDG 8 (Promote sustained, inclusive and sustainable economic growth, full and productive employment and decent work for all), shipowners can play an important role in supporting the development of social security schemes for workers, including fully functioning compensation payment system.

---

[33] Jason Lee Byas, 'Rectification and Historic Injustice' in *The Routledge Companion to Libertarianism* (Routledge, 1st ed, 2022) 427–441.

[34] Ibid.

[35] Ibid.

[36] Ibid.

[37] Robert Nozick, *Anarchy, State, and Utopia* (Basic Books & Oxford, 1974) 152; James S. Coleman, Boris Frankel and Derek L. Phillips, 'Robert Nozick's Anarchy, State, and Utopia' (1976) 3(3) *Theory and Society* 437, 438.

John Rawls' 'difference principle' asserts that social and economic inequalities are only justifiable if they result in tangible benefits for the most disadvantaged members of society.[38] Within this framework, any unequal distribution of risks or resources must be evaluated based on its impact on the 'worst off'. Rawls further acknowledges that individuals may be influenced by personal motivations—shaped by factors such as income, social class, gender, or innate abilities—which inevitably colour their perceptions of justice. Nevertheless, he maintains that certain fundamental values must remain universally applicable: liberty, fair opportunity, the social foundations or self-respect, and access to meaningful employment.[39]

Rawls' propositions are particularly relevant to the global shipbreaking industry. While shipowners in developed nations may be motivated by economic incentives to offload obsolete ships and externalise the environmental and human costs of breaking to South Asian countries, such decisions must be evaluated through a justice-oriented lens. In accordance with Rawlisian ethics, shipowners bear a moral and practical obligations to assume responsibility for the adverse consequences of shipbreaking—including fatalities, injuries, and occupational diseases—borne disproportionately by vulnerable workers in developing nations. Upholding justice in this context requires aligning industrial practices with the core values of fairness, accountability, and respect for human rights.[40]

Similarly, according to Sen, 'practical reasoning must include ways of judging how to reduce injustice and advance justice, rather than aiming only at the characterisation of perfectly just societies'.[41] A goal of the theory of justice is to identify an injustice, which is remediable. If not in full, at least a society should try to eliminate this remediable injustice.[42] In doing so, a legal system should focus on human lives and the people who suffer from injustice.[43] In other words, Sen argues for reflecting people and their sufferings in a legal system with the aim of providing adequate and prompt remedies in each context.

The aspects of remedying injustice proposed by Aristotle, Rawls, and Sen are relevant to the South Asian shipbreaking industry for two reasons. First, following Aristotle and Rawls' propositions, as shipbreaking is an externalisation of risk to developing nations, the focus should be on the 'worst off', i.e., the workers of the shipbreaking industry. Second, following Sen's proposition, as the current shipbreaking laws discussed in Chaps. 4 and 5 are not enough to prevent shipbreaking

---

[38] John Rawls, *A Theory of Justice* (Oxford University Press, 1999 rev ed) 101–109; Philosophy Overdose, Rawl's Theory of Justice (September 12, 2016) https://www.youtube.com/watch?v=zhVByiXBxi4.

[39] Ibid.

[40] Martin Siecker and Richard Adams, *Report on the Shipbreaking and the Recycling* Society, CCMI/145-EESC (19 October 2016).

[41] Amartya Sen, *The Idea of Justice* (The Belknap Press of Harvard University Press, 2009) 7.

[42] Ibid, 7–8; see also Amartya Sen, 'Rawls versus Bentham: An Axiomatic Examination of the Pure Distribution Problem' (1974) 4 *Theory and Decision* 301, 301–309.

[43] Sen (n 41) 10.

accidents,[44] shipowners must undertake responsibility through a civil liability framework to remedy the injustice in their business relationships. Given that shipowners are the main beneficiaries of shipbreaking in terms of wealth accumulation,[45] an argument for applying rectificatory global justice that leads to a proposal to introduce a mandatory civil liability mechanism is reasonable and necessary.

Rectificatory global justice is not a new theory used in inter-State issues, such as shipbreaking. Some studies have used this theory to compensate for past injustices in cases of border closure,[46] debt relief,[47] slave trade,[48] and climate change.[49] In relation to the debt burden of developing countries, a study conducted by Justin and others has convincingly argued that debt is the financial consequence of the colonisation of previous centuries. The study has also claimed that the reason behind the poverty of many developing countries in Asia and Africa is that 'they have been robbed of their wealth in the past'.[50] Because of this taking away of assets by past colonisers, developing countries, which are now struggling with many poverty-related issues, including industrial development, are required to borrow wealth from developed countries. It is argued that the responsibility lies with the colonial powers to release developing countries' debt burden and rectify past injustice.[51] In relation to past injustices, such as slavery and racial discrimination, studies argue to obtain compensation for slavery by European countries.[52] Compensation to States that have fallen victim to climate change caused by historical emissions by developed countries.[53]

International law principles, such as good faith duty, due diligence duty, and corporate social responsibility have also aimed at remedying these issues using the principles of rectifying global injustices. The following sections explain the doctrinal basis for remedying future harm by compensation in light of these international law principles.

---

[44] See Chaps. 4 and 5 that discuss why current shipbreaking laws are not enough to prevent shipbreaking accidents.

[45] See Chaps. 3 and 5 for detailed discussion on the question of profit.

[46] Alexander Sager, 'The Implications of Migration Theory for Distributive Justice' in *Philosophy Faculty Publications and Presentations* (Portland State University, PDXScholar, 2012) 56, 56–58.

[47] Wilfred Onyekachi Aniago, 'International Debt Cancellation and the Question of Global Justice: A Case Study of Nigeria' (Master Thesis, Linkoping University, 2006).

[48] Justin Reedy et al., 'Deliberative Democracy and Historical Perspectives on American Indian/Alaska Native Political Decision Making Practices' (Online ed, June, 2021) *Humanit Soc Sci Commun* 10.1057/s41599-020–0506-4

[49] Peter Newell et al., 'Towards Transformative Climate Justice: An Emerging Research Agenda' (online 2021) 12 (6) *WIREs Climate Justice* https://wires.onlinelibrary.wiley.com/doi/epdf/10.1002/wcc.733.

[50] Justin et al. (n 48).

[51] Ibid.

[52] Maeve Mckeown, 'Backward-Looking Reparations and Structural Injustice' (February 2021) 20 *Contemporary Political Theory* 771–794.

[53] Peter Newell et al. (n 49).

Doctrinal Basis for Shipowners' Responsibility

Benefit and knowledge are linked to the responsibility of shipowners under international law principles. For the argument, the following sections use three grounds. First, shipowners breach the international principles of good faith and prevention of abuse of rights. Second, shipowners promote shipbreaking in developing countries despite having knowledge of poor shipbreaking practices. Third, shipowners keep tight control of the total business process of selling ships. The next three sub-sections explain these grounds.

Justification Based on the Principles of Good Faith and Prevention of Abuse of Rights

Promoting the shipbreaking industry in South Asian developing countries is a breach of the international principles of good faith and prevention of abuse of rights duties (principles). In addition to shipbreaking incidents, activities involving shipbreaking cause environmental pollution and harm human health, which indicates that shipowners violate these principles. This reinforces the argument of rectifying the injustice in the shipbreaking industry and taking responsibility of shipowners.

Owing to good faith and prevention of abuse of rights duties, a person cannot abuse the rights of others and cause damage or harm. If they do so, the abuser is required to take responsibility for his abusive actions. Joseph defines the duty to prevent abuse of rights as a 'legal mechanism designed to ease the inflexibility of the legal relationships derived from statutory, judicial, or treaty rules'.[54] According to this definition, the duty of good faith and abuse of rights are interrelated, which means that the duty of preventing abuse of rights is an expansion of the good faith principle.[55]

Inter-State environmental and human rights treaties have also explicitly incorporated these principles. For example, art 300 of the 1982 *United Nations Convention on the Law of the Sea* provides that 'State Parties shall fulfil in good faith, the obligations assumed under this Convention and shall exercise the rights, jurisdiction, and freedoms recognised in this Convention in a manner, which would not continue as abuse of right'.[56] Moreover, the amended art 17 of the *Convention for the Protection of Human Rights and Fundamental Freedoms* reads as follows:

> Nothing in this Convention may be interpreted as implying for any state, group, or person any right to engage in any activity or perform any act aimed at the destruction of any of the

---

[54] Joseph M Perillo, 'Abuse of Rights: A Pervasive Legal Concept' (1995) 27 *Pacific Law Journal* 37–55.

[55] Clive Parry, John P Grant, and John Craig Barker, *Parry and Grant Encyclopaedic Dictionary of International Law* (Oxford University Press, 2009) vol 5, 224–30.

[56] *United Nations Convention on the Law of the Sea*, opened for signature10 December 1982, 21 ILM 1261 (entered into force 16 November 1994).

> rights and freedoms set forth herein or at their limitations to a greater extent than is provided for in the Convention.[57]

In addition to the endorsement of the principles in the treaties, Judges referred to the principles in several international disputes. For instance, Weeramantry J in *Gabcikovo-Nagymaros*, recognised the principles as a 'well-established area of international law'.[58] In deciding the question of whether Hungary's environmental concerns violated Slovakia's treaty right leading to human harm, Parra-Aranguren J in the same case held that Slovakia should not give compensation to Hungary, unless evidence can prove a manifest abuse of rights on its part.[59] With clearer objectives, the Appellate Body of the World Trade Organisation (WTO) relied on the duty to prevent abuse of rights in *Shrimp-Turtle*. In this case, the Appellate Body stated that the duty to prevent abuse of rights controls a State's abusive practice over another State.[60] It is therefore clear that neither a State nor a group or person can misuse the rights of other States or their citizens.

Accountability lies with the responsible parties if they breach the duty to prevent abuse of rights. In the context of shipbreaking, as shipowners deliberately send their ships to developing countries, principles of good faith and prevention of abuse of rights duties are the key international principles for them to undertake responsibility.[61] The next sections shed light on associative duties,[62] the *OECD Guidelines for Multinational Enterprises* (the *OECD Guidelines*) and the *United Nations Guiding Principles for the Implementation of the United Nations 'Protect, Respect and Remedy Framework'* (the *United Nations Guiding Principles*) to further elaborate this argument.[63]

---

[57] *Convention for the Protection of Human Rights and Fundamental Freedoms*, opened for signature 4 November 1950, 213 UNTS 222 (entered into force 4 November 1953).

[58] The *Gabcikovo-Nogumoaros Project (Hungary v Slovakia)* [1997] ICJ Rep 7, 22.

[59] Ibid Parra-Aranguren J [25].

[60] Appellate body Report, *United States – Import Prohibition of Certain Shrimp and Shrimp Products*, WTO Doc WT/DS58/AB/R (6 November 1998) [10].

[61] Fernando Felipe Basch, 'The Doctrine of the Inter-American Court of Human Rights regarding States' Duty to Punish Human Rights Violations and its Dangers' (2007) 23 *American University International Law Review* 195.

[62] Lea YPI, Robert E. Goodin, and Christian Barry, 'Associative Duties, Global Justice, and the Colonies' (2009) 37(2) *Philosophy and Public Affairs* 103, 103.

[63] Organisation for Economic Co-operation and Development (OECD), *OECD Guidelines for Multinational Enterprises*, 2nd ed, 2000, Part II, para 2, http://www.oecd.org/daf/investment/guidelines/mnetext.htm ≥ and *OECD Guidelines for Multinational Enterprises, Recommendations for Responsible Business Conduct in a Global Context 2011* http://www.oecd.org/investment/mne/1922428.pdf; John Ruggie, *Guiding Principles for the Implementation of the United Nations 'Protect, Respect and Remedy Framework,* Report of the Special Representative of the Secretary-General on the issue of human rights and transnational corporations and other business enterprises, UN Doc A/HRC/17/31 (March 2011). (*the United Nations Guiding Principles*).

Other Grounds for Shipowners' Responsibility?

Shipbreaking is an international business that involves chains of owners, including shipowners and their States; shipbreaking yards and their States; open registry countries; and cash buyers as intermediary shipowners (see Chap. 3 for details). The question is who should, and under which legal principles, take responsibility and what the nature of the remedy would be. This section contends that shipowners should be responsible for deaths, injuries, or work-related diseases, taking into account their business associations with the shipbreaking industry.

As stated before, justice requires one to pay what one owes to others in a range of areas, where injustice occurs.[64] There are three schools of thought in relation to ensuring justice when inter-State parties are involved. First, international justice considers the duty of everyone to remedy victims, irrespective of their involvement in any breach.[65] Second, domestic justice argues that the principle of justice applies only among citizens of the State.[66] Third, the middle ground that also argues that responsibility must be taken for global problems, but the extent of responsibility is neither too high as the first school contends nor too low as the second school contends.[67] The argument for civil liability follows the third position. It posits that the responsibility of the actors in a business arises on the basis of associative duties. As discussed before, shipbreaking is a value chain of the shipping industry that eventually leads to the conversion of an unwanted ship into valuable steel products, thereby adding value to the materials found in an old ship through a series of activities or processes. Shipbreaking aims to create profitable value for end-of-life ships, which would otherwise remain burdens for shipowners.

On a similar issue of 'business association' account, people generally have more duties to those with whom they have a business association than to outsiders.[68] Everyone within the same business association has associated duties (associative duties) with each other.[69] The duty exists only among the participants in the business. The associative duties do not decrease merely on the ground of distance, regardless of how far the advantaged group is from those who are adversely affected.

In the context of shipbreaking, the associated duty lies with shipowners from the beginning because of their knowledge of poor working conditions and profit from shipbreaking industries in South Asia.[70] This is evident in a recent case law decided

---

[64] Mohammad Ali, 'Injustice to Workers in the Shipbreaking Industry in South Asia: A Quest for a Civil Liability Framework in International Law' (PhD Thesis, Curtin University).

[65] YPI, Goodin, and Barry (n 62) 104.

[66] Matthew Groves, 'Exclusion of the Rules of Natural Justice' (2013) 39 (2) *Monash University Law Review* 285–318.

[67] Gerald Gaus, 'Coercion, Ownership, and the Redistributive State: Justificatory Liberalism's Classical Tilt' (2010) 27 (1) *Social Philosophy and Policy* 233–275.

[68] YPI, Goodin, and Barry (n 62) 103.

[69] Ibid.

[70] See Chap. 3 for understanding business profit of shipowners.

by the Court of Appeal of England and Wales.[71] The Court found a UK shipping industry broadly responsible for paying compensation to the family of a deceased worker, who died from the fall while working in a Bangladeshi shipbreaking yard. The UK shipping industry sold its ship despite having knowledge about the poor working conditions in the Bangladeshi shipbreaking yard (see section 'Duty of Care for Creating a Danger Principle' below).

Like a hazardous waste management company, a shipowner can hardly escape responsibility by severing ties with a ship. For example, if a company exposes its workers to asbestosis for many years and later the workers start showing symptoms of serious health problems, the owners cannot simply avoid responsibility by selling the company and retaining no relationship with the affected workers.[72] The same argument would apply where a shipowner intends to sever the tie with the human harms caused in breaking an old ship by transferring ownership to a shipbreaking yard or a cash buyer company, such as Global Marketing System (GMS).[73] 'Cash buyer' refers to an intermediate buyer of a ship who may purchase a ship 'as it is' paying cash to a shipowner. The responsibility to pay compensation does not end with the transfer of ships. Primarily, shipowners' duty to safeguard the right to life and health of workers in their value chain continues and any failure to meet these associatively grounded duties leads to paying compensatory damage.[74]

In relation to the changes in ownership and value chain connections during shipbreaking, a reasonable question is as follows: if there are duties, what should be their philosophical basis? In fact, a compensation mechanism that creates an incentive to prevent accidents in the workplace is important. One good example of this is the readymade garment (RMG) sector in Bangladesh.

The Bangladeshi RMG sector acts as a supply chain that manufactures garment products for many global brand companies. As people use the readymade garments produced in Bangladesh for multinational brand companies, the sense of responsibility is greater than that in the shipbreaking industry. Owing to the use of RMG and therefore, a greater sense of responsibility and concern for the RMG sector and the consensus on the responsibility of foreign buyers, two key global regulatory frameworks were established by multinational companies after the collapse of a building named 'Rana Plaza' in Bangladesh on 24 April 2013. Rana Plaza housed a number of small garment industries, which were in operation at the time of its collapse. Eleven hundred workers died, and 2500 workers were injured in that industrial accident.[75] This event forced multinational companies to introduce and implement the *Accord on*

---

[71] *Hamida Begum (on behalf of MD Khalil Mollah) v Maran (UK) Limited* [2021] EWCA Civ 326. (10 March 2021). *(Maran Shipping).*

[72] The example is cited in YPI, Goodin, and Barry (n 62) 124.

[73] See Chaps. 4 and 5; Established in USA in 1992, GMS is the world's largest buyer of ships and Offshore Assets: see GMS Leadership, *World's Largest Buyer of Ships and Offshore Assets* (Webpage, 2019) http://www.gmsinc.net.

[74] YPI, Goodin, and Barry (n 62) 124.

[75] International Justice and Human Rights Clinic, 'In the Dark: Bringing Transparency to Canadian Supply Chains' (Allard School of Law, June 2017) https://allard.ubc.ca/sites/default/files/2020-06/In%20the%20Dark%20-%20IJHR%20TSC%20Report.pdf

Fire and Building Safety in Bangladesh (the Accord) and *the Alliance for Bangladesh Worker Safety (the Alliance)* in 2013 (Agreements). They are binding agreements, and they focus both on prevention and on compensation.[76] *The Accord* is between the brand companies and the trade unions of Bangladesh for a safe environment and *the Alliance* is among the leading North American apparel companies, retailers, and brands for safer RMG industries in Bangladesh.[77]

Since the implementation of these agreements, there have been no major industrial accidents in the RMG sector of Bangladesh. This indicates that although the focus of the Agreements is to pay adequate compensation to the victims, they also have a slipover effect on preventing catastrophic industrial accidents.[78]

These instruments have introduced a very important aspect of the corporate responsibility of business enterprises such as those in the global shipping industry.[79] However, as yet shipping industries have not introduced any effective mechanism for shipbreaking. Perhaps unsurprisingly, the reason is that shipbreaking involves different activities from those of the RMG sector. People use garments produced by the RMG sector, whereas people have nothing to use from shipbreaking in a direct sense. People are attached to ships during their commercial life for shipping goods, parcels, et cetera, but no one keeps track of what happens to ships at the end of their life or of what consequences shipbreaking has for workers and the environment. However, in both the RMG sector and the shipbreaking sector, owners have responsibility due to their knowledge, and profits from their business relationships.

As discussed in the following sections, the knowledge about the poor shipbreaking practices and profit of shipowners can be followed by court actions if shipowners do not undertake responsibility. The profit motive of shipowners is already under increasing scrutiny under tort law's duty of care principle, which can form the basis of duty and compensation payments.

---

[76] The Accord is a legally binding agreement between brands and trade unions for improving safety environment and the Alliance is a legally binding five years initiative among leading North American apparel companies, retailers, and brands for safer Readymade Garments industries in Bangladesh. Business and Human Rights Resource Centre, *The Accord on Fire and Building Safety in Bangladesh* (Web Page) https://www.business-humanrights.org/en/latest-news/the-accord-on-fire-and-building-safety-in-bangladesh/ ; Clean Clothes Campaign, *Alliance for Bangladesh Worker Safety Overstates Progress while Workers Lives Remain at Risk* (Web Page) https://cleanclothes.org/news/2016/11/21/alliance-for-bangladesh-worker-safety-overstates-progress-while-workers-lives-remain-at-risk.

[77] Juliane Reinecke and Jimmy Donaghey, 'After Rana Plaza: Building Coalition Power for Labour Rights between Unions and (Consumption-based) Social Movement' 2015 (22) 5 *Organisations* 72–740.

[78] Ibid.

[79] Jennifer Bair, Mark Anner, and Jeremy Blasi, 'The Political Economy of Private and Public Regulation in Post-Plaza Bangladesh' (2020) 73 (4) *ILR Review* 969–994.

Duty of Care for Creating a Danger Principle

The Court of Appeal of England and Wales (Civil Division) has recently used the principle of duty of care to create a danger principle to find a UK shipping industry liable for the death of a worker in a shipbreaking industry in Bangladesh. According to this principle, if 'X' does something that creates an opportunity for 'Y' to exploit and cause harm to 'Z', then to create the danger, 'X', being the person in control of the transaction, is liable to pay compensation.

The Court of Appeal of England and Wales established the principle in *Hamida Begum v Maran (UK) Limited.*[80] The Court reached this conclusion after hearing an appeal that upheld an interim order passed by the High Court of Justice (Queen's Bench Division), stating that the defendant-shipowner would owe the legal duty of care to a shipbreaking worker in Bangladesh and pay compensation subject to full trial of the case.[81]

Initially, Hamida Begum, wife of a shipbreaking worker, Khalil Mollah, who fell from a height to death while breaking the ship named the *Maran Centaurus*, made a compensation claim before the High Court of Justice arguing that the shipowner, Maran (UK) Limited, had a duty of care. This was because the defendant retained full control over the ship's sale arrangement, including the transfer to its final destination and the purchase price.[82] On Appeal, the Court of Appeal had to decide whether the defendant-Maran (UK) Limited had a legal duty of care to the plaintiff and was liable to pay compensation.

The defendant, by contrast, argued that the shipowner had no duty of care, for not being the last owner of the ship. The facts, however, showed that the defendant maintained tight control for selling the disputed ship but followed a non-transparent process, as discussed in Chaps. 1 and 3. Maran (UK) Limited acted as an agent to sell the disputed ship on behalf of the principal company, Centaurus Special Maritime Enterprise.[83] Finally, Hsaejar Maritime, Inc., the intermediary cash buyer used by the defendant, purchased the ship with cash from the defendant and sold it to the

[80] *Maran Shipping* (n 71).

[81] Earlier, the defendant-appellant filed a petition before the High Court of Justice (Queen's Bench Division). The Court rejected the petition. In rejecting the petition, the Court primarily ordered that the plaintiff had a good case to claim compensation and the matter should go for trial. The defendant-appellant, Maran (UK) Limited, appealed against the order to the Court of Appeal for England and Wales (Civil Division): at *Hamida Begum (on behalf of MD Khalil Mollah) v Maran (UK) Limited* [2020] EWHC 1846 (QB) (13 July 2020) Jay J.

[82] *Maran Shipping* (n 71).

[83] The defendant, Maran (UK) Ltd. is a British company that acted as a broker for the original registered owner, Centaurus Special Maritime Enterprise (CSME), a Liberian company that is a part of the Angelicoussis shipping group. Full share of the registered owner, Centaurus Special Maritime Enterprise, belongs to another company within the same group, Maran Tankers Ship Holdings Limited (MTS), incorporated in the Cayman Islands, UK. Another related Liberian company, Maran Tankers Management was the operational and management company of the ship. Maran (UK) Ltd. acted as an agent to sell ships on behalf of the principal company, Centaurus Special Maritime Enterprise. Alongside 28 other ships, defendant-Maran (UK) Limited signed an agency agreement with the operator, Maran Tankers Management on 1 August 2013: at Ibid [7].

Bangladeshi business enterprise, the Zuma shipbreaking yard, which purchased the ship to break in Bangladesh.

Arguing against the non-transparent selling process of the ship, the plaintiff claimed that the defendant had a legal duty of care under the neighbourhood principle established in *Donoghue v Stevenson*.[84] According to the neighbourhood principle, a defendant owes a duty of care to a claimant if the defendant has knowledge and control over the act causing harm. The plaintiff accordingly claimed that the defendant owed a duty of care, as they had knowledge of unsafe shipbreaking practices in Bangladesh and foreseen the danger involved in breaking the ship.

The defendant-appellant, on the contrary, argued that the defendant had no legal duty of care because the accident had happened due to a third-party intervention and, in this case, it was the Zuma shipbreaking yard in Bangladesh. The defendant had no control over the shipbreaking practices of the third party, the Zuma shipbreaking yard in Bangladesh. The victim faced death after he fell from the height that occurred because of the unsafe shipbreaking practices of a third party, the Zuma shipbreaking yard. However, the defendant's argument of third-party intervention could not succeed before the court, as the evidence was that the defendant-appellant had complete control over the sale of the vessel, its last destination, and price.

After hearing, the Court of Appeal accepted the plaintiff's appeal affirming the decision of the High Court of Justice and sent the matter back for trial. The court found that the shipowner would 'owe a legal duty of care to a shipbreaking worker in Bangladesh' because 'the shipowner created the danger for not foreseeing a state of danger which may be exploited by a third party'.[85] Moreover, referring to *Smith v Littlewoods*, the Court stated that the creation of danger is an exception to the third-party intervention principle.[86] Under this danger principle established in *Smith v Littlewoods*, a defendant may be held liable if it is reasonably foreseeable that third parties may exploit it, and for 'sparking off the danger'.[87] Coulson LJ also found that the shipowner's duty did not extinguish by the intervention of a third party—Zuma shipbreaking yard. Importantly, Coulson LJ further found that the shipowner would owe a legal duty because between a substandard shipbreaking yard in Bangladesh and a standard shipbreaking yard in China, the owner preferred selling the ship to Bangladesh to earn extra profit.

The Court further emphasised the issue of the profit motivation of the shipowner. The Court found that for the same ship, China was ready to pay USD 10 million whereas the Zuma shipbreaking yard, a shipbreaking company in Bangladesh, agreed to pay USD 16 million because the yard did not have to bear the expense of and arrange for providing safe conditions for its workers.[88] Coulson LJ explicitly mentioned that

---

[84] [1932] UKHL 100.

[85] *Maran Shipping* (n 71) [53]-[73] (Coulson J).

[86] *Smith v Littlewoods Organisation Ltd.* [1987] UKHL 18.

[87] *Maran Shipping* (n 71) [53].

[88] Ibid [121].

'the defendant-Maran (UK) Limited decided to prefer taking the money to workers in Bangladesh, to take the risk'.[89] The Court concluded that:

> The defendant was responsible for sending the ship to Bangladesh, knowing that this would expose workers such as the Claimant's husband to the risk of death or serious injury as a result of the negligence of the shipbreaker which employed him. It was not a case where there was merely a risk that the shipbreaker would fail to take reasonable care for the safety of its workers. In contrast, this was a certainty, as the defendant knew.[90]

The judgement has used the profit motivation of shipowners in establishing the responsibility of shipowners for the compensation payment. Although this decision was based on tort law principle, it reinforces the debate that a party that controls the business process and earns extra profit must follow due diligence and corporate responsibility to pay compensation in a given business context.

The Due Diligence Principle

The due diligence principle in the global context is derived from the common law of due diligence that has been accepted as a general principle recognised by civilised nations.[91] Owing diligence serves as an objective standard for introducing an obligation to the responsible parties aiming to ensure a minimum standard of protection,[92] and remediation. During the second half of the twentieth century, national courts used the due diligence principle as a principle of good faith in good neighbourly relations.[93]

For international issues, such as shipbreaking, the application of due diligence requires an additional legal mechanism. The principle itself does not create any binding obligation in relation to an inter-State business relationship. As discussed above, the RMG sector adopted this principle in the *Accord* after the Rana Plaza incident, which indicates that although the due diligence depends on the foreseeability of harm from international parties, it can only be applied subject to its inclusion in the regulatory mechanism of the industry under which it operates.[94] Without a specific mechanism to that end, introducing a direct link between value chains, where unsafe practices cause harm, and the international parties who control the business is highly unlikely. In other words, only knowledge of the abusive practice is not enough in the absence of a regulatory mechanism that incorporates the due diligence principle.

---

[89] Ibid [64].

[90] Ibid [124].

[91] This is a source of international law under art 38(1)(c) of the Statute of the ICJ: see the *Statute of the International Court of Justice*, opened for signature 26 June 1945, 33 UNTS 993, entered into force 18 April 1946.

[92] *Corfu Channel Case (United Kingdom v Albania)* [15 December 1949] ICJ Rep 1, 244; *Pulp Mills on the River Uruguay (Argentina v Uruguay)* [2006] ICJ Rep 113, 200.

[93] Robert McCorquodale et al., 'Human Rights Due Diligence in Law and Practice: Good Practices and Challenges for Business Enterprises' (2017) 2(2) *Business and Human Rights Journal* 195–224.

[94] Ibid.

The *Hong Kong Convention* does not provide any mechanism for applying the due diligence principle. Hence, the Convention does not provide a mechanism to ensure sound shipbreaking management in shipbreaking countries under the control and supervision of shipowners despite the deliberate use of substandard shipbreaking practices in South Asia. This is an indication that unless the shipbreaking industry adopts a treaty-based approach to introduce the due diligence principle, business as usual will continue. This means that uncompensated deaths and injuries in the industry will continue in the future, and there will be limited scope to apply other relevant principles, such as the principle of corporate responsibility.

The Principle of Corporate Responsibility

The corporate responsibility principle is an extension of the due diligence principle when a business involves several business entities. By the parameters of corporate responsibility, a business should respect human rights, included in fundamental human rights instruments such as the *Universal Declaration of Human Rights*,[95] and the *Declaration of Fundamental Principles and Rights at work*.[96] The *OECD Guidelines* and *United Nations Guiding Principles* promote corporate responsibility to respect human rights in the supply chain of an international business.

Under the *OECD Guidelines*, companies that have business connections with an entity directly responsible for violating the rights of workers bear a responsibility to prevent or mitigate its impact on violations of rights. The *OECD Guidelines* require companies to engage with their value chain to address systemic issues. Importantly, the *OECD Guidelines* recommend that companies should seek to mitigate and prevent adverse impacts by engaging with 'impacted or potentially impacted parties'.[97]

The *OECD Guidelines*, which include important labour rights and human rights, are similar to the *United Nations Guiding Principles*.[98] The *United Nations Guiding Principles* suggest that corporations are committed to respecting human rights and should refrain from performing any act or acts that may affect the core standard of human rights by avoiding and mitigating loss. Corporations therefore need to take steps that minimise adverse effects on humans.[99]

The *OECD Guidelines* and *United Nations Guiding Principles* are directly relevant to the shipbreaking industry and are therefore applicable to shipowners. With respect to the parameters of due diligence and corporate social responsibility, shipowners should respect the fundamental human rights of shipbreaking

---

[95] *Universal Declaration of Human Rights*, GA Res 217 A (III) UN GOAR, UN Doc A/810 (10 December 1948).

[96] *The ILO Declaration on Fundamental Principles and Rights at Work*, International Labour Conference, 86th Session, Geneva, 18 June 1998 (Annex revised 15 June 2010).

[97] *OECD Guidelines* [12].

[98] Some of the key rights are trade union rights, abolition of child labour, elimination of all forms of forced or compulsory labour, equal opportunity consultation, and co-operation between employers and workers, *OECD Guidelines*, ch V.

[99] The *United Nations Guiding Principles* [11], [12] and [13 (a)-(b)].

workers and refrain from selling ships unless shipbreaking facilities adopt safety measures to prevent accidents. If the prevention of accidents is not possible because of inherent dangers involved in the shipbreaking industry, shipowners should take steps to minimise human harms and provide adequate remedies to victims.[100] The *United Nations Guiding Principles*, in particular, recommend an effective judicial and administrative remedy contemplating the dangerous nature of an industry, such as shipbreaking.[101]

Doctrinal Basis of the Remedy System with Compensation

Broadly, in the context of business and human rights, the *United Nations Guiding Principles* suggest that 'remedies may include financial or nonfinancial compensation, apologies, restitution, rehabilitation, and punitive sanctions'.[102] According to the *United Nations Guiding Principles*, an aggrieved party may seek four different kinds of remedies depending on the facts of his or her case. One may seek restoration for one's full loss; compensation if the complete return of the loss is not possible; a person may want an apology to acknowledge and address the wrongness of an injustice grounded on a moral basis; or a person may want that the perpetrator suffers due punishment.[103]

In the context of shipbreaking, given that the death or serious injury of a worker demanding restitution for full loss is not possible, compensation is more acceptable than restoration, apology, and punishment. Apology or punishment falls short of addressing the economic loss of a victim worker, whereas compensation addresses the unaccounted loss. This means that it supplements a victim's loss of earnings due to a workplace accident. It also attempts to counterbalance an unjust loss with something equivalent in value to that loss. Broadly, shipbreaking would balance the profit earned by shipowners and the loss suffered, if any, by the victims.

However, as the *United Nations Guiding Principles* (*Principles*) are not mandatory laws, a question arises regarding the effectiveness of the *Principles*.[104] Moreover, the payment of compensation following an international mechanism is controversial because many international instruments shift responsibility to the concerned States where the violation has occurred. For instance, art 8 of the *Universal Declaration of Human Rights* states that 'everyone has the right to an effective remedy by the

---

[100] *The United Nations Guiding Principles* [11]-[12].

[101] Ibid [25]-[30].

[102] Ibid [25].

[103] Commentary, *The United Nations Guiding Principles* [111.A.25].

[104] International Federation of Human Rights (FIDH), *Joint Civil Society Statement on the Draft Guiding Principles on Business and Human Rights* (Web Page, 3 March 2011) http//www.fidh.org/UN-Forum-on-Business-and-Human-1259 ; Robert C. Blitt, 'Beyond Ruggie's Guiding Principles on Business and Human Rights: Charting an Embracive Approach' (2012) 48(1) *Texas International Law Journal* 33, 35.

competent national tribunals for acts violating the fundamental rights granted by the constitution of law'.

In contrast, from the perspective of a victim, in the absence of an effective mechanism for compensation in the national context, an international system is more appropriate for compensation for two main reasons. First, when the constitution guarantees the rights of workers but the national judiciary and tribunals are not legally able to enforce rights due to the loopholes in national laws and the unequal bargaining power between shipbreaking yards and workers, it becomes the associative duty of shipowners as international parties to follow international law and remedy victims in their value chain.[105] Second, as victimisation is the indirect effect of business the profit of shipowners, shipowners, both individually and collectively, have a moral obligation to remedy victims by introducing an appropriate financial system. To assess the claim for an international remedy system with a financial mechanism, the next section investigates several international human rights laws that in principle have focused on a global remedy with a financial mechanism.

Financial Compensation in the International Human Rights Law

International human rights laws emphasise on the financial reparation of victims. As a principle of customary international law, international human rights laws even suggest paying additional compensation to victims following an international mechanism.

Importantly, art 2(3) of the *International Covenant on Civil and Political Rights* (ICCPR) provides that 'each person whose rights or freedoms as herein recognised are violated shall have an effective remedy for granting financial reparation to victims of human rights violation'.[106] This provision is controversial. Some scholars argue that the ICCPR provides no ground for financial remedies since it focuses only on procedural rights,[107] whereas the International Law Commission's *Drafts Articles on the Responsibility of States for Internationally Wrongful Acts* and Human Rights Committee maintain that 'customary international law recognises the duty

[105] See Chap. 4.

[106] *International Covenant on Civil and Political Rights*, opened for signature 16 December 1966, 999 UNTS 171 (entered into force 23 March 1976) art 6.

[107] Walter Kalin and Jorg Kunzli, *The Law of International Human Rights Protection* (Oxford University Press, 2019) 192.

to pay compensation'.[108] Duty to pay compensation as a principle, not a procedure, became clearer when the United Nations General Assembly (UNGA) in 1999 declared that 'everyone has the right to benefit from an effective remedy, including any compensation due'.[109]

Moreover, some international laws also recommend paying compensation in addition to the remedies available from the courts of the State where the shipbreaking yards are located (State remedies). Art 14 of the *Convention Against Torture* states that 'the individual victim or his or her dependents in the case of death shall have a direct right to financial compensation from the responsible parties and states must ensure this'.[110] An important development of the provision is that it adds to State remedies, that is, irrespective of remedies available from the State courts, victims can seek remedies from the parties who profit from the industry. The *United Nations Declaration of Basic Principles of Justice for Victims of Crime and Abuse of Power* also recognises the general principle of compensation specifically in the case of 'unlawful detention and acts of political brutality'.[111]

These declarations and documents demonstrate that there is a quest to form an international principle under the UN to impose responsibility for human harm with a financial mechanism on international parties in addition to or in absence of State remedies. This is also evident in the regional mechanisms where the Member States have commonly accepted that compensation is the most suitable remedy for human harm. For instance, art 13 of the *European Union Convention on Human Rights* and Art 41 of the *European Union Court of Human Rights* allows the *European Union Court of Human Rights* to order financial remedies for human harm.

Importance of a Special Responsibility Framework for Global Issues

It follows from the above international law principles that there is a recognised need to introduce a special responsibility framework to address global injustice, where

[108] International Law Commission, *Drafts Articles on Responsibility of States for Internationally Wrongful Acts*, November 2001, Supplement No. 10 (A/56/10), chp.IV.E.1, art 31,34, and 36; Human Rights Committee, *Ann Maria Garcia Lanza de Netto* v *Uruguay* Communication No 8/1977, UN Doc CCPR/C/OP/1 (1984) 45(*'Weissmann Communication')*. A principle becomes a customary international law if it satisfies two criteria. First, the principle must be well-settled and practised by the States and second, States obey the rule because they consider themselves legally bound by it, not just because of tradition, politeness, or convenience, see Monica Hakimi, 'Making Sense of Customary International Law' (2020) 118(8) *Michigan Law Review* 1487, 1488.

[109] *Declaration on the Rights and Responsibility of Individuals, Groups and Organs of Society to Promote and Protect Universally Recognised Human Rights and Fundamental Freedoms*, UN Doc GA Res 53/144 (8 March 1999) art 9(1).

[110] *Convention against Torture and Other Cruel, Inhuman or Degrading Treatment or Punishment*, opened for signature 10 December 1984, 1465 UNTS 85 (entered into force 26 June 1987).

[111] *The United Nations Declaration of Basic Principles of Justice for Victims of Crime and Abuse of Power*, UN Doc, GA Res 40/34 (29 November 1985) art 12.

business related deaths, injuries, and diseases are issues. Although, in principle, the abovementioned instruments have established a strong basis for compensation, the mechanisms have not introduced a direct procedure so that a victim can pursue an individual claim against a non-State actor or a State.

There are two ways to access a financial remedy. One of the ways to access a financial claim rests with State actions. A concerned State party can initiate a complaint or communication procedure, where a State brings the matter to an international tribunal or communicates directly with another country to seek compensation in the event of a mass violation of human rights.[112] Both American and African Human Rights Courts follow this approach.[113]

Another process involves filing an individual complaint before the concerned regional human rights court to decide on a victim's remedy.[114]The European Union Court of Human Rights follows this approach. Nevertheless, the problem is that both approaches may lead to traditional litigation processes and the concerned courts finally have to decide on the remedy. Without a direct remedy system, the traditional State action or litigation approach has created a weak procedure for an individual victim to enforce their rights, especially against a State or a non-State actor.[115] Owing to the weakness of the law, there is a growing demand within the legal community to introduce a special responsibility framework for compensating for specific human consequences.[116] Importantly, Bachmann argues for a global instrument to impose civil responsibility in the context of gross human rights violation.[117] Shipbreaking falls into the category of a special regime that causes regular human rights violations because of the hazardous nature of the industry itself.[118]

---

[112] *The Basic Principles and Guidelines on the Right to A Remedy and Reparation for Victims of Gross Violations of International Human Rights Law and Serious Violations of International Humanitarian Law*, UN Doc, GA Res 60/147 (16 December 2005) ch 7 [12] & ch 9 [15]; *American Convention on Human Rights*, opened for signature 22 November 1969, 1144 UNTS 123 (entered into force 18 July 1978) art 25.

[113] *American Convention on Human Rights*, opened for signature 22 November 1969, 1144 UNTS 123 (entered into force 18 July 1978) art 25; *Protocol to the African Charter on Human and People's Rights on the Establishment of An African Court on Human and Peoples' Rights*, opened for signature 10 June 1998, AU Doc, Assembly/AU/Dec.45 & Assembly/AU/Dec.83(V) (entered into force 25 January 2004) arts 28–30. Under the regional human rights instruments, the Inter-American Court of Human Rights and the African Court of Human Rights have not been entrusted with the duty to hear and decide individual claims.

[114] Art 47(1) of the *Charter of Fundamental Rights of the European Union*, opened for signature 2000, EU Doc, OJ C 326/ 391 (entered into force December 2009) provides the power to European Union Human Rights Court to hear individual claims.

[115] Sascha-Dominik Bachmann, *Civil Responsibility for Gross Human Rights Violations – The Need for a Global Instrument* (Pretoria University Law Press, 2007) 11–12.

[116] Ibid.

[117] Ibid.

[118] Okechukwu Ibeanu, *Report of the Special Rapporteur on the Adverse Effects of the Movement and Dumping of Toxic and Dangerous Products and Wastes on the Enjoyment of Human Rights*, UN Doc. A/HRC/12/26 (15 July 2009).

Argument for a Treaty-Based Civil Responsibility Approach for the Shipbreaking Industry

Chap. 9 of this book discusses the feature of a treaty-based civil liability framework, tailored to the unique and hazardous conditions of the shipbreaking industry—an industry marked by frequent fatalities, injuries, and chronic illnesses resulting from prolonged exposure to toxic substances. The rational for such a framework rests on two foundational arguments.

The first justification lies in the need to provide affected workers—or the families of those who have died as a result of unsafe working conditions—with a direct legal avenue to seek compensation from shipowners or their designated shipbreaking insurers. While international instruments such as the *OECD Guidelines* and the *United Nations Guiding Principles* provide important normative expectations, they remain non-binding. Their effectiveness is therefore contingent upon integration into a legally binding regime. Addressing this normative—enforcement gap, the proposed shipbreaking liability certificate (SLC) would function as a binding legal instrument, obligating shipowners to maintain insurance or financial security to cover liabilities arising from harm to workers. This mechanism would not only operationalise the policy goals of existing international principles but also ensure that accountability is not evaded through jurisdictional fragmentation or corporate opacity.

Nevertheless, a philosophical basis for such an enforceable mechanism is subject to debate in relation to regulating business and human rights in the global context. For example, while Rawls acknowledges the role of human rights in regulating international conduct, his framework largely confines responsibility within a State that does not extend liability to transnational corporate actors.[119] Conversely, Pogge offers a more compelling normative foundation through his theory of rectificatory global justice. Pogge contends that when powerful actors—such as shipowners from industrialised nations—benefit from systemic structures that disadvantage weaker communities, they incur a moral and legal obligation to rectify the resulting harms.[120] This perspective is particularly salient in the context of shipbreaking, where the economic benefits of maritime commerce are concentrated in the Global North, while the human and environmental costs are disproportionately borne by workers in the Global South.

The second rationale for endorsing a treaty-based civil liability framework lies in its capacity to offer a robust and compulsory safety net for individuals harmed by the inherently dangerous process of shipbreaking. In contrast, Yujuico has proposed a corporate social responsibility (CSR) model tailored to the shipbreaking sector in South Asia. His approach envisions a voluntary funding mechanism aimed at improving safety and environmental standards within the region's ship recycling yards.[121] However, the application of the CSR model for the shipbreaking industry is

---

[119] John Rawls, *A theory of Justice* (Oxford University Press, 1999, rev ed) 109.

[120] Thomas Pogge, 'World Poverty and Human Rights' (2005) 19(1) *Ethics and International Affairs* 1–7.

[121] Emmanuel Yujuico, 'Demandeur Pays: The EU and Funding Improvements in South Asian Ship Recycling Practices' (2014) 67 *Transportation Research Part A: Policy and Practice* 340, 348–349.

not suitable for two reasons. First, CSR model fails to assign binding obligations to international stakeholders—particularly shipowners and flag States from developed nations—whose decisions and practices significantly shape the industry. The model's reliance on voluntary participation renders it vulnerable to the shifting political and economic priorities of wealthier States, thereby undermining its reliability and reach. Second, the CSR framework lack enforceability.[122] It does not establish any legal consequences for non-compliance, nor does it provide mechanisms for redress or accountability. That said, the proposed civil liability framework does not dismiss the broader value of CSR in promoting ethical business conduct. However, within the specific context of shipbreaking—where systemic non-compliance by shipowners has been well documented—a voluntary model is insufficient. The persistent failure of industry actors to adhere to CSR commitments underscores the need for a binding legal structure that compels compliance and ensures that victims are not left without recourse.[123] Thus, the SLC offers a more effective and just alternative. By mandating financial responsibility and enabling direct claims by affected individuals, it is aimed at transforming abstract ethical obligations into enforceable legal duties.

Chapters 7 and 8 examine civil liability as an effective approach for compensation where the insurance and other responsible parties share the burden for compensation as used in inter-State oil transport, the waste trade, and the mining business. The incorporation of the features within the SLC is required to meet five important objectives. First, it is easy to facilitate claims. Second, it can protect the industry from excessive claims. Third, it allows a victim to claim compensation directly. Fourth, the insurance industry will be directly responsible for the victims on behalf of the shipowner, and at last, the victim will not require proving the fault of any party or party for one's claim.[124]

Conclusion

The global legal framework governing shipbreaking is an example of a postcolonial legal order that perpetuates structural injustices against workers in the Global South. Instruments such as the *Hong Kong International Convention* predominantly reflect the interests of developed marine nations—historically the colonial powers—and their shipping corporations. This legal architecture, while ostensibly aimed at regulating environmental and labour standards, disproportionately safeguards the economic interests of shipowners while failing to adequately address the human costs of shipbreaking operation in countries like India, Bangladesh, and Pakistan. Overall, the *Hong Kong Convention*'s failure to impose binding obligations on shipowners to

[122] Ibid.

[123] Ishtiaque Ahmed, 'Safe and Environmentally Sound Recycling of Ships' (20,200) 31 (1) *Fordham Environmental Law Review* 60–106.

[124] Chapter 9 discusses these objectives in detail.

compensate for workplace fatalities and injuries reveals a critical gap in the international regime. Without structural reform that centres the lived realities of shipbreaking workers, the industry will remain mired in systemic injustice.[125] It is argued in this chapter that the theory of rectificatory global justice can address this offering a compelling normative foundation.

It posits that actors who have historically benefited from exploitative global practices—such as shipowners—bear a moral and legal responsibility to rectify the hams caused to workers. This is reinforced by the duty of care principle articulated in *Maran Shipping*, as well as established norms in international law concerning due diligence and corporate accountability. These principles collectively affirm that shipowners, who possess both the technical knowledge and financial capacity, must be held liable for the risks and harms associated with shipbreaking. However, while international legal instruments increasingly acknowledge the need for equitable treatment and worker protection, many of these commitments remain aspirational. Soft law mechanisms, such as voluntary guidelines and non-binding principles, lack the enforceability necessary to compel compliance or provide redress. As such, a shift towards a treaty-based legal framework is essential.

A binding international treaty should establish a direct right of action for affected workers, enabling them to seek compensation from shipowners. The mechanism should mandate shared financial responsibility between shipowners and shipbreaking enterprises, ensuring that the burden of remediation does not fall solely on the economically weaker parties. Such a framework should allow individuals to claim compensation directly from shipowners, with costs shared between shipowners and shipbreaking industries. The next chapter presents the statistics and analyses the problems of the shipbreaking industry in detail.

Bibliography

Articles/Books/Reports

Alam, Shawkat and Abdullah Faruque, 'Legal Regulation of the Shipbreaking Industry in Bangladesh: The International Regulatory Frameworks and Domestic Implementation Challenges' (2014) 47 *Marine Policy* 46

Alcadidea, Juan Ignacio, Francisco Piniella and Emilio Rodriguez-Diaza, 'The Mirror Flags: Ship Registration in Globalised Shipbreaking Industry' (2016) 48 *Transportation Research Part D* 378

Amighetti, Sara and Alaisa Nuti, 'Towards Shared Redress: Achieving Historical Justice Through Democratic Deliberation' (2015) 23(4) *The Journal of Political Philosophy* 385

Blake, Michael and Patrick Taylor Smith, 'International Distributive Justice' in Edward N. Zalta (ed) *The Stanford Encyclopaedia of Philosophy* (Stanford University, Summer 2021) 40

Blake, Michael, 'Distributive Justice, State Coercion, and Autonomy' (2001) 30 *Philosophy and Public Affairs* 257

---

[125] Lavanya Rajamani, *The Changing Fortunes of Differential Treatment in the Evolution of International Environmental Law* (2012) 88 (3) *International Affairs* 605–623.

Byers, Michael 'Abuse of Rights: An Old Principle, New Age' (2002) 47 *McGill Law Journal* 389
Cairns, George, 'Return to Chittagong: Ten Years since the "Postcard"' (2017) 13(4) *Critical Perspectives on International Business* 340
Campbell, Tom D., 'Humanity before Justice in Global Perspective' (1974) 4 *British Journal of Political Science* 219
Donaghey, Jimmy and Juliane Reinecke, 'When Industrial Democracy Meets Corporate Social Responsibility – A Comparison of the Bangladesh Accord and Alliance as Responses to the Rana Plaza' (March 2018) 56(1) *British Journal of Industrial Relations* 14
Frey, Robert Scott, 'Breaking Ships in the World-System: An Analysis of Two Ship Breaking Capitals, Alang-Sosiya, India and Chittagong, Bangladesh' (2015) 21(1) *Journal of World System Research* 25
Gardiner, Stephen M., 'Ethics and Global Climate Change' (April 2004) 114(4) *University of Chicago Press Journals* 580
George M. Cairns, 'Return to Chittagong: Ten Years since the "Postcard" (2017) 13(4) *Critical Perspectives on International Business* 340
Hadjiyianni, Ioanna and Anna Kloni, 'Regulating Shipbreaking As a Global Activity: Issues of Fragmentation and Injustice' (2021) *Journal of Environmental Law* 211
Hakimi, Monica, 'Making Sense of Customary International Law' (2020) 118(8) *Michigan Law Review* 1487
Jageuken, Christian et al, 'The EU Circular Economy and Its Relevance to Metal Recycling' (Special Issue 2016) 1(2) *Public Policy Directions for Directions for Recycling, Waste Management, Resource Recovery and Circular Economy* 242
Jaggar, Alison M., 'Vulnerable Women and Neo-Liberal Globalisation: Debt Burdens Undermine Women's Health in the Global South,' (2002) 23 *Theoretical Medicine* 425
James S. Coleman, Boris Frankel and Derek L. Phillips, 'Robert Nozick's Anarchy, State, and Utopia' (1976) 3(3) *Theory and Society* 437
Jonathan Bonnitcha and Robert McCorquodale, 'The Concept of 'Due Diligence' in the Guiding Principles on Business and Human Rights' (2017) 28(3) *The European Journal of International Law* 899
Karim, Md. Saiful, 'Environmental Pollution from the Shipbreaking Industry: International Law and National Legal Response' (2010) 22 *Georgetown International Law Review* 185
Kecskes, Gabos, 'The Concept of State Responsibility and Liability in Nuclear Law' (2008) 49(2) *Acta Jurdica Hungarica* 221
Meyer, Lukas H. and Dominic Roser, 'Climate Justice and Historical Emissions' (2010) 13(1) *Critical Review of International Social and Political Philosophy* 229
Pogge, Thomas, 'World Poverty and Human Rights' (2005) 19 (1) *Ethics and International Affairs* 1
Renzo, Mossimo, 'Why Colonialism is Wrong' (2019) 72(1) *Current Legal Problems* 347
Robert C. Blitt, 'Beyond Ruggie's Guiding Principles on Business and Human Rights: Charting an Embracive Approach' (2012) 48(1) *Texas International Law Journal* 33
Roy, Alpana, 'Postcolonial Theory and Law: A Critical Introduction' (2008) 29 *Adelaide Law Review* 315
Sangiovanni, Andrea, 'Global Justice, Reciprocity, and the State' (2007) 35 *Philosophy and Public Affairs* 3
Sen, Amartya, 'Rawls versus Bentham: An Axiomatic Examination of the Pure Distribution Problem' (1974) 4 *Theory and Decision* 301
Voyame, Joseph, Bertil Cottier and Boliver Rocha, 'Abuse of Right in Comparative Law' (Conference Paper, European Union Law, 6-9 November 1989) 23
YPI, Lea, Robert E. Goodin, and Christian Barry, 'Associative Duties, Global Justice, and the Colonies' (2009) 37(2) *Philosophy and Public Affairs* 103
Yujuico, Emmanuel, 'Demandeur Pays: The EU and Funding Improvements in South Asian Ship Recycling Practices' (2014) 67 *Transportation Research Part A: Policy and Practice* 340

Bachmann, Sascha-Dominik, *Civil Responsibility for Gross Human Rights Violations – The Need for a Global Instrument* (Pretoria University Law Press, 2007)
Brian Barry, 'Humanity and Justice in Global Perspective' in James Ronald Pennock and James Wack Chapman (eds), *Ethics, Economics and the Law* (New York University Press, 1982) 219
Brock, Gillian, 'Global Justice' in Edward N. Zalta (ed) *The Stanford Encyclopaedia of Philosophy* (Stanford University, Spring 2017)
Collste, Goran, *Global Rectificatory Justice* (Springer Link, 2014)
Farooque, Mohiuddin, 'Regulatory Framework and Some Examples of Environmental Contamination in Bangladesh' in Bangladesh Environmental Lawyers Association (ed), *Selected Writings of Mohiuddin Farooque: Environmental Order the Security of Survival* (BELA, 2004) 20
Karim, Md Saiful, *Recycling of Ships in* 'Prevention of Pollution of the Maritime Environment from Vessels: Potential Limit of the International Maritime Organisation' (Springer, 2015)
Karim, Saiful, *Shipbreaking in Developing Countries: A Requiem for Environmental Justice from the Perspectives of Bangladesh* (Taylor and Francis Group, 2018)
Nozick, Robert, *Anarchy, State, and Utopia* (Basic Books & Oxford, 1974)
Pevnick, Ryan, *Immigration and the Constraints of Justice: Between Open Borders and Absolute Sovereignty* (Cambridge University Press, New York, 2011)
Rajamani, Lavanya, *Differential Treatment in International Environmental Law* (Oxford University Press, 2006)
Rajamani, Lavanya, *Differential Treatment in International Law* (Oxford University Press, 2006)
Rawls, John, *A Theory of Justice* (Oxford University Press, 1999 rev ed)
Roberts, Rodney C. (ed), *Injustice and Rectification* (Peter Lang, 2002)
Sen, Amartya, *The Idea of Justice* (The Belknap Press of Harvard University Press, 2009)
Walker, Gordon, *Environmental Justice, Concepts, Evidence and Politics* (Routledge, 2012)
Weeramanty, Christopher George, *Universalising International Law* (Brill Publications, 2004) vol 48
Whiteman, M., *Digest of International Law* (Washington DC: Government Printing Office, 1965) vol 5, 224–30
Appellate body Report, *United States – Import Prohibition of Certain Shrimp and Shrimp Products*, WTO Doc WT/DS58/AB/R (6 November 1998)
Clean Cloth Campaigns, 'Human Rights Due Diligence' (Position Paper, March 2016)
Human Rights Committee, *Ann Maria Garcia Lanza de Netto* v *Uruguay* Communication No 8/ 1977, UN Doc CCPR/C/OP/1 (1984)
Ibeanu, Okechukwu, *Report of the Special Rapporteur on the Adverse Effects of the Movement and Dumping of Toxic and Dangerous Products and Wastes on the Enjoyment of Human Rights*, UN Doc. A/HRC/12/26 (15 July 2009)
International Law Commission, *Drafts Articles on Responsibility of States for Internationally Wrongful Acts*, November 2001, Supplement No. 10 (A/56/10)

Cases

Corfu Channel Case (United Kingdom v Albania) [15 December 1949] ICJ Rep 1, 244
Hamida Begum (on behalf of MD Khalil Mollah) v Maran (UK) Limited [2021] EWCA Civ 326. (10 March 2021). *(Maran Shipping)*
Hamida Begum (on behalf of MD Khalil Mollah) v Maran (UK) Limited [2020] EWHC 1846 (QB) (13 July 2020)
Pulp Mills on the River Uruguay (Argentina v Uruguay) [2006] ICJ Rep 113, 200
Smith v Littlewoods Organisation Ltd. [1987] UKHL 18
The *Gabcikovo-Nogumoaros Project (Hungary v Slovakia)* [1997] ICJ Rep 7, 22

Treaties

American Convention on Human Rights, opened for signature 22 November 1969, 1144 UNTS 123 (entered into force 18 July 1978)

American Convention on Human Rights, opened for signature 22 November 1969, 1144 UNTS 123 (entered into force 18 July 1978)

Charter of Fundamental Rights of the European Union, opened for signature 2000, EU Doc, OJ C 326/ 391 (entered into force December 2009)

Convention against Torture and Other Cruel, Inhuman or Degrading Treatment or Punishment, opened for signature 10 December 1984, 1465 UNTS 85 (entered into force 26 June 1987)

Convention for the Protection of Human Rights and Fundamental Freedoms, opened for signature 4 November 1950, 213 UNTS 222 (entered into force 4 November 1953)

Declaration on the Rights and Responsibility of Individuals, Groups and Organs of Society to Promote and Protect Universally Recognised Human Rights and Fundamental Freedoms, UN Doc GA Res 53/144 (8 March 1999)

European Commission, *Communication from the Commission to the European Parliament, the Council, the European Economic and Social Committee and the Committee of the Regions: Closing the Loop – A EU Action Plan for the Circular Economy*, COM (2015) 614/2

International Covenant on Civil and Political Rights, opened for signature 16 December 1966, 999 UNTS 171 (entered into force 23 March 1976)

John Ruggie , *Guiding Principles for the Implementation of the United Nations 'Protect, Respect and Remedy Framework,* Report of the Special Representative of the Secretary-General on the issue of human rights and transnational corporations and other business enterprises, UN Doc A/ HRC/17/31 (March 2011). (*the United Nations Guiding Principles*)

OECD Guidelines for Multinational Enterprises, Recommendations for Responsible Business Conduct in a Global Context 2011 http://www.oecd.org/investment/mne/1922428.pdf

Organisation for Economic Co-operation and Development (OECD), *OECD Guidelines for Multinational Enterprises*, 2nd ed, 2000 http://www.oecd.org/daf/investment/guidelines/mnetext.htm

Protocol to the African Charter on Human and People's Rights on the Establishment of An African Court on Human and Peoples' Rights, opened for signature 10 June 1998, AU Doc, Assembly/ AU/Dec.45 & Assembly/AU/Dec.83(V) (entered into force 25 January 2004)

Statute of the International Court of Justice, opened for signature 26 June 1945, 33 UNTS 993, entered into force 18 April 1946

The Basic Principles and Guidelines on the Right to A Remedy and Reparation for Victims of Gross Violations of International Human Rights Law and Serious Violations of International Humanitarian Law, UN Doc, GA Res 60/147 (16 December 2005

The Hong Kong International Convention for the Safe and Environmentally Sound Recycling of Ships, opened for Signature 1 September 2009, IMO Doc. SR/CONF45 (not yet in force)

The ILO Declaration on Fundamental Principles and Rights at Work, International Labour Conference, 86th Session, Geneva, 18 June 1998 (Annex revised 15 June 2010)

The United Nations Declaration of Basic Principles of Justice for Victims of Crime and Abuse of Power, UN Doc, GA Res 40/34 (29 November 1985)

United Nations Convention on the Law of the Sea, opened for signature10 December 1982, 21 ILM 1261 (entered into force 16 November 1994)

Universal Declaration of Human Rights, GA Res 217 A (III) UN GOAR, UN Doc A/810 (10 December 1948)

Others

Alyssa Ayress, 'A Guide to the Rana Plaza Tragedy, and Its Implications, in Bangladesh', *the Forbes* (online at 24 April 2014) https://www.forbes.com/sites/alyssaayres/2014/04/24/a-guide-to-the-rana-plaza-tragedy-and-its-implications-in-bangladesh/#62b4d3b62c50

Bangladesh. Bangladesh Accord, *Accord on Fire and Building Safety in Bangladesh* (Web Page) http://bangladeshaccord.org/

Bangladesh Worker Safety, *Alliance for Bangladesh Worker Safety* (Web Page) http://www.bangladeshworkersafety.org/

GMS Leadership, *World's Largest Buyer of Ships and Offshore Assets* (Webpage, 2019) http://www.gmsinc.net

International Federation of Human Rights (FIDH), *Joint Civil Society Statement on the Draft Guiding Principles on Business and Human Rights* (Web Page, 3 March 2011) http://www.fidh.org/UN-Forum-on-Business-and-Human-1259

Philosophy Overdose, Rawl's Theory of Justice (September 12, 2016) https://www.youtube.com/watch?v=zhVByiXBxi4

Chapter 3
The Shipbreaking Industry in South Asia: Economic Gains and Profit-Making at the Cost of Workers' Health and Safety

Abstract This chapter provides factual background to argue that workers' deaths, injuries, and occupational diseases that occur in the shipbreaking industry are the issues of transnational injustice. It aims to conceptualise how the shipbreaking industry in South Asia and the global maritime industry, which represents shipowners, are inextricably linked to business profit, i.e., the profits that the maritime industry receives from the sale of ships to the shipbreaking industry in South Asia. Although the global maritime industry earns millions of dollars per annum from the sale of ships to the South Asian shipbreaking market, the industry has yet to call for, or contribute to, any scheme to provide adequate compensation to workers for death, injury, or disease-related economic loss.

Keywords Business and shipbreaking · Human harms · Transnational injustice · Sale of ships · Scheme of compensation · Beaching · Hazardous materials · Dry dock method · Socio-economic benefit · Environmental harms

Introduction

This chapter places evidence based on facts for a treaty-based civil liability framework specific, namely the shipbreaking liability certificate (SLC). It argues that the shipbreaking in South Asia is mainly a question of the maritime industry's business profit.

This chapter is organised as follows. Section "Overview of the Shipbreaking Industry" explores the commercial interconnection between the shipbreaking sector and the broader global maritime industry. Section "The Role of the Shipbreaking Industry in South Asian Economies" then examines the financial profitability of the global maritime industry and highlights the economic advantages that South Asian nations derive from shipbreaking activities, contending that maritime stakeholders benefit most when vessels that are no longer fit for commercial trading exported to South Asia for disposal. Section "Business Profit of the Maritime Industry, Cash Buyers, and Open Registry Countries" investigates human rights issues within the

M. Z. Ali, *Worker Injustices in the South Asian Shipbreaking Industry*, International Law in Asia, https://doi.org/10.1007/978-981-95-8325-6_3

South Asian shipbreaking landscape, drawing on findings from international and non-governmental bodies regarding occupational hazards and health risks. Section "Analyses of Labour, Environmental Standards, and Human Rights Abuses in South Asian Shipbreaking Industry" concludes by inciting the debate for a global legal framework aimed at addressing human harms, including injuries, deaths and diseases at workplace) particularly within the cross-border shipbreaking industry.

Overview of the Shipbreaking Industry

Life Cycle of Ships

The maritime industry operates globally that typically ends in the breaking of ships. Maritime commercial activities are extensive, with roughly 80% of global trade reliant on international shipping.[1] Presently, over 50,000 merchant ships are engaged in cross-border transportation of diverse range of goods.[2] But the question is: what does happen to these ships when they are no longer fit for commercial trading? Once ships reach end of their operational life and are deemed unsuitable for commercial use, they are primarily sent to South Asian shipbreaking facilities. Given that approximately 80–90% of a ship's structure consists of steel, these vessels become valuable sources of recyclable metal, making them attractive investments for South Asian buyers.[3]

The growth of shipbreaking is closely intertwined with fluctuations in scrap metal prices within these regions. For instance, during the 2007 financial crisis, scrap rates in South Asia surged from USD 200 to USD 300 per Light Displacement Tonnage (total weight of a ship excluding any cargo and fuel stored in a ship, which is only used for the shipbreaking market) over a ten-month span, leading to the sale of more than 700 ships for breaking.[4] Furthermore, between 2019 and 2021, market data indicated a 19.5% increase in the cost of end-of-life ships, reflecting broader inflationary trends in the global iron market.[5]

---

[1] United Nations Conference on Trade and Development, 'Review of Maritime Transport 2024' (Annual Report, 2024) https://unctad.org/publication/review-maritime-transport-2024.

[2] International Chamber of Shipping, 'Shipping and World Trade: World Seaborne Trade' https://www.ics-shipping.org/shipping-fact/shipping-and-world-trade-world-seaborne-trade/.

[3] Bisma Mannan, Md Jahir Rizvi, and Yong Ming Dai, 'Ship Recycling in Developing Economies of South Asia: Changing Liability to a Commodity' (2024) 2(2) *Green Technology and Sustainability* (online) https://doi.org/10.1016/j.grets.2023.100064 .

[4] Thanasis Karlis, Dionysios Polemis, and Anastasios Georgakis, 'Ship Demolition Activity: An Evaluation of the Effect of Currency Exchange Rates on Ship Scrap Values' (2016) 66(3) *Journal of Economics and Business* 53–70.

[5] Sam Chambers, 'Second Hand Ship Prices and Sales Volumes Scale Heights' *Splash247.com* (Webpage, 4 March 2024) https://splash247.com/secondhand-ship-prices-and-sales-volumes-scale-heights/.

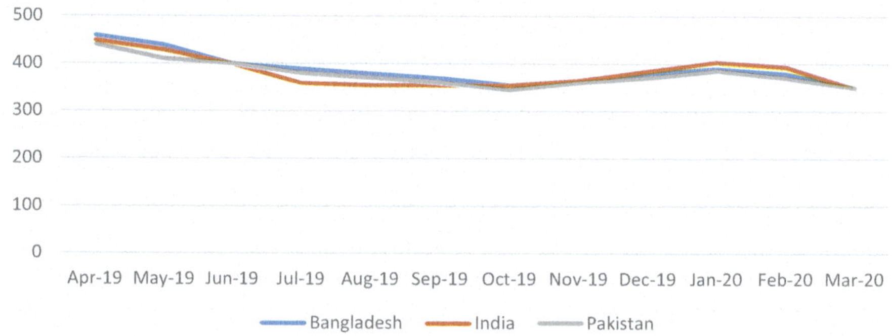

Fig. 3.1 Scrap prices in South Asian countries (April 2019–March 2020) (*Source* Allied Shipbroking—Monthly Report April 2020)

Table 3.1 Prices of steel scraps of different classes of ships in 2019

Rank	Location	Dry Bulk USD per LDT	Tanker USD per LDT	Container USD per LDT
1	India	375	USD 385/LDT	USD 395/LDT
2	Bangladesh	365	USD 375/LDT	USD 385/LDT
3	Pakistan	355	USD 355/LDT	USD 375/LDT
4	Turkey	280	USD 270/MT	USD 280/MT

Source Global Maritime Services April 2020

The upward trajectory of scrap metal princes is influenced by various other factors, notably domestic demand from the construction sector. For instance, between 2019 and 2021, the rise in scrap valuations was strategically aligned with efforts to stimulated steel consumption within Bangladesh's infrastructure development. According to data compiled from the Global Maritime Service and Allied Shipbroking sources (refer to Fig. 3.1 and Table 3.1), steel prices began to stabilise in mid-2019, averaging around USD 350 to 400 per Light Displacement Tonnage (LDT.[6]

Methods Used for Shipbreaking

Besides domestic demand from the construction sector, labour availability and regulatory compliance costs significantly influence operations within the shipbreaking sector.[7] Because South Asian countries can sustain offering low wages and relatively lax enforcement of environmental and safety protocols (refer to Chap. 4) and thus

[6] Allied Shipbroking, *Weekly SnP Statistics Report Week 34 2022* (Web Page) https://www.hellenicshippingnews.com/allied-shipbroking-weekly-snp-statistics-report-week-34-2022/.

[7] Ibid.

low compliance costs, it is a privilege for their shipbreaking companies. Accordingly, shipbreaking companies in South Asia can offer higher prices for ships for breaking than those in other locations. In addition, shipbreaking companies across South Asia frequently employ the beaching method (ships are run on and broken on the beaches), which offers a more economical solution compared to higher-cost approaches such as dry docking, or lay-up or reefing.

The dry dock method of shipbreaking involves stripping vessels within a sealed and drained enclosure, distinguishing it from lay-up and reefing approaches, which mainly involve submerging intact ships. While dry dock method is considered the safest and most controlled method of shipbreaking, it is also the costliest. Industrialised nations such as China, the UK, and the US have adopted this method,[8] yet its financial impractically limits the number of vessels processed annually, especially given the stringent oversight imposed by national regulatory authorities. This method requires the systematic segregation of hazardous and non-hazardous substances and their sound disposal prior to the hull of a ship is cut. For example, hazardous materials such as asbestos, commonly found in engine compartments, are extracted, encased in specialised containment materials, and disposed of in accordance with rigorous occupational health and safety protocols, mainly through secure burial.[9]

The lay-up process, although considered a safe practice, is not utilised for breaking ships, rather, it serves as a temporary suspension of operations when market conditions result in excess shipping capacity.[10] This inactive phase can span from several weeks to multiple years, during which ships are anchored in appropriate coastal zones.[11] Nevertheless, due to the substantial infrastructure required, shipowners often avoid this method.[12] Reefing represents another method of disposing a ship, involving the removal of hazardous components and deliberate sinking at designated sites.[13] Despite its safety benefits, this technique is rarely implemented owing to the significant expenses liked to the cleaning, decontaminating, and secure sinking of ships.

Conversely, the common beaching method employed in South Asia, entails driving ships ashore during high tide, followed by breaking them in open conditions without

---

[8] Suman Barua et al., 'Environmental Hazards Associated with Open-Beach Breaking of End-of-Life Ships: A Review' (2018) 25 *Environmental Science and Policy Research* 30,880–30,993 https://link.springer.com/article/10.1007/s11356-018-3159-8.

[9] Ibid.

[10] Teekay, 'Step-by-Step: A Glimpse into the Dry-Docking Process' (Web Page, 18 April 2016) https://www.teekay.com/blog/2016/04/18/step-step-glimpse-dry-docking-process/#:~:text=What%20is%20Dry%2Ddocking%20and,best%20ships%20in%20the%20industry.

[11] Jun-Ki Choi et al., 'Economic and Environmental Perspective of End-of-Life Ship Management' (2016) 107 *Resources, Conservation and Recycling* 82, 83.

[12] Shipowners, 'What Steps should a Prudent Shipowner Take When Placing Vessels in Layup?' (Web Page, 13 December 2016) https://www.shipownersclub.com/latest-updates/news/what-steps-should-prudent-shipowner-take-when-placing-vessels-layup/.

[13] Choi et al. (n 9) 85.

Table 3.2 Costs and profit from breaking a ship in Bangladesh and Pakistan

	Bangladesh		Pakistan	
Revenues from selling steel and other reusable materials	USD 5,613,600		USD 5,505,500	
Total costs	4,692,200	(82%)	5,340,900	(82%)
Purchase of ships	3,848,000	(1.97%)	3,848,000	(4.97%)
Labour Costs (salary is 2 euros a day) Platform	92,700	(6.44%)	233,400	(4.91%)
report 2010	302,200	(3.15%)	230,000	(5.66%)
Consumables	147,900	(5.61%)	265,700	(14.7%)
Financial Costs	263,000	(0.81%)	693,600	(1.4%)
Taxes, Tariffs, and duties	38,400		70,200	
Other costs				
(Including rents, investment costs, etc.)				
Profit	921,400 (16%)		164,600 (3%)	

Source World Bank report 2010[17]

the need for storage facilities.[14] As characterised by the Norwegian Shipowners' Association, this method relies on the absence of fixed infrastructure and frequently results in improper containment of harmful wastes. However, compared to alternatives such as dry docking, lay-up, or reefing, beaching offers economic advantages, particularly due to its low operational and environmental compliance costs.[15]

End-of-life ships often contain substantial quantities of harmful substances, including asbestos and mercury, embedded within their structures. When breaking occurs along coastal or beach zones, these toxic materials are frequently deposited on the shore or beach areas around ships. While this approach significantly reduces waste management expenditures, it poses considerable risks to both human health and the surrounding ecosystem. According to World Bank, certain shipbreaking operations in South Asia allocate merely 2% to 5% of their overall shipbreaking costs to labour, while disregarding protocols related to environmental protection and worker safety (refer to Table 3.2). Moreover, comparative figures indicate that the beaching method commonly employed in the region results in a 30% reduction in labour expenses and a 50% decrease in compliance costs required for safety and environmental regulations compared to dry dock shipbreaking method (see Table 3.3).[16]

Accordingly, due to lower expenditures on labour and regulatory compliance, shipbreaking companies in South Asia are able to allocate a substantially larger proportion of their overall operational costs—approximately 82% towards purchasing end-of-life ships from global shipowners. In contrast, industries employing the dry dock method can dedicate only around 30% of their total

[14] Rov Watkinson, 'Case Study to Develop Models for Compliant Ship Recycling Facilities' for Ship (Research Report, RWEC Environmental Consulting, July 2012) 11.

[15] Ibid.

[16] Choi et al. (n 9) 87.

[17] Maria Sarraf et al., 'Ship Breaking and Recycling Industry in Bangladesh and Pakistan,' (Report No. 58275-SAS, World Bank, 2010) 20. *(World Bank Report 2010).*

Table 3.3 Cost distribution between a dry dock and the beaching method of shipbreaking

Cost	Dry dock method (%)	Beaching method (%)
Environmental and safety regulation	50	00
Labour cost	10	4.97
Ship purchase	30	82
Other cost	10	13.03

Source: Jun-Ki Choi[18]

shipbreaking costs to purchase a ship (see Table 3.3). As illustrated in Table 3.2, when the aggregate shipbreaking expenditure amounts to USD 4,692,200, South Asian companies such as those in Bangladesh may spend roughly USD 3,848,000 on purchasing the ship. On the other hand, for an identical ship, dry dock operations in the US would allocate just USD 1,407,600 for the ship's purchase, reflecting the more demanding cost structure inherent to compliant and safe breaking practices.

The increased price offered by South Asian shipbreaking companies contribute to increased revenue for shipping companies, providing a compelling financial advantage. This pricing dynamic plays a pivotal role in enabling South Asian nations to consistently secure leading positions within the global shipbreaking sector, surpassing competitors such as China. Additionally, ship disposal is often driven by economic rationales[19]: either when the cost of operations, including expenditures on maintenance, certifications, and insurance surpasses the revenue generated, or when continued commercial service becomes economically unfeasible for the age of a vessel or unfavourable market conditions.[20]

The Shift of the Shipbreaking Industry to South Asia

In the 1980s, shipping companies relied on a highly mechanised task for breaking their old ships using dry docks (breaking ships in a contained area to avoid escaping

[18] Choi et al. (n 9) 87–88.

[19] Nafisa Mehtaj et al., 'Ship Recycling Process in Bangladesh and a Survey-based Risk Assessment with Mitigation Proposal' (2024) 10 (20) *Heliyon* (Online) https://www.cell.com/heliyon/fulltext/S2405-8440(24)15375-3.

[20] Nafisa et al. (n 19).

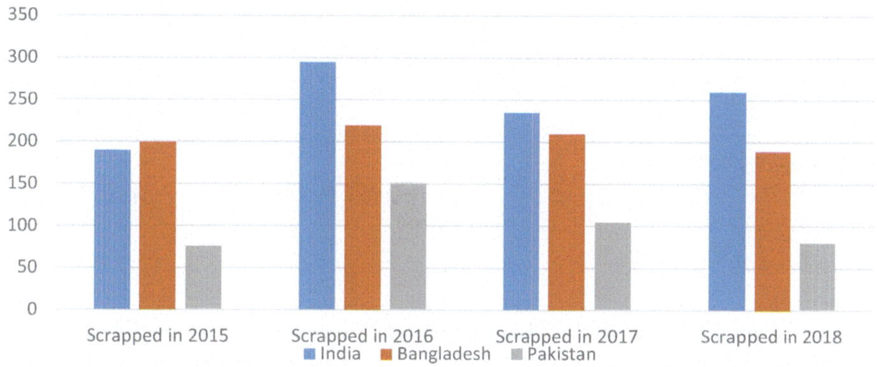

Fig. 3.2 Total number of ships broken between 2015 and 2018 in South Asia (*Source* NGO shipbreaking platform reports from 2010 to 2018[26])

of hazardous materials of a ship),[21] along with providing sophisticated safety equipment to their shipbreaking workers.[22] Within major shipping countries, it was expensive since the industry was required to comply with high standards for health, the environment, and safety regulations.

In the 1990s, shipbreaking activity shifted from developed countries to India, Bangladesh, Pakistan, China, and Turkey.[23] By 2010, these five countries had managed to break 98% of end-of-life ships. Recently, the focus of shipbreaking has become concentrated in South Asia, such that by 2018, the three South Asian countries jointly broke 90% of unused ships—518 (Bangladesh 222, India 305, and Pakistan 141) of 744 ships broke globally (see Fig. 3.2). In terms of the LDT, 80% of ships required breaking.[24] Most of the ships came from shipping companies based in the China ($n = 56$), Switzerland = (16), South Korea ($n = 13$), United Arab Emirates ($n = 20$), and Russia ($n = 18$).[25]

[21] A dry dock is a secure and environmentally safe facility where hazardous materials from ships are contained, removed using cranes, and cleaned after the breaking process to prevent any toxic spills from mixing with seawater.

[22] SS Sejan and MI Muhfuz, 'A Critical Analysis of Legal Regime of Shipbreaking and Ship Recycling in Bangladesh' (2024) 4 *Journal of Environmental Law and Policy* 54.

[23] Safety4Sea, 'Report: EU Ship Recycling Yards more than enough to Handle Demand' (Online News, 25 September 2018) https://safety4sea.com/report-eu-ship-recycling-yards-more-than-enough-to-handle-demand/.

[24] NGO Shipbreaking Platform, 'Platform Publishes List of Ships Dismantled Worldwide in 2024' (Press Release, 3 February 2025) https://shipbreakingplatform.org/platform-publishes-list-2024/#:~:text=Press%20Release%20%E2%80%93%20Platform%20publishes%20list,due%20to%20unsafe%20working%20practices.

[25] Ibid.

[26] NGO Shipbreaking Platform, *Impact Report 2018–2019* (Biennial Report, 2018–2019) https://shipbreakingplatform.org/wp-content/uploads/2020/06/NGOSBP-Bi-Annual-Report-18-19.pdf 3–8.

Table 3.4 Differences in purchase price and profit

	Revenue (USD)	Cost (USD)	Profit (USD)
Standard method (USA)	466	370	96
Substandard method (Bangladesh)	379	317	62
		Loss of profit by substandard method	34

Source Choi et al.[32]

China's and Turkey's shipbreaking industries, meanwhile, have declined sharply to only approximately 10% of global ships.[27] In general, shipping companies are unwilling to send a large number of ships to Turkey and China because companies based in Turkey and China cannot offer as high a purchase price as companies based in India, Bangladesh, and Pakistan (see Fig. 3.2). For example, China can offer only USD 210 per Light Displacement Tonnage (LDT),[28] which is less than half the price (USD 450) offered by South Asian yards. Turkey can offer USD 280 per LDT. Because of the price difference, a large container ship that weighs approximately 25 000 LDT can earn approximately USD 11.80 million for a ship purchased by India, but only USD 7 million from Turkey and USD 5.25 million from China.[29] One estimate shows that a shipowner earns USD 3–9 million more USD by sending a ship to South Asian shipbreaking countries than by sending a ship elsewhere.[30] This price is just conjecture; however, it may rise at any time depending on the steel demand.

The profit margins for South Asian shipbreaking companies are not as high as those for companies based elsewhere (see Table 3.4), mainly because of the high purchase price, they offer. A standard shipbreaking industry located in Norway may earn approximately USD 96/LDT, whereas the profit may be only USD 62/LDT in Bangladesh. This means that a South Asian shipbreaking company sacrifices approximately 34 USD/LDT to provide a high purchase price to shipowners.[31] On the other hand, the shipping industry remains the key beneficiary of the current state of the South Asian shipbreaking industry since its part of the business gives little or no consideration to the environmental and human rights impacts involved in the breaking of ships.

---

[27] Ibid.

[28] Light Displacement Tonnage refers to actual weight of a ship without any crew, passengers, cargo, water or fuel onboard: at VS&B Containers Group, 'All that You Ought to Know on Tonnage in Shipping' (Webpage, 8 July 2023) https://www.vsnb.com/all-you-ought-know-tonnage-shipping .

[29] Matt Miller, *Shipbreaking: Breaking Badly* (Web Page, 23 April 2018) http://www.ajot.com/news/channel/maritime.

[30] Chris White, 'Two Years Since Pakistan's Gadani Shipbreaking Disaster, Why are Workers Still dying?' *This Week in Asia* (online at 28 October 2018) (https://www.scmp.com/week-asia/health-environment/article/2170256/two-years-pakistans-gadani-ship-breaking-disaster-why.

[31] Choi et al. (n 9) 87.

[32] Choi et al. (n 9) 87.

The information outlined in Table 3.4 highlights the profit-driven interests of all stakeholders engaged in ship sales. This includes not only shipowners but also affiliated entities such as cash buyers and nations utilising open registries. These profit motivations serve as a central force propelling the involvement of South Asian shipbreaking facilities in the in the international shipbreaking market (see section "Business Profit of the Maritime Industry, Cash Buyers, and Open Registry Countries" of this chapter).

According to forecasts, the volume of ships broken in South Asian is set to rise.[33] A May 2025 report from Hellenic Shipping News anticipate an influx of ships entering the shipbreaking sector, citing the region's scrap prices—reaching around 500 per Light Displacement Tonnage, which is set to be the highest global price before 2025.[34] Consequently, analysts foresee a surge in activity within South Asian shipbreaking markets in the future.[35]

This optimistic economic outlook prompts two pivotal inquiries. First, what factors have led South Asia to dominate the global shipbreaking market, and in what ways does the maritime sector benefit financially from this regional concentration? Second, given the anticipated increase in shipbreaking, can the industry ensure safe working conditions, which will be free from fatal accidents, injuries, and occupational diseases?[36] Sections "The Role of the Shipbreaking Industry in South Asian Economies" and "Business Profit of the Maritime Industry, Cash Buyers, and Open Registry Countries" of the chapter dig into the first question by exploring profitability dynamics. Section "Business Profit of the Maritime Industry, Cash Buyers, and Open Registry Countries" addresses the second question, assessing the sector's capacity to manage growth responsibly.

The Role of the Shipbreaking Industry in South Asian Economies

The shipbreaking industry is the biggest single contributor to the steel supply in South Asia that substantially supports their construction activities and rerolling mills. Because of limited domestic iron ore reserves and accelerated infrastructure expansion, there is a pressing demand for alternative steel sources.[37] End-of-life ships yield

---

[33] Hellenic Shipping News Worldwide, Ship Demolition Still Stagnant (Webpage, 22 May 2025) https://www.hellenicshippingnews.com/ship-demolition-still-stagnant/.

[34] Ibid.

[35] Fortune Business Insights, 'Ship Breaking Market' (Research Report no. FBI108231, 30 June 2025) https://www.fortunebusinessinsights.com/ship-breaking-market-108231#:~:text=The%20ship%20breaking%20market%20size,8.2%25%20during%20the%20forecast%20period.&text=Ship%20breaking%20refers%20to%20the,estimated%20end%2Dof%2Dlife.

[36] Mohammad Zulfikar Ali, 'Injustice to Workers in the Shipbreaking Industry in South Asia: A Quest for a Civil Liability Framework in International Law' (PhD Thesis, Curtin University, 2022) 74–75.

[37] Nafisa et al. (n 19).

substantial quantities of scrap metal, which are reprocessed into high-quality steel products. In addition to steel, shipbreaking operations generate approximately 20 million tonnes of valuable reusable materials—ranging from durable furniture and ship hulls to machinery,[38] electronic devices, and various industrial and household tools. Once refurbished or reconditioned, these items find robust commercial demand across South Asian markets.[39]

The shipbreaking sector plays a positive role in generating employment across South Asia. Characterised by its labour-intensive nature, particularly when utilising the beaching method, it engages large number of workers in the extraction and handling of steel and second-hand materials. Support for the industry from policymakers and business leaders is largely driven by socio-economic challenges such as dense population growth, widespread poverty, a significant proportion of unskilled and uneducated workers, and persistent unemployment. Moreover, the industry's expansion is enabled by limited environmental regulations along coastal zones and the absence of comprehensive legal frameworks, as outlined in Chap. 4.[40] The following sections explore the sector's socio-economic relevance in Bangladesh, India, and Pakistan.

Socio-economic Benefit of the Shipbreaking in Bangladesh

Between 2004 and 2008, Bangladesh led the global shipbreaking industry, a position that deeply embedded the sector into its national economy. Since 2009, the volume of ships broken has surged by an estimated 36% annually,[41] resulting in the import of 130 vessels for breaking in 2025 alone.[42] Profit margins are considerable, with each ship generating roughly USD 921,400.[43]

---

[38] Staffan Appelgren, 'Growing in Motion: The Circulation of Used Things on Second-hand Markets' (2015) 7 (1) *Journal of Current Cultural Research* 143–168 https://doi.org/10.3384/cu.2000.1525.1571143.

[39] Ibid.

[40] Ljubomir Jeftice, Seba Sheavly, and Ellik Adler, 'Marine Litter: A Global Challenge' (Report, United Nations Environmental Program, April 2009).

[41] Mosabbir Pasha et al., 'Assessment of Shipbreaking and Recycling Industries in Bangladesh—an Effective Step Towards the Achievement of Environmental Sustainability'(Conference Paper, International Conference on Agriculture, Environmental and Biological, May 2012).

[42] NGO Shipbreaking Platform, 'Platform Publishes List of Ships Dismantled Worldwide in 2024' (Press Release, 3 February 2025) https://shipbreakingplatform.org/platform-publishes-list-2024/#:~:text=Press%20Release%20%E2%80%93%20Platform%20publishes%20list,due%20to%20unsafe%20working%20practices.

[43] World Bank Report 2010 (n 18) 1.

The shipbreaking sector has positively contributed to Bangladesh's national steel demand,[44] meeting over 70% of the country's annual demand.[45] This self-reliance helps conserve foreign exchange and supports small-scale rerolling operations, which rely exclusively on metal scraps recovered from end-of-life ships. Over 350 rerolling mills benefit directly from these supplies.[46] The shipbreaking industry also underpins Bangladesh's expanding shipbuilding industry, providing between 35,000 and 45,000 tonnes of recycled steel annually.[47] This steady influx of affordable raw materials enables local shipyards to produce more than 200 vessels per year at reduced construction costs.[48] The industry's contribution to generating national revenue is huge, which is estimated at over USD 130 million annually.[49] The annual revenue income from shipbreaking accounts for nearly 15% of all tax income as of 2016. Taxes and duties levied on shipbreaking activities help the government project a potential annual revenue stream of up to USD 2.4 billion.[50] The revenue is generated by imposing duties (7.5%), a yard tax (2.5%), and other imposts.[51]

Employment figures in the industry are substantial, with over 25,000 individuals directly engage in shipbreaking as of 2017.[52] Some estimates suggest that the wider businesses,[53] including retail outlets and rerolling mills linked to this industry supports employment for more than one million people across the nation.[54]

Socio-economic Benefits of the Shipbreaking Industry in India

India holds the top position with its ability to break the highest number of ships. With over 180 operational shipbreaking facilities spread along a 12-km stretch of the Gujarat coastline, Indian shipbreaking sector breaks nearly half of the world's

---

[44] Mizanur Rahman Yousuf, 'How Shipbreaking is Contributing to Bangladesh's Economy' *Bangladesh Standards* (online at 29 October 2024) https://www.tbsnews.net/supplement/how-shipbreaking-contributing-bangladeshs-economy-978836.

[45] Pasha et al. (n 41).

[46] Georgy Abraham, 'Ship Breaking- Will the Industry Sink' *RecycleInMe Scrap Market Place* (online at 24 November 2015) https://www.recycleinme.com/scrap-news/newsdetails-283.

[47] Yousuf (n 44).

[48] Ibid.

[49] Khandakar Akhter Hossain, Shahriar Iqbal, and N.M. Golam Zakaria, 'Ship Recycling Prospects in Bangladesh' (Conference Paper, The International Conference on Maritime Technology, 11–12 December 2010) 297- 302.

[50] Nafisa et al. (n 19).

[51] Moutushi Tanha et al., 'Shipbreaking in Bangladesh: Organisational Responses, Ethics, and Varieties of Employee Safety' (2022) 80 *Journal of Safety Research* 14–26.

[52] Moutushi et al. (n 51).

[53] Das and Shahin (n 52).

[54] World Bank report (n 18) 27.

end-of-life ships.[55] According to recent estimates, the industry yields approximately 4.5 million tonnes of steel per year through the processing of around 400 ships, which is comparable in scale to output from a large domestic steel producer.[56] Until 2013, the Indian shipbreaking industry broke more than 6000 ships.[57]

Having settled over several decades, the industry now contributes 10–15% of India's total yearly steel demand.[58] Direct employment from shipbreaking activities exceeds 60,000 workers. Similar to Bangladesh, the sector supports a vast network of ancillary industries, such as rerolling mills, foundries, oxygen plants, logistics companies, and a wide array of small-scale retail operations.[59] Altogether, the industry provides livelihood for over 500,000 individuals.[60] The annual turnover generated by Indian shipbreaking industry stands at approximately USD 756 million, highlighting its integral role within the broader industrial and economic framework of the country.[61]

Socio-economic Benefit of the Shipbreaking Industry in Pakistan

Pakistan's shipbreaking industry began in 1965 and gradually expanded into a significant supplier of steel by 1980s. In 2009 and 2010 following increased rate of taxation on scrap steel, it experienced a downturn.[62] In response, Pakistan's government adjusted their fiscal policies in 2010,[63] reducing taxes and enabling a gradual recovery. The reduced tax policy led Pakistan ascending to third place globally in shipbreaking volume.[64] Gadani, located along the coast, emerged as the country's primary location for shipbreaking, employing over 30,000 individuals and yielding

---

[55] Saurabh Battacharjee, 'From Basel to Hong Kong: International Environmental Regulation of Ship Recycling Takes One Step Forward and Two Steps Back' (2009) 1 *Trade Law and Development* 193.

[56] Bisma Mannan, Md Jahir Rizvi, and Yong Ming Dai, 'Ship Recycling in Developing Economies of South Asia: Changing Liability to a Commodity' (May 2024) 2 (2) *Green Technologies and Sustainability* (online edition) https://doi.org/10.1016/j.grets.2023.100064.

[57] Geetanjoy Sahu, 'Workers of Alang-Sosiya: A Survey of Working Conditions in a Ship-Breaking Yard, 1983–2013'(2014) 49 (50) *Economic and Political Weekly* 52–59.

[58] Mannan, Rizvi, and Dai (n 57).

[59] Das and Shahin (n 52).

[60] Sahu (n 58).

[61] Mannan, Rizvi, and Dai (n 57).

[62] Mannan, Rizvi, and Dai (n 57).

[63] Kumar (n 63) 6.

[64] Allauddin et al., 'Elevated Concentrations of Mercury and Methylmercury in the Gadani Shipbreaking Area, Pakistan' (2021) 165 *Marine Pollution Bulletin* (online edition) https://doi.org/10.1016/j.marpolbul.2021.112048.

more than one million tonnes of steel annually during its early peak.[65] At present, the sector supplies around 500,000 tonnes of recycled steel each year that helps meeting up to 15% of the nation's steel requirements. This output directly supports other industries, with downstream operations such as rerolling mills employing half a million people through indirect links to shipbreaking activities.[66] The average financial return from breaking a ship in Pakistan is estimated to be USD 164 600.[67]

While profitability remains steady, the industry drew widespread concern following two deadly incidents at Gadani in 2016 and 2017. These explosions resulted in the deaths of over 50 workers and serious injuries to more than 100 others.[68] Despite, these tragedies, available data suggests that industry operations and profit levels were not substantially disrupted. The next section explains this situation.

Business Profit of the Maritime Industry, Cash Buyers, and Open Registry Countries

Shipbreaking is highly profitable for the global maritime industry, both for shipping companies and for associated parties, including cash buyers and open registry countries. Although they receive a high sale price, shipping companies and shipowners do not sell ships directly to a shipbreaking yard. Instead, they use brokerage services of cash buyers. Cash buyers are dedicated brokers who base themselves in 'open registry' countries and pay a registration fee to open registry countries to provide their nationality to foreign vessels just before a ship is sailed to a shipbreaking yard. The use of cash buyers and open registry countries raises important questions of transparency in the global maritime shipbreaking industry and is examined later in Chaps. 5 and 6. These associated parties benefit financially from the South Asian shipbreaking industry (see Table 3.5) and are referred to as shipowners or short-term shipowners throughout the book.

Table 3.5 shows the annual revenues that the maritime industry receives from the sale of ships into the South Asian shipbreaking market. Data on the revenue of shipping companies from shipbreaking are difficult to acquire because the original owners sell ships via cash buyers paying a commission of 1% of the sale price.[69] Table 3.5 also shows that between 2007 and 2018, the annual revenue derived by shipping industries and shipowners varied between USD 905 million and USD 4150

---

[65] Ramapati Kumar, *Ship Dismantling: A Status Report on South Asia and the EU*, eds Johan Bentinck and Dr Paul R Halmos (Euroconsult Matt Macdonald and World Wildlife Fund-India, 2018) 6.

[66] Ibid.

[67] Ibid.

[68] Human Rights Commission of Pakistan, 'Horror in Gadani' (Fact Finding Mission Report, November 2016) 5.

[69] Nikos E. Mikelis, *The Recycling of Ships* (Global Maritime Services (GMS) Leadership, 2nd ed, 1 October 2019) 7.

Table 3.5 Average revenue income of the global maritime industry from the South Asian shipbreaking market between 2007 and 2018

Year	LDTs	Bangladesh Price in USD/LDT	Indian Price in USD/LDT	Pakistani Price in USD/LDT	Avg. Price	Shipowners' Annual Income from the Industry	Cash buyers' income (1%)
Ships broken in million				USD/LDT		Shipowners' income and Cash buyers' earning as 1% commission	
2007	1.9	500	470	460	476.66	905.65	9.056
2008	2.6	770	745	690	735	1911	19.11
2009	6.2	340	320	320	326.66	2025.35	20.25
2010	4.3	480	480	480	480	2064	20.64
2011	6.1	520	550	510	510	3111	31.11
2012	8.3	500	500	500	500	4150	41.50
2013	6.4	435	440	440	438.34	2805.38	28.05
2014	6	480	500	480	486.67	2920.02	29.20
2015	4.4	300	320	320	313.34	1378.70	13.78
2016	8.1	310	310	310	310	2511	25.11
2017	5.9	380	390	380	383.34	1955.03	19.55
2018	5.8	430	420	420	423.34	2455.34	24.55
Average income –USD 2349.37 million/per year for shipowners and USD 23.49 million for cash buyers							23.49

Source of Data Nikos Mikelis[70]

million. On average, the industry earns approximately USD 2350 million per year. Cash buyers derived an annual revenue of USD 23.49 million during that period (on the basis of a 1% share in sale prices).

Open registry countries also earn revenue from the inter-State transfer of ships for breaking. Although data on their earnings are not readily available, an investigative report by a UK-based non-government organisation (NGO) revealed a close connection between open registry countries and cash buyers, from which open registry countries earn a registration fee of approximately USD 6750 per ship. Altogether, it can be roughly estimated that in 2018 open registries, such as those from Palau, Comoros and the Caribbean Islands of St. Kitts and Nevis, earned approximately USD 1.8 million by registering 266 ships.[71] However, these countries are not directly

[70] Nikos E. Mikelis, *The Recycling of Ships* (Global Maritime Services (GMS) Leadership, 2nd ed, 1 October 2019) 2, 8, 10, 12, 13, 17; Nikos E. Mikelis, A Statistical Overview of Ship Recycling (2008) 7(1) *World Maritime University Journal of Maritime Affairs* 227, 233. Nikos E. Mikelis, *The Recycling of Ships* (Global Maritime Services (GMS) Leadership, 1st ed, 1 April 2018 1–2, 9–11, 14.

[71] Margot Gibbs, 'Revealed: The UK Company and Caribbean Tax Haven Cashing in on One of the World's Deadliest Trades – Shipbreaking' *F:Uncovered* (Web Page, 20

involved in transactions. Instead, their registration service is outsourced to private companies incorporated in large shipping nations. For example, a private company named Skanreg, incorporated in the UK, arranges registration and port documentation for several open registry countries, such as St Kitts and Nevis. The company takes a service and registration charge from shipowners. Through the company's services, 143 ships flagged at St. Kitts and Nevis were sold to South Asian yards between 2016 and 2019. In 2016, by way of example, St Kitts and Nevis earned USD 500,000 from this company.[72]

Analyses of Labour, Environmental Standards, and Human Rights Abuses in South Asian Shipbreaking Industry

While the shipbreaking industry is South Asia offers substantial economic advantages, these come with significant human costs. Workers breaking end-of-life ships often lack sufficient safety gear and proper training resulting in regular exposure to hazardous materials. The following sections investigate the labour and environmental standards of the South Asian shipbreaking industry and examine whether the South Asian shipbreaking industry manages to break the high number of ships without deaths, injuries, or diseases to workers. The subsequent analysis draws upon findings from major international organisations, including the International Labour Organisation, the United Nations Human Rights Council, the European Union Commission, the World Bank, the International Metal Works Federation, and the NGO Shipbreaking Platform collectively highlights that environmental degradation and workplace accidents remain persistent and unresolved across the region. On the other hand, representatives from the shipping industry argue that conditions have improved due to their interventions. The claim leads to a critical evaluation of current casualty rates as an indicator of progress. Section H assesses these conflicting positions by reviewing recent data on fatalities and injuries within South Asian shipbreaking industry, offering insight into whether preventative measures have been effectively implemented.

International Labour Organisation (ILO) Report, 2001

A 2001 ILO published by the International Labour Organisation (ILO) identified occupational safety as the primary challenge in South Asia's shipbreaking sector. The study highlighted a lack of financial investment in enhancing workplace safety, particularly in major shipbreaking sites across the region. These operations generally

February 2019) https://www.financeuncovered.org/investigations/tax-haven-flags-of-convenience-stkitts-nevis-shipbreaking-toxic-ships-skanreg-chittagong/.

[72] Ibid.

do not employ dry dock systems for managing waste, nor do they utilise advanced technological methods. Instead, they rely heavily on manual labour, supported by traditional old tools and outdated machinery. The ILO classified such facilities as 'first-generation' or 'non-facilitated beach yards', indicating minimal infrastructure and safety provisions. Consequently, inadequate health and safety protocols have contributed to elevated rates of worker injuries and fatalities.

The ILO's findings emphasise that addressing the persistent challenges in shipbreaking necessitates a collaborative approach among all actors involved. Given the industry's entrenched role in both the maritime trade and the economies of South Asian countries, it is not feasible to relocate the maritime shipbreaking activities elsewhere. The sector remains economically viable and includes a wide spectrum of participants, which ranges from shipowners, intermediary cash buyers, and nations allowing open registries to shipbreaking countries and their shipbreaking companies. The report argues that these stakeholders must acknowledge their shared responsibility in helping developing countries navigate the tension between financial benefit and the imperative to uphold human and environmental rights.[73] Accordingly, the ILO recommends imposing clear accountability across the industry to ensure ethical and sustainable practices are pursued collectively.[74]

European Commission Report, 2001–2016

European shipowners represent nearly 40% of the global shipbreaking market. The European Union (EU) has in response implemented robust regulatory and policy measures targeting its shipping operators (refer to Chap. 6). Since the early 2000s, several studies have examined European strategies, consistently acknowledging the international scope of shipbreaking and recommending alignment between EU regulations and broader global standards.[75] A notable 2001 study, 'Technological and Economic Feasibility Study of Ship Scrapping in Europe', recognised the substantial contribution of South Asian shipbreaking operations to the maritime economy.[76] It

[73] Aage Bjorn Anderson, 'Worker Safety in Shipbreaking, Sectoral Activities Program' (Working Paper No 167, International Labour Organisation, 2001). *(ILO Report).*

[74] Ibid, 60.

[75] European Commission, 'Study on "Ship Dismantling and Precleaning of Ships"' (Final Report, Directorate General for Environment, June 2007) http://ec.europa.eu/environment/waste/ships// index.htm; The European Commission, 'Study on Oil Tanker Phase Out and the Ship Scrapping Industry' (Research Report, DG Transport and Energy, 2004) http://europa.eu.int/comm/transport/maritime/safety/doc/prestige/2004_06_scrapping_study_en.pdf; Department of Environment, Food and Rural Affairs (DEFRA) 'Regulatory Impact Assessment for the UK Ship Scrapping Industries' (Research Report, February-2007) http://www.defra.gov.uk/ENVIRONMENT/WASTE/strategy/ship.htm; The European Commission, 'Ship Recycling: Reducing Human and Environmental Impacts' (Thematic Issue 55, Director General Environment by the Science Communication Unit Environmental Policy, 2016) http://ec.europa.eu/science-environment-policy.

[76] Det Norske Veritas, 'Technological and Economical Feasibility of Ship Scrapping in Europe' (Research Report No. 2000–3527, 13 February 2001) 46.

also highlighted that conducting shipbreaking within the EU lacks economic viability, chiefly due to limited demand for reuseable materials.

The report underscores the high operational costs associated with conducting shipbreaking within the European Union, primarily for the region's stringent safety and environmental standards. The European Union policymakers have therefore introduced legislative procedures grounded in the 'polluter pays' principle. This framework places accountability on the producers, requiring them to ensure that waste disposal is executed by a licenced disposer using environmentally responsible practices.[77] The report also highlights the critical role of South Asian shipbreaking facilities in sustaining global maritime profitability. Without access to these more economically viable shipbreaking markets, European shipowners would likely incur substantial financial losses. For this reason, shipowners preferred selling ships to South Asia's shipbreaking industry. However, the report revealed that the shipbreaking industry in South Asia lacks adequate plans and policies, facilities, procedures, skill requirements, and an appreciation of training needs that represent sufficient inadequacies to draw conclusions about their general non-compliance.[78]

Importantly, the report identifies the shipbreaking industry's regulatory imbalance is nothing but a global market failure. The European Union, in response, undertook a comprehensive policy review in 2008 and published its report entitled 'Impact Assessment for a EU Strategy for Better Ship Dismantling'. This analysis evaluated four policy pathways, including one that proposed alignment with the international legal framework established under the *Hong Kong Convention*.[79] The EU's 2007 Green Paper on Ship Dismantling emphasised the necessity for uniform global standards. It cautioned that even with improvements to safety and environmental protocols in South Asian countries, those regions would likely retain a dominant role in the sector due to structurally lower labour costs and a robust internal demand for second-hand ship materials.[80]

World Bank Report, 2010

The World Bank's 2010 assessment of shipbreaking industries in Bangladesh and Pakistan highlights critical structural issues within the sector. Despite documenting severe working conditions, the report attributes South Asia's dominance in shipbreaking to economic advantages, including a substantial domestic demand for scrap materials and the prevalence of low-cost labour. Crucially, it emphasises that the

---

[77] Ibid.

[78] Det Norske Veritas, 'Technological and Economical Feasibility of Ship Scrapping in Europe' (Research Report No. 2000-3527, 2001) 51.

[79] Commission of the European Community, *Impact Assessment for a EU Strategy for Better Ship Dismantling*, EU Doc. COM (2008) 765 final, Brussels, 19 November 2008.

[80] Commission of the European Community, *Green Paper on Better Dismantling*, Com SEC (2007) 645, Brussels 22 May 2007.

industry operates entirely in private domain, receiving no investment from national governments to support adherence to international labour rules.

In line with findings of the EU and ILO, the report raises serious concerns regarding occupational health and environmental safety. It details chronic health risks associated with inadequate workplace standards, noting that nearly 9 out of 10 workers sustain accidental injuries. It also points to the financial pressures exerted by shipowner's elevated sale prices, which compel shipbreaking facility owners to resort to cost-cutting methods such as beaching and traditional techniques to break ships. Alarmingly, the report also reveals the absence of compensation mechanisms for workers facing fatalities, injuries, or illness linked to their employment.[81]

United Nations Human Rights Council Reports, 2009 and 2010

In two separate reports issued in July 2009 and September 2010, the UN Human Rights Council's Special Rapporteur, Okechukwu Ibeanu, examined the transboundary movement and disposal of hazardous materials and their impact on human rights.[82] The second report focused specifically on shipbreaking activities in India.[83] Both reports emphasised that shipbreaking is a globally interconnected issue that demands coordinated intervention from all stakeholders, such as the flag States, shipbreaking nations, and shipowners.

A primary concern highlighted was the systemic exclusion of shipbreaking workers from formal social protections frameworks, largely because of the unregulated and informal nature of the sector. Individuals who sustain injuries or developed illnesses as a result of workplace accidents rarely receive meaningful compensation. Financial remedies are limited to emergency medical costs for injuries and funeral expenses in cases of death. Long-term support for occupations diseases, which often rendered workers unable to return to the workforce, is notably absent.

The reports also underscored the shared responsibility among global actors, pointing out that economic and logistical limitations make the relocation of shipbreaking operations to more industrialised regions improbable. As a result of this, South Asia is expected to remain the centre for such activities. Despite the adoption of the *Hong Kong Convention*, international efforts to address safety and labour

---

[81] World Bank Report (n 18) 4.

[82] Okechukwu Ibeanu, *Report of the Special Rapporteur on the Adverse Effects of the Movement and Dumping of Toxic and Dangerous Products and Wastes on the Enjoyment of Human Rights*, UN Doc. A/HRC/12/26 (15 July 2009). (*UN Special Report on Shipbreaking*).

[83] Calin Georgescu, *Report of the Special Rapporteur on the Adverse Effects of the Movement and Dumping of Toxic and Dangerous Products and Wastes on the Enjoyment of Human Rights – Preliminary Assessment of Whether the Hong Kong Convention Establishes an Equivalent Level of Control and Enforcement as that Established under the Basel Convention*, UN Doc. UNEP/CHW/OEWG/7/21 (2 September 2010).

rights concerns remain inadequate. The reports warned against using the low operational costs and labour availability in South Asian as justification for disregarding internationally recognised labour and health standards.[84]

The International Metal Workers Foundation Report, 2005

A 2005 field study conducted by the International Metalworkers Federation (IMF)—a global labour organisation representing metal industry workers across over 100 countries examined the working conditions within shipbreaking facilities in Alang and Mumbai, India. The report categorically described shipbreaking as among the most hazardous occupation.[85] It further characterised workers in this sector as functioning under exploitative and quasi-bonded conditions lacking formal protections or regulatory oversight regarding their employment terms. The study illuminated systemic failures in the provision of compensation for workplace related injuries and fatalities. Injured workers face regular job termination without receiving any form of financial redress. In cases of death, the monetary support extended to bereaved families range between USD 205.2 and USD 1370.13. This compensation range is significantly below statutory entitlements, and often contingent upon external media advocacy to paid at all. In particular, the report revealed the following:

> Workers have some knowledge of their compensation in the case of fatal injuries, but the total amount that actually the family of the deceased or injured receives is much lower than the legal amount prescribed by law.[86]

NGO Shipbreaking Platform Report, 2020

In addition to many other international reports published between 2001 and 2020 on South Asia's shipbreaking industry, the reports of the NGO Shipbreaking Platform have played a key role in reinforcing the debate over the liability of shipowners. The NGO Shipbreaking Platform is an international NGO established in 2005. One of its goals is to expose the international shipowners and shipping industries who have a record of sending ships for breaking after changing flags and names. In early 2020, the NGO Shipbreaking Platform published an online report providing detailed information on which countries and their registered shipowners have sent their ships to South Asia. The online report noted that, irrespective of a new EU *Ship Recycling Regulation* that prohibits ships from being sent to recycling facilities that use the

---

[84] UN Special Report on Shipbreaking (n 85).

[85] International Metalworkers Federation, 'Special Report – Cleaning Up Shipbreaking is the Most Dangerous of the World' (Research Report, 15 December 2015) 1.

[86] Ibid, 11.

beaching method, several EU ships hit beaches in South Asia (see Chap. 6). Many of them had reflagged their ship to non-EU countries just before the last journey.[87]

The report stated that the government and multinational corporations have failed to recognise the problems in South Asia, noting concerns with human rights to life, the enjoyment of sound health in the workplace, and the large-scale degradation of the coastal environment. The report also questioned whether *the Hong Kong Convention* is going to solve all the problems and ensure social security for workers. The report further noted that although the *Hong Kong Convention* will help to upgrade the standards of a shipbreaking yard, it will do little to compensate workers when the standard fails. It also argues that deaths, injuries, and diseases in the shipbreaking industry are statistically certain and require an adequate legal standard that imposes liability on all parties along the way.

The main recommendation of the NGO Shipbreaking Platform is that shipowners must respect workers' rights and apply for due diligence when they decide to sell ships. These corporations are obliged to ensure that no one is harmed due to their business practices, although to date, this had happened only in rare cases.[88]

Recent Reports, 2023–2025

A report published by the Human Rights Watch in 2023 demonstrates that Bangladesh Shipbreaking sector has not shown a sign of substantial improvement.[89] According to the report, the industry remains beyond regulation. For instance, there is no authority to check whether pipes in a ship are free from fuel residues and whether the 'gas-free for hot work certificate' has been issued.[90] A shipbreaking worker is paid only around USD 160 for emergency treatment.

The report also suggests how badly workers are treated in the shipbreaking facilities. They are not provided with any emergency transport services to send workers to hospitals even in cases when workers have lost their legs and other important parts of their body from explosion or falling from height. According to the report, the injuries mainly occur because of inadequate personal protective equipment such as a device or clothing worn used by worker to protect them from specific hazards in t their work environment.[91]

---

[87] NGO Shipbreaking Platform, *Toxic Tide: 2019 Shipbreaking Records* (Web Page) http://www.offthebeach.org/.

[88] Ibid.

[89] Human Rights Watch is an international, independent organisation that investigates and reports abuse of internationally recognised human rights worldwide: at Human Rights Watch, *Trading Lives for Profit: How the Shipping Industry Circumvents Regulations to Scrap Toxic Ships on Bangladesh's Beaches* (Report, 28 September 2023) https://www.hrw.org/report/2023/09/28/trading-lives-profit/how-shipping-industry-circumvents-regulations-scrap-toxic.

[90] Ibid.

[91] Ibid.

It is also document in the report that EU shipowners are regularly evading *EU Waste Shipment Regulation* that prohibits the shipment of waste—including end-of-life ships to non-OECD countries like Bangladesh. Moreover, it is not allowed to send EU ships to an unregistered EU shipbreaking facility under the *EU Ship Recycling Regulation*, but by changing ships' flag to a non-EU country, EU shipowners are sending their ships to Bangladesh.[92] This finding corresponds with the NGO shipbreaking Platform's report discussed above.

Pakistan shipbreaking is still at crossroads without much improvement. The sector remains a major hotspot for damage to the coastal environment and human rights breach. Workers cannot expect to earn more than USD 4 daily. They are always at risk of health hazards such as exposure to lead paint and asbestos.[93] Indian shipbreaking sector has seen positive changes in the last few years, but they are yet to conform with the standards set under the *EU Ship Recycling Regulation*.[94] The sector continues to use the beaching practice arguing that the *Hong Kong Convention* does not ban the practice. According to National Maritime Foundation's report published in 2024, it is challenging to enforce the accountability of employers and application of the domestic labour laws in Indian shipbreaking sector.[95]

Opposite View

Despite these well-documented reports on unsafe conditions in South Asia's shipbreaking industry published between 2001 and 2025, shipping companies and their associated parties refute these reports. They argued that the maritime industry has policies for on-site assessment and that the situation is improving in India, Bangladesh, and Pakistan[96] since shipbreaking processes are closely monitored.[97] The shipping industry also claims that, in a number of cases, it has provided financial assistance to the shipbreaking industry in South Asia to improve standards.[98] The

---

[92] Ibid.

[93] Arab News Pakistan, 'Pakistan Approves USD 42 million to Transform Shipbreaking Yard into Model Green Facility,' *The Arab News* (online), (online at 25 June 2025) https://www.arabnews.com/node/2605790/pakistan.

[94] Aarushi Rai, Abhas Sinha, and Atul Mudaliar, *Turning the Tide: Ship Recycling as a Source of Green Steel in India* (Climate Group Steel Zero Report, 2024), 50. https://climatecatalyst.org/wp-content/uploads/2024/12/Turning-the-Tide-Ship-Recycling-as-a-Source-of-Green-Steel-in-India.pdf.

[95] MS Rhythma Kaul and Debesh Lahiri, *Sustainable Ship Recycling in India- Legal, Economic and Political Analysis* (National Maritime Foundation Report, 17 January 2025) https://maritimeindia.org/sustainable-ship-recycling-in-india-legal-economic-and-political-analysis/.

[96] Maersk, 'Breaking the Stalemate' *Case Studies* (Web Page, 25 October 2019) https://www.maersk.com/news/articles/2017/01/03/breaking-the-stalemate.

[97] Inderpreet Walia, 'India Ratifies the Hong Kong Convention on Ship Recycling', *Lloyd List Maritime Intelligence* (Online at 21 November 2019) http://www.gmsinc.net/gms_new/assets/pdf/IndiaHC.pdf http://www.gmsinc.net/gms_new/assets/pdf/2019-09-10bwM_org.pdf.

[98] Ibid.

Global Marketing System (GMS), one of the largest cash buyers in the world, claims that, utilising their support in preparing a ship-recycling plan and a ship recycling facility plan and monitoring the ship recycling process,[99] approximately 70 Indian shipbreaking yards have already obtained a statement of compliance certificates from classification societies, such as ClassNK from Japan and RINA from Italy. A classification society is a non-governmental organisation that assists the maritime industry in following regulatory standards.[100] Classification societies act as private consultants and assess the standards of a yard. Obtaining a Statement of Compliance (SoC) certificate means that the safety standard of a yard meets a safety standard. A shipbreaking company from Bangladesh has also obtained a statement of a compliance certificate.

In contrast, the NGO Shipbreaking Platform contends that the classification societies have been issuing SoC certificates without field visits. The shipbreaking industry in South Asia uses SoC certificates for window dressing to show that the facilities are 'green', whereas the actual conditions may not be safe enough.[101] UN Special Rapporteur Baskut Tuncak has gone even further, questioning the certification power of a classification society. He argues that the classification societies are simply extensions of the shipping industry and are not independent organisations.[102]

The EU takes a slightly different approach to the issue of SoC certificates issued by classification societies. Peter Koller, a policy officer at the European Commission's director-general for the environment, agreed that there have been many improvements in the South Asian industry.[103] However, he calls for an impartial investigation of standards since he believes that the quality of all the certified shipbreaking yards is not equal and that some do not meet the *Hong Kong Convention* standard.[104] Norway's Greig Green, which audits shipbreaking yards and helps shipbreaking yards follow safety and environmental standards, has also argued that the yards with statements of compliance certificates have varying standards. Risks are still high without providing enough protective equipment or training.[105] The above contesting claims of the international organisations and shipping industries led examining the recent data on deaths and injuries in South Asian shipbreaking industry.

---

[99] GMS Leadership, *Overview* (Web Page) https://www.gmsinc.net/gms_new/index.php/about.

[100] International Association of Classification Societies, *Classification Societies- What, Why and How* (Web Page) http://www.iacs.org.uk/media/3785/iacs-class-what-why-how.pdf.

[101] NGO Shipbreaking Platform, *HKC Statement of Compliance* (Web Page) https://www.shipbreakingplatform.org/issues-of-interest/the-law/hkc-soc/.

[102] Ibid.

[103] Julian Bray, 'Ship Recycling Forum', *TradeWinds News* 13 March 2020, 25–26.

[104] Ibid 28.

[105] Ibid.

Environment and Human Harms from Shipbreaking

Many scientific and media reports confirm that a significant number of ships beached and broken in South Asia contain high quantities of toxic chemicals,[106] and their release into seawater contaminates marine life and the surrounding workplace of a yard.[107] Pollution of thc workplace from such hazards has long-term adverse effects on workers.[108] For example, long-term exposure to asbestos and polychlorinated biphenyl (PCB) is responsible for causing lung cancer, asbestosis and mesothelioma, birth defects, and reproductive and neurological damage.[109] A 2008 study reported that workers suffer from abdominal, urinary, muscle and skin problems, in addition to nutritional deficiencies caused by toxic metal, oil, and chemical contamination.[110] Another study revealed that 16% of Indian shipbreaking workers had symptoms of asbestosis and were at risk of developing mesothelioma, a type of cancer, in the future.[111] Table 3.6 shows the nature of the symptoms due to long-term exposure to the hazardous materials found in old ships.

Shipbreaking is also a cause of immediate threat to workers' lives. The shipbreaking industry in South Asia has caused a number of deaths and injuries due to the limited use of technical standards. A recent study suggested that between 1000 and 2000, people died, and many more suffered grievous injuries over the last 20 years from various accidents in this industry.[112] Figure 3.3 depicts data on deaths and injuries between 2005 and 2019. In particular, the overall number of deaths was 456 in the three countries from 2005 to 2019. According to these figures, 53 workers died in 2016 alone, equalling the total death rate for the years 2011–2015. In 2016, Bangladesh recorded 22 deaths and 29 serious injuries, and India reported two deaths.[113] The second highest death toll was reported for 2011, with 43 deaths. The figure also ranks that year with the highest number of injuries, reaching 150. In terms of the ratio between the number of ships and accidents, 2018 was at the top, with 39 deaths and injuries. In 2019, 21 deaths and 11 injuries were reported in South Asia. Overall, the South Asian shipbreaking industry records two accidents per 1000 workers, which corresponds with the claims of the reports discussed above.[114]

---

[106] Mannan, Rizvi, and Dai (n 57).

[107] Syed Robayet Ferdous and Md Ikra, 'Industrial Killing in Bangladesh: State Policies, Common-Law Nexus, and International Obligations' (2023) 35 (4) *Employee Responsibilities and Rights Journal* 601–618.

[108] OH Parsons, 'Understanding the Effects of Occupational Hazards on Your Health'(Webpage, 2 January 2025) https://ohparsons.co.uk/understanding-the-effects-of-occupational-hazards-on-your-health/ .

[109] Mannan, Rizvi, and Dai (n 57).

[110] Mohammad Shahadat Hossain et al., 'Occupational Health Hazards of Ship Scrapping Workers at Chittagong Coastal Zone, Bangladesh' (2008) 35(2) *Chiang Mai Journal of Science* 370, 376.

[111] Mannan, Rizvi, and Dai (n 57).

[112] Syed and Ikra (n 102).

[113] Mohammad Zulfikar Ali, 'Shipbreaking Industry: Responsibility of the Maritime Industry' (November 2020) *Perspective Australian New Zealand Society of International Law* 20-26.

[114] NGO Shipbreaking Platform, *India* (Web Page) https://www.shipbreakingplatform.org/our-work/the-problem/india/.

Table 3.6 Long-term adverse effects on the health of workers

Hazardous materials	Available in	Symptoms
Asbestos	Engine room	Lung cancer, asbestosis and mesothelioma
Polychlorinated biphenyls (PCBs)	Cable insulation, transformers, capacitors, switches, some paints, pumps, cranes etc	Cancer, liver damage, neurological and immune system damage
Ozone depleting substances (CFCs, HCFC, etc.)	Insulation of LNG carriers, extinguishing agent, refrigerant for refrigerating machine	Large-scale pollution of the environment
Organotin compounds (TBT, TPT, TBTO)	Anti-fouling paint on ship's bottoms	Sea product contamination, potential hazardous effect on human health
Glass wool	Glass wool board, glass wool felt, glass wool pipe, shell of glass fibre products	Toxic as asbestos
Heavy metal-lead	Paints, cabling, batteries, motors, and generators	The neurological system, hearing, vision, reproductive system, blood vessels, kidneys and heart damage especially children's physical and neurological development
Heavy metal-mercury	Light fittings, luminescent lamps, switches, thermometers	Toxic, bio accumulative and affect nervous system
Oil and fuel (including hydraulic and lubricating oils, engine oil and grease)	Bunkers, bilges, fuel systems and engine room	Poisonous through inhalation or consumption of contaminated water or fish. May also result in fire and explosion
Blige water	Accumulated stagnant water in bilges	Contains a range of pollutants: oil, inorganic salt, heavy metals, etc
Ballast water	Fresh or salt water taken on board ballast tanks to adjust ship's trim and stability	May contain bacteria and viruses, also persistent invasive organisms and sediments
Polyvinyl chloride (PVC)	In a number of materials, including plastics, cable coatings, floor coverings	May induce cancers, asthma, and impairment to human reproduction systems. Burning may generate carbon monoxide, and highly toxic dioxins, etc. Burials may release chemicals to groundwater

(continued)

Table 3.6 (continued)

Hazardous materials	Available in	Symptoms
Polycyclic aromatic hydrocarbons (PAHs)	In high quantity in ship's body and due to beaching the material is available on the sediments and water surface	Soil and water pollution. A long-term exposure by ingestion, inhalation may cause lung, skin and bladder cancer

Source World Bank Report 2010[115]

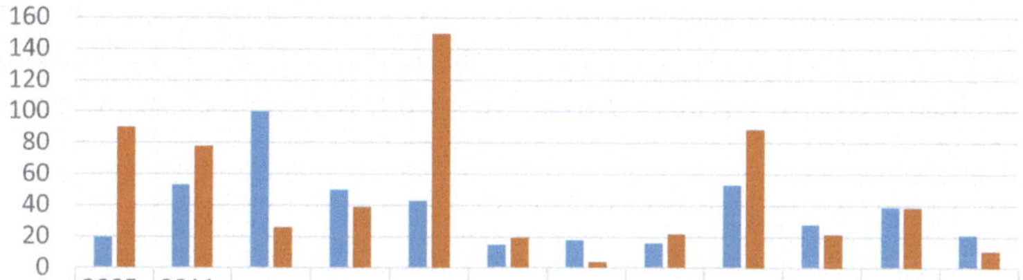

	2005-2012	2011-2015	2008	2009	2011	2012	2014	2015	2016	2017	2018	2019
Number of deaths	20	53	100	50	43	15	18	16	53	28	39	21
Number of Injuries	90	78	26	39	150	20	4	22	89	22	39	11

Fig. 3.3 Rate of deaths and injuries from 2005 to 2019 in South Asian shipbreaking yards (*Source* NGO shipbreaking platform reports[116])

Following the discussion of the profit of the shipowners and their associates and the accident data, it is logical to submit that the responsibility to protect from these

[115] World Bank Report 2010 (n 18) 28–35.

[116] The figure was developed by using information from the following sources: Karim (n) 20; Young Power in Social Action, Death Trap? A List of Dead Workers from the Year of 2005 to 2012 (September 2012) Death Trap I Shipbreaking in Bangladesh (shipbreakingbd.info) ; NGO Shipbreaking Platform, *Annual Report 2009* (Annual Report, 2009) NGO_Shipbreaking_Platform_Annual_Report-2009.pdf (shipbreakingplatform.org) 3; NGO Shipbreaking Platform, *Annual Report 2010* (Annual Report, 2010) Rapport_Annuel_2010.pdf (shipbreakingplatform.org) 5; NGO Shipbreaking Platform, *Annual Report 2011* (Annual Report, 2011) https://shipbreakingplatform.org/wp-content/uploads/2018/02/AR-2011-light-version.pdf 10; NGO Shipbreaking Platform, *Annual Report 2012* (Annual Report, 2012) Annual-Report-2012-NGO-Shipbreaking-Platform.pdf (shipbreakingplatform.org) 3; NGO Shipbreaking Platform, *Annual Report 2013* (Annual Report, 2013) NGO-Shipbreaking-Platform-annual-report-2013.pdf (shipbreakingplatform.org) 6; NGO Shipbreaking Platform, *Annual Report 2014* (Annual Report, 2014) NGO-Shipbreaking-Platform-Annual-Report-2014.pdf (shipbreakingplatform.org) 6; NGO Shipbreaking Platform, *Annual Report 2015* (Annual Report, 2015) https://shipbreakingplatform.org/wp-content/uploads/2018/02/NGO-Shipbreaking-Platform-Annual-Report-2015.pdf 9; NGO Shipbreaking Platform, *Annual Report 2016* (Annual Report, 2016) NGO_Shipbreaking_Platform_Annual_Report_2016_05.indd (shipbreakingplatform.org) 12–15; NGO Shipbreaking Platform, *Annual Report 2017* (Annual Report, 2017) https://shipbreakingplatform.org/wp-content/uploads/2018/07/Annual-Report-2017-Final-Spreads.pdf 6–12; NGO Shipbreaking Platform, *Impact Report 2018–2019* (Biennial Report, 2018–2019) https://shipbreakingplatform.org/wp-content/uploads/2020/06/NGOSBP-Bi-Annual-Report-18-19.pdf 6–13.

human consequences and to provide a remedy in cases of death, injury, and disease lies primarily with the shipping industry. While shipbreaking is an economic necessity for shipbreaking countries in South Asia, it is also a business for the shipping industry. The shipping industry, which represents foreign shipowners, should therefore undertake responsibility either to provide protection from human harm or to pay adequate compensation to victims. However, recent accident data show that the shipping industry has thus far failed to protect workers from these extreme consequences or to pay adequate compensation. One of the underlying causes for not providing adequate safety standards and compensation is the lack of adequate mechanisms in the national and international laws that govern the shipbreaking industry. The next chapter examines the deficiencies in the national laws of India, Bangladesh, and Pakistan, followed by an examination of the deficiencies in international laws in Chap. 5.

Conclusion

Shipbreaking industry has become well established in South Asian countries despite its negative impacts on the environment and the welfare of workers. The key factor for sustaining the industry in South Asia is the revenue earned by the global shipping industry and their associates, namely cash buyers and open registry countries, from the sale of ships to South Asian shipbreaking yards. A second factor is the socio-economic benefits of the industry to Bangladesh, Pakistan, and India.

The South Asian shipbreaking industry is a significant contributor to the global shipbreaking market and a major source of income for the shipping industry. It is expected that in the future more ships will be sent for breaking in South Asia because shipbreaking in large shipping nations is not economically viable due to high labour, safety, and environmental regulatory costs. The shipbreaking industry in South Asia therefore benefits the shipping industry in terms of both the economy and the environment. But the problem is despite generating millions of USD, overall, the shipping industry has done nothing to address the human consequences of the shipbreaking industry practices in these countries.

In the eye of law, such a harmful industry in one part of the planet—South Asia—should not provide a source of revenue for companies and countries located elsewhere without a robust global system to prevent the abuse of human rights and to compensate workers. An analysis of the national laws in South Asia that govern the shipbreaking industry is presented in Chap. 4 to examine whether South Asian shipbreaking countries have adequate legal mechanism to prevent and compensate the work-related deaths, injuries and diseases occur in their shipbreaking industry.

Bibliography

Articles/Books/Reports

Alcadia, Juan Ignacio, Francisco Piniella and Emilio Rodriguez-Diaz, '"The Mirror Flags": Ship Registration in Globalised Ship Breaking Industry' (2016) 48 *Transportation Research Part D* 378

Ali, Mohammad Zulfikar, 'How Effective are the International and Domestic Laws in Protecting Workers' Occupational Health and Safety Rights in the Shipbreaking Industry of Bangladesh? What Role Could the National Court Play in Accordance With Their Constitution' (Master's Thesis, University of New South Wales, 2013)

Choi, Jun-Ki et al, 'Economic and Environmental Perspective of End of Life Ship Management' (2016) 107 *Resources, Conservation and Recycling* 82

Demaria, Federico, 'Shipbreaking at Alang-Sosiya (India): An Ecological Distribution Conflict' (2010) 70(2) *Ecological Economics* 250

Demaria, Federico, 'Shipbreaking at Alang-Sosiya (India): An Ecological Distribution Conflict' (2010) 70(2) *Ecological Economics* 250

Deshpande, Paritosh C. et al, 'A Novel Approach to Estimating Resources Consumption Rates and Emission Factors for Ship Recycling Yards in Alang, India, (2013) 59(15) *Journal of Cleaner Production* 251

Deshphande, Paritosh Chakor, Atit K Tilwankar, and Shyam R Asolekar, 'A Novel Approach to Estimating Potential Maximum Heavy Metals Exposure to Ship Recycling Yard Workers in Alang, India' (2012) 438C *Science of the Total Environment* 304

Hiremath, Anand M., Sachin Kumar Panday, and Shyam R. Asolekar, 'Development of Ship-specific Recycling Plan to Improve Health Safety and Environment in Ship Recycling Yards' (2016) 116 *Journal of Cleaner Production* 279

Hossain et al, Mohammad Shakhaoat, 'Impact of Shipbreaking Activities on the Coastal Environment of Bangladesh and a Management System for Its Sustainability,' (2016) 16 *Environmental Science and Policy Journal* 84

Hossain, Khandakar Akhter, 'Overview of Ship Recycling Industry of Bangladesh' (2015) 5(5) *Journal of Environmental and Analytical Toxicology* 7

Hossain, Mohammad Shahadat et al, 'Occupational Health Hazards of Ship Scrapping Workers at Chittagong Coastal Zone, Bangladesh' (2008) 35(2) *Chiang Mai Journal of Science* 370

John, Johsin and Sushil Kumar, A Locational Decision Making Framework For Shipbreaking Under Multiple Formula (2016) 7(1) *International Journal of Strategic Decision Sciences* 76

Karim, Md. Saiful, 'Violation of Labour Rights in the Ship-Breaking Yards of Bangladesh: Legal Norms and Reality' (2009) 25(4) *International Journal of Comparative Labour Law and Industrial Relations* 379

Mahindrakar, Amit B. et al, 'Shipbreaking industry in India: Assessment of Opportunity and Challenges' (January 2008) *eLaw Journal: Journal of Air and Waste Management Association*, 1

Mikelis, Nikos E., A Statistical Overview of Ship Recycling (2008) 7(1) *World Maritime University Journal of Maritime Affairs* 227

N. Gregson et al, 'Following Things of Rubbish Value: Retired Ships, Chock-Chocky Furniture and the Bangladesh Middle Class Consumer' (2010) 41(6) *Geo Forum* 846

Rabbi, Hasan Ruhan and Aevelina Rahman, 'Shipbreaking and Recycling Industries in Bangladesh; Issues and Challenges' 194 (2017) *Prodcedia Engineering* 254

Zakaria, N. M. Golam, Mir Tareque Ali and Khandakar Akhter Hossain, 'Underlying Problems of Ship Recycling Industries in Bangladesh and Way Forward' (2012) 9(2) *Journal of Naval Architecture and Marine Engineering* 91

Galley, Michael, *Shipbreaking: Hazards and Liabilities* (Springer International Publishing, 2014)

Hossain, Mohammad Maruf and Md. Atikur Rahman, 'Shipbreaking Activities: Threat to Coastal Environment and Fish Biodiversity' in M.E Yousuf Haroon and A. K Hussain (eds), *Eco-system Health and Management of Pollution in the Bay of Bengal* (Bangladesh Fisheries Research Institute, 2011) 23

Karim, Saiful, *Shipbreaking in Developing Countries: A Requiem for Environmental Justice from the Perspectives of Bangladesh* (Taylor and Francis Group, 2018)

Kumar, Ramapati, *Ship Dismantling: A Status Report on South Asia and the EU*, eds Johan Bentinck and Dr Paul R Halmos (Euroconsult Matt Macdonald and World Wildlife Fund-India, 2018)

Mikelis, Nikos E., *The Recycling of Ships* (Global Maritime Services (GMS) Leadership, 2nd ed, 1 October 2019)

Mikelis, Nikos E., *The Recycling of Ships* (Global Maritime Services (GMS) Leadership, 2nd ed, 1 October 2019)

Mikelis, Nikos E., *The Recycling of Ships* (Global Maritime Services (GMS) Leadership, 1st ed, 1 April 2018

Oxford University Press, *The Oxford Encyclopaedia of Economic History* (online at 25 April 2020) 4 Economic History, 'India'

Oxford University Press, *The Oxford Encyclopaedia of Economic History* (online at 25 April 2020) 5 Economic History, 'Pakistan'

Oxford University Press, *The Oxford Encyclopaedia of Economic History* (online at 25 April 2020) 4 Economic History, 'Bangladesh'

Puthurcherril, Tony George, *From Shipbreaking to Sustainable Ship Recycling: Evolution of a Legal Regime* (Matinus Nijhoff Publishers, 2010)

Aage Bjorn Anderson, 'Worker Safety in Shipbreaking, Sectoral Activities Program' (Working Paper No 167, International Labour Organisation, 2001)

Commission of the European Community, *Green Paper on Better Dismantling*, Com SEC (2007) 645, Brussels 22 May 2007

Commission of the European Community, *Impact Assessment for a EU Strategy for Better Ship Dismantling*, EU Doc. COM (2008) 765 final, Brussels, 19 November 2008

Department of Environment, Food and Rural Affairs (DEFRA) 'Regulatory Impact Assessment for the UK Ship Scrapping Industries' (Research Report, February-2007) http://www.defra.gov.uk/ENVIRONMENT/WASTE/strategy/ship.htm

European Commission, 'Study on "Ship Dismantling and Precleaning of Ships"' (Final Report, Directorate General for Environment, June 2007) http://ec.europa.eu/environment/waste/ships//index.htm

Georgescu, Calin, *Report of the Special Rapporteur on the Adverse Effects of the Movement and Dumping of Toxic and Dangerous Products and Wastes on the Enjoyment of Human Rights – Preliminary Assessment of Whether the Hong Kong Convention Establishes an Equivalent Level of Control and Enforcement as that Established under the Basel Convention,* UN Doc. UNEP/CHW/OEWG/7/21 (2 September 2010)

Government of India Ministry of Labour and Employment, 'The Second National Commission on Labour Report' (New Delhi: Ministry of Labour and Employment, 2002)

Hossain, Md. Maruf, *Shipbreaking Activities: Threat to Coastal Environment and Fish Biodiversity and Fisherman Community in Chittagong, Bangladesh* (Young Power in Social Action, 2010)

Human Rights Commission of Pakistan, 'Horror in Gadani' (Fact Finding Mission Report, November 2016)

Ibeanu, Okechukwu, *Report of the Special Rapporteur on the Adverse Effects of the Movement and Dumping of Toxic and Dangerous Products and Wastes on the Enjoyment of Human Rights*, UN Doc. A/HRC/12/26 (15 July 2009)

International Federation for Human Rights, 'Where Do the "Floating Dustbins" End Up? Labour Rights in Shipbreaking Yards in South Asia – The Cases of Chittagong (Bangladesh) and Alang (India)' (Investigative Mission Report No 348/2, International Federation for Human Rights, December 2002)

International Maritime Organisation, 'Report on International Shipping Facts and Figures – 2012' (Information Resources on Trade Safety, Security, Environment, 2012)

International Metalworkers Federation, 'Special Report – Cleaning Up Shipbreaking is the Most Dangerous of the World' (Research Report, 15 December 2015)

Margot Gibbs, 'Revealed: The UK Company and Caribbean Tax Haven Cashing in on One of the World's Deadliest Trades – Shipbreaking' *F:Uncovered* (Web Page, 20 February 2019) https://www.financeuncovered.org/investigations/tax-haven-flags-of-convenience-stkitts-nevis-shipbreaking-toxic-ships-skanreg-chittagong/

NGO Shipbreaking Platform, *Annual Report 2009* (Annual Report, 2009) NGO_Shipbreaking_Platform_Annual_Report-2009.pdf(shipbreakingplatform.org)

NGO Shipbreaking Platform, *Annual Report 2010* (Annual Report, 2010) Rapport_Annuel_2010.pdf(shipbreakingplatform.org)

NGO Shipbreaking Platform, *Annual Report 2011* (Annual Report, 2011) https://shipbreakingplatform.org/wp-content/uploads/2018/02/AR-2011-light-version.pdf

NGO Shipbreaking Platform, *Annual Report 2012* (Annual Report, 2012) Annual-Report-2012-NGO-Shipbreaking-Platform.pdf(shipbreakingplatform.org)

NGO Shipbreaking Platform, *Annual Report 2013* (Annual Report, 2013) NGO-Shipbreaking-Platform-annual-report-2013.pdf (shipbreakingplatform.org)

NGO Shipbreaking Platform, *Annual Report 2014* (Annual Report, 2014) NGO-Shipbreaking-Platform-Annual-Report-2014.pdf (shipbreakingplatform.org)

NGO Shipbreaking Platform, *Annual Report 2015* (Annual Report, 2015) https://shipbreakingplatform.org/wp-content/uploads/2018/02/NGO-Shipbreaking-Platform-Annual-Report-2015.pdf

NGO Shipbreaking Platform, *Annual Report 2016* (Annual Report, 2016) NGO_Shipbreaking_Platform_Annual_Report_2016_05.indd (shipbreakingplatform.org)

NGO Shipbreaking Platform, *Annual Report 2017* (Annual Report, 2017) https://shipbreakingplatform.org/wp-content/uploads/2018/07/Annual-Report-2017-Final-Spreads.pdf

NGO Shipbreaking Platform, *Impact Report 2018–2019* (Biennial Report, 2018–2019) https://shipbreakingplatform.org/wp-content/uploads/2020/06/NGOSBP-Bi-Annual-Report-18-19.pdf

NGO Shipbreaking Platform, *Impact Report 2018–2019* (Biennial Report, 2018–2019) https://shipbreakingplatform.org/wp-content/uploads/2020/06/NGOSBP-Bi-Annual-Report-18-19.pdf

Overgaard, S., 'Feasibility Study for Ship Dismantling' (Research Report, Litehauz, 2013) 27–28.

Sarraf, Maria et al, 'Ship Breaking and Recycling Industry in Bangladesh and Pakistan,' (Report No. 58275-SAS, World Bank, 2010)

The European Commission, 'Ship Recycling: Reducing Human and Environmental Impacts' (Thematic Issue 55, Director General Environment by the Science Communication Unit Environmental Policy, 2016) http://ec.europa.eu/science-environment-policy

The European Commission, 'Study on Oil Tanker Phase Out and the Ship Scrapping Industry' (Research Report, DG Transport and Energy, 2004) http://europa.eu.int/comm/transport/maritime/safety/doc/prestige/2004_06_scrapping_study_en.pdf

Tradewinds, 'Watershed Looms for Recyclers After 15% Drops in Prices' (Research Paper, 19 August 2019) 29.

United Nations Conference on Trade and Development, 'Review of Maritime Transport 2018' (Annual Report, 2018) 3 https://unctad.org/en/pages/PublicationWebflyer.aspx?publicationid=2245

United Nations Conference on Trade and Development, 'Review of Maritime Transport 2016' (Annual Report, 5 March 2017) 3 http://unctad.org/en/pages/PublicationWebflyer.aspx?publicationid=1650

Veritas, Det Norske, 'Technological and Economical Feasibility of Ship Scrapping

Veritas, Det Norske, 'Technological and Economical Feasibility of Ship Scrapping in Europe' (Research Report No. 2000–3527, 13 February 2001)

Others

Allied Shipping Research, *Monthly SnP Statistics* (Web Page) https://www.bluverve.com/wp-content/uploads/2020/04/ALLIED-SnP-Statistics-Week-15-12_04_2020.pdf

Bray, Julian, 'Ship Recycling Forum', *TradeWinds News* 13 March 2020

Costa, Sara and Geetanjoy Sahu, 'The Ship Recycling Industry Must Move Towards a Sustainable Future' *The Wire* (online at 03 August 2020) https://thewire.in/environment/shipbreaking-ship-recycling-industry-sustainable-future-environment

Daems, Ebe and Gie Goris, *Behind the Hypocrisy of Better Beaches, Shipbreaking in India, Shipowners in Switzerland Lobbying in Belgium*, ed Linda A Thompson (MO Magazine, 2019)

Dastageer, Ghulam, Subuk Hasnain and Ayesha Binte Rashid, 'The Ugly Side of Pakistan's Ship-Breaking Industry at Gadani' *The WIRE* (online at 28 December 2016) https://thewire.in/south-asia/ugly-gadani-ship-breaking

gCaptain, *The Unwanted Ships: How to Lay-up a Vessel* (Web Page, 20 May 2016) https://gcaptain.com/the-unwanted-ships-how-to-lay-up-a-vessel/

GMS Leadership, *Overview* (Web Page) https://www.gmsinc.net/gms_new/index.php/about

Hansen, Jan Moller, 'Shipbreaking in Bangladesh', *Lensculture* (Web Page) https://www.lensculture.com/articles/jan-moller-hansen-ship-breaking-in-bangladesh

Henrikson, Sturla, 'Says No to Beaching Ships' *Norwegian Shipowners' Association* (Web Page, 17 August 2015) https://www.rederi.no/aktuelt/2015/nei-til-beaching-av-skip

International Association of Classification Societies, *Classification Societies- What, Why and How* (Web Page) http://www.iacs.org.uk/media/3785/iacs-class-what-why-how.pdf

Maersk, 'Breaking the Stalemate' *Case Studies* (Web Page, 25 October 2019) https://www.maersk.com/news/articles/2017/01/03/breaking-the-stalemate

Milad, Masud, '25 Years Old Ship, Cost 24.564 Million' *Prothom Alo* (9 July 2021)

Miller, Matt, *Shipbreaking: Breaking Badly* (Web Page, 23 April 2018) http://www.ajot.com/news/channel/maritime

NGO Shipbreaking Platform, 'Europe Has Capacity to Recycle Its ships, New Data shows – However, shipowners Want to Use Dangerous, Polluting Yards Abroad' (Press Release, 24 September 2018)

NGO Shipbreaking Platform, *HKC Statement of Compliance* (Web Page) https://www.shipbreakingplatform.org/issues-of-interest/the-law/hkc-soc/

NGO Shipbreaking Platform, *India* (Web Page) https://www.shipbreakingplatform.org/our-work/the-problem/india/

NGO Shipbreaking Platform, *Toxic Tide: 2019 Shipbreaking Records* (Web Page) http://www.offthebeach.org/

Roussanoglou, Nikos, *Shipbreaking Expected to Roar Ahead in 2020, as More Ships Could Head for Demolition* (Blog Post, 8 January 20) https://www.hellenicshippingnews.com/shipbreaking-expected-to-roar-ahead-in-2020-as-more-ships-could-head-for-demolition/

Safety4Sea, '90% of Tonnage Scrapped on South Asian Beaches in 2018' *Ship Recycling* (Web Page, 30 January 2019) https://safety4sea.com/ngo-90-of-tonnage-scrapped-on-south-asian-beaches-in-2018/

Schular, Michael, 'NGO shipbreaking Platform Slams Shipping Industry Scaremongering to Undermine European Ship Recycling Regulation', *gCaptain* (online at 22 June 2018) https://gcaptain.com/ngo-shipbreaking-platform-slams-shipping-industry-scaremongering-to-undermine-european-ship-recycling-regulation/

Sultana, Munima 'Bangladesh Ship Breakers Left Out to Sea', *Equal Times* (online at 11 January 2013) http://www.equaltimes.org/wp-content/uploads/2013/01/Shipbreaking_021-WP.jpg

Syed, Md Abu, 'Shipbreaking in South Asia: Impact on Environment and Health', *The Daily Star* (online at 23 April 2011) http://archive.thedailystar.net/newDesign/news-details.php?nid=182721

Tuscar Lloyds, *Breaking Bad? The Story of Alang Shipbreaking Yards* (Web Page, 18 November 2016) https://www.tuscorlloyds.com/alang-ship-breaking-yards/

Veritas, Det Norske, *Key Factors to Consider When Assessing Lay-up Options* (Web Page, 2 April 2020) https://www.dnv.com/expert-story/maritime-impact/Key-factors-to-consider-when-assessing-lay-up-options.html

Walia, Inderpreet, 'India Ratifies the Hong Kong Convention on Ship Recycling', *Lloyd List Maritime Intelligence* (Online at 21 November 2019) http://www.gmsinc.net/gms_new/assets/pdf/IndiaHC.pdf

White, Chris, 'Two Years Since Pakistan's Gadani Shipbreaking Disaster, Why are Workers Still dying?' *This Week in Asia* (online at 28 October 2018) (https://www.scmp.com/week-asia/health-environment/article/2170256/two-years-pakistans-gadani-ship-breaking-disaster-why

Young Power in Social Action, Death Trap? A List of Dead Workers from the Year of 2005 to 2012 (September 2012) Death Trap | Shipbreaking in Bangladesh (shipbreakingbd.info)

Chapter 4
Deficiencies Within the Regulatory Framework in South Asia

Abstract Domestic regulatory frameworks are critical in governing high-risk sectors such as shipbreaking. Nevertheless, in Bangladesh, India, and Pakistan's shipbreaking industries, workers face significant obstacles in accessing legal remedies. The informal and precarious nature of their employment, compounded by the absence of formal contracts and identity documentation, renders these workers unable to effectively invoke national labour laws or pursue compensation for occupational injuries and fatalities. The chapter conducts a legal analysis of the national compensation laws applicable in these jurisdictions, employing a descriptive research methodology, the underlying objective of which is to offer commentary on relevant statutory provisions by elucidating their scope and implementation challenges.

Keywords Risky industry · Compensation and regulation · Shipbreaking liability certificate · Approach differences to regulation · Deficiencies in regulation · Precleaning · Conventional shipbreaking methods

Introduction

This chapter conducts a critical assessment of the structural and judicial decisions within the existing legal framework in India, Bangladesh, and Pakistan. Through a comparative analysis of national regulations and judicial interventions, it seeks to advance the dialogue surrounding the adoption of a transnational civil liability system—a shipbreaking liability certificate (SLC) to ensure accountability and compensation for victims of shipbreaking-related harm. A key component of the legal discourse in South Asian shipbreaking sector involves the role of Supreme Courts in these jurisdictions, which have issued relevant rulings on issues such as the transboundary movement and environmentally responsible shipbreaking.[1]

---

[1] Hajime Sato, 'The Universality, Peculiarity, and Sustainability of Indian Public Interest Litigation Reconsidered' (2017) 100 *World Development* 59–68; There are no equivalent cases from the Supreme Court of Pakistan giving such decisions.

M. Z. Ali, *Worker Injustices in the South Asian Shipbreaking Industry*, International Law in Asia, https://doi.org/10.1007/978-981-95-8325-6_4

These decisions often initiated by NGO-led public interest litigation (PIL) that have played a key role in guiding legal policy. In particular, the courts have interpreted laws in ways that promote environmental protection and safeguard worker health and safety, even in face of economic considerations. Their judicial activism often acts as a catalyst for legal reform: where community interest is strong and judicial directives highlight deficiencies, governments are prompted either to enact new legislation or authorise relevant ministries to issue sector specific rules and standards.[2] Thus, the judiciary not only serves as an adjudicative body but also indirectly outlines regulatory architecture by drawing attention to gaps in existing laws. The intersection of comparative statutory analysis and judicial engagement underscores the need for a harmonised global liability mechanism—one that transcends national limitations and ensures equitable redress for affected individuals in shipbreaking operations.[3]

This chapter is divided into five parts. Following the introductory remarks, section "Where India, Bangladesh, and Pakistan's National Approaches Fall Short" critically explores juridical strategies employed by Supreme Courts of the South Asian nations in overseeing maritime import regulation, particularly through four landmark judgements from India and Bangladesh. These cases illuminate judicial engagement with issues of occupational safety, environmental sustainability, and the balancing act with economic priorities.

Section "Analysing the Deficiencies in the Laws and Policies of Bangladesh, India, and Pakistan" turns to statutory frameworks governing shipbreaking across South Asia. It evaluates notable instruments such as the *Shipbreaking Code 2013* (India) and the *Ship Recycling Act 2019* (India), *the* Ship Recycling Act, 2018 (Bangladesh), *the Shipbreaking and Recycling Rules, 2011* (Bangladesh), the *Hazardous Waste and Shipbreaking Management Rules, 2011 (*Bangladesh), the *Balochistan Environmental Protection Act 2012* (Pakistan), and general labour laws. The analysis identifies four systemic shortcomings: the absence of mandatory precleaning requirements, inadequate oversight of onboard hazardous materials, and the lack of constraints on substandard shipbreaking methodologies. This part further engages with the relevant case of *Bangladesh Environmental Lawyers Association (BELA) v Janata Steel Corporation* (*Janata Steel)*, which holds particular resonance in the context of Bangladesh.[4] The nation's Supreme Court adopted a progressive interpretive stance on the *Hazardous Waste and Shipbreaking Management Rules, 2011,* advancing judicial environmentalism and labour protection.[5]

---

[2] Ridwanul Hoque, *Judicial Activism in Bangladesh: A Golden Mean Approach* (Cambridge Scholars Publishing, 2011) 3.

*Part of this chapter was published as a Book Chapter entitled 'Comparative Legal Analysis of Shipbreaking Regulations in Bangladesh, India, and Pakistan: Implication on Human Tragedy and Compensation to Victims' in Jushua Aston et al. (eds) *Comparative Law* (Thomson Reuters, 2021).

[3] Taqbir Huda, 'Why is the Price of Killing a Worker Only Tk 2 Lakh' *The Daily Star e-paper* (online at 11 July 2021) E-paper (http://epaper.thedailystar.net).

[4] Malcolm Langford, 'The Impact of Public Interest Litigation: the Case of Socio-economic Rights' (2021) 27 (3) *Australian Journal of Human Rights* 505–531.

[5] *The Hazardous Wastes and Shipbreaking Waste Management Rules, 2011* (Bangladesh) r 19; *The Shipbreaking and Recycling Rules, 2011* (Bangladesh) r 11; *The International Convention for the*

Section "Issues in Relation to the Compensation Claim" interrogates the compensation regimes across these jurisdictions, observing that recourse for victims relies chiefly on national labour legislation. These laws, however, fall short in addressing the precarious employment status and limited legal protections afforded to shipbreaking workers, prompting concerns about the adequacy of redress mechanisms.

The final section underscores the chapter's central thesis: the urgent need for an international compensation architecture that remedies existing legal inadequacies and ensures equitable remedies for affected individuals in South Asian shipbreaking counties.

Where India, Bangladesh, and Pakistan's National Approaches Fall Short

The lack of mandatory precleaning protocols before a ship is imported for breaking in a South Asian shipbreaking country has emerged as a central factor contributing to environmental harm and public health risks.[6] But rather than following uniform regulatory standards, India, Bangladesh, and Pakistan have adopted conflicting approaches. India relies on Industry-specific regulations that tend to favour economic interests; Pakistan employs a broad legal framework that similarly prioritises commercial gains, while Bangladesh has enacted special legislation that integrates both environmental safeguards and labour protections. These contrasting governance models have led to uneven regulatory environments, undermining efforts to coordinate oversight across borders and enabling competitive imbalance. As a result, shipowners incline to deal with jurisdictions offering lenient oversight and higher financial returns, often at the expense of human health. Bangladesh's emphasis on sustainable practices and worker rights, which is reinforced by Supreme Court decisions mandating comprehensive precleaning before entry of ships—has rendered it less attractive to international shipowners, who are generally unwilling to incur the additional costs associated with responsible shipbreaking.[7]

Safe and Environmentally Sound Recycling of Ships, opened for signature 1 September 2009, IMO Doc. SR/CONF/45 (19 May 2009) (entered into force 26 June 2025). (*The Hong Kong Convention).*

[6] Ship recycling activities in India, Bangladesh and Pakistan is one of the main sources of marine pollution in South Asia: See Ljubomir, Jeftic, Seba Sheably and Ellik Adler, *Marine Litter: A Global Challenge*, ed Nikki Meith (United Nations Environment Program, April 2009) 13; On an average, 2 workers face accidents out of 1000 workers in the shipbreaking industry everyday: at Stara Srinivas, 'Breaking Down the Ship Recycling Industry' *The Ship Recycling Industry in India* (Research Report, Part I- Issue Brief, Social and Political Research Foundation, 20 June 2020) 3.

[7] *Bangladesh Environmental Lawyers Association (BELA) v Bangladesh and others*, [Writ Petition No 3916 of 2006] High Court Division (6 July 2006) (*MT Alfaship*); *Bangladesh Environmental Lawyers Association (BELA) v Bangladesh, Represented by the Secretary, Ministry of Shipping and Others* [Writ Petition No. 7260 of 2008] High Court Division (5 March 2009, 17 March 2009, 31 May 2010 and 7 March 2011). (*MT Enterprise*).

In the shipbreaking sector, regulatory frameworks that prefer occupational safety and environmental sustainability tend to elevate social and environmental protections above profit-driven motives. Bangladesh serves as a prominent example of this rights-focused model, implementing rigorous standards aimed at safeguarding both workers and the natural environment. Conversely, India and Pakistan operate under legal regimes that allow ship imports without compulsory decontamination, signalling a preference for economic expediency. This disparity incentivises shipowners to opt for destinations with lower compliance costs and weaker enforcement of labour rights, making India and Pakistan more commercially attractive than Bangladesh, within this context, a pro-business approach denotes the elevation of financial interests over environmental and human welfare. The subsequent three sections offer an in-depth analysis of each country's legal approach, supported by pertinent judicial pronouncements from their respective Supreme Courts.

Indian Approach—Blue Lady and the Exxon Valdez

The evolution of India's legal framework governing shipbreaking can be divided into two distinct phases. Before 2012, the country maintained a relatively protective stance towards both labour conditions and environmental standards in relation to ship imports. Subsequent legal advancements were largely shaped by rulings from the Indian Supreme Court, which drew upon the foundational principles of the *Basel Convention on the Control of Transboundary Movements of Hazardous Wastes and their Disposal (Basel Convention).*[8] From 2012 onwards, changes to the law have followed the *Hong Kong Convention* principles and a pro-business approach as applied by the Supreme Court of India in *Research Foundation for Science Technology and Natural Resource Policy v Union of India and Others, Supreme Court of India* (*Blue Lady*) and *Research Foundation for Science Technology and Natural Resource Policy v Union of India and Others, the Supreme Court of India* (*Exxon Valdez*).[9]

In its initial decision in *Research Foundation,*[10] the Supreme Court of India restricted the import of hazardous wastes and issued comprehensive regulatory directives to the central government. The litigation was initiated by the Research Foundation for Science, Technology and Natural Resources, which sought judicial scrutiny over the widespread dumping of toxic waste within India. While adjudicating this

---

[8] *Basel Convention on the Control of Transboundary Movements of Hazardous Wastes and their Disposal*, opened for signature 22 March 1989, 1673 UNTS 126 (entered into force 5 May 1992). *(Basel Convention).*

[9] [Civil Original Jurisdiction Writ Petition No 657 of 1995) (November 2007) *(Blue Lady)*; [Civil Original Jurisdiction Writ Petition No 657 of 1995 interim application no. 61 and 62] (12 October 2012). *(Exxon Valdez).*

[10] *Research Foundation for Science Technology and Natural Resource Policy v Union of India and Others, Supreme Court of India,* [Civil Original Jurisdiction Writ Petition no. 657 of 1995] 4 SCC 647. *(Research Foundation).*

broader environmental concern, the Court also addressed the legal dimensions of shipbreaking activities.

Research Foundation operates as a continuing mandamus under art 226 of the *Constitution of India*, 1950, which is a provision that empowers higher courts to compel subordinate bodies or public authorities to fulfil their statutory responsibilities.[11] In a 2003 order within the ongoing proceeding, the Supreme Court acknowledged that India's legislative framework was adequate to meet its international commitments, but highlighted systemic failures in enforcement by regulatory agencies.[12] The petitioner contended that, as a signatory to the *Basel Convention*, India was obligated to prohibit the entry of ships into its territorial waters unless they had undergone prior documentation.[13] The Supreme Court accepted the argument issuing a directive that authorities must rigorously adhere to the standards outlined in the *Basel Convention* or any future regulations adopted by the central government to ensure a clean and safe maritime environment before allowing ships suspected of containing hazardous substances to enter Indian waters.[14]

Subsequent legal developments over the next five years demonstrated the Court's role in regulating precleaning issue, as outlined in Table 4.1.

Following *Research Foundation*, the Gujrat (where Indian shipbreaking facilities are mainly located) State government enacted regulations aimed at improving environmental and health safety in shipbreaking operations. However, these measures raised serious issues for India's shipbreaking industry. International shipowners, deterred by the high costs associated with mandatory precleaning to eliminate hazardous substances, became reluctant to sell ships to Indian companies. In response to declining business and economic setbacks, the Indian government adopted a more pro-business approach to retain its position in the global shipbreaking market. This was reflected in India's decision to import hazardous ships. Despite widespread domestic opposition, India permitted the entry of highly toxic ships, notably the Blue Lady in September 2007 and the Exxon Valdez in May 2012.[15]

The import of the Blue Lady ship, a former French ship, came as a great opportunity for India to revive its industry.[16] The Blue Lady, originally a French-built cruise

[11] A continuing mandamus is a judicial remedy that extends beyond the issuance of a final judgement, functioning as an ongoing directive that obliges the responsible authority to fulfil its legal obligations over time. In mandamus cases, the court assumes an oversight role, monitoring compliance with specific duties outlined in the writ. The proceedings remain active indefinitely, allowing the judiciary to periodically assess whether the respondent is adhering to its mandated responsibilites: see Shreemanshu Kumar Dash, Writ of Continuing Mandamus in Matters of PILs: A Step towards Development of Environmental Jurisprudence (August 2017) 22 (8) *Journal of Humanities and Social Science* 26, 29–32.

[12] *Research Foundation for Science Technology and Natural Resource Policy V Union of India and Others,* [Civil Original Jurisdiction Writ Petition no. 657 of 1995] Supreme Court of India (12 April 2003). (*Research Foundation—2003).*

[13] See Chap. 5.

[14] *Research Foundation—2003* (n 10).

[15] Ibid.

[16] Ibid.

Table 4.1 Precleaning regulations passed by the Gujarat Provincial Government and the Central Government of India

Name of the regulations	Principles	Objective	Influence on the industry
Gujarat Maritime Board (Prevention of Fire and Accidents for the Safety and Welfare of Workers and Protection of Environment during Shipbreaking Activities) Regulations 2000	The international conventions issued by the IMO and the International Labour Organisation	To direct industry good practices, but they had no binding obligations	Little influence on the non-compliant industry
Hazardous Waste (Management, Handling and Transboundary Movement) Rules 2008	Ensuring sound management by exporter	Compulsory precleaning requirement	Decreased import of ships
Gujrat Maritime Board (Prevention of Fire and Accidents for Safety of Workers and Protection of Environment during Shipbreaking Activities) Regulation, 2003 and the Gujarat Maritime Board (Conditions and Procedures for Granting Permission for Utilising Ship Recycling Plots) Regulation, 2006	Empowering local authorities to issue clearance	Local authorities can deny entry or breaking of toxic ships	Decreased import of old ships

Source Florent Pelsy[17]

ship, had become a financial and operational burden for its last owner, the Norwegian Cruise Lines (NCL), after boiler explosion in 2006 at Miami in Florida. The incident resulted in killing several workers and rendered the ship inoperative. NCL subsequently sold the ship to an Indian firm for USD 14.5 million, thereby avoiding the estimated USD 17 million cost of asbestos removal.[18] Because of the risks involved in breaking this hazardous ship, import of the Blue Lady was challenged before Indian Supreme Court. In the litigation, petitioner, Union of India sought a ban on breaking the ship, citing severe risks to worker safety and environmental health. The Court, however, permitted its breaking,[19] finding that the ship would yield approximately 41,0000 metric tonnes of steel and generate employment for around 400 individuals.

In its decision, the Court introduced the principle of proportionality in the context of development, ostensibly aiming to balance economic growth with environmental and social concerns.[20] The decision suggests that the Court clearly

[17] Florent Pelsy, 'The Blue Lady Case and the International Issue of Ship Dismantling' (2008) 4(2) *Law, Environment and Development Journal* 135, 137.

[18] NGO Shipbreaking Platform, 'Comments on the Indian Committee Inspection Report on the Hazardous Materials On-board the SS Blue Lady' (Research Report, 31 July 2006).

[19] *Blue Lady* (n 9).

[20] The concept of proportionality is used as a threshold to limit the interference with human or fundamental rights. It requires that the interference with rights must be reasonable and it must not cross boundary in relation with the intensity of the interference: Jam Sieckmann, 'Proportionality

preferred economic benefits over environmental and worker safety. Although, the Court acknowledged the need for equilibrium between developmental priorities and environmental safeguards, its decision failed to reflect such a balance. The precedent has since left room for similar pro-business decisions, potentially at the expense of sustainable and ethical practices later in *Exxon Valdez*.[21]

The breaking of the Exxon Valdez in 2012 further underscored the Indian Supreme Court's approach to prefer commercial interests.[22] Originally infamous for its catastrophic oil spill in Alaska's Prince William Sound in 1989, the ship was subsequently barred from docking at ports in both the US and the European Union because of the pollution risk involved in anchoring the damaged ship. Hong Kong based Bloom Shipping Ltd., changed the name of the ship several times between 1989 and 2011 to conceal the ship's infamous identity. As the ship neared the end of its operational life, Priya Blue Industries Private Limited, the same Indian firm that had previously acquired the Blue Lady, purchased the Exxon Valdez paying approximately USD 16 million.[23] Although, the Supreme Court initially denied permission for its entry, the ship eventually arrived in Indian waters in May 2012 without a national flag, which effectively helped the shipowner to conceal its original identity. Its prior registration under Sierra Leone had also lapsed by that time.

An environmental advocacy group, Toxic Watch Alliance uncovered the ship's concealed identity and filed a legal petition praying to the Supreme Court to halt its breaking in India. Nevertheless, because the ship had already entered India's maritime jurisdiction, the Court permitted its breaking. In its ruling, the Court cited earlier precedents and emphasised the need for a unified national framework. It recommended transferring regulatory authority over the shipbreaking sector from State governments to the central government for ensuring more consistent regulatory oversight.[24]

The unregulated importation of the Blue Lady and Exxon Valdez—both lacking prior cleaning of inbuilt hazardous substances remained inside—represented core legal and environmental concern in their respective cases. The Supreme Court's rulings in these matters contributed constructively by prompting the Indian government to establish a unified legal framework governing shipbreaking across the country. Conversely, since 2007, these judicial decisions have departed from the stricter precedents set in *Research Foundation*. They effectively permitted the entry of ships containing inbuilt hazardous materials, which eventually relaxed earlier environmental and safety regulations. Following these decisions, the Indian Parliament

---

as Universal Human Rights Principle' in Duarte D. and Silva Sampson (eds), *Proportionality in Law* (Springer International Publishing, 2018) 3–24. https://doi.org/10.1007/978-3-319-89647-2_1.

[21] Pelsy (n 15) 141.

[22] *Exxon Valdez* (n 9); Michael Galley, *Shipbreaking: Hazards and Liabilities* (Springer International Publishing, 2014) 155.

[23] Ibid 155–157.

[24] *Exxon Valdez* (n 9). *Research Foundation* was the original ruling and in 2003, 2007, and 2012, the Indian Supreme Court delivered further decisions disposing more petitions.

enacted shipbreaking specific regulations, including the *Ship Recycling Code, 2013* and the *Ship Recycling Act 2019.*

The Bangladeshi Approach—MT Alfaship and Enterprise

In 2012, the Supreme Court of Bangladesh decided two leading cases—*MT Alfaship* and *MT Enterprise,* in which the Court diverged from the Indian Judiciary's stance by prohibiting the import and breaking of both ships.[25] These ships were part of a compilation prepared by Greenpeace International, identifying them as two of the 50 most environmentally hazardous ships slated for breaking, which was the basis of *MT Alfaship* and *MT Enterprise.*[26] The purpose of this list was to exert pressure on shipbreaking facility owners to compel shipowners to undertake proper decontamination prior to dispatching ships to Bangladesh.[27]

In *MT Alfaship,* the purchaser attempted to bring the ship into Bangladesh for breaking. Despite lacking official environmental clearance from the Department of Environment (DoE), the ship arrived at outer anchorage.[28] The Bangladesh Environmental Lawyers Association (BELA), a prominent legal advocacy group, which works on the protection of environment, intervened to halt the import, citing that the ship was a source of hazardous waste.[29] Before the ship could be brought ashore, the High Court Division of the Supreme Court issued an injunction directing government agencies to prevent the MT Alfaship from entering Bangladesh's territorial waters.[30]

[25] The decisions came in response to litigations filed by an environmental policy-based NGO, Bangladesh Environmental Lawyers Association (BELA), on behalf of the people and environment affected by the industry activities. These types of litigations are called Public Interest Litigation (PIL), when someone from the society has the right to sue and get the issue addressed by the Apex Court. As with India and Pakistan, the judicial guidelines from the Courts on shipbreaking followed this common approach: at *MT Alfaship.*

[26] Michael Galley, 'Shipbreaking-a Convenient Washing of Hands?' (2008) 12 (2) *Mountbatten Journal of Legal Studies* 96–121.

[27] Ibid.

[28] 'Toxic Ship Barred from Chittagong Port', *The Daily Star* (online at 15 January 2007) http://www.thedailystar.net/2007/01/.

[29] *MT Alfaship* (n 7).

[30] Being the highest Court and guardian of the constitution, the Bangladesh Supreme Court is empowered to review and strike down any law if the concerned law does not corroborate the mandate of the constitution. The Bangladesh Supreme Court is divided into High Court and Appellate Division. The High Court division has some original jurisdiction along with the power of deciding appeal from the lower courts. This division decides writ petitions of all kinds. Against the decision of the High Court, an aggrieved person can file appeal to the Appellate Division whose decision is final: see generally *Constitution of the Peoples' Republic of Bangladesh Constitution* (Bangladesh) 1972, arts 94–117. *(Bangladesh Constitution).*

Unlike India, the judgement imposed a legal duty on public bodies to prohibit the entry of a hazardous ship to Bangladesh.[31] Furthermore, the Court's order emphasised that the government was required to follow its international obligations in order to improve the sound management capacity of its shipbreaking industry in accordance with the *Basel Convention*.[32]

Following the Supreme Court's decision in *MT Alfaship*, the ship ultimately departed from Bangladesh waters. However, in the subsequent years, the government did not enact new legislation or revise existing policies to reflect the Court's findings. This inaction may be attributed to the absence of a specific judicial directive mandating legislative reform. Consequently, while the judgement marked a step forward, its impact was limited in scope.[33] Nonetheless, it served as a catalyst, triggering increased governmental attention to the regulatory challenges within the shipbreaking industry and laying the groundwork for future legal interventions, including *MT Enterprise*.[34]

In *MT Enterprise*, the ship entered Bangladesh despite an official prohibition issued by the Department of Environment. After substantial dismantling occurred at a local shipbreaking facility, BELA filed a petition before the High Court Division of the Supreme Court in September 2008. BELA requested that the Court compel the Ministry of Environment and Forest, along with the Department of Environment, to shut down all shipbreaking facilities operating without formal environment approval, including the facility responsible for breaking the ship, MT Enterprise.

Mirroring the legal reasoning of MT Alfaship, MT Enterprise scrutinised government policy on shipbreaking and its intersection with constitutional rights, in particular the right to life and the right to safe and sustainable working environment. The High Court ruled in favour of BELA, affirming that shipbreaking facilities must obtain valid environment clearance certificated from the Department of Environment.[35]The Court issued a binding order requiring:

- All shipbreaking operations lacking environmental clearance to cease operation within two weeks of the judgement.
- The Ministry of Environment and the Department of Environment to take immediate action to enforce the closure of all non-compliant shipbreaking facilities, in accordance with statutory requirements.

---

[31] Mohammad Zulfikar Ali and Prafula Pearce, 'Comparative Legal Analysis of Shipbreaking Regulations in Bangladesh, India, and Pakistan: Implication on Human Tragedy and Compensation to Victims' in Jushua Aston et al. (eds) *Comparative Law* (Thomson Reuters, 2021).

[32] *MT Alfaship* (n 7).

[33] Ibid.

[34] 'Promoting fundamental rights, impartial administration of justice, application of rule of law are the issues in which the Supreme Court acts as the final interpreter as guardian of the Constitution. The Judiciary can shape principle of law according to the need of the society by taking resort from International law when there is gap in national law': at Md Mizanur Rahman, Can Ordinary People Seek Environmental Justice in Bangladesh' (2021) 29 (2) *Bangladesh Journal of Public Administration* (online) https://doi.org/10.36609/bjpa.v29i2.226.

[35] *MT Enterprise* (n 7) (17 March 2009) directions no 2–4.

After this order of ban in shipbreaking operation, importers of old ships were barred from bringing old ships into Bangladesh unless shipowners had first undertaken thorough decontamination to remove inbuilt hazardous substances.[36] The Court also considered BELA's principal point of argument: the urgent necessity for a cohesive national framework to govern the shipbreaking sector.

The order effectively halted all shipbreaking activities in Bangladesh for an indefinite period. In response, the Bangladesh Shipbreakers Association (BSBA), expressing dissatisfaction with the ruling, submitted applications for leave to appeal to the Appellate Division (superior court to the High Court of Bangladesh) in January 2011.[37] The BSBA contended that the High Court Division had rendered its decision without providing them an opportunity to be heard. Because BSBA was the industry representative who could not get an opportunity to place their argument, the one sided decision was illegal and not sustainable. Upon review, the Appellate Division granted permission for the appeal in March 2011 and suspended the High Court's prohibition order pending the outcome of the appeal. The matter was ultimately resolved when the Appellate Division heard the appeal and passed its final verdict.[38] The Appellate Division finally lifted any restriction to conduct shipbreaking operations,[39] following the government's enactment of two regulatory instruments: the *Shipbreaking and Recycling Rules of 2011* and the *Hazardous Waste and Shipbreaking Management Rules of 2011.*

The Pakistani Approach—the Shehla Zia Case

A key concern regarding Pakistan's shipbreaking sector is the absence of a dedicated and comprehensive legal framework governing its operations. Although Pakistan adopts a liberal and business-oriented approach akin to India that allows unrestricted importation of end-of-life ships without restriction, it diverges significantly in its regulatory approach. India manages this activity under specific regulatory framework, whereas Pakistan lacks any dedicated statutory provisions, which eventually fails to institutionalise safeguards or oversight mechanisms. This legislative gap undermines Pakistan's obligations under both international treaties and its own constitutional provisions.

As a signatory to the *Basel Convention* and multiple International Labour Organisation (ILO) conventions, Pakistan has pledged to uphold standards related to

---

[36] Ibid, direction no 8.

[37] Bangladesh Supreme Court has two divisions, namely, High Court Division and Appellate Division. Appellate Division has the power to hear appeal against the High Court Division and decision of the Appellate Division is final in Bangladesh Legal System: at art 94(1) of *Bangladesh Constitution.*

[38] *MT Enterprise* (n 8) (17 March 2009) directions 2–4.

[39] *MT Enterprise* (n 8) (17 May 2010) 5 [4].

hazardous waste management and labour protections.[40] These international instruments require Member States to implement domestic measures that reflect their commitments to environmental sustainability and worker welfare. Domestically, Pakistan's Constitution, the supreme law of the country enshrines the protection of fundamental rights, including the right life, health, and a clean environment. Article 141 imposes a duty on the State to preserve the dignity, autonomy, and well-being of its citizens, and any legislative action must align with these constitutional guarantees.[41] Pakistan's judiciary reinforced this principle in deciding the leading case of *Shehla Zia and Others v Water Resources and Power Development Authority*. In this case, the Supreme Court of Pakistan expanded the scope of the right to life to encompass environmental and public health considerations.[42] This precedent affirms that individuals affected by environmental harm have a legitimate claim to legal remedy. Given these legal foundations, Pakistan cannot justify regulatory inaction in hazardous industries on economic grounds. The government is obligated to reform its legislative framework and enforce rigorous compliance standards, particularly in sectors like shipbreaking that pose significant risks to both human health and the environment.[43]

Calls for legislative reform in Pakistan's shipbreaking industry intensified in late 2016, following a devastating explosion at the Gadani shipbreaking site on 1 November.[44] The tragic incident unfolded when over 250 workers were instructed to break the oil tanker, MT ACES (IMO # 8,021,830) while it remained afloat and uncleansed of residual gases. The ship's lower compartments contained a volatile mixture of oil and water, which released hazardous and combustible fumes. Despite these conditions, the shipbreaking facility owner instructed the workers to start cutting the ship using oxy-acetylene torches.[45]

The ignition of one torch triggered a massive explosion upon contact with the flammable gases, resulting in the deaths of at least 29 workers and injuring more than 50 others. Eyewitnesses' accounts suggested that the actual death toll may

---

[40] Pakistan has ratified 36 ILO Conventions, such as *Labour Inspection Convention*, 1947 (No. 81) adopted on 19 June 1947, entered into force 10 October 1953, 13th Session, Governing Body of the International Labour Office: at International Labour Organisation, 'Ratifications for Pakistan' (Web Page) https://www.ilo.org/dyn/normlex/en/f?p=1000:11200:0::NO:11200:P11200_COUNTRY_ID:103166.

[41] The Supreme Court of Pakistan has the power to review the laws and examine whether they are in conformity with the fundamental rights guaranteed in the Constitution: at arts 184 and 190 of *the Constitution of the Islamic Republic of Pakistan,* 1973 (Pakistan).

[42] PLD 1994 SC 963 (12 February 1994). (*Shehla Zia).*

[43] Josh and Mak International, 'Legal Insights into the Shipbreaking Industry in Pakistan' (Webpage) https://joshandmakinternational.com/recent-cases-on-ship-breaking-in-pakistan/.

[44] Akbar (41).

[45] In most cases, the inside of a ship's chamber contains unseen and flammable gases. Therefore, degassing is a process used to remove the remaining gas from the hold in an environmentally sound way. It basically means to remove the gas from a tanker's hold: at Super Flox, *Why are Degassing Regulations Becoming Stricter for Chemical Tankers*? (Web Page) https://superflox.com/2025/06/12/why-are-degassing-regulations-becoming-stricter-for-chemical-tankers/.

have exceeded 80.[46] This explosion incident in a Pakistan shipbreaking facility starkly revealed the systemic regulatory deficiencies within Pakistan's shipbreaking sector. Subsequent investigations by civil society organisations identified multiple contributing factors: the absence of mandatory precleaning protocols for imported vessels, the failure to degas ships prior to breaking, reliance on outdated and unsafe cutting techniques, and minimal intervention or oversight from relevant government bodies.[47] Despite the scale of the disaster and the widespread condemnation that followed, Pakistan has yet to enact a dedicated statute addressing these critical safety and environmental concerns. Nearly five years after the shocking incident, the regulatory landscape in Pakistan remains unchanged, leaving workers vulnerable and the industry largely unaccountable.

Analysis of the Approaches of India, Bangladesh, and Pakistan

Despite employing similar operational methods in shipbreaking, India and Pakistan have failed to implement meaningful reforms in response to the catastrophic explosion at Gadani. Both nations continue to permit the entry of ships filled with oil residues and flammable gases, reflecting a persistent disregard for safety and environmental standards. In contrast, Bangladesh has taken notable steps towards regulatory improvement, largely influenced by landmark rulings from its Supreme Court. However, the decisions in *MT Alfaship* and *MT Enterprise* have raised debate. The Bangladesh Shipbreakers Association contended that the Judicial intervention effective brought the industry to a standstill,[48] arguing that the Court's position prohibited shipbreaking activities until comprehensive regulations were enacted by the government.[49] An alternative interpretation suggests that the Court did not impose an outright ban but rather permitted the continuation of shipbreaking operations under stricter oversight by the Ministry of Environment and Forest. The perspective views the Court's rulings as an attempt to reconcile economic imperatives with the imperative of ensuring safe and environmentally responsible working conditions. Through these decisions, the Supreme Court of Bangladesh sought to strike a regulatory equilibrium between economic needs and workplace safety.[50]

---

[46] Human Rights Commission of Pakistan, 'Horror in Gadani' (Fact-finding Report, November 2016) 30.

[47] BBC, 'Gadani Shipbreaking Yard Blast Kills at least 11 in Pakistan' *BBC* (online at 1 November 2016) https://www.bbc.com/news/world-asia-37834414.

[48] NGO Shipbreaking Platform, 'Bangladesh High Court Issues Contempt Rule against 14 Government Officials: Ministers and Shipbreakers Asked to Account for Non-compliance with 2009 Judgement' (Press Release, 12 April 2016) https://shipbreakingplatform.org/press-release-bangladesh-high-court-issues-contempt-rule-against-14-government-officials-ministries-and-shipbreakers-asked-to-account-for-non-compliance-with-2009-judgement/.

[49] Ibid.

[50] *MT Enterprise* (n 7) (7 March 2011).

Both India and Bangladesh share two common judicial directives concerning the shipbreaking sector: the call for dedicated national legislation and the endorsement of continued industrial activity. However, a key divergence lies in the manner of implementation. The Indian Supreme Court permitted the breaking of the Blue Lady and Exxon Valdez without imposing specific regulatory conditions or requiring environmental clearances. In contrast, Bangladesh's Supreme Court adopted a more stringent stance. It prohibited the entry of the vessel, MT Alfaship and halted the breaking of the MT Enterprise until formal approval was obtained from the Department of Environment (DoE). This precautionary approach, while aimed at safeguarding environmental and occupational standards, inadvertently disrupted the industry's operations. Particularly, the decision in *MT Enterprise* led to a temporary cessation of shipbreaking activities, posing significant challenges to the sector's continuity and economic stability.

Unlike its counterparts in South Asia, Pakistan's Supreme Court has articulated broad principle concerning waste management but has yet to engage directly with the specific regulatory challenges posed by the shipbreaking industry.[51]

In *Shehla Zia*, the Court affirmed Pakistan's obligation to uphold its international commitments and to manage hazardous waste in a manner that protects public health and preserves life. The catastrophic explosion in 2016 underscored the risks inherent in Pakistan's generalised regulatory approach, particularly strategy, such as requiring precleaning of ships prior to their entry into national waters, which might have mitigated the likelihood of such incidents. Moreover, the tragedy serves as a cautionary tale for Bangladesh, highlighting the potential consequences of failing to enforce judicial directives effectively. Considering these developments, the subsequent sections examine the legal intricacies involved in implementing Supreme Court decisions across Pakistan, India, and Bangladesh. This analysis is followed by a comparative evaluation of legislative progress in regulating shipbreaking activities within these jurisdictions.

Analysing the Deficiencies in the Laws and Policies of Bangladesh, India, and Pakistan

Challenges in Seeking Compulsory Precleaning

Following different judicial directives in India and Bangladesh, each country adopted distinct legislative approaches to shipbreaking. In response to its Supreme Court's guidance, India introduced the *Shipbreaking Code* in 2013 (India), which notably did not mandate the precleaning of ships prior to import.[52] The decision effectively placed the burden of precleaning and breaking on domestic facilities. Conversely,

[51] *Shehla Zia* (n 44).

[52] *Shipbreaking Code 2013* (India).

the original version of the *Hazardous Waste and Shipbreaking Management Rules, 2011* (Bangladesh), directed by its Supreme Court, imposed clear restrictions on the importation of ships containing hazardous substances in the body of a ship.

India's regulatory framework, while ambitious in its scope, was criticised in a filed study for its limited effectiveness in practice.[53] A persistent challenge across South Asia's shipbreaking sector lies in the inadequate infrastructure and technical capacity to manage toxic wastes safely. Many shipbreaking facilities lack standardised procedures for handling inbuilt substances such as asbestos and residual flammable gases. Improper disposal and unsafe handling of these substances pose serious environmental risks, including degradation of local air, water, and soil quality.[54] Moreover, the absence of rigorous safety protocols has led to frequent accidents, with an estimated annual fatality rate of over 300 workers due to explosions and other hazardous incidents.[55]

A critical shortcoming of India's *Shipbreaking Code 2013* lies it its omission of mandatory precleaning requirements for ships prior to their arrival in Indian waters.[56] The regulation stipulates that hazardous materials must be removed only after the ship has entered Indian waters and is awaiting authorisation to proceed to a shipbreaking facility.[57] This approach in practice permits the transboundary movement of toxic waste, as contaminated ships are allowed to anchor within India's territorial limits without prior decontamination at their point of origin.

The lack of a precleaning requirement conflicts with India's commitments under the *Basel Convention*, which requires Member States to implement legal measures ensuring that hazardous waste is treated at its source before international transfer.[58] The absence of this requirement in the *Shipbreaking Code 2013* (India) suggests a possible alignment with the *Hong Kong International Convention for the Safe and Environmentally Sound Recycling of Ships Hong Kong Convention (Hong Kong Convention).*[59] While the *Hong Kong Convention* serves as a specialised framework for shipbreaking, it notably does not mandate precleaning at the exporting country, thereby reinforcing a regulatory model that overlooks upstream waste management responsibilities (see Chap. 5).

---

[53] See details for understanding the Indian shipbreaking standards: at Industrial Global Union, Cleaning up Shipbreaking the World's Most Dangerous Job' (Special Report, 15 December 2015) https://www.industriall-union.org/cleaning-up-ship-breaking-the-worlds-most-dangerous-job.

[54] Camelia Dewan and Elizabeth A. Sibilia, 'Global Containments and Local Leakages: Structural Violence and Toxic Flows of Shipbreaking' (2024) 42 (1) *Environmental and Planning C: Politics and Space* 80–101.

[55] Ibid.

[56] Ishtiaque Ahmed, 'The Origin and Evolution of the Shipbreaking Regime in India: A Critical Perspective' (23 May 2022) *Ocean Book Online* https://brill.com/view/journals/ocyo/36/1/article-p551_18.xml.

[57] *Shipbreaking Code 2013* (India), s 4(3).

[58] *Basel Convention*, arts 4(2)(d)-4(2)(e), 4(2)(9)(a).

[59] *The Hong Kong International Convention for the Safe and Environmentally Sound Recycling of Ships*, opened for Signature 1 September 2009, IMO Doc. SR/CONF45 (entered into force 26 June 2025)). *(Hong Kong Convention).*

The limitations in India's *Shipbreaking Code 2013* (India) had negative consequences for the environmental credibility of the nation's shipbreaking sector. Criticism emerged from both international environmental organisations and European shipowners, with groups such as the NGO Shipbreaking Platform and the EU Community Shipowners' Association calling for substantial revisions to the *Shipbreaking Code 2013* (India).[60] In response, India enacted the *Ship Recycling Act 2019* (India), which intended to reinforce and expand upon the provisions of the earlier *Shipbreaking Code 2013* (India).[61] The legislative move coincided with India's formal accession to the *Hong Kong Convention.* Accordingly, the *Ship Recycling Act 2019* (India) was structured to align with the standards set forth by the *Hong Kong Convention.* Despite these developments, the new legislation continues to fall short in one critical area: it does not impose a definitive obligation on shipowners to undertake precleaning prior to exporting ships for breaking. Such regulatory loophole raises concerns about the effectiveness of India's compliance with international environmental norms.

Under the provisions of India's *Ship Recycling Act 2019*, ships that are newly constructed or less than five years old are required to maintain a documented inventor of hazardous materials (IHM).[62] This inventory is subject to inspection by designated National Authority or an authorised entity, which may verify its accuracy and determine whether a ship qualifies for a recycling certificate.[63] The legislation further requires shipowners to ensure that vessels are free from cargo remnants and that any residual fuel oil or onboard waste is reduced to the minimum possible level.[64]

A detailed analysis of the *Ship Recycling Act 2019*, however, reveals that it does not establish a precise requirement for comprehensive precleaning of ships prior to breaking. The *Ship Recycling Act 2019* only requires the shipowner 'to clean the cargo residues and minimise any remaining fuel oil and waste on board kept in loose condition', but does not define the term 'cargo residues and remaining fuel oil and waste on board'.[65] Without a formal definition of these terms, shipowners may interpret their obligations narrowly, focusing only on surface-level contaminants such as leaked oil, while neglecting the waste remaining in a ship's body.[66] The ambiguity undermines the effectiveness of the regulation, as it leaves room for inconsistent compliance. Moreover, the *Ship Recycling Act 2019* fails to specify which authority

---

60 Platform News, 'EU Must Take Action to End Dumping of Toxic Ships and Support Capacity Building' *NGO Shipbreaking Platform* (online at 25 March 2025) https://shipbreakingplatform.org/eu-must-take-action-to-end-toxic-ship-dumping/.

61 *Ship Recycling Act 2019* (India) Preamble para 4.

62 Ibid s 16.

63 Ibid s 28.

64 Ibid s 19.

65 Ibid s 19(iii).

66 Mohammad Zulfikar Ali and Prafula Pearce, 'Comparative Legal Analysis of Shipbreaking Regulations in Bangladesh, India, and Pakistan: Implication on Human Tragedy and Compensation to Victims' in Jushua Aston et al. (eds) *Comparative Law* (Thomson Reuters, 2021) 17–42.

or professional body is responsible for issuing the inventory of hazardous materials, creating further uncertainty in implementation and oversight.[67]

Similarly, as discussed, Pakistan currently lacks a dedicated legal framework governing the shipbreaking sector, resulting in a regulatory void concerning environmental safeguards. What it means is that there is no statutory obligation for exporters to provide a precleaning certificate prior to a vessel's arrival. As a result, ships containing hazardous materials can be permitted to beach without undergoing any prior decontamination, exposing a critical deficiency in Pakistan's maritime import controls.[68]

While several laws such as the *Shipbreaking Industry (Special Procedure) Rules 1997* (Pakistan),[69] the *Balochistan Environmental Protection Act 2012* (Pakistan) and the *Balochistan Development Authority Act 1974* (Pakistan) indirectly applies to the industry, they primarily address administrative concerns related to national security, taxation, and insurance. As an instance, security agencies, including the Pakistan Navy, are authorised to issue clearances based on advance information about a ship's origin, classification, and navigational codes. However, these assessments do not extend to the ship's internal hazardous content. Although authorities may deny entry on security grounds, they lack the jurisdiction to reject ships on the grounds of storing hazardous substances within its body.[70]

In the absence of a formal mechanism to request precleaning documentation from exporting parties, Pakistan continues to accept contaminated ships based solely on voluntary clearance applications.[71] This stands in contrast to Bangladesh, whose legislative reforms demonstrate a more proactive approach on worker safety and environmental responsibility. Nevertheless, Bangladesh faces ongoing challenges in enforcing these legal standards, particularly in balancing between its commercial interests and labour rights.[72]

Bangladesh shipbreaking industry is governed by a set of dedicated legal instruments, including the Ship Recycling Act, 2018 (Bangladesh), *the Shipbreaking and Recycling Rules, 2011* (Bangladesh), and the *Hazardous Waste and Shipbreaking Management Rules, 2011* (Bangladesh). These laws collectively empower the Department of Environment to authorise the beaching and breaking of ships, with particular focus on regulating hazardous wastes.

Initially, the *Hazardous Waste and Shipbreaking Management Rules, 2011* (Bangladesh) introduced a stringent requirement of precleaning, mandating that exporting nations furnish official certification issued either by a government agency

---

[67] Ibid.

[68] Mohammad Zulfikar Ali, 'Injustice to Workers in the Shipbreaking Industry in South Asia: A Quest for a Civil Liability Framework in International Law' (PhD Thesis, Curtin Law School, 2022) 116.

[69] *Shipbreaking Industry (Special Procedure) Rules, 1997* (Pakistan) (vide SRO Sales Tax notification S.R.O 1283(I)/97; amended vide notifications SRO 313(I)/2001, 23 May 2001, SRO 699(I)/2002, 12 October 2002, and SRO 887(I)/2003, 5 September 2003.

[70] Human Rights Commission of Pakistan (n 47) 19–20.

[71] Ibid.

[72] Ali (n 68) 117.

or an accredited expert verifying that the ship had been decontaminated prior to export.[73] This regulatory measure led to a marked decline in the number of ships entering Bangladesh for breaking.

In response to the downturn in imports, the government revised the rule in 2012, removing the mandatory precleaning clause. Under the amended framework, Bangladeshi authorities may issue a precleaning certificate in accordance with the country's National Policy.[74] The revised *Import Policy Order (2012–2015)*, specifically Annex 1, stipulates that for ships classified under HS Heading No. 89.08, importers must submit documentation from the last exporter or shipowner confirming that the ship does not carry toxic or hazardous wastes, except for materials inherently built into the ship. Additionally, importers are required to provide a formal declaration alongside shipping documents.[75]

The National Import Policies of Bangladesh for periods 2012–2015 and 2016–2019 also contain largely identical provisions regarding shipbreaking. Following the regulatory amendments, importers are only required to submit a documented inventory of hazardous substances present on the ship to secure environmental clearance from the Department of Environment.[76] However, this inventory pertains only to surface-level or accessible waste and excludes contaminants embedded within the ship's structural components. As a result, exporters are not obliged to remove internal residues such as residual oil and volatile gases prior to shipment. This regulatory gap has contributed to a risk in workplace incidents and significant environmental degradation in coastal areas where shipbreaking occurs. The growing frequency of accidents and pollution has intensified calls for reform, prompting legal authorities in Bangladesh to consider more robust and transparent guidelines for safer shipbreaking practices.[77] In the absence of a formal labour union representing shipbreaking workers, civil society organisations and environmental NGOs have taken the lead in advocating for improved safety standards and regulatory oversight. An example of which is the intervention of the Supreme Court of Bangladesh by being pressured by NGOs working in shipbreaking sector in *Janata Steel*. *Janata Steel* provided important guidance on the Department of Environment's (DoE) power to conduct a formal assessment of both the inbuilt waste and the IHM of a ship.

In Bangladesh, the Department of Environment (DoE) holds primary authority over environmental regulation, including oversight of shipbreaking activities. However, in *Janata Steel*, a jurisdictional dispute arose between the DoE and the Ministry of Industry regarding the issuance of operational clearances for breaking a

[73] *Hazardous Waste and Shipbreaking Management Rules, 2011* (Bangladesh) r 17.

[74] *Amendment to the Hazardous Waste and Shipbreaking Management Rules, 2011* (Bangladesh) SRO no. 386-ain/2012, subs 15(gha).

[75] *Import Policy Order 2012-2015* (Bangladesh) (No. SRO 411-Ain/2012) (No. SRO 411-Ain/2012); *Import Policy Order 2015-2019* (No. S.R.O. No. 28-Law/2016 of 15 February 2016) ("Import Policy 2015-2019").

[76] *Environment Conservation Act 1995* (Bangladesh), s 12.

[77] Muhammad Muhibullah, 'Health Hazards and Risks of Ship Breaking Workers: A Case Study on Sitakunda Ship Breaking Industrial Area of Bangladesh' (2013) 2 (8) *Global Advanced Research Journal of Geography and Regional Planning* 172-184.

ship. The issue was whether the defendant had violated r 15(d) of the *Hazardous Waste and Shipbreaking Management Rules 2011* and *Import Policy Order 2015–2018* item 39,[78] by not disclosing the presence of toxic substances not declaring the hazardous substances that remained in the ship's structure. Rule 15(d) of the *Hazardous Waste and Shipbreaking Management Rules 2011* stipulates that a shipbreaking clearance cannot be granted by the DoE for any imported ship (either be a cargo ship, oil tanker, or fishing boat) unless the exporting nation's government or its designated authority certifies that the ship is substantially free of hazardous materials. Under Bangladeshi law, environmental clearance is a pre-requisite for breaking ships, and such a clearance must be supported by a comprehensive report from an inspector approved by the DoE, detailing the types and quantities of hazardous substances on board.[79]

Aiming at enforcing this regulatory framework, the Ministry of Environment and Forests is empowered to establish inspection committees tasked with examining old ships anchored offshore. These committees are responsible for identifying and labelling hazardous components, collecting samples, and compiling inventories of toxic waste found on the ships.[80] In contrast, the Ministry of Industry possesses independent authority to grant operational permissions, which may be exercised without even consulting with other regulatory bodies. This autonomous power given to the Ministry of Industry has led to concerns that shipbreaking approvals could be issued independently of the DoE preferring business profit to environmental and health safety. This overriding power given to the Ministry of Industry created the possibility of providing clearances for breaking ships without the DoE's detailed assessment report.[81]

In *Janata Steel*, the Ministry of Industry authorised to break the disputed ship, the MT producer based on an application submitted by Janata Steel Industries' (identified as Defendant no. 17), despite the absence of prior environmental clearance from the DoE. This approval was justified through a resolution adopted during an inter-ministerial meeting convened on 14 January 2017, which was well after the ship had arrived in Bangladeshi waters.[82] The resolution effectively served as a mechanism to circumvent the DoE's regulatory oversight.

After widespread media attention, Bangladesh Environmental Lawyers Association (BELA) filed a petition challenging the legality of the clearance. BELA's contention was that an internationally verified inventory of hazardous materials is needed to authenticate the internal wastes of the ship. In absence of such inventory, the clearance issued by the Ministry of Industry was illegal.[83] Specifically, BELA argued that the clearance lacked the requisite documentation to verify the ship's internal toxic components. On the other hand, Janata Steel Industries argued that their disclosure of

[78] Import Policy Order 2015-2019 (No. S.R.O. No. 28-Law/2016 of 15 February 2016)

[79] *The Hazardous Wastes and Shipbreaking Waste Management Rules, 2011* (Bangladesh) r 19.

[80] Ibid.

[81] *The Shipbreaking and Recycling Rules, 2011* (Bangladesh) r 11.

[82] Janata Steel (n 4) [11]

[83] *Janata Steel* (n 4) [11].

onboard substances satisfied the requirements under r 15(d) of the *Hazardous Waste and Shipbreaking Management Rules 2011* and *Import Policy Order 2015–2018* item 39. They asserted that a formal declaration from the shipowner regarding the ship's hazardous contents was not required under the relevant legal framework.[84]

The High Court Division of the Bangladesh Supreme Court ultimately determined that the Ministry of Industry had acted beyond its legal authority in granting the permission to break the ship. In deciding the issue, the court ruled that.

> It is mandatory to provide true information on the materials found in a ship's structure, systems, and equipment that may be hazardous to health or the environment, and the description and standards of the inventory of hazardous materials should be recognised globally,[85] and any false declaration concerning the true nature of the inventory of hazardous materials is a criminal offence.[86]

Moreover, the Court held that the Ministry of Industry lacked the jurisdiction to authorise shipbreaking activities in the absence of a prior environmental clearance from the DoE, rendering its intervention procedurally and legally invalid.[87]

Limited Power of the National Authorities to Check Inbuilt Wastes of a Ship

Another deficiency in the domestic laws of South Asia is the limited power of the National Authorities to check inbuilt wastes of a ship, which is against the *Hong Kong Convention*'s objective of promoting a responsible shipbreaking industry and strengthening the national institutions in shipbreaking States.

The *Ship Recycling Code 2013* (India) is a consolidated version of all the previous laws. It includes a systematic legal requirement to authorise the process of shipbreaking but does not address the extent of power of the national authorities in checking inbuilt substances of a ship.[88] Owing to the weaknesses in the *Ship Recycling Code 2013* (India), Indian public bodies may be unable to stop breaking a ship or avoid shipbreaking accidents.[89]

The *Ship Recycling Act 2019* (India) also provides limited power to local authorities. With respect to the inspection of the Inventory of Hazardous Materials (i.e., a written document that provides information on the internal materials of a ship), the

---

[84] *Janata Steel* (n 4) [21].

[85] An inventory of hazardous materials has to be submitted in line with the government's import policy order and international conventions ratified by Bangladesh: at *Shipbreaking and Recycling Rules 2011* (Bangladesh) r 2(xv).

[86] *Shipbreaking and Recycling Rules* 2011 (Bangladesh) r 46(2).

[87] *Janata Steel* (n 4).

[88] Ahmed (n 57).

[89] Bisma Mannan, Md Jahir Rizvi, and Yong Ming Dai, 'Ship Recycling in Developing Economies of South Asia: Changing Liability to a Commodity' (2024) 2(2) *Green Technologies and Sustainability* https://doi.org/10.1016/j.grets.2023.100064.

National Authority or Administration has the power to dismiss, exclude, or detain the ship from its ports or within Indian waters in case of failure to carry a valid certificate of the Inventory of Hazardous Materials. Nevertheless, this power is not absolute. The Central Government can take away this detaining power by considering the facts and circumstances of each case.[90] By applying this power, a toxic ship with no valid inventory of hazardous materials may be permitted entry on the grounds of economic benefit, such as in the *Blue Lady* case. Unlike Bangladesh, India is a federal State, and the *Ship Recycling Code 2013* (India) sets up elaborate administrative arrangements. Thus, as far as the implementation of environmental law is concerned, it involves authorities at the federal and State levels. Even in the case of shipbreaking, there are involvements of authorities at both the federal and State levels, with the Central Government having overriding power over other authorities. This overriding power of the Central Government is a major weakness, which is fatal for proper checks and balances of power in regulating the shipbreaking industry in India.

Moreover, *the Ship Recycling Act 2019* (India) provides limited power to the National Authorities to regulate the breaking of unclean ships. The *Act* does not address this problem. It neither specifies a method of detailed assessment of ships before breaking nor bans the import of ships that may include built-in hazardous materials.[91] It is therefore uncertain whether the National Authorities can reject an application for beaching a ship that is likely to contain hazardous materials. It is also uncertain whether the national authorities can reject permission to break a ship for having a false inventory of hazardous materials issued by an unrecognised institution.

Pakistan also follows India's approach. After a ship reaches a shipbreaking yard, the provincial regulatory body, the Balochistan Environmental Protection Agency (the Agency), is legally responsible for inspecting the ship. When applying power, the agency must test whether a ship is hazard-free for safety purposes.[92] However, the agency can issue a no-objection certificate (NOC) following an initial environmental examination (IEE) to ensure that it is fire hazard-free or free from risk or other potential damage to the environment from onboard waste rather than the waste contained in a ship's body. Moreover, before the test, the agency can verify only the no-objection certificate issued by the customs,[93] but has no legal authority to seek a precleaning certificate from the importer.

The Balochistan Environment Protection Agency also has limited power for examination. It can only examine a shipbreaking yard after its owner voluntarily applies for an examination. As discussed above in section "The Pakistani Approach—The Shehla Zia Case", the shipbreaking yard in which the ship exploded at Gadani in 2016 had no environmental certificate obtained because it did not apply for clearance

[90] *Ship Recycling Act 2019* (India) s 29.

[91] Ali and Pearce (n 31).

[92] The Balochistan Environmental Protection Agency was established in 1992 and worked under the Department of Environment, Wildlife, Livestock and Tourism and the Secretary for Environment and Sports. However, now it is an independent department under the new *Balochistan Environmental Protection Act 2012* (Pakistan): at Balochistan Environmental Protection Agency, *About Us* (Web Page) https://bepa.gob.pk/

[93] Human Rights Commission of Pakistan (n 47) 18.

in the first place and the agency had no official information about the ship.[94] The incident also demonstrates that if ship sellers do not identify and preclean a ship, the ship can become explosive, and a small amount of flame may result in a number of deaths and permanent injuries.[95]

In relation to the local authority's power in assessing the built-in substances of a ship,[96] Bangladesh's approach is superior to those of Pakistan and India. The Bangladesh Supreme Court in *Janata Steel* convincingly decided that before a shipbreaking yard can submit an application for beaching, the DoE must have the power of a formal and detailed assessment of the inbuilt and onboard hazardous materials or wastes of an end-of-life ship.[97] The Court also ordered that the Ministry of Industry or other National Authorities could not encroach on the DoE's power under any circumstances whatsoever and provide permission for beaching and cutting.[98] Thus, the Court has interpreted that the DoE is empowered to examine the hazardous materials contained in a ship's body, despite r 3(3) of the *Ship Breaking and Recycling Rules*, 2011 (Bangladesh), providing that the DoE is not empowered to do so before issuing environmental clearance certificates. The Court established a new and strict principle in light of *MT Enterprise* and *MT Alfaship*, which was the foundation of the *Ship Breaking and Recycling Rules*, 2011 (Bangladesh).

The Court further ruled that after examining the hazardous waste of a scrap vessel, including waste in structures and on board, the DoE can agree or decline to issue an environmental clearance certificate prior to beaching. The Ministry of Industry cannot override this power. In relation to the decision of the interministerial meeting, the Court found that such a decision is illegal in the presence of enforceable rules.[99]

The consequence of the order is that the importer and owner of the ship for breaking, Janata Steel Industries, eventually has no permission to start breaking the ship. This is an enormous setback to the business profit of the shipbreaking yard owner for not properly understanding and following the existing legal principles.[100] In the legal sense, however, it appears from the decision that Bangladesh has recognised that the National Authorities must have the power to check inbuilt wastes of a ship, which is important for establishing a fair balance among economic, human, and environmental interests. This decision is pivotal in ensuring that Bangladesh may be able to maintain a green shipbreaking image. Enforcement of the decision, however, depends on the will of the executive organs, including the Bangladesh Ship Recycling Board (Board), a government body proposed under the Ship Recycling Act 2018 in

[94] Ibid 6.

[95] Gizem Elidou et al., 'Quantitative Failure Analysis for Static Electricity-related Explosion and Fire Accidents on Tanker Vessels under Fuzzy Bow-tie CREAM Approach' (2022) 131 *Engineering Failure Analysis* 105917: 1–10 https://doi.org/10.1016/j.engfailanal.2021.105917.

[96] The *Hazardous Wastes and Shipbreaking Waste Management Rules 2011* (Bangladesh) rr 3(3), 15, 18, 19(4),19(5).

[97] *Janata Steel* (n 4) [73].

[98] *Janata Steel* (n 4) [76].

[99] Ibid [79].

[100] Ingvild Jenssen et al., 'Biennial Report – 2018–2019' (Research Report, NGO Shipbreaking Platform, 2020) 11.

Bangladesh. An important purpose of the Bangladesh Ship Recycling Board is to deliver one-stop service for all matters with respect to shipbreaking.[101]

Bangladesh has yet to form the Ship Recycling Board, but subject to its formation, the proposed Board will be able to exercise absolute power for every issue related to shipbreaking, such as beaching and shipbreaking permissions. The main problem with the ship recycling board is its constitution. The majority of Board members are bureaucrats and shipbreaking yard owners who can dominate in making any decision (the implications of which are discussed below). In other words, as seen in *Janata Steel*, it is obvious that, holding the majority, bureaucrats and shipbreaking yard owners may have the tendency to prefer business interests to those of people and the environment. It is therefore a matter of doubt whether the Board would enforce the decision of *Janata Steel*.[102]

Under the Ship Recycling Act 2018 (Bangladesh), the Bangladesh Ship Recycling Board consists of 15 members,[103] but one-third of the members complete the quorum to hold a valid meeting,[104] and a simple majority in a Board meeting can make any decision.[105] Any decision of the Board is final, and no one can raise a question against a decision made by the Board.[106] One third is equivalent to five members, and interestingly, among 15 members of the Board, three represent the owners of shipbreaking yards, and by adding two bureaucrats from the Ministry of Industry, a quorum completes. Therefore, if a ratio of three from industry representatives and two from the bureaucracy sit in a meeting and decide to disregard the legal requirements of taking compulsory clearance for shipbreaking from the DoE established in *Janata Steel*, it is unclear whether the DoE can enforce the decision of *Janata Steel*.

Conventional Shipbreaking Practice

Problems with the Use of the Beaching Method

The beaching method is one of the main concerns for Indian shipbreaking, but there is no provision in the *Ship Recycling Code 2013* (India) to prohibit this method. Rather, the *Ship Recycling Code 2013* (India) implies that beaching is subject to certifications from several government bodies. In the pre-beaching process, the customs authority

---

[101] Ship Recycling Act 2018 (Bangladesh), s 7. See s 11 that provides details on function and powers of the Bangladesh Ship Recycling Board.

[102] Bangladesh Ship Recycling Board consists of eight members from the different government departments, one member from the Police department, one member from the Bangladesh Navy, and three members from the shipbreaking industry owners: at the Ship Recycling Act 2018 (Bangladesh), s 10.

[103] Ship Recycling Act 2018 (Bangladesh), s 13.

[104] Ship Recycling Act 2018 (Bangladesh), s 12(6).

[105] Each member has one vote, and a simple majority can decide any matter: at *Ship Recycling Act*, s 12(5).

[106] Ship Recycling Act 2018 (Bangladesh), s 12(7).

has the power to inspect a ship upon arrival at an Indian port. There are three flaws with inspection for beaching. First, the customs authority is only empowered to check loose materials stored in a ship[107] and thus mainly inspects hazardous waste in 'loose' conditions on board the ship.[108] Along with the customs department's inspection, the shipbreaking yard has a voluntary duty to obtain a copy of the gas-free and fit-for-work certificate from the competent authority,[109] but the customs department cannot reject a gas-free and fit-for-work certificate (i.e., the certificate ensures that the inside of a ship is free from flammable gas), even if it finds that the ship has a high volume of inbuilt hazardous substances, such as oil and unseen gases.

Second, the State Maritime Board or Port authority can issue beaching permission to a shipbreaking yard only on the production of the document issued by other authorities, including the Petroleum and Explosives Safety Organisation, the State Pollution Control Board, or the Customs authority. The State Maritime Board or port authority has no duty to check anything other than these documents.[110] Third, without being gas-free and fit-for-work certificates, a ship can beach on an Indian shipbreaking yard, which is subject to clearing the toxic materials contained in a ship's structure at an Indian port. However, it is important to note that India has recently initiated the move to construct dry docks. India's National Green Tribunal, a special environmental court, has also given a green signal to the project.[111] However, a recent report revealed that the situation has not yet improved.[112]

Pakistani laws also do not stop dangerous beaching practices, which involve cutting ships on open beaches and releasing toxic substances into seawater. All shipbreaking yards are located at Gadani beach in the State of Balochistan. Owing to its location, under *the Balochistan Shipbreaking Industry Rules 1979* (Pakistan), the Balochistan Development Authority (BDA) controls shipbreaking yards.[113] Under the *Balochistan Shipbreaking Rules of 1979* (Pakistan), a person or industry can lease a plot of the beach for breaking ships from the BDA by paying an annual rent.[114] Upon leasing, the BDA allows all shipbreaking yards in Pakistan to officially follow common beaching practices, which creates difficulties in the application of sound waste management and safe operations. In the 2016 incident at Gadani beach, which

---

[107] *Ship Recycling Code 2013* (India), s 3(6).

[108] Ibid ss 3(6)(7)(xvii).

[109] *Factories Act 1948* (India), s 2(c)(a).

[110] For example, in case of petroleum oil cargo and petroleum slop tanks; 'on production of gas-free for hot work certificate issued by the Petroleum and Explosives Safety Organisation (PESO)': at *the Ship Recycling Code 2013* (India), s 4(2)(a).

[111] Premal Balan, 'NGT Nod for Beaching Method of Ships at Alang', *Times of India* (online at 28 November 2020).

[112] Foote (n 54).

[113] The issue of environmental protection and labour rights now rests with the provincial government, Balochistan. The authority of the federal government is limited: International Labour Organisation, 'Pakistan Moves to Strengthen Hazardous Waste Management in Ship Recycling Sector' (Press Release, 17 June 2025) https://www.ilo.org/resource/news/pakistan-moves-strengthen-hazardous-waste-management-ship-recycling-sector.

[114] Human Rights Commission of Pakistan (n 47) 6.

killed dozens of workers, the executive director of the Sustainable Development Policy Institute (SDPI), a social and policy research body that works on behalf of the NGO shipbreaking platform, raised concerns about conventional beaching practices:

> If health and safety would come first, the terrible blast could have been avoided. There is a lack of infrastructure and equipment in Gadani to prevent such a deadly incident. Rescue operations are extremely difficult due to the lack of ambulances and firefighting equipment and because rapid access to ships and workers who are still stuck inside is extremely challenging.[115]

In principle, Bangladesh also allows beaching, although it is one of the major hindrances to ensuring sound waste management.[116] The *Ship Recycling Act of 2018* (Bangladesh) provides a 'zoning' system for shipbreaking on beaches. The *Ship Recycling Act of 2018* (Bangladesh) provides that the government can declare an area to a zone or can extend an existing zone for shipbreaking.[117] Any person or institution can establish a yard in the zone by gaining permission from the government.[118] Any yard established before the Ship Recycling Act 2018 (Bangladesh) has to gain permission from the government.[119] These provisions, in relation to the zoning system, encourage more beaching by allocating more space to coastal beaches. However, a good provision against beaching is 6(7) of the Ship Recycling Act 2018 (Bangladesh), which provides a voluntary requirement that the government and yard owners can take necessary action to apply alternative methods to beaching. However, as the requirement to shift from beaching to an alternative safer method, i.e., the dry dock method of breaking ships using a built structure, is not mandatory, this optional provision may not have any practical impact on the profitable practice of beaching.

Problems in the Use of Other Conventional Shipbreaking Methods

Cutting ships with bare hands or using an oxy torch has also been a major concern for the South Asian shipbreaking industry, but none of the South Asian countries has stopped this practice. As discussed in section "The Pakistani Approach—The Shehla Zia Case", the accident that occurred at Gadani in 2016 demonstrated the problem with this conventional shipbreaking practice in Pakistan, but Pakistani laws still have not addressed the problem. One way to address this problem would be to declare shipbreaking a formal industry to ensure a better enforcement and compliance

---

115 Ibid, 24.

116 Ingvild Jenssen, Martine Mork, and Nicola Mulinaris, 'Recycling Outlook: Decommissioning of North Sea Floating Oil and Gas Units' (NGO Shipbreaking Platform, Research Report, 2019) 6.

117 Ship Recycling Act 2018 *(Bangladesh)*, s 4.

118 Ibid ss 5(1)-5(3).

119 Ibid.

monitoring system. As Pakistan is yet to do so,[120] the industry is out of the scope of the general health and safety laws applicable to formal industries.

Some of the legislation that would be applicable to the shipbreaking sector upon such a declaration includes the *Workmen Compensation Act 1923, the Labourers Act, 1934*, and *the Factories Act 1934*. Pakistan significantly developed its *Workmen Compensation Rules in 1961*, the *West Pakistan Hazardous Occupation Rules in 1963*, the *Provincial Employees Social Security (Occupational Diseases) Regulations in 1967*, and the *Labour Laws Ordinance (amendment)* in *1972*. These domestic laws cover safety issues in hazardous work with a detailed procedure for handling explosive or inflammable dust, gas, and other materials. A fundamental legal restriction related to shipbreaking is the mandatory duty of every factory to provide effective management for the disposal of wastes and effluents in the manufacturing process.[121] However, as an informal sector, a shipbreaking yard in Pakistan has limited motivation to follow these legal standards.

Similarly, the *Ship Recycling Code 2013* (India) does not prohibit dangerous conventional shipbreaking practices. As mentioned before, cutting a ship using an oxy torch is one of the most dangerous methods, but the Indian Port Authority has the power to permit such a method.[122] The port authority may authorise cutting a ship upon submission of a gas-free certificate so that the ship is free of unseen gases, installation of firefighting pumps and compliance with the provisions for the management of occupational health and safety.[123] The *Ship Recycling Code 2013* (India), in s 6, contains specific provisions and procedures to conduct the cutting operation, such as the use of appropriate personal protection equipment (PPE) for 'ships of special concern', but the *Ship Recycling Code 2013* (India) does not interpret what it means by the term 'ships of special concern'.[124]

Bangladesh also has no legal restrictions on the use of the same conventional shipbreaking practice. Bangladeshi laws allow this practice to be subject to some technical documents. For example, upon submission of a ship recycling plan (SRP), yard environment clearance certificate, certificate from the Bangladesh Navy, workers' registration and proof of cleaning oil from all bunker tanks, and gas-free test certificate issued by the Department of Arms and Explosives, a shipbreaking yard owner can obtain cutting permission from the Ministry of Industry.[125]

Because of the deficiencies in the laws discussed in this section, workers are at high risk of shipbreaking accidents and exposure to hazardous substances. It is unlikely that domestic laws would succeed in preventing shipbreaking accidents in the future.

---

[120] Saleem Shahid, 'Federal Government Urged to Grant Formal Status to Shipbreaking Industry' *Dawn* (online at 15 April 2025) https://www.dawn.com/news/1904327#:~:text=updates%20from%20Dawn-,Federal%20govt%20urged%20to%20grant%20formal%20status%20to%20ship%2Dbreaking,introduce%20ship%2Dbreaking%20legislation%20soon.

[121] The *Factories Act* (Pakistan) 1934, ss 9–11.

[122] *Shipbreaking Code* (India), s 6(2) (3).

[123] Ibid 6(2)(1)-6(2)(2).

[124] Jenssen, Mork, and Mulinaris (n 112).

[125] *The Shipbreaking and Recycling Rules 2011* (Bangladesh), r 11.

This leads to a logical conclusion that these countries require a special compensation mechanism for workers to ensure prompt and adequate financial compensation should they fall victim to a shipbreaking incident and pollution. The next section examines this proposition.

Issues in Relation to the Compensation Claim

Tortious remedies against private parties are not available in Bangladesh, India, or Pakistan.[126] If a tort claim could be lodged against the supplier or seller of ships that are broken in South Asia, the injured or ill or families of deceased workers could receive adequate compensation by judicial enforcement. Indeed, because of this absence, Hamida Begum sued a British ship in English courts for adequate compensation for the death of her husband while working in a Bangladeshi shipbreaking yard (see Chap. 5 for a detailed discussion). This is a significant legal gap in imposing liability on foreign shipowners for the human harm caused by shipbreaking yards.

Moreover, the challenge of establishing a compensation mechanism in South Asia lies in the fact that labour laws in these countries do not consider the casual nature of work, as is the case in their shipbreaking industry. This gap limits workers' enjoyment of compensation rights under labour laws, as the laws are silent on the legal status of shipbreaking workers who do not have an employment contract or an identity card.

India's Compensation Laws

India has a comprehensive set of laws that only apply to permanent and registered workers employed in a factory.[127] Some of the important rights provided under the special *Shipbreaking Code 2013* (India) include insurance, but for enforcing the rights, the *Shipbreaking Code 2013* (India) has high reliance on the application of the *Factories Act 1948* (India) which is itself problematic to apply in case of shipbreaking.

For proper application of the *Factories Act 1948* (India), a shipbreaking yard must fall within the definition of a 'Factory'. 'If the manufacturing process is carried out with the aid of power', 'Factory' is a premise 'where ten or more workers work', and

[126] Manjeri Subin Sundar Raj, Ujal Kumar Mookherjee, and Aman Deep Borthakur, 'Tort Law in India' (2021) in eds Mauro Bussain and Anthony J. Sebak *Comparative Tort Law* 427–442; Taqbir Huda, 'Bangladesh: A Constitutional Solution for a Tort Law Deficit' (2022) in eds Ekaterina Aristova and Uglijesa Grusic *Civil Remedies and Human Rights in Flux: Key Legal Developments in Selected Jurisdictions* (Hart Publishing 2022); Farukh Usman, 'Torts Can be the Perfect Solution for Redressing the Negligence Committed by Public Authorities in Pakistan' (2022) 5 (4) *Pakistan Journal of International Affairs* 682–694.

[127] A permanent worker means a worker who has been appointed following a permanent recruitment process. He has an identifiable employer, a job contract, and registration or passbooks with details.

if the 'manufacturing process is carried out without the aid of power', 'Factory' is a premise where twenty or more workers work.[128] Under this definition, workers mean permanent and registered workers. Casual or seasonal workers are beyond the ambit of the definition and because of this limitation, it is problematic for the shipbreaking workers to enforce the *Factories Act 1948* (India).

The *Shipbreaking Code 2013* (India) also provides that the workers engaged in shipbreaking are required to have registration under either the *Employees State Insurance Corporation Act* or *Workmen Compensation Act*.[129] In order to protect injured workers from losing income, the *Shipbreaking Code 2013* (India) mandates the shipbreaking yard owner to re-employ them in safer areas of the shipbreaking process,[130] but for the principles to apply, a shipbreaking worker has to prove his legal status as a worker. As in Bangladesh and Pakistan, shipbreaking yards in India often employ hundreds of workers through contractors. Shipbreaking workers in Alang, India are mainly migrant workers. The contractors hire the workers on a casual basis, subject to ships being available for breaking,[131] and can suspend a worker at any time. The workers shift from one yard owned by one company to another yard owned by a different company. Thus, the absence of a job contract and permanent recruitment process by an identifiable employer makes it very complicated to enforce workers' rights.[132] India could address the problem by introducing a mandatory requirement of registration, or by issuing passbooks with details of employment, wage rates etc., as provided in the *Inter-State Migrant Workmen Act (Regulation of Employment and Conditions of Service) Act 1979* (India).[133] Again, as the *Shipbreaking Code 2013* (India) does not explicitly mention the *Inter-State Migrant Workmen Act (Regulation of Employment and Conditions of Service) Act 1979* (India), shipbreaking workers cannot enforce these laws.[134]

Bangladesh's Compensation Laws

Bangladesh also has different laws on compensation for workers, but they are insufficient to provide an adequate amount of compensation to victims due to a lack of mandatory direction for shipbreaking yard owners.

---

[128] Ibid s 2(m).

[129] The *Ship Recycling Code 2013* (India) sub-s 6(2) (1) (i).

[130] Ibid, sub-ss 6(12) (2).

[131] Peter Rousmaniere, 'Shipbreaking in the Developing World: Problems and Prospects' (2007) 13 (4) *International Journal of Occupational and Environmental Health* 359–368.

[132] Mayzar Ahmad, 'Ship Recycling in India-Environmental Stock Taking' (2022) 6 (3) *Indian Law Review* 465–478.

[133] *Inter-State Migrant Workmen Act (Regulation of Employment and Conditions of Service) Act 1979* (India).

[134] Poddar and Sood (n 129) 258.

The umbrella legislation includes the *Labour Act* of *2006* (Bangladesh) and the *Labour Rules of 2015* (Bangladesh). The *Labour Act 2006* (Bangladesh) has provisions of compensation for injured workers[135] and obligations for the yard owners to reemploy them.[136] Importantly, the insurance of workers is mandatory under the *Labour Rules* of *2015*.[137] Every yard owner must maintain insurance for each worker. The *Labour Act 2006* (Bangladesh) and *Labour Rules 2015* (Bangladesh) are the only applicable laws concerning compensation. However, the compensation amount is too low under the *Labour Act of 2006* (Bangladesh), with, for example, the highest value for death in an accident at only USD 2357.93. In addition to the *Labour Act* of *2006* (Bangladesh), 20(1) of the *Ship Recycling Act* of *2018* (Bangladesh) provides that yard owners may pay extra compensation to injured workers or their families over and above the amount provided in the *Labour Act of 2006* (Bangladesh). As the section uses the term 'may' instead of 'shall', however, it implies that the requirement for extra compensation is not mandatory. Without a binding obligation, this provision is weak. Therefore, the extra payment option provided under the *Labour Act* of *2006* (Bangladesh) should be made mandatory to be effective, as shipbreaking yard owners rarely pay the amount willingly.[138]

The Ship Recycling Act 2018 (Bangladesh) also does not provide for the consequence of paying no compensation or for a way to enforce payment of compensation. The rate of complaints filed by victims for compensation is only 0.2%, and in the case of shipbreaking, the rate is zero.[139] This is because employers are not accountable since they have no mandatory obligation to provide adequate compensation.

Pakistan's Compensation Laws

Pakistan has a set of comprehensive rules related to compensation payments, but these rules are applicable only to formal industries. Pakistan has yet to include shipbreaking in its list of formal industries.[140] According to the *Employers Liability Act, in 1938*, a worker can sue an employer for damage with respect to an injury at a workplace.[141] More specifically, the *Workmen Compensation Act 1923* provides injury and death

[135] *The Labour Act 2006* (Bangladesh), s 151.

[136] Ibid, s 21.

[137] *The Labour Rules 2015* (Bangladesh), r 98.

[138] Saiful Karim, *Shipbreaking in Developing Countries: A Requiem for Environmental Justice from the Perspectives of Bangladesh* (Taylor and Francis Group, 2018) 105.

[139] A.K.M Mahatab Uddin, Md, Zillur Rahman, 'Nature and Pattern of Recent Submitted Disputes at Labour Courts in Bangladesh', (Research Report, Institute of Social Welfare and Research, University of Dhaka, March 2019) 29.

[140] Sayed Asghar Shah, Hussain Hadi and Mujahed Hussain, 'Skill Gap Analysis in the Ship Breaking Industry of Pakistan' (2017) 7 (11) *American Journal of Industrial and Business Management* 1244, 1253.

[141] *The Employers Liability Act 1938* (Pakistan), s 3.

grants for different classes of accidents.[142] There is also a provision for an insurance scheme for workers. Under the *Industrial and Commercial Employment (Standing Orders) Ordinance, 1968*, a permanent worker must be insured at least for the amount specified, which varies between USD 1244 and 2488.[143] Unless the country declares shipbreaking as a formal industry and provides workers with permanent statues, a shipbreaking yard in Pakistan has a limited incentive to follow these legal standards.

The 2016 shipbreaking accident at Gadani Port in Pakistan highlighted the struggle of injured workers to receive adequate and prompt compensation.[144] As there was no legal compulsion to pay, the workers received compensation only after a series of protests and seminars organised by the workers' community, although the amount they received was unsatisfactory. Three months after the incident, each family of a deceased worker received approximately USD 18,000 one-off payment from the government, the Workers' Welfare Board and the employer of the shipbreaking yard. The injured workers only received USD 1500 as compensation, which could not satisfy the workers.[145] The dissatisfaction was demonstrated by an industry leader from Pakistan with the following statement:

> We are disappointed that the compensation is less than what we demand. We are concerned that even after such a horrific accident, workers at the Gadani shipbreaking yard are still working in dangerous conditions, and safe protective equipment is not provided to workers.[146]

Conclusion

Using the example of the Gadani incident, the analysis in this chapter has shown that shipbreaking workers are not safe because the countries have not stopped hazardous methods of beaching or other conventional shipbreaking methods. The three countries discussed also have different approaches related to the responsibility of identifying and precleaning onboard and built-in wastes guided by their Supreme Courts' decisions. This is a major problem. As these three countries are not taking a coordinated approach, one country cannot enact better laws to protect workers and the environment, since if they do, they face the reality of losing business. Bangladesh's approach is superior to that of India and Pakistan since Bangladesh's DoE has enough power to check inbuilt wastes found on a ship before accepting or rejecting it. However, the enforcement of this approach is dependent upon the questionable structure of the

---

[142] *The Workmen's Compensation Act 1923* (Pakistan) s 4 read with sch I.

[143] International Labour Standards Units, 'Occupational Safety and Health: Legal Framework and Statistical Trend Analysis (2010–2015)' (Research Report, Ministry of Overseas Pakistanis and Human Resources Development, April 2016) 33–34.

[144] IndustriALL Global Union, Pakistan: Shipbreaking Accident Victims Receive Compensation (Web Page, 23 February 2017) http://www.industriall-union.org/pakistan-shipbreaking-accident-victims-receive-compensation.

[145] Ibid.

[146] Ibid.

Bangladesh Ship Recycling Board's membership, by which it can make any decision to favour business interests over those of the population.

The worker- and environmentally friendly approach in Bangladesh provides enough power to its Department of Environment to conduct a formal assessment before a shipbreaking clearance sourced from the Bangladesh Supreme Court's decision in *Janata Steel* is issued. Thus, the problem for Bangladesh is to portray this better legal environment, at the same time offering a high purchase price to shipowners and allowing them to externalise their costs for precleaning. The result is that if India and Pakistan are able to secure a better market share than Bangladesh by allowing ships without precleaning beyond their territorial waters, Bangladesh will lose the market. Bangladesh is not willing to take risks. This is arguably why the country did not stop beaching and conventional shipbreaking practices, similar to Pakistan and India, and introduced the Bangladesh Ship Recycling Board to bypass the worker- and environmentally friendly approach to precleaning. What it means is that injuries and deaths of workers are not going to be stopped soon.

Compensatory framework available for shipbreaking workers is also weak. The countries have introduced domestic laws that are aimed at prevention rather than compensation. General laws regulate the compensation for which workers must prove their legal status as workers. The casual nature of their employment, however, makes it very difficult for shipbreaking workers to claim compensation. The national standard of compensation amount is also very low in these countries.

Therefore, as the injuries and deaths in the shipbreaking industry are not going to end soon and workers' claim of compensation relies on their weak domestic laws, it is important to explore whether under the existing international laws workers have adequate protection and means of claiming adequate compensation. The next chapter examines whether international laws have provided a good safety net and compensatory mechanism to shipbreaking workers, who sacrifice their valuable lives in pursuit of profit for these international parties.

Bibliography

Articles/Books/Reports

Abeyratne, Rehan, 'Ordinary Wrongs as Constitutional Rights: The Public Law Model of Torts in South Asia' (2018) 54 (1) *Texas International Law Journal* 1

Ahmed, Rukhsar and Kamran Siddiqui, 'Shipbreaking Industry in Pakistan – Problems and Prospects' (September 2013) 3 (9) *International Journal of Management, IT and Engineering* 140

Dash, Shreemanshu Kumar, Writ of Continuing Mandamus in Matters of PILs: A Step towards Development of Environmental Jurisprudence (August 2017) 22 (8) *Journal of Humanities and Social Science* 26

Hoque, Ridwanul, *Judicial Activism in Bangladesh: A Golden Mean Approach* (Cambridge Scholars Publishing, 2011) 3

Hoque, Ridwanul, 'Taking Justice Seriously: Judicial Public Interest and Constitutional Activism in Bangladesh' 2006 15(4) *Contemporary South Asia* 399

Karim, Saiful, 'Environmental Pollution from Shipbreaking Industry: International Law and National Legal Response' (2010) 12(2) *Georgetown International Law Review* 185

Mohammad Shahanwaz, 'The Effective Enforcement of National Ship recycling Regulations in India' (Master's Thesis, World Maritime University Dissertation, 2017) 65

Pelsy, Florent, 'The Blue Lady Case and the International Issue of Ship Dismantling' (2008) 4(2) *Law, Environment and Development Journal* 135

Poddar, Paridhi and Sarthak Sood, 'Revisiting the Shipbreaking Industry in India: Axing Out Environmental Damage, Labour Rights' Violation and Economic Myopia' (2015) 8 *National University of Juridical Science Law Review* 245

Razzaque, Jona, 'Access to Environmental Justice: Role of the Judiciary in Bangladesh' (2000) *Bangladesh Journal of Law* 1

Shah, Sayed Asghar, Hussain Hadi and Mujahed Hussain, 'Skill Gap Analysis in the Ship Breaking Industry of Pakistan' (2017) 7 (11) *American Journal of Industrial and Business Management* 1244

Galley, Michael, *Shipbreaking: Hazards and Liabilities* (Springer International Publishing, 2014)

Karim, Saiful, *Shipbreaking in Developing Countries: A Requiem for Environmental Justice from the Perspectives of Bangladesh* (Taylor and Francis Group, 2018)

Ljubomir, Jeftic, Seba Sheably and Ellik Adler, *Marine Litter: A Global Challenge*, ed Nikki Meith (United Nations Environment Program, April 2009)

Sieckmann, Jam, 'Proportionality as Universal Human Rights Principle' in Duarte D. and Silva Sampson (eds), *Proportionality in Law* (Springer International Publishing, 2018) 3

Anderson, Aage Bjorn, 'Worker Safety in the Shipbreaking Industries' (Issues Paper No WP 167, International Labour Office, February 2001) 13–14, 39–40. http://www.ilo.org/safework/info/publications/WCMS_110357/lang--en/index.htm

Greenpeace International, 'Playing Hide and Seek: How the Shipping Industry, Protected by Flags of Convenience, Dumps Toxic Waste on Shipbreaking Beaches' (Research Report, December 2003)

Human Rights Commission of Pakistan, 'Horror in Gadani' (Fact-finding Report, November 2016)

Ibeanu, Okechukwu, Special Rapporteur, *Report on the Adverse effects of the Movement and Dumping of Toxic and Dangerous Products and Wastes on the Enjoyment of Human Rights*, UN Doc A/HRC/15/22/Add.3 (2 September 2010)

Ingvild Jenssen et al, 'Biennial Report – 2018–2019' (Research Report, NGO Shipbreaking Platform, 2020) 11

International Labour Standards Units, 'Occupational Safety and Health: Legal Framework and Statistical Trend Analysis (2010–2015)' (Research Report, Ministry of Overseas Pakistanis and Human Resources Development, April 2016)

International Metal Workers' Federation, 'Status of shipbreaking workers in India' (Research Report, 6 March 2006)

Iqbal, Kanwar Muhammad Javed, Patrizia Heidegger, 'Pakistan Shipbreaking Outlook: The Way Forward for a Green Ship Recycling Industry – Environmental, Health, and Safety Conditions Pakistan Outlook' (Fact Finding Report 1st ed, Sustainable Development Policy Institute and NGO Shipbreaking Platform, October 2013)

NGO Shipbreaking Platform, 'Comments on the Indian Committee Inspection Report on the Hazardous Materials On-board the SS Blue Lady' (Research Report, 31 July 2006)

NGO shipbreaking Platform, 'Substandard Shipbreaking: A Global Challenge' (Research Report, 2016)

Srinivas, Stara, 'Breaking Down the Ship Recycling Industry' *The Ship Recycling Industry in India* (Research Report, Part I- Issue Brief, Social and Political Research Foundation, 20 June 2020)

Uddin, A.K.M Mahatab, Md, Zillur Rahman, 'Nature and Pattern of Recent Submitted Disputes at Labour Courts in Bangladesh', (Research Report, Institute of Social Welfare and Research, University of Dhaka, March 2019)

Cases

Bangladesh Environmental Lawyers Association (BELA) v Janata Steel Corporation, [Writ Petition No 8466 of 2019] High Court Division (26 February 2020)

Research Foundation for Science Technology and Natural Resource Policy v Union of India and Others, [Civil Original Jurisdiction Writ Petition No 657 of 1995] Supreme Court of India (11 September 2007) (*Blue Lady*)

Research Foundation for Science Technology and Natural Resource Policy v Union of India and Others, Supreme Court of India, [Civil Original Jurisdiction Writ Petition No 657 of 1995 interim application No 61 and 62] (12 October 2012) (*Exxon Valdez*)

Research Foundation for Science Technology and Natural Resource Policy v Union of India and Others, Supreme Court of India, [Civil Original Jurisdiction Writ Petition no. 657 of 1995] 4 SCC 647 *(Research Foundation)*

Research Foundation for Science Technology and Natural Resource Policy V Union of India and Others, [Civil Original Jurisdiction Writ Petition no. 657 of 1995] Supreme Court of India (12 April 2003) *(Research Foundation—2003)*

Bangladesh Environmental Lawyers Association (BELA) v Bangladesh and others, [Writ Petition No 3916 of 2006] High Court Division (6 July 2006)

Bangladesh Environmental Lawyers Association (BELA) v Bangladesh, Represented by the Secretary, Ministry of Shipping and Others [Writ Petition No. 7260 of 2008] High Court Division (5 March 2009, 17 March 2009, 31 May 2010 and 7 March 2011)

Ms. Shehla Zia v WAPDA PLD 1994 SC 693 (12 February 1994) (*Shehla Zia)*

Legislation

Amendment to the Hazardous Waste and Shipbreaking Management Rules, 2011 (Bangladesh) SRO no. 386-ain/2012

Balochistan Environmental Protection Act 2012 (Pakistan)

Constitution of the Islamic Republic of Pakistan, 1973 (Pakistan)

Constitution of the Peoples' Republic of Bangladesh Constitution (Bangladesh) 1972

Environmental Conservation Act 1995 (ECA)

Factories Act 1948 (India)

Import Policy Order 2012–2015 (Bangladesh) (No. SRO 411-Ain/2012) (No. SRO 411-Ain/2012)

Import Policy Order 2015–2019 (No. S.R.O. No. 28-Law/2016 of 15 February 2016)

Inter-State Migrant Workmen Act (Regulation of Employment and Conditions of Service) Act 1979 (India)

Ship Recycling Act 2018 (Bangladesh)

Ship Recycling Act 2019 (India)

Shipbreaking Code 2013 (India)

Shipbreaking Industry (Special Procedure) Rules, 1997 (Pakistan) (vide SRO Sales Tax notification S.R.O 1283(I)/97; amended vide notifications SRO 313(I)/2001, 23 May 2001, SRO 699(I)/2002, 12 October 2002, and SRO 887(I)/2003, 5 September 2003

The Employers Liability Act 1938 (Pakistan)

The *Factories Act 1934* (Pakistan)

The *Hazardous Wastes and Shipbreaking Waste Management Rules 2011* (Bangladesh)

The Hazardous Wastes and Shipbreaking Waste Management Rules, 2011 (Bangladesh)

The Labour Act 2006 (Bangladesh)

The Labour Rules 2015 (Bangladesh)

The Shipbreaking and Recycling Rules, 2011 (Bangladesh)

The Workmen's Compensation Act 1923 (Pakistan)

Treaties

Basel Convention on the Control of Transboundary Movements of Hazardous Wastes and their Disposal, opened for signature 22 March 1989, 1673 UNTS 126 (entered into force 5 May 1992)
Labour Inspection Convention, 1947 (No. 81) adopted on 19 June 1947, entered into force 10 October 1953, 13th Session, Governing Body of the International Labour Office
The Hong Kong International Convention for the Safe and Environmentally Sound Recycling of Ships, opened for Signature 1 September 2009, IMO Doc. SR/CONF45 (not yet in force). *(Hong Kong Convention)*
The International Convention for the Safe and Environmentally Sound Recycling of Ships, opened for signature 1 September 2009, IMO Doc. SR/CONF/45 (19 May 2009) (not yet in force)

Others

'Toxic Ship Barred from Chittagong Port', *The Daily Star* (online at 15 January 2007) http://www.thedailystar.net/2007/01/
Baloch, Saher, 'Shipbreaking Activities at Gadani Suspended', *Dawn* (online at 11 January 2017)https://www.dawn.com/news/1307621
Block, Ben, *Bangladeshi Lawyer Fights Toxic Shipbreaking* (Web Page, World Watch Institute) http://www.worldwatch.org/node/6084
Feature Story, *Ship-sized Loophole Closed: Victory- Toxic Ships Export Controlled*, Green Peace International (1 November 2004) http://www.greenpeace.org/international/en/news/features/victory-toxic-ship-export-co/
Foote, Chris, 'Breaking Bad: Uncovering The Oil Industry's Dirty Secret' (Investigative Report, BBC, 17 March 2020) https://www.bbc.co.uk/news/extra/ao726ind7u/shipbreaking
Huda, Taqbir, 'Why is the Price of Killing a Worker Only Tk 2 Lakh' *The Daily Star e-paper* (online at 11 July 2021) E-paper(http://epaper.thedailystar.net)
IndustriALL Global Union, Pakistan: Shipbreaking Accident Victims Receive Compensation (Web Page, 23 February 2017) http://www.industriall-union.org/pakistan-shipbreaking-accident-victims-receive-compensation
Gieseke, Jens 'European Union Ship Recycling Rules: Carrot, Stick or Illusion' European Community Shipowners Association (5 May 2021) https://www.youtube.com/watch?v=BY1jfhJj3lI
NFB, Shipbreakers (21 June 2017) https://www.youtube.com/watch?v=5jdEG_ACXLw&feature=emb_rel_pause, 46.52–47, 1:12:51
NGO Shipbreaking Platform, 'Bangladesh Succumbs to Shipping Industry Pressure: Bangladesh Temporarily Allows Toxic Ships Pending Final Ruling' (Press Release, 9 March 2011) http://www.shipbreakingplatform.org/bangladesh-succumbs-to-shipping-industry-pressure/
NGO Shipbreaking Platform, 'NGO Denounces Dangerous Working Conditions After Major Explosion At Gadani Shipbreaking Yard In Pakistan Killing At Least 21 Workers' (Press Release, 2 November 2016). https://www.shipbreakingplatform.org/press-release-ngos-denounce-dangerous-working-conditions-after-major-explosion-at-gadani-shipbreaking-yard-in-pakistan-killing-at-least-21-workers/
NGO Shipbreaking Platform, 'Why ships are Toxic?' *Issues of Interest* (Web Page) https://shipbreakingplatform.org/issues-of-interest/why-ships-are-toxic/.
Norma J. Martinez, Claus Nordahi, and Louise Maria Shottle Moller, 'Maersk and The Hazardous Waste in
Bangladesh', DANWATCH (Web Page, 15 October 2016) https://old.danwatch.dk/en/undersogelse/maersk-og-det-farlige-affald-i-bangladesh/

Port of Rotterdam, *First Steps in Environmentally Responsible Degassing of Ships* (Web Page, 7 September 2020) https://www.portofrotterdam.com/en/news-and-press-releases/first-steps-in-environmentally-responsible-degassing-of-ships

Balan, Premal, 'NGT Nod for Beaching Method of Ships at Alang', *Times of India* (online at 28 November 2020)

Seatrade Maritime News, Marcus Hand, Five Workers Dead in Blast at Alang shipbreaking yard, (June 28 2014) https://www.seatrade-maritime.com/asia/five-workers-dead-blast-alang-shipbreaking-yard

Bharucha, Zarir, 'Hong Kong: Ship Recycling in India- Hong Kong Convention', *Mondaq-Connecting Knowledge and People* (Web Page, 11 August 2020) https://www.mondaq.com/hongkong/environmental-law/974864/ship-recycling-in-india-hong-kong-convention

Chapter 5
Existing International Laws—Relevance in Ensuring Rectificatory Global Justice

Abstract This chapter examines the international regulatory frameworks governing shipbreaking. It describes the frameworks and critically questions the moral validity of these laws based on the theoretical foundation global injustice. This chapter specifically employs the concept of 'global injustice' as its theoretical basis. As shipbreaking workers mainly suffer from the poor shipbreaking practices in South Asia, this chapter examines whether the preventive system introduced under the international legal frameworks is enough to ensure justice to workers. It argues that the *Hong Kong Convention* is fundamentally flawed, as it disproportionately transfers burden of implementing safe shipbreaking practices onto developing countries. This chapter concludes raising the debate of introducing a transnational compensation framework.

Keywords Global injustice · Wastes · Exporters' liability · Shipbreaking yard · South Asian shipbreaking countries · European Union · Notification and hazardous management system · Preventive model · Legal foundation for compensation

Introduction

Focusing on three grounds, this chapter establishes the case to introduce a global civil liability mechanism. First, it argues that the *Hong Kong Convention* focuses mainly on a preventive system, which is inadequate to protect the workers from work-related fatalities, injuries, or diseases.[1] Second, it shows that in absence of a system to regulate the business using a compensation-based regulation, the regulatory

[1] *The International Convention for the Safe and Environmentally Sound Recycling of Ships*, opened for signature 1 September 2009, IMO Doc. SR/CONF/45 (19 May 2009) (entered into force on 26 June 2025). *(Hong Kong Convention)*.

Part of this chapter has been published in Curtin Law and Taxation Review Journal in 2020. The reference is mentioned below.

'Effectiveness of the Hong Kong Convention on Ship Recycling in India and Bangladesh' (2019) 5*Curtin Law and Taxation Review* 69–87.

M. Z. Ali, *Worker Injustices in the South Asian Shipbreaking Industry*, International Law in Asia, https://doi.org/10.1007/978-981-95-8325-6_5

framework introduced by the *Hong Kong Convention* diverges from other global industries,[2] which would presumably weaken the effectiveness of the international legal framework for shipbreaking (section "Lack of Compensatory Mechanism for Victims"). Third, it contends that the *Hong Kong Convention* does not provide a strong legal system by failing to shift the cost burden to shipowners and their States.

This chapter is divided into six parts. Section "The Classification of 'Ships' for Breaking as 'Wastes' Within the *Basel Convention*" explores the regulatory approaches introduced by the *Basel Convention* and examines the challenges in applying them to shipowners, particularly in the context of imposing legal responsibility for harm caused to individuals and environment within South Asia's shipbreaking sector. It further contends that the *Basel Convention* was primarily designed to govern the transboundary movement of hazardous wastes between nations, rather than the disposal of ships. Given that shipowner often obscure their shipbreaking intentions by altering ownership and reflagging ships at sea, identifying the precise moment when a 'ship' comes within the definition of 'wastes' is highly problematic. This ambiguity undermines the *Basel Convention*'s applicability to end-of-life ships.

Section "Shortcomings in the Hong Kong Convention's Approach to Prevention" evaluates the International Maritime Organisation's (IMO) initiative to establish a distinct legal framework for shipbreaking, focusing on the preventive mechanisms provided by the *Hong Kong Convention.* It critically assesses the Convention's shortcomings, particularly its inadequate provisions for prior notification and the management of hazardous materials. It argues that the Convention's regulatory structure falls short of effectively mitigating the risks or fatalities, injuries, and occupational illnesses associated with shipbreaking activities.

Section "Implication on Future Shipbreaking for Shifting the Liability on Shipbreaking Yards and Their States" contends that the legal architecture introduced by the *Hong Kong Convention* is fundamentally flawed, as it disproportionately transfers burden of implementing safe shipbreaking practices onto developing countries. This part also highlights the imbalance in benefit distribution, noting that shipowners, who profit most from the process are largely absolved of responsibility. It further underscores that South Asian shipbreaking facilities bear nearly 82% of the total costs involved in breaking ships, leaving them with minimal financial capacity to enhance safety and environmental standards.

Section "Lack of Compensatory Mechanism for Victims" identifies a critical gap in the *Hong Kong Convention*: the absence of a transnational compensation framework. The Hong *Kong Convention*'s failure to impose clear liability on shipowners for the environmentally and socially responsible disposal of their ships perpetuates hazardous working conditions in shipbreaking facilities. Workers continue to suffer fatalities, injuries, and occupational illnesses without any legal recourse to claim damages from the entities that profit from the practice. This part also analyses the decision given by the Court of Appeal of England and Wales in *Hamida Begum (on*

[2] Mining and Waste Trade as discussed in Chapter 7.

behalf of MD Khalil Mollah) v Maran (UK) Limited (*Maran Shipping*).[3] The matter involved a claim for damages brought by the widow of a Bangladeshi shipbreaking worker who died while breaking a ship originally owned by a UK-based company. The Appellate Court held that the UK shipowner could be held liable under tort law for failing to ensure the safety of the worker. However, *Maran Shipping* also illustrates the limitations of pursuing cross-border tort claims, which are infrequent, legally complex, and procedurally burdensome.

Section "Conclusion" concludes the chapter advocating for the establishment of a civil liability regime to fill the void left by existing international instruments. Otherwise, the systemic risks and inequities embedded in the global shipbreaking industry will continue to exist.

The Classification of 'Ships' for Breaking as 'Wastes' Within the *Basel Convention*

The importation of ships that are not free from hazardous substances and widespread practice of beaching raise serious question about the sustainability of South Asian shipbreaking sector.[4] A central problem lies in the presence of inbuilt toxic substances within a ship's body, which the regional industry generally fails to handle in an environmentally sound manner. Shipowners are not interested in extracting and managing residual waste of end-of-life ships because of logistical and technical challenges. Moreover, stringent international regulations govern both the responsible treatment of waste and its cross-border movement, add further complexity to the process.[5]

Before the International Maritime Organisation (IMO) Member States adopted the *Hong Kong Convention* in 2009, the *Basel Convention* served as the sole international legal instrument applicable to the shipbreaking sector. As the primary global treaty governing the transboundary movement of hazardous waste, the *Basel Convention* aims to reduce both the volume and international movement of hazardous wastes, promoting its management as close as possible to their place of production. Ships designated for breaking are, by definition, considered wastes, when they have reached their end of operational life and no longer serving a maritime operation. One of the *Basel Convention*'s goals is to impose strict controls on the international trade of waste, emphasising the reduction of waste generation and its associated risks. It obliges waste producers and exporting nations to adopt and enhance policies aimed at minimising waste. Aiming at facilitating this, the *Basel Convention* encourages

---

[3] *Hamida Begum (on behalf of MD Khalil Mollah) v Maran (UK) Limited* [2021] EWCA Civ 326. (*Maran Shipping*).

[4] See Chapter 3 that has explained the major issues in the shipbreaking industry.

[5] Ioanna Hadjiyianni and Kleoniki Pouikli, 'The Regulatory Landscape of Ship Recycling: Justice, Environmental Principles, and the European Union as a Global Leader' (2024) in *The Regulatory Landscape of Ship Recycling* (Edward Elgar Publishing, 2024) 46–75.

participating countries to strengthen their technical capabilities,[6] including the development of appropriate infrastructure and methodologies. Furthermore, it establishes a framework of accountability, holding exporting parties liable for any adverse impacts in case their wastes cause to human health or the environment.[7]

Liability of exporters under the *Basel Convention* is ensured by its requirement for prior informed consent (PIC) and the submission of a formal movement document from the exporting country.[8] The PIC mechanism functions as a formal assurance that the exporting country has been notified by the private exporter of the intended waste transfer and has secured written approval from the receiving country.[9] The waste movement document requires disclosure of 14 (fourteen) items,[10] including a declaration from the exporter affirming the accuracy of the information,[11] confirmation of non-objection from relevant authorities, and a comprehensive description of the waste.[12] Additionally, all private importers must hold national authorisation to handle waste,[13] as stipulated in art 4(7)(a), which prohibits any individual or entity from processing waste without legal approval under domestic law. A further safeguard provided in the *Basel Convention* requires that, in cases where the importing country fails to achieve environmentally sound disposal, the exporting nation must ensure the waste is returned.[14]

Broadly speaking, the *Basel Convention* prohibits the transboundary movement of ships unless the exporting party can guarantee their proper treatment within the importing jurisdiction. Nonetheless, the *Basel Convention* has not been successful to regulate ships destined for breaking, primarily because of the contested classification of such ships as 'waste' under its legal framework. Given the operational and definitional complexities outlined in subsequent sections, it remains uncertain

---

[6] *Basel Convention,* art 4.

[7] Kathrina Kummer Peiry, 'The Basel Convention on the Control of Transboundary Movements of hazardous Wastes and their Disposal: The Basel Convention at a Glance' (2013) 107 *Proceedings of the ASIL Annual Meeting* (Cambridge University Press, 2013) 434–436.

[8] *Basel Convention,* arts 6(1), 6(3).

[9] Ibid art 6(4).

[10] Article 4(7)(c) of the *Basel Convention* states that a waste movement document is a list of hazardous materials that are travelling inter-State. The starting point of the transboundary movement issues the document that has to be maintained until final disposal of the hazardous materials. In effect, the document provides a complete idea about the wastes that are moving inter-State and their consequences.

[11] *The Basel Convention on the Control of Transboundary Movements of Hazardous Wastes and their Disposal,* opened for signature 22 March 1989, 1673 UNTS 126 (entered into force 5 May 1992) annex V B ('Information to be provided on the Movement Document') item 12.

[12] Ibid item no 8.

[13] International Chamber of Shipping, 'Shipping Industry Guidelines on Transitional Measures for Shipowners Selling Ships for Recycling' (Marisec Publications, Second Edition, 2016).

[14] *Basel Convention,* art 8; Ibid.

whether the *Basel Convention* was ever intended to encompass shipbreaking within its scope.[15]

Definition of Wastes in the Basel Convention and Associated Issues with the Definition Related to Shipbreaking

In applying to shipbreaking sector, *Basel Convention*'s principal challenge is the ambiguity surrounding its definition of 'waste'—specifically, whether this term encompasses ships. Shipowners generally evade the *Basel Convention*'s requirements by asserting that it governs only the movement of waste materials, and that a ship does not qualify as waste at its point of export.[16] Art 2(1) of the *Basel Convention* defines 'wastes' as 'substances or objects, which are disposed of, are intended to be disposed of, or are required to be disposed of by the provisions of national law'.[17] Consequently, the classification of a ship as waste hinges on the shipowner's intention: whether the ship is being exported with the purpose of disposal. As the determination of a ship's status depends on internal decisions that may not be transparently disclosed, this subjective element complicates the enforcement of the *Basel Convention*.

The concept of 'intention' provided in art 2(1) of the *Basel Convention* is inherently subjective, relying on the explicit or inferred conduct of the shipowner.[18] In the absence of clear actions or communications suggesting that a ship is destined for breaking, establishing the requisite intent becomes highly problematic. In an effort to assess an owner's intent, various legal or operational indicators may be examined, such as documented correspondence regarding shipbreaking procedures or directives to limit fuel reserves to minimal levels, which may imply preparation for breaking. However, without such evidence, discerning whether a ship is being sent for final disposal is challenging. This ambiguity is compounded by the fact that ships often continue to carry cargo even during their final voyage to a breaking facility, further obscuring their status. As a result, pinpointing the moment a ship transitions from being a functional ship to qualify as waste under the *Basel Convention* is fraught with uncertainty.[19] This definitional vagueness enables shipowners to circumvent

[15] Shannen Trout, 'First World Problems, Developing World Impacts: An Assessment of the Adequacy of the Law on Shipbreaking' (2018) 10 *The Plymouth Law and Criminal Justice Review* 43–66.

[16] International Chamber of Shipping (n 13).

[17] *Basel Convention*, art 2(1).

[18] Tony George Puthurcherril, 'Contemporary International Law and Ship Recycling' in David Freestone (ed), *From Shipbreaking to Sustainable Ship Recycling: Evolution of a Legal Regime* (Martinus Nijhoff Publishers, 2010) 9.

[19] Ibid 144.

regulatory obligations, for instance, by withholding information from the exporting country or altering the ship's registration and identity (see Chap. 1).[20]

Shipowners Concealing Intentions to Break Ship and Circumvent the Basel Convention on Shipbreaking

A relevant illustration of deliberate evasion of regulatory mechanism occurred in August 2016, involving the transfer of the ship, the North Sea Producer from a port of London to Bangladesh. The ship's original owner, Maersk—a UK-based maritime company sold the ship to a shell corporation registered in Saint Kitts, a Caribbean country, under the pretence that it would be repurposed for commercial operations in Nigeria. Contrary to this claim, the ship was ultimately sent to Bangladesh for breaking.[21] Although Maersk denied any involvement in the shipbreaking process, investigative findings revealed that the company had orchestrated the transaction and employed an obscure intermediary to circumvent the *Basel Convention*'s requirements.[22]

Because of the procedural complexities in establishing a shipowner's intent to dispose of a ship, one viable enforcement strategy involves initiating legal proceedings in the domestic courts of the ship's flag State.[23] In certain cases, courts within the European Union have intervened to block export of EU-owned end-of-life ships to South Asia and have imposed financial penalties on the responsible parties (see Chap. 6).[24]

In prosecuting such cases, authorities, particularly public prosecutors have faced challenges in demonstrating the shipowner's intent to discard the ship. Evidence such as internal email correspondence and unusually low fuel reserves has been used to substantiate claims of intended disposal (see *Seatrade* in Chap. 6). Where intent has been successfully proven, national courts in shipowners' jurisdictions (discussed in detail in Chaps. 4 and 6) have held owners liable for directing ships to South Asian

---

[20] Ibid.

[21] North Sea Producer was primarily used in transporting oil in a North Sea Oil Extracting field. It was used for oil transport for more than 17 years. After that, it was sold with a false claim that it was going to be used for commercial operation in Nigeria. Under the *Basel Convention*, it was illegal to sell a ship for breaking without informing her flag States. The original owner had knowledge about the ultimate destination of the ship but due to the enormous profit, used the fraudulent practice. The issue is still under investigation by the UK government: at Shipbreaking Platform, *Spotlight North Sea Producer Case* (Web Page). http://www.shipbreakingplatform.org/spotlight-north-sea-producer-case.

[22] Ibid.

[23] Ibid.

[24] Norton Rose Fullbright, *Seatrade: A New Approach to Violations of Regulations on Ship Recycling in the European Union* (Web Page, May 2018) https://www.nortonrosefulbright.com/en-gb/knowledge/publications/f686f825/seatrade-a-new-approach-to-violations-of-regulations-on-ship-recycling-in-the-european-union.

shipbreaking facilities and have exercised legal authority to curb unsafe practices by invoking principles derived from the *Basel Convention.*[25] These decisions have emphasised compliance with mandatory precleaning requirements (see Chap. 4).[26] Nevertheless, the ongoing flow of hazardous ships to South Asia underscores the limitations of relying solely on judicial remedies to deter shipowners from bypassing international waste regulations.

Use of Reflagging to Circumvent the Basel Convention

An essential and often problematic aspect of the shipbreaking industry involves the practice of reflagging, whereby a ship changes its registration from one national jurisdiction to another either during its operational life or shortly before breaking. This process is frequently used by shipowners to break the legal and administrative connections between the ship and its original owner, complicating efforts to trace ownership and apply the *Basel Convention*'s principles. Under arts 92 and 94 of the *United Nations Convention on the Law of the Sea* (1982), flag States hold administrative authority over a ship. Consequently, when a ship is reflagged, regulatory oversight transfers to the new flag State.[27]

The reflagging mechanism is frequently exploited to avoid compliance with international waste regulations. Both the initial owner and new flag State can evade obligations under the *Basel Convention.* If a ship is sold with the intent of disposal and subsequently reflagged, the new owner operating under a different jurisdiction may not bear any responsibility under the *Basel Convention* for two primary reasons.[28] First, the *Basel Convention* applies only to transboundary movements of wastes,

---

[25] See for example *Cemsan Ship Dismantling Metal and Steel Industry Trade Limited Company V Ministry of Environment, Ankara* (IZmr 2nd Administrative Court), case no. 2002/496, Decision no. 2003/1184, 30 September 2003; *Stichting Greenpeace Nederland V Secretary of Housing, Spatial Planning and the Environment* [Council of State], Case No. 200606332/1, 21 February 2007, *Research Foundation for Science Technology and National Resource policy V Union of India & another* [Supreme Court of India], Writ Petition (civil) No. 657 of 1995, 30 July 2012; *Le Clemenceau, Council d'Etat* [French Administrative Court] Decision No. 288801, 15 February 2006 reported in Rec Labon.

[26] See for example *Cemsan Ship Dismantling Metal and Steel Industry Trade Limited Company V Ministry of Environment, Ankara* (IZmr 2nd Administrative Court), case no. 2002/496, Decision no. 2003/1184, 30 September 2003; *Stichting Greenpeace Nederland V Secretary of Housing, Spatial Planning and the Environment* [Council of State], Case No. 200606332/1, 21 February 2007, *Research Foundation for Science Technology and National Resource policy V Union of India & another* [Supreme Court of India], Writ Petition (civil) No. 657 of 1995, 30 July 2012; *Le Clemenceau, Council d'Etat* [French Administrative Court] Decision No. 288801, 15 February 2006 reported in Rec Labon.

[27] Puthutcherill (n 18) 115; The *United Nations Convention on the Law of the Sea*, adopted on 7 October 1982, UN Doc. A/CONF.62/122 (entered into force 16 November 1994).

[28] Michael Galley, 'Hazardous Materials in Shipbreaking—Where Do Liabilities Lie?' (Doctoral Thesis, Nottingham Trent University and Southampton Solent University, May 2013).

which requires the involvement of at least two distinct national jurisdictions.[29] If the waste transfer does not cross border from one State to another State, the *Basel Convention* 's provisions are not applicable.[30] Second, the decision to break a ship generally occurs outside the territorial jurisdiction of the new flag State, further distancing it from liability under the *Basel Convention.*[31]

The term 'area under national jurisdiction' refers to a geographic zone where a State holds administrative and regulatory authority, particularly in relation to safeguarding public health and environmental standards. As an illustration, consider a scenario in which Panamanian shipowner acquires a ship docked in Singapore and subsequently transfers it to a shipbreaking facility in Pakistan. Although the vessel is registered under Panama's flag, the physical movement of the ship originates from Singapore, a location outside Panama's jurisdiction. As a result, the Panamanian owner is not obliged to comply with the *Basel Convention*'s stipulations regarding precleaning prior to disposal.[32]

If the basic principles of the *Basel Convention*, namely prior informed consent (PIC), precleaning, and environmentally sound waste management were effectively applied to shipbreaking process, the volume of hazardous substances handled by shipbreaking workers would be reduced significantly. The *Basel Convention* prohibits the export of hazardous ships to developing nations unless waste minimisation and safe disposal practices are ensured within the receiving country. Further, the duty to mitigate occupations hazards, including fatalities, injuries, and disease rests directly with shipowners, thereby assigning them financial accountability for unsafe shipbreaking operations, particularly in South Asian shipbreaking facilities.[33] The subsequent part examines whether the *Hong Kong Convention* has positively integrated the *Basel Convention*'s principles and whether it sufficiently mandates protections against occupational harm in shipbreaking activities.[34]

---

[29] *Basel Convention,* art 2(3).

[30] Thomas Ormond, 'Hong Kong Convention and EU Ship Recycling Regulation: Can They Change Bad Industrial Practices Soon?' (2012) 2 *Environmental Law Network International* https://doi.org/10.46850/elni.2013.007.

[31] Ibid.

[32] Mohammad Zulfikar Ali, 'Injustice to Workers in the Shipbreaking Industry in South Asia: A Quest for a Civil Liability Framework in International Law' (PhD Thesis, Curtin University, 2022) 149.

[33] Ibid.

[34] Ibid.

Shortcomings in the Hong Kong Convention's Approach to Prevention

Challenges in implementing the *Basel Convention* within the context of shipbreaking led the International Maritime Organisation (IMO) to act. Aiming at establishing a special instrument and clarifying obligations specific to shipbreaking, IMO Member States convened a diplomatic conference in Hong Kong in May 2009, resulting in the adoption of the *Hong Kong Convention.* The final agreement was shaped through collaboration among the IMO Member States, non-government organisations (NGOs), the International Labour Organisation (ILO) and the Parties to the *Basel Convention.*[35]

In contrast to the broader scope of the *Basel Convention*, the *Hong Kong Convention* is specific to shipbreaking. It introduces a global structure grounded in national level reporting and domestic waste management protocols to address persistent issues in shipbreaking operations (see Chap. 3). Although, the *Hong Kong Convention* has entered into force on 26 June 2025 after two years of meeting the requirements on 26 June 2023,[36] arguably, the success of the *Hong Kong Convention* for South Asian countries depends on the effective operation of systems that include national notification and waste management.

The national notification framework established under the *Hong Kong Convention* imposes a mandatory duty on both shipowners and shipbreaking facilities to inform their respective national authorities of any planned shipbreaking activities.[37] In ensuring environmentally responsible practice, the *Hong Kong Convention* restricts the transfer of ships to shipbreaking facilities unless they are devoid of hazardous substances, such as mercury and radioactive elements identified in Appendix I of the *Hong Kong Convention.*[38] Most importantly, the *Hong Kong Convention* requires a shipbreaking yard to increase its technical capacity. Article 15 of the *Hong Kong Convention* requires each State Party to develop and enforce appropriate legal instruments to ensure that shipbreaking facilities meet the required standards for technical

---

[35] Ibid.

[36] *The Hong Kong Convention,* art 17 provides the requirements for entry into force of the Convention. The requirements are ratification (without reservation) from 15 States who by gross tonnage represent 40% of the world merchant fleets, and by recycling tonnage represent 3% of end-of-life ships for the previous 10 years. The requirements were met on 26 June 2023 when Bangladesh being the hub of many shipbreaking facilities and Siberia as a large flag State ratified the *Hong Kong Convention*: Deutsche Flagge, *The Hong Convention Enters into Force in 2025* (Webpage) https://www.deutsche-flagge.de/en/news/news-archive/news-2023/hong-kong-convention-enters-into-force-in-2025#:~:text=More%20than%2015%20years%20after, force%20on%2026%20June%202,025.

[37] *The International Convention for the Safe and Environmentally Sound Recycling of Ships*, opened for signature 1 September 2009, IMO Doc. SR/CONF/45 (19 May 2009) (entered into force on 26 June 2025) annex *(Regulation for Safe and Environmentally Sound Recycling of Ships)*, reg 24(1). *(Annex Regulation on Ship Recycling)*.

[38] Ibid, reg 17.

competence.[39] Following sections will critically assess the limitations inherent in the *Hong Kong Convention*'s notification procedures and its mechanisms for ensuring safe and effective waste management.

Problems in Applying the Hong Kong Convention's Notification System

A major weakness of the *Hong Kong Convention* is its private notification system for mandatory precleaning requirements. The crux of the problem is that the notification is voluntary in nature; therefore, the Convention provides no mechanism to enforce the requirement. There is no legal or other consequence in case of failure to comply with the reporting requirement, and because of this substantial gap, the reporting merely becomes a directory, rather than a mandatory, requirement. Consequently, shipbreaking countries and shipowners may be reluctant to follow reporting obligations if their industries provide employment and greater revenues for their government.

According to the *Hong Kong Convention*, shipowners and shipbreaking yards are required to notify their own State about their intention to break a ship.[40] The notification enables the administration of a flag State to prepare for the necessary survey of a ship's Inventory of Hazardous Materials (IHM),[41] before issuing an International Ready for Recycling Certificate (IRRC).[42] Notification from a shipowner follows the survey of an IIHM, and the survey follows the IRRC to authorise the breaking of a ship by a flag State, the state of registration that registers a ship. With respect to a shipowner, a shipbreaking yard is required to notify a competent authority of its own State government in three stages:

1. The intention to break a ship when the company is preparing to receive a ship[43];

[39] States are bound to introduce adequate inspection, monitoring, and enforcement provisions that may include sampling and entry powers. Moreover, such a mechanism may include an audit scheme to be carried out by the competent authority or an organisation recognised by the Party': at *Annex Regulation on Ship Recycling*, ibid reg 15(1)-(2).

[40] Ibid reg 24(1).

[41] The IHM is specific to each ship and shall at least identify as Part I, Hazardous Materials listed in Appendices 1 and 2 to the Hong Kong Convention and contained in a ship's structure or equipment, their location and approximate quantities: at ibid reg 5(1).

[42] Ibid reg 24(1).

[43] *Annex Regulation on Ship Recycling* provides the detailed information that has to be included in the notification: at ibid reg 24(2); the *Hong Kong Convention* provides that 'Competent Authority(ies)' means a 'governmental authority or authorities designated by a Party as responsible, within specified geographical area(s) or area(s) of expertise, for duties related to Ship Recycling Facilities operating within the jurisdiction of that Party as specified in this Convention': at *the Hong Kong Convention* art 2(3).

2. The planned start of shipbreaking after the shipbreaking yard has obtained the IRRC[44]; and
3. At the time of completion of the intended shipbreaking activity, that is, when the shipbreaking will be completed following the requirements of the Convention.[45]

The notification requirement established by the *Hong Kong Convention* serves primarily to ensure that shipowners remain answerable to their national authorities. However, unlike the prior informed consent procedure under the *Basel Convention*, the *Hong Kong Convention* does not require shipowners or the countries in which they are registered to secure approval from the destination country prior to exporting a ship for breaking. The omission results in a lack of formal intergovernmental coordination aimed at regulating the transboundary movement of hazardous ships. Had the *Hong Kong Convention* adopted a PIC-style mechanism provided in the *Basel Convention*, it would have necessitated that the receiving country explicitly authorise the import of a ship intended for breaking. Such a requirement would shift responsibility to the importing State to verify the presence of dangerous substances using the ship's inventory of hazardous materials before their arrival in the territory of a shipbreaking country.[46]

The PIC requirement under the *Basel Convention* is fundamentally different from the reporting obligations outlined in the *Hong Kong Convention*. While the PIC system demands prior consent from the importing State before any hazardous waste is accepted, the *Hong Kong Convention* merely requires that information be provided, without requiring approval from any governmental authority in the receiving country.[47] Consequently, shipbreaking facilities may proceed with breaking operations on ships containing toxic materials without oversight or intervention from public regulatory bodies. This practice risks normalising the arrival of hazardous ships, leaving the importing State with little recourse but to permit breaking once the vessel has entered its jurisdiction.[48]

---

[44] *Annex Regulation on Ship Recycling* (n 37), reg 24(3).

[45] Ibid reg 25.

[46] Some of the international environmental agreements are: *The Convention on Biological Diversity* opened for signature 5 June 1992. 1760 UNTS 79 (entered into force 29 December 1993);

The Stockholm Convention on Persistent Organic Pollutants, opened for signature 23 May 2001, UNEP/POPS/CONF/4 (Appendix II) (entered into force 17 May 2004); *The Rotterdam Convention on the Prior Informed Consent Procedure for Certain Hazardous Chemicals and Pesticides in International Trade*, opened for signature 10 September 1998, UNEP/FAO/PIC/CONF/5 (entered into force 24 February 2004).

[47] According to the *Hong Kong Convention* a shipbreaking company means 'the owner of the ship recycling or shipbreaking facility or any other organisation that is under the authority to operate the recycling or shipbreaking yards'; at *the Hong Kong Convention*, art 2(12).

[48] Ishtiaque Ahmed, 'Safe and Environmentally Sound Recycling of Ships: A Stocktaking of the Current State of International Law' (2020) 31 (1) *Fordham Environmental Law Review* 60–106.

Problems with Satisfying the Requirement of Sound Waste Management Under the Hong Kong Convention

The *Hong Kong Convention* also contains a requirement of sound management. Regulation 15 (Controls on Ship Recycling Facilities) provides:

> Each party shall establish legislation, regulations, and standards that are necessary to ensure that ship recycling facilities (shipbreaking yards) are designed, constructed, and operated in a safe and environmentally sound manner in accordance with the regulations of this Convention.

Similarly, Regulation 20 (Safe and environmentally sound management of hazardous materials) provides the following:

> Ship recycling facilities (shipbreaking yards) authorised by a party ensure safe and environmentally sound removal of any hazardous material contained in a ship certified in accordance with regulations 11 or 12.

As discussed in Chap. 3, the increasing number of ships sent for breaking in South Asia demonstrates an opposing view that shipowners and shipbreaking facilities are slowly looking to enforce the above regulatory requirements. International pressure to that effect is also growing slowly. This is an indication that South Asian countries are unlikely to adhere to sound management principles (see below) as long as their business-as-usual runs without interruption. The number of shipbreaking yards has increased dramatically between 2009 and 2023 in these countries without even following the above regulations.[49] Except for a few exceptions, shipbreaking facilities in South Asia that use beaching practices do not appear to have any urgency to build dry docks to ensure safe shipbreaking practices.[50]

The lack of urgency to build dry docks is related to the limited financial capacity of both the shipbreaking facilities and their government involved.[51] The financial constraint contributes to the inadequate compensation provided to workers who suffer fatalities, illness, or occupational illnesses. This is since South Asian shipbreaking facilities are compelled to offer elevated purchase prices to international shipowners in order to remain competitive and retain business. A substantial portion of the total cost associated with breaking ships, approximately 82% as outlined in section "The Role of the Shipbreaking Industry in South Asian Economies" of Chap. 3 is

---

[49] Beaching refers to cutting vessels on coastal beaches with no use of a contained or covered area that makes it impossible to stop toxic substances from affecting workers (see Chapter 3). Beaching is mainly 'responsible for the degradation of the coastal environment because with beaching it is not possible to stop toxic substances from directly mixing with seawater': at Okechukwu Ibeanu, Special Rapporteur, *Report on the Adverse Effects of the Movement and Dumping of Toxic and Dangerous Products and Wastes on the Enjoyment of Human Rights*, UN Doc A/HRC/15/22/Add.3 (2 September 2010) 8.

[50] MS Rhythma Kaul and Debesh Lahiri, *Sustainable Ship Recycling in India- Legal, Economic and Political Analysis* (National Maritime Foundation Report, 17 January 2025) https://maritimeindia.org/sustainable-ship-recycling-in-india-legal-economic-and-political-analysis/.

[51] Ali (n 32) 150.

transferred to shipowners as the sale value.[52] This leaves only 18% of the total expenditure available for operational revenue, labour wages, and miscellaneous expenses, severely restricting the funds that could be allocated towards improving safety and environmental standards. Governments in the region are also unable to allocated public resources to develop infrastructure specific to the shipbreaking sector, such as dry docks or to enforce regulatory frameworks and provide worker compensation. This limitation stems from the fact that shipbreaking is predominantly a privately operated industry, making it difficult to justify targeted public investment.[53]

Although, the *Hong Kong Convention* recognises the financial burden imposed by the high payment to shipowners, it nonetheless requires that shipbreaking facilities must secure adequate funding and implement effective management systems to construct dry docks.[54] Additionally, it places responsibility on national governments to address the human and environmental costs associated with the industry. These provisions, however, impose disproportionate obligations on South Asian countries, resulting in a regulatory framework that is misaligned with their economic realities.

Burden on Shipbreaking Yards for Ensuring Sound Management

The sound management of an end-of-life ship is the responsibility of everyone involved in the business, but the *Hong Kong Convention* shifts the burden solely onto shipbreaking yards.

A shipbreaking yard can only accept a ship that is free from the hazardous substances (for example, asbestos, PCBs and ozone-depleting substances) listed in Appendix I of the *Hong Kong Convention*.[55] Importantly, the *Hong Kong Convention* introduces a 'cradle-to-grave' approach,[56] meaning that a ship must protect the marine environment throughout its lifetime and that a shipbreaking yard cannot receive a ship that does not comply with such requirements.[57] Regulation 17 (General requirements) provides the following:

> Ship recycling facilities (shipbreaking yards) authorised by a party shall establish management systems, procedures and techniques that do not pose health risks to the workers concerned or to the population in the vicinity of the ship recycling facility and that will prevent, reduce, minimise and eliminate adverse effects on the environment caused by ship recycling, taking into account guidelines developed by the organisation.

---

[52] Ibid 154.

[53] Ibid.

[54] Ibid.

[55] *Annex Regulation on Ship Recycling* (n 37), reg 17.

[56] Under the *Hong Kong Convention* both 'ship recycling facilities operating under the jurisdiction of a party' and 'ships entitled to fly the flag of a party' are under the purview of the Convention: at *the Hong Kong Convention* (n 1) art 3.1.

[57] *Annex Regulation on Ship Recycling* (n 37) regs 17(2) and 4.

The *Guidelines for the Authorisation of Ship Recycling Facilities*, 2012, also provide the detailed rules for a shipbreaking yard to obtain approval.[58] Only shipbreaking yards, which can provide these yards, can accept a ship.[59] Linked to these requirements, the *Hong Kong Convention* has introduced 'green shipbuilding and design', for which State Parties are required to introduce restrictions on the use of hazardous materials, including asbestos, ozone-depleting substances, PCBs and prohibited anti-fouling compounds on their ships.[60]

The State Parties are also required to 'prohibit and/or restrict the installation or use of such materials on ships visiting their ports, shipyards, ship repair yards, or offshore terminals'. These restrictions lead to a number of surveys that are required before actual shipbreaking can commence.

A shipowner must conduct the first survey prior to putting a ship into the business of transportation or before an internationally recognised Classification Society issues the International Certificate on IHM.[61] A Classification Society certifies the seaworthiness of a ship upon a shipowner's request. Each new ship maintains a certificate of IHM once it starts operation.[62] In addition, a shipowner must conduct a periodic survey of a ship every five years.[63] Furthermore, an additional survey is required upon the request of the shipowner in case of any change, replacement, or significant repair of the structure.[64] Finally, a shipowner must conduct a survey before recycling or shipbreaking commences.[65]

A flag State can issue an IRRC following the final report before a ship ends up in a shipbreaking yard.[66] The IRRC proves that a ship is free from any hazardous materials listed in the *Hong Kong Convention*.[67]

To accept a ship, a shipbreaking yard must obtain survey reports from the owner[68] and improve its physical and technical capacity to manage the reported hazardous

---

[58] *The Hong Kong Convention* (n 1), art 16; *Guidelines for the Authorisation of Ship Recycling Facilities*, 2012 (Resolution MEPC.211 (63)), IMO Doc. MEPC 63/23 (14 March 2012) Annex 5.

[59] *The Hong Kong Convention*, art 17(2).

[60] *Annex Regulation on Ship Recycling* (n 34), reg 4(1) and Appendix 1 (*Controls of Hazardous Materials*).

[61] Ibid reg 10(1)(1).

[62] The *Hong Kong Convention*, Appendix 2 (*Minimum List of Items for the Inventory of Hazardous Materials*). See *Guidelines for the Development of the Inventory of Hazardous Materials* replaced in 2015; *Guidelines for the Development of the Inventory of Hazardous Materials, 2011* (Resolution MEPC.197 (62)), IMO Doc. MEPC 62/24 (26 July 2011) Annex 3; *Guidelines for the Development of the Inventory of Hazardous Materials, 2015* (Resolution MEPC.269 (68)), IMO Doc. MEPC 68/21/Add.1 (29 May 2015) Annex 17.

[63] *Annex Regulation on Ship Recycling* (n 37), reg 10(1)(2).

[64] Ibid reg 10(1)(3).

[65] Ibid reg 10(1)(4).

[66] Ibid reg 11(11).

[67] It means to comply with the conditions of safety as laid down in the Convention such as proper oxygen and removal of explosive substances: at ibid reg 1(6) – 1(7).

[68] Ibid regs 17(1) and 17(1)(3).

materials in a sound manner.[69] The *Hong Kong Convention*, however, is silent on the problem of the financial ability of a shipbreaking yard in South Asia. Surprisingly, the *Hong Kong Convention* does not address how a shipbreaking yard, or the government of a State party such as Bangladesh, can demand that shipowners internalise the costs of implementing the guidelines. Without any explicit provision of funding, how a financially capable shipowner shares the cost with shipbreaking yards in developing countries is therefore not clear.[70]

Burden on Shipbreaking States

Providing no funding mechanism in the *Hong Kong Convention* does not address the financial problems faced by shipbreaking yards and their States to enforce the guidelines. Legally, under the *Hong Kong Convention*, it is the duty of each party to establish proper legal mechanisms to enforce regulatory requirements in a shipbreaking yard.[71]

The *Hong Kong Convention* provides requirements for a ship recycling plan safeguarding human health and the environment; safe management of ships' hazardous materials; emergency response and preparedness; safety of workers and their training; and reporting on incidents, accidents, and occupational diseases and their chronic effects.[72] As principles, requirements are very important, but their practical implementation is subject to the financial ability of a shipbreaking State. The problem of financial ability begs the question of whether developing countries in South Asia can enforce these requirements.

These countries still face development-related challenges, including a high rate of illiteracy, unemployment, and lack of communication infrastructure, sanitary facilities, and shortages of other necessities. The governments of these countries have therefore preferred to invest their State budget in these areas of national importance rather than in the single shipbreaking industry.

The main impact of the *Hong Kong Convention*, to date, has been to shift responsibility for environmentally sound management of wastes to developing countries

---

[69] *The Hong Kong Convention* (n 1) art 6 read with *Annex Regulation on Ship Recycling* (n 5) reg 8(1).

[70] Gabriela Arguello Moncayo, 'International Law on Ship Recycling and Its Interface with EU Law' (2016) 109 (1) *Marine Pollution Bulletin* 301–308.

[71] A State Party is required 'to establish effective use of inspection, monitoring and enforcement provisions, including powers of entry and sampling. Such a mechanism may include an audit scheme to be carried out by the competent authority or an organisation recognised by the Party': at *Annex Regulation on Ship Recycling*, reg 15(1)-(2).

[72] *Annex Regulation on Ship Recycling* (n 34) regs 18–23 read with *Guidelines for Safe and Environmentally Sound Ship Recycling*, 2012 (Resolution MEPC. 210(63)), IMO Doc. MEPC 63/23 (14 March 2012) Annex 4.

and their industries.[73] This is the main difference between the *Basel Convention* and the *Hong Kong Convention* as instruments for regulating the transfer of ships from shipowners to intermediaries to shipbreaking companies in developing countries. The *Basel Convention* makes shipowners responsible for the environmentally sound management of waste within a ship's structure, whereas *the Hong Kong Convention* shifts responsibility to shipbreaking yards to ensure the sound management of this waste.

The *Hong Kong Convention* is also silent on shipowners' responsibility for precleaning inbuilt wastes of ships at any designated place beyond the territorial waters of shipbreaking States because Reg 8(2) (Preparation for Ship Recycling—General Requirements) provides the following:

> Ships destined to be recycled should conduct operations in the period prior to entering the ship recycling facility to minimise the amount of cargo residues, remaining fuel oil, and waste remaining onboard.[74]

In fact, a clear meaning of the above regulation is that it does not require shipowners to preclean the inbuilt waste of a ship in their own State jurisdiction. The next section evaluates the implications of this gap.

Implication on Future Shipbreaking for Shifting the Liability on Shipbreaking Yards and Their States

The above analysis demonstrates that mainly shipbreaking yards and their States are responsible for enforcing the standards of the *Hong Kong* Convention. Shipowners have no responsibility for ensuring the sound management of a ship.[75] The *Hong Kong Convention* is also silent on how the corresponding State of a shipowner is to monitor the sound management of a ship. Art 10(2) of the *Hong Kong Convention* provides the following:

> In the case of a ship recycling facility (shipbreaking yard), sanctions should be established under the law of the Party having jurisdiction over the ship recycling facility.

This is a clear deviation from the *Basel Convention*. Under the *Basel Convention*, an exporting State must monitor the environmentally sound management of hazardous waste. The *Basel Convention* elaborates the restriction and provides that an exporting State can allow a waste transfer only if the exporting State has a lack of technical expertise and capacity to dispose of the waste or if a State of import has a

---

[73] Ahmed (n 48) 214–215; art 10(2) of the *Hong Kong Convention* (n 1), *Annex Regulation on Ship Recycling* (n 37), reg 15(1)-(2), 8(2), 10(1)-(3), 19.

[74] Ibid reg 8(2).

[75] Tone George Puthucherril, 'Trans-boundary Movement of Hazardous Ships for Their Last Rites: Will the Ship Recycling Convention Make a Difference?' in David Freestone (ed), *From Shipbreaking to Sustainable Ship Recycling: Evolution of a Legal Regime* (Martinus Nijhoff Publishers, 2010) 283, 314.

demand for the waste as raw materials for its industrial production. The *Hong Kong Convention* provides no such qualifying terms or restrictions for importing a ship.[76]

Furthermore, under the *Basel Convention*, it is the duty of an exporting State to ensure sound management practices, and an exporting State cannot shift the duty to the importing State.[77] According to art 4(2)(e) of the *Basel Convention*, the exporting States have a mandatory obligation to stop a waste transfer if they are not capable of ensuring the environmentally sound management capacity of the importing States.

In particular, the *Hong Kong Convention* unjustly requires shipbreaking yards and their states to ensure the prevention of shipbreaking-related accidents and diseases, as it provides no limitation on beaching practices.[78] Regulation 19 (prevention of adverse effects to human health and the environment) provides the following:

> Ship recycling facilities (shipbreaking yards) authorised by a party should establish and utilise procedures to prevent explosions, fires, and other unsafe conditions by ensuring that safe-for-hot work conditions and procedures are established, maintained and monitored throughout ship recycling; prevent other accidents, occupational diseases and injuries or other adverse effects on human health and the environment; and prevent spills or emissions throughout ship recycling, which may cause harm to human health and/or the environment, taking into account the guidelines developed by the organisation.

Without restrictions on beaching practices, shifting responsibility to shipbreaking yards and their states may make the application of the above requirements doubtful. Greenpeace International, an international non-government organisation, voiced reservations around the issue during the negotiation process of the *Hong Kong Convention*. Greenpeace International proposed the following provision to add to Reg 19 of the *Hong Kong Convention*:

> Ship recycling facilities (shipbreaking yards), authorised by a party, establish and utilise procedures to ensure that ship recycling operations take place on intertidal flats, ocean beaches or other working platforms, which prevent rapid access to ships by emergency equipment; the ability to utilise cranes and lifting equipment at all times alongside vessels; and the possibility of full containment of pollutants during all cutting and stripping operations, which are prohibited.[79]

This proposal did not receive acceptance during the negotiation phase of the *Hong Kong Convention*. This is an indication that the international community has accepted beaching practices but has failed to address the legal gap, meaning that the *Hong Kong Convention* would bring about no significant change in ongoing industry practices, although they are not safe for workers or the environment.[80]

---

[76] Ishtiaque Ahmed, 'Ungovernable Ships at the End of their Lives and the Response of the Hong Kong Convention: A Critical Appraisal of the Treaty on Shipbreaking from the Perspective of South Asian Shipbreaking Nations '(2020) 18 *Santa Clara Journal of International Law* 124–174.

[77] *Basel* Convention, art 4(8).

[78] *Annex Regulation on Ship Recycling* (n 34), reg 15.

[79] *Ensuring Sustainable Green and Safe Ship Dismantling – Concerning Beaching and the Establishment of a Mandatory Fund (Submitted by Greenpeace International and FOEI)*, IMO Doc. SR/CONF/14 (9 February 2009) cited in Karim (n 47) 85.

[80] Ahmed (n 76).

In fact, the *Hong Kong Convention* also does not recognise the reality of shipbreaking workers.[81] Ignoring the reality of shipbreaking workers is a denial of rectificatory global justice. Objectively, the rectificatory justice theory extends liability to responsible parties for any cost related to rectifying an injustice (see Chap. 2).[82] Specifically, for a proper application of the theory, the concerned law must identify responsible parties and propose a mechanism for remedying the risk between the responsible parties and victims.[83] It is evident that shipowners are the responsible parties whose commercial use contributes to the generation of waste and who control the sale of a ship mainly for profit,[84] but the *Hong Kong Convention* does not recognise this.

This is an indication that 'business as usual' will continue to cause deaths and injuries in the future, without justification. These foreseeable future risks from shipbreaking lead to the question of a compensation system and whether the *Hong Kong Convention* has a compensatory mechanism to remedy any potential harm.

Lack of Compensatory Mechanism for Victims

Workers in South Asian shipbreaking sector serves the purpose of global maritime industry by disposing of their unwanted ships, but the silence in the *Hong Kong Convention* about responsibility of shipowners for any work-related fatalities, injuries, or occupational diseases is problematic. One may, however, argue that compensation is something, which is available under ILO conventions, but in absence of a mechanism to claim compensation, workers injured in their workplace have limited recourse to these ILO instruments.[85] Since shipbreaking requires efficient administrative procedure, legal enforcement, and proper technical capacity, international community realised the demand of a separate mechanism.[86] Moreover, because shipbreaking is a unique, but inherently dangerous industry, sustainability of the industry is compromised having inadequate knowledge of safety and health issues of labourers in facilities used for shipbreaking.[87] The ILO addressed these concerns

[81] Camelia Dewan and Elizabeth A. Silbia, 'Global Containments and Local Linkages: Structural Violence and the Toxic Flows of Shipbreaking' (2024) 42(1) *Environmental and Planning C: Politics and Space* 80, 84–90.

[82] Ali (n 32) 157.

[83] Principle 16 of *Rio Declaration* provides that National authorities should endeavour to promote the internalisation of environmental cost and the use of economic instruments, taking into account the approach that the polluter should, in principle, bear the cost of pollution, with due regard to the public interest and without distorting international trade and investment: at *Rio Declaration on Environment and Development*, UN Doc. A/CONF.151/26 (Vol. I) 1992.

[84] NGO Shipbreaking Platform, *Annual Report 2017* (Web Page) https://www.shipbreakingplatform.org/wp-content/uploads/2018/07/Annual-Report-2017-Final-Spreads.pdf.

[85] Ali (n 32) 158.

[86] Ibid.

[87] Ibid.

framing a distinct framework, *Safety and Health in Shipbreaking: Guidelines for Asian Countries and Turkey (ILO Guidelines)* in 2004.[88] But it is not a binding legal framework with strict enforcement process and it is only used to encourage responsible States to implement the guidelines introducing practical guidelines or amending their labour laws and rules. However, like the *Hong Kong Convention*, the issue with the *ILO Guidelines* is that it neither includes a compensation-based enforcement mechanism nor asks State parties to focus on a mechanism to introduce a separate platform to claim compensation for shipbreaking workers.[89]

The *ILO Guidelines* in fact makes the same mistake focusing only on the preventive strategy rather than compensation-based model. Aiming at upgrading shipbreaking standards, some of the fundamental yardsticks in framing national laws include considering shipbreaking is one of the most dangerous professions,[90] making sure that the wastes are disposed of in a sound manner,[91] taking into account social protection of workers,[92] and identifying the problematic aspects to enforce the shipbreaking laws to shipbreaking locations.[93]

As *ILO Guidelines* are short of mandatory requirements, if States are willing to implement *ILO Guidelines* voluntarily, they need to address the issues on relevant types of shipbreaking facilities and improve the status of workers changing their national legal framework.[94] The *ILO Guidelines* is the most important step taken by the ILO,[95] but requirements of *ILO Guidelines* are not mandatory in nature, and their implementation is aimed at prevention.

The *ILO Guidelines* is therefore limited to just providing a roadmap for national actions introducing no scope for forcing the shipbreaking facilities to pay compensation if its preventive mechanism fails.[96] Overall, as the *ILO Guidelines* and the *Hong Kong Convention* do not provide a compensatory mechanism, there is no international system to make the shipowners accountable for the payment of adequate compensation. In such a context, claiming compensation from international shipowners by workers of the South Asian shipbreaking sector would need to rely on interstate compensation claims under the tort of negligence law before the home State court of a shipowner. But as argued in the paragraphs below, such a claim is not beyond criticism.

---

[88] See generally International Labour Organisation, *Recycling of Ships: Safety and Health in Shipbreaking: Guidelines for Asian Countries and Turkey* (2004) www.ilo.org/public/english/region/asro/beijing/download/ship_breaking.pdf

[89] Ibid art 3(2)(2).

[90] Ibid art 2(3)(1).

[91] Ibid art 2(3)(2).

[92] Ibid art 2(3)(3).

[93] Ibid art 2(3)(4).

[94] Ibid 3(2)(2).

[95] Puthucherril (n 13)120.

[96] Duncan Graham-Rowe, 'Ship Scrapping: Breaking up is Hard to Do' (2004) 429 *Nature: International Weekly Journal of Science* 800, 802.

As discussed in Chap. 2, *Maran Shipping* is a recent example of an inter-State compensation claim under tort law in the UK.[97] The matter was concerned primarily with the liability of a foreign shipowner to pay compensation to the wife of a Bangladeshi shipbreaking worker, who died in breaking a ship owned by a UK shipowner.

For reasons set out at length in the judgement, Coulson J accepted the proposition that Maran (UK) Limited would owe a duty of care to the worker for its knowledge about poor shipbreaking practices and the greater amount of profit received from selling the ship.[98] The Court also stated that 'the issue must go for a full trial to decide finally on the matter of the amount of compensation'.[99] This statement appears from the fact that the plaintiff, Hamida Begum, the wife of the victim, MD Khalil Mollah, has a good case under the tort of negligence, but the shipping company may defend the liability for compensation payment, providing evidence that the victim, in fact, did not die breaking the company's ship in the concerned shipbreaking yard.

The High Court of Justice (Queens Division) has the original jurisdiction to try the matter and is yet to decide the matter of compensation. Until a final decision is reached, the implications of the decision for shipbreaking are not clear. However, the interim decision has more negative implications than positive implications for global shipbreaking.

On the one hand, the decision implies a good basis for victims establishing that court actions will follow each shipbreaking-related fatality or injury because the international framework of shipbreaking has no compensatory mechanism, and the national mechanism of shipbreaking countries is not sufficient to provide adequate compensation (see Chap. 4). With hundreds of unskilled workers in South Asia and with the continuous risk of more casualties, however, the decision demonstrates that companies are responsible for providing meaningful remedies to workers.

On the other hand, despite being a wake-up call for other shipowners, the decision risks the business of shipbreaking in developing countries. South Asia may lose the growing shipbreaking market if foreign shipowners do not send ships to South Asia because of the fear of similar court actions. The decrease in the number of ships that broke in South Asia from 90% in 2018–2019 to 76% in the first quarter of 2021 is likely a sign of such consequences.[100] The shipowners will also be mindful about the decision that may lead to an unlimited amount of compensation if the claim is proved before the Court.

From the standpoint of shipbreaking workers, it is exceptionally rare to see an injured, ill worker, or surviving family members to pursue a compensation claim from an international shipowner. *Maran Shipping* is such a rare case among many which

---

[97] *Hamida Begum (on behalf of MD Khalil Mollah) v Maran (UK) Limited* [2021] EWCA Civ 326. (10 March 2021). *(Maran Shipping).*

[98] Ibid [116].

[99] Ibid [116].

[100] Compared to 90% ships broken in 2015–2020, in the first quarter of 2021, South Asia broke 76% of ships: at Safety4Sea, '155 Ships Sold to South Asian Shipbreaking Yards in Q1 2021' (online at 29 April 2021) https://safety4sea.com/155-ships-sold-to-south-asian-shipbreaking-yards-in-q1-2021/?

reached to the Court of Appeal of England and Wales. But that could not be possible without taking support from intermediaries, including local and international NGOs and the very expensive law firm, Leigh Day.[101]

Whereas compensation claim should be restricted between wrongdoer and a victim, the involvement of third parties, such as law firms, has financial consequences for all parties. The legal proceeding is also not equally applicable to shipowners from other countries unless courts of other developed countries deny applying the principle established in *Maran Shipping* that eventually will result in imposing no liability on their shipowners.

Broadly, tort claims are localised mechanisms which differ from one country to another that underscores the urgent need for an international civil liability mechanism. In the context of compensation claims, a mechanism will only be effective if it covers all shipowners around the world and ensures their responsibility to pay adequate compensation irrespective of the location where fatality, injury, or occupational disease has taken place.

Conclusion

The *Hong Kong Convention* has created an unequal distribution of the waste burden of old ships and that developing countries have to accept this burden while not having a mechanism in place to compensate the most vulnerable shipbreaking workers. The *Hong Kong Convention,* which has not yet entered into force, is the only specific legally binding international legal instrument for shipbreaking, and the international community relies heavily on this instrument.

This chapter has argued that the *Hong Kong Convention* is not beyond criticism, largely because it is not seen as imposing an obligation on any of the beneficial entities, such as shipowners and shipping industries, involved in the business. Instead, the *Hong Kong Convention* shifts the burden onto flag States and ship recycling facilities unequally and establishes an unequal waste burden. Although the *Hong Kong Convention* canvasses the idea that its primary concern is to protect the occupational health and safety of workers, it does not have sufficient mechanisms for accomplishing this goal. The principles of sustainable development (considering shipbreaking as a green activity by emphasising an inventory for containing hazardous materials) introduced by the *Hong Kong Convention* portray safety as an important issue in shipbreaking. However, the Convention fails to accomplish its goal of promoting safe recycling because the responsibility for safety and enforcement lies mainly in under resourced ship recycling States and their under resourced facilities.[102]

---

[101] John Vidal, 'Mollah's Life was Typical: the Deadly Ship Graveyards of Bangladesh' *The Guardian* (online at 31 January 2020) https://www.theguardian.com/global-development/2020/jan/31/khalid-mollah-life-was-typical-the-deadly ship-graveyards-of-bangladesh.

[102] Ibid.

Moreover, the industry is not justified under justice theory because it does not focus on supporting those most in need with a compensation mechanism. Instead, the *Hong Kong Convention* focuses mainly on national notification and sound management systems that follow a number of surveys and certifications for protecting workers from shipbreaking accidents. Section "Implication on Future Shipbreaking for Shifting the Liability on Shipbreaking Yards and Their States" has therefore questioned whether the *Hong Kong Convention*'s ability to regulate inter-State movement of contaminated ships is sufficient to protect the rights of workers at recycling or shipbreaking yards in South Asia. Section "Lack of Compensatory Mechanism for Victims" has questioned the Convention's ability to provide adequate compensation to victim workers. This leads to a logical conclusion that an appropriate policy is required to remedy the abuse of rights within the industry.

Since the international community has established the *Hong Kong Convention* as the single most important instrument, the first place where regulatory control should be introduced is where it would have the least impact on regulatory standards. The next chapter explores existing regulatory and financial mechanisms implemented by the EU and its Member States so that lessons can be learned that can help in designing a legal framework to control the abuse of human and environmental rights within the global shipbreaking industry.

Bibliography

Articles/Books/Reports

Anderson, H Edwin, 'The Nationality of Ships and Flags of Convenience: Economic, Politics and Alternatives' (1996) 21 *Tulane Maritime Law Journal* 139

Battacharjee, Saurabh, 'From Basel to Hong Kong: International Environment Regulation of Ship Recycling Takes One Step Forward and Two Steps Back' (2009) 1(2) *Journal of Trade Law and Development* 193

Choksi S. 'The Basel Convention on the Control of Transboundary Movement of Hazardous Wastes and their Disposal: 1999 Protocol on Liability and Compensation' (2001) 28(2) *Ecology Law Quarterly* 509

Graham-Rowe, Duncan, 'Ship Scrapping: Breaking up is Hard to Do' (2004) 429 *Nature: International Weekly Journal of Science* 800

Karim, Md. Saiful, 'Environmental Pollution from the Shipbreaking Industry: International and National Legal Response' (2010) 22 *Georgetown International Environmental Law Review* 185

Moncayo, Gabriela Agguuiello, 'International Law on Ship Recycling and its Interface with EU Law' (2016) 109 *Marine Pollution Bulletin* 301

Galley, Michael, *Shipbreaking: Hazards and Liabilities* (Springer International Publishing, 2014)

Karim, Md. Saiful, *Shipbreaking in Developing Countries: A Requiem for Environmental Justice from the Perspectives of Bangladesh* (Taylor and Francis Group, 2018)

Puthurcherril, Tony George, *From Shipbreaking to Sustainable Ship Recycling: Evolution of a Legal Regime* (Matinus Nijhoff Publishers, 2010)

Ali, Mohammmad Zuflikar, 'How Effective Are International and Domestic Laws in Protecting Workers' Occupational Health and Safety Rights in the Shipbreaking Industry of Bangladesh?

What Role Could the National Court Play in Accordance with Their Constitutional Power?' (Master's Thesis, The University of New South Wales)

Chircop, 'A law of the Sea and International Environmental Law Considerations for Places for Refuge in Need of Assistance' in Aldo Chircop and Olof Linden (eds), *Places of Refuge for Ships: Emerging Environmental Concerns of a Maritime Custom* (Marinus Nijhoff Publishers, 2005) 231

Kalkbrenner, Astrid, 'Compensating for Catastrophic Harm: Civil Liability Regimes and Compensation Fund' (PhD Thesis, University of Calgary, 2015)

Puthucherril, Tony George, 'Trans-boundary Movement of Hazardous Ships for Their Last Rites: Will the Ship Recycling Convention Make a Difference?' in David Freestone (ed), *From Shipbreaking to Sustainable Ship Recycling: Evolution of a Legal Regime* (Martinus Nijhoff Publishers, 2010) 283

Puthurcherril, Tony George, 'Contemporary International Law and Ship Recycling' in David Freestone (ed), *From Shipbreaking to Sustainable Ship Recycling: Evolution of a Legal Regime* (Martinus Nijhoff Publishers, 2010) 9

Rummel-Bulska, Iwona, 'The Basel Convention and the UN Convention on the Law of the Sea' in Henrick Ringdom (ed), *Competing Norms in the Law of Marine Environmental Protection – Focus on Ship Safety and Pollution Prevention* (Kluwer Law International, 1997) 83

Ibeanu, Okechukwu, Special Rapporteur, *Report on the Adverse Effects of the Movement and Dumping of Toxic and Dangerous Products and Wastes on the Enjoyment of Human Rights*, UN Doc A/HRC/15/22/Add.3 (2 September 2010)

International Chamber of Shipping, *Communication to the Use of Basel Convention in the Context of Shipbreaking*, 9 January 2004

Ulfstein, Juris Geir, Legal Aspects of Scrapping of Vessels (Research Report, the Norwegian Ministry of Environment, 9 March 1999)

Cases

Cemsan Ship Dismantling Metal and Steel Industry Trade Limited Company V Ministry of Environment, Ankara (IZmr 2nd Administrative Court), case no. 2002/496, Decision no. 2003/1184, 30 September 2003

Hamida Begum (on behalf of MD Khalil Mollah) v Maran (UK) Limited [2021] EWCA Civ 326. (10 March 2021) *(Maran Shipping)*

Le Clemenceau, Council d'Etat [French Administrative Court] Decision No. 288801, 15 February 2006 reported in Rec Labon

Research Foundation for Science Technology and National Resource policy V Union of India & another [Supreme Court of India], Writ Petition (civil) No. 657 of 1995, 30 July 2012

Stichting Greenpeace Nederland V Secretary of Housing, Spatial Planning and the Environment [Council of State], Case No. 200606332/1, 21 February 2007

Treaties

Convention Concerning Occupational Health Services, adopted on 25 June 1985, ILO Convention 161 (entered into force 17 February 1988)

Convention Concerning Occupational Safety and Health and the Working Environment, adopted on 22 June 1981 ILO Convention 155 (entered into force August 1983)

Convention Concerning Prevention and Control of Occupational Hazards Caused by Carcinogenic Substances and Agents, adopted on 24 June 1974, ILO Convention 139 (entered into force 10 June 1976)
Convention Concerning Safety in the Use of Asbestos, adopted on 24 June 1986, ILO Convention 162 (entered into force 16 June 1989)
Convention Concerning Safety in the Use of Chemicals at Work, adopted on 25 June 1990, ILO Convention 170 (entered into force 4 November 1993)). See also *Safe Work Codes of Practice*, online: International Labour Organisation http://www.ilo.org/public/english/protection/safework/cops/english/index.htm
Convention Concerning the Promotional Framework for Occupational Safety and Health, adopted on 15 June 2006, ILO Convention 187 (entered into force 20 February 2009)
Convention Concerning the Protection of Workers against Occupational Hazards in the Working Environment Due to Air Pollution, Noise and Vibration, adopted on 20 June 1977, ILO Convention 148 (entered into force 11 July 1979)
Ensuring Sustainable Green and Safe Ship Dismantling – Concerning Beaching and the Establishment of a Mandatory Fund (Submitted by Greenpeace International and FOEI), IMO Doc. SR/CONF/14 (9 February 2009)
Guidelines for Safe and Environmentally Sound Ship Recycling, 2012 (Resolution MEPC. 210(63)), IMO Doc. MEPC 63/23 (14 March 2012)
Guidelines for the Authorisation of Ship Recycling Facilities, 2012 (Resolution MEPC.211 (63)), IMO Doc. MEPC 63/23 (14 March 2012)
Guidelines for the Development of the Inventory of Hazardous Materials, 2011 (Resolution MEPC.197 (62)), IMO Doc. MEPC 62/24 (26 July 2011)
Guidelines for the Development of the Inventory of Hazardous Materials, 2015 (Resolution MEPC.269 (68)), IMO Doc. MEPC 68/21/Add.1 (29 May 2015)
Rio Declaration on Environment and Development, UN Doc. A/CONF.151/26 (Vol. I) 1992
The Basel Convention on the Control of Transboundary Movements of Hazardous Wastes and their Disposal, opened for signature 22 March 1989, 1673 UNTS 126 (entered into force 5 May 1992)
The Convention on Biological Diversity opened for signature 5 June 1992. 1760 UNTS 79 (entered into force 29 December 1993)
The International Convention for the Safe and Environmentally Sound Recycling of Ships, opened for signature September 2009, IMO Doc. SR/CONF/45 (19 May 2009) (not yet in force)
The International Convention for the Safe and Environmentally Sound Recycling of Ships, opened for signature 1 September 2009, IMO Doc. SR/CONF/45 (19 May 2009) (not yet in force) annex *(Regulation for Safe and Environmentally Sound Recycling of Ships) (Annex Regulation on Ship Recycling)*
The Rotterdam Convention on the Prior Informed Consent Procedure for Certain Hazardous Chemicals and Pesticides in International Trade, opened for signature 10 September 1998, UNEP/FAO/PIC/CONF/5 (entered into force 24 February 2004)
The Stockholm Convention on Persistent Organic Pollutants, opened for signature 23 May 2001, UNEP/POPS/CONF/4 (Appendix II) (entered into force 17 May 2004)
The *United Nations Convention on the Law of the Sea*, adopted on 7 October 1982, UN Doc. A/CONF.62/122 (entered into force 16 November 1994)

Others

Flagge, Deutsche, *The Hong Convention Enters into Force in 2025* (Webpage) https://www.deutsche-flagge.de/en/news/news-archive/news-2023/hong-kong-convention-enters-into-force-in-2025#:~:text=More%20than%2015%20years%20after,force%20on%2026%20June%202025
Midshipman (MIDN), 'End of Life Ships' (Report, Inter-Departmental Committee on the Dismantling of Civilian and Military End of life Ships, March 2007) 19. http://www.shipbreakingplatform.org/shipbrea_wp2011/wp-content/uploads/2011/12/2007-06-18_-_Rapport_MIDN_english_version.pdf.

Mikelis, Nikos, *Developments and Issues on Recycling of Ships 3* (Web Page, 16 December 2006) http://www.imo.org/includes/blastDataOnly.asp/data_id%3D17980/Developments.pdf.

NGO Shipbreaking Platform, *Annual Report 2017* (Web Page) https://www.shipbreakingplatform.org/wp-content/uploads/2018/07/Annual-Report-2017-Final-Spreads.pdf

Safety4Sea, '155 Ships Sold to South Asian Shipbreaking Yards in Q1 2021' (online at 29 April 2021) https://safety4sea.com/155-ships-sold-to-south-asian-shipbreaking-yards-in-q1-2021/?

Shipbreaking Platform, *Spotlight North Sea Producer Case* (Web Page) http://www.shipbreakingplatform.org/spotlight-north-sea-producer-case

See generally International Labour Organisation, *Recycling of Ships: Safety and Health in Shipbreaking: Guidelines for Asian Countries and Turkey* (2004) www.ilo.org/public/english/region/asro/beijing/download/ship_breaking.pdf

Vidal, John, 'Mollah's Life was Typical: the Deadly Ship Graveyards of Bangladesh' *The Guardian* (online at 31 January 2020) https://www.theguardian.com/global-development/2020/jan/31/khalid-mollah-life-was-typical-the-deadly ship-graveyards-of-bangladesh

Chapter 6
Case Studies to Explore Responsibility within the Shipbreaking Industry—An Analysis of Regulatory Measures of the EU and Its Member States

Abstract This chapter aims to derive lessons for the global shipbreaking industry from the regulatory measures of the European Union (EU). A principal objective of this chapter is to critically review the literature on the *European Union Ship Recycling Regulation, 2013* (the *EU Ship Recycling Regulation*), through the lens of global justice theory, questioning its application in the current context. This chapter further examines three financial liability mechanisms—Capital Fund, Ship Recycling Licence, and Ship Recycling Insurance—evaluated by the EU Commission since 2005, which aim to impose financial liability on the EU shipowners for recycling ships in substandard shipbreaking yards. Additionally, it investigates the criminal liability approach introduced by the District Court of Rotterdam in the Netherlands. Overall, this chapter finds that the regulatory approaches introduced by the EU are insufficient given that they do not address the rectification of global injustice faced by shipbreaking workers.

Keywords EU regulation · Waste shipment · Flag State approach · Off-the-beach · EU listed shipbreaking yards · Ship recycling licence · Ship recycling fund · Ship recycling insurance · Financial liability · EU shipowners · Criminal liability · Regulatory approaches · Reflagging

Introduction

European Union (EU) is the major supplier of ships to South Asian shipbreaking yards. Because of this, the European Union's regulatory approaches (EU) play an influential role to introduce changes for global shipbreaking regulation. This chapter attempts to answer the question: What can the global shipbreaking industry learn from regulatory and financial measures of the EU in relation to shipbreaking? It investigates the impact of EU regulations and approaches on the international regulation

M. Z. Ali, *Worker Injustices in the South Asian Shipbreaking Industry*, International Law in Asia, https://doi.org/10.1007/978-981-95-8325-6_6

of shipbreaking.[1] With this objective in mind, discussion in this chapter proceeds as follows. Section "The EU Ship Recycling Regulation, 2013" argues that the *European Union Ship Recycling Regulation, 2013* (the *EU Ship Recycling Regulation*) has failed to address the reflagging issue.[2] Reflagging refers to any change in the flag of a ship from the country of original registration to another country. Shipowners use it to hide the identity of the original owner (see Chap. 1). This part also argues that the EU follows the flag State approach, and since the reflagging practice is not prohibited within the *EU Ship Recycling Regulation*, the flag State approach allows shipowners to circumvent the *EU Ship Recycling Regulation.* An EU owner can change flag from its EU jurisdiction to a non-EU jurisdiction when a ship is on its last journey. But without addressing the reflagging issue, the EU is planning to introduce several financial mechanisms. Table 6.1 summarises the major approaches, which will be discussed in detail in this chapter, from which lessons can be learned for the global shipbreaking industry.

Section "Analysis of the Proposals Within the EU to Impose Financial Liability on EU Shipowners" argues that the approaches for a financial mechanism proposed for the EU are also problematic since they aim at discouraging the reflagging practice, but they leave out civil liability of the EU shipowners for reportedly breaking ships on South Asian beaches. Section "Imposition of Criminal Liability by the District Court of Rotterdam" of this chapter argues that the criminal liability approach of the Netherlands imposes liability on its ships in limited cases. Learning from these approaches, each of these parts develops a section under the heading of 'Lessons for the Global Shipbreaking Industry'.

Section "Lesssons Learned From the EU Approaches and Stimulating the Debate on IMO Leadership in Shipbreaking" argues that the EU has played a pioneering role in reinforcing the debate over the introduction of financial liability to shipowners for end-of-life ships globally. By thoroughly discussing EU approaches, this section further argues that a global liability framework should learn from the ship recycling licence and ship recycling insurance proposed within the EU. However, the aim of a global ship recycling licence, i.e., the shipbreaking liability certificate (SLC), together with insurance should be to address the global injustice inflicted on shipbreaking workers who suffer regular deaths, injuries, and diseases while breaking foreign ships. Section "Conclusion" provides a brief conclusion of this chapter. The lessons learned from this chapter will be applied later in Chap. 9 to critically examine shipbreaking liability certificates (SLCs) with insurance as a liability framework for the global shipbreaking industry.

---

[1] News Agencies, 'European Companies Dumping Toxic Ships on Bangladesh beaches' *ALJAZEERA* (online, 27 Sep 2023) https://www.aljazeera.com/news/2023/9/28/european-companies-dumping-toxic-ships-on-bangladesh-beaches-hrw-says .

[2] *Regulation (EU) No. 1257/2013 of the European Parliament and of the Council of 20 November 2013 on Ship Recycling and Amending Regulation (EC) No. 1013/2016 and Directive 2009/16/EC, 2013*, OJ (L 330) 1. (*EU Ship Recycling Regulation).*

Table 6.1 Measures to impose liability on EU shipowners

Approach	Measures	Region/Country	Discussion
The EU ship recycling regulation	Off-the-beach shipbreaking, listing and flag State approach that restrict EU shipowners to sell ships to South Asian shipbreaking facilities	The EU	section "The EU Ship Recycling Regulation, 2013"
Capital fund	Accumulation of fund charging from ships as a precondition to enter into an EU port (Port Levy)	The EU	section "Capital Funds"
Ship recycling licence	Ship recycling licence paying levy for entry into EU ports	The EU	section "Ship Recycling Licence"
Ship recycling insurance	Insurance certificate paying levy for entry into EU ports	The EU	section "The Ship Recycling Insurance"
Criminal liability	Judicial enforcement imposing criminal liability	Netherlands[3]	section "Imposition of Criminal Liability by the District Court of Rotterdam"

[3] *State v Seatrade* [Rotterdam District Court, three-judge economic division for criminal cases], Public Prosecutor Office 10/994550–15, 15 March 2018 reported in (2018) Rechtspraak.nl 1, ECLI:NL:RBROT:2018:2108 https://www.rechtspraak.nl/Organisatie-en-contact/Organisatie/Rechtbanken/Rechtbank-Rotterdam/Nieuws/Documents/English%20translation%20Seatrade.pdf

The EU Ship Recycling Regulation, 2013

Background and Essential Features

Involvement of several international parties in the business chain of shipbreaking makes it an international business.[4] Ships operated profitability throughout their commercial life on international waters arrive South Asian shipbreaking facilities at the end of their life. This international nature of shipbreaking business has triggered renewed investigation into the *International Convention for the Safe and Environmentally Sound Disposal of Ships* (*Hong Kong Convention*), specially its challenges in shifting legal responsibility on shipowners dealing internationally and the International Maritime Organisation (IMO) itself.[5] As global shipbreaking market is substantially loaded by ships owned by the EU shipowners, the EU adopted its own law, the *EU Ship Recycling Regulation* in 2013. Advancing its own standards within the *EU Ship Recycling Regulation*, the EU is advocating for renewed focus on regulating the industry.

The primary objective of the *EU Ship Recycling Regulation* centres on incorporating the *Hong Kong Convention* within the EU frameworks.[6] This specialised legislation became necessary because of disputes concerning the applicability of existing *Waste Shipment Regulation* to ships reaching end-of-life status, particularly when shipowners selling ships for breaking provide no clear evidence of their intention to dispose (see Chap. 5).[7] Fundamentally, the *Waste Shipment Regulation* prohibits ship transfers outside the EU territorial control unless the exporting nation or ship owner removes toxic substances from the ship's structure beforehand.[8]

The mandatory precleaning requirement was established by a Dutch District Court decision in *Otopan*.[9] This litigation challenged the Netherlands Secretary of State's authorisation to move the hazardous ship, the Otopan from Amsterdam to a Turkish

---

[4] Tony George Puthurcherril, *From Shipbreaking to Sustainable Ship Recycling: Evolution of a Legal Regime* (Matinus Nijhoff Publishers, 2010) 10.

[5] *The International Convention for the Safe and Environmentally Sound Recycling of Ships*, opened for signature 1 September 2009, IMO Doc. SR/CONF/45 (19 May 2009) (entered into force on 26 June 2025). (*The Hong Kong Convention*); see Chap. 5 of the book.

[6] The Preamble of the *EU Ship Recycling Regulation* provides that 'this Regulation is aimed at facilitating early ratification of Hong Kong Convention both within the Union and in third countries by applying proportionate controls to ships and ship recycling facilities on the basis of that Convention': at *EU Ship Recycling Regulation* (n 1) Preamble para 5.

[7] *Regulation (EC) No 1013/2006 of the European Parliament and of the Council of 14 June 2006 on Shipments of Waste* OJ (L 190) 1 (*Waste Shipment Regulation*); *The Sandrien Case* (Council of State, Case Number 200105168/2, 19 June 2002); the Clemenceau Case (2005) (Council of State, Case Number 288801, 15 February 2006).

[8] Tomi Solakivi et al., 'The European Ship Recycling Regulation and its Market Implications: Ship-Recycling Capacity and Market Potential' (2021) 294 *Journal of Cleaner Production* 126,235 https://doi.org/10.1016/j.jclepro.2021.126235 .

[9] *Stitching Greenpeace Nederland v The Minister of Housing, Spatial Planning and The Environment* (Council of State, Case No. 2200606331/1, 21 February 2007. (*Otopan Case*).

shipbreaking facility. Greenpeace, the international environmental organisation, initiated legal proceedings, contending that since Turkey lacks EU membership status unlike the Netherlands, transferring the ship without prior waste removal violated the *Waste Shipment Regulation*. The Court accepted this position and determined that Dutch officials lacked authority to send the ship to Turkey for breaking without eliminating approximately 441 tonnes of asbestos and related contaminated materials.[10] This ruling imposed significant financial burdens on the Netherlands government, requiring expenditure of roughly 4 million Euros for waste removal before the ship's transfer to Turkey. But the judgement established the fundamental requirement that EU shipowners must preclean ships before their final journey.[11]

The decision illustrates that the *Waste Shipment Regulation* operates through stringent mechanisms preventing ships from being dispatched to India, Bangladesh, or Pakistan without adequate management of their internal waste. Nevertheless, practical application differs substantially, primarily because of challenges in establishing EU shipowner disposal intention for ships sent beyond European boundaries. In actual practice, from 2006 to 2011, approximately 91% of EU ships avoided these restrictions through reflagging,[12] a standard and legitimate maritime industry procedure that alters ship's nationality and administrative oversight. While international maritime law requires vessels to display flags for international navigation, EU shipowners exploit reflagging practice to conceal their identities and circumvent stringent *Waste Shipment Regulation* requirements. This approach results in insufficient evidence to classify ships as 'waste', thereby preventing *Waste Shipment Regulation*'s enforcement.

The Danish ferry Frederik IX also exemplifies how reflagging practices enable circumvention of *Waste Shipment Regulation* by concealing EU shipowners' identities. Following multiple flag and name changes, the Danish owner sold this ferry to India for breaking.[13] Despite India's intention to purchase the ship was for recycling, the owner falsely reported to Danish authorities that the ship was sold for commercial operations in the Middle East. Ultimately, lacking substantial evidence proving the ship was sent to India as waste for breaking, Danish authorities could not apply the *Waste Shipment Regulation*. Similar enforcement difficulties occurred with ships like the Sandrein in 2002 and the Clemenceau in *2008*.[14]

The EU addressed challenges in applying *Waste Shipment Regulation* by transitioning focus from general *Waste Shipment Regulation* towards specialised EU frameworks.[15] On March 23, 2012, the European Commission proposed introducing

---

[10] Ibid.

[11] Michael Galley, *Shipbreaking: Hazards and Liabilities* (Springer International Publishing, 2014) 127.

[12] Frederik Scholaert and Karin Smit Jacobs, Addressing ship Reflagging to Avoid Sanctions (European Parliamentary Research Service, Research Report, PE 745.686 –March 2023).

[13] See for a detail discussion on this case in Galley (n 11) 124–127.

[14] Ibid 117–136.

[15] NGO Shipbreaking Platform, 'The EU Agrees: The Recycling of Ships is a matter of Global Environmental Justice' (Press Release online at 1 December 2021) https://shipbreakingplatform.org/eu-agrees-shiprecycling-is-a-matter-of-global-environmental-justice/ .

a binding regulatory system of law.[16] The European Parliament and Council endorsed this proposal in 2013, enacting the *EU Ship Recycling Regulation*. This instrument seeks to advance sustainable shipbreaking practices for EU-flagged vessels, accelerate the adoption of the *Hong Kong Convention* throughout the EU, and incorporate the *Hong Kong Convention* principles into EU legislation.[17] Aiming at these objectives, the *EU Ship Recycling Regulation* supersedes the *Waste Shipment Regulation*.[18] The European Commission justified this override as necessary for preventing confusion, regulatory overlap, and administrative burden restricting EU shipowners to send ships to only EU-approved facilities either located within the EU or elsewhere.[19]

As the *EU Ship Recycling Regulation* restricts EU shipowners to utilising only EU-approved facilities, European Commission maintains that superseding the existing regulations does not compromise the promotion of developing more sound shipbreaking operations. This means shipbreaking facilities operating outside EU jurisdiction must discontinue conventional beaching methods and obtain European Commission approval. Given that beaching practices cause direct environmental and health concerns through discharge of wastes directly into coastal waters,[20] the *EU Ship Recycling Regulation* adopts an 'off the beach' shipbreaking requirement. The next section examines implications of this requirement comprehensively.

Regulatory Standards Under the EU Ship Recycling Regulation

Off-the-Beach Shipbreaking

The *EU Ship Recycling Regulation* adopts a methodology known as 'off-the-beach' shipbreaking process that refers to breaking ships on platforms rather than on the beach. This process aims to prevent the discharge of dangerous ship materials onto shoreline areas (refer to Chap. 3 for a detailed examination of the distinctions between beach-based and off-the-beach, e.g., dry dock shipbreaking methods).

---

[16] See Denmark, 'Proposal for an Enforceable Legally Binding System for the Recycling of Ships', Submission to the IMO Maritime Environment and Protection Committee (IMO MEPC 53/3/7).

[17] Committee Draft Report on the proposal for a regulation of the European Parliament and of the Council on ship recycling, 2012/0055 (COD), (12 November 2012) 80.

[18] It is worthy to mention art 27 of the *EU Ship Recycling Regulation* excludes vessels from the scope of the *Waste Shipment Regulation*. Art 1(3) of the *Waste Shipment Regulation* adds that (i) 'Ships flying the flag of a Member State falling under the Scope of Regulation (EU) No 1257/2013 of the European Parliament and of the Council are excluded'.

[19] Art 1(3) of the *Waste Shipment Regulation* is an exclusion clause that covers the areas where the *EU Ship Recycling Regulation* is not applicable.

[20] The *EU Ship Recycling Regulation*, art 15(2)(a).

The *EU Ship Recycling Regulation* fundamentally utilises the *Hong Kong Convention* as its foundational framework; however, regarding the 'off-the-beach' shipbreaking approach,[21] it establishes supplementary criteria beyond those specified in the *Hong Kong Convention*. The three most critical criteria include (a) the obligation for breaking facilities to secure placement on an EU registry of approved shipbreaking facilities (refer to section "The EU Ship Recycling Regulation, 6.2013" of this part), (b) the mandate for 'built structure' corresponding to the dry dock method, and (c) the management of hazardous waste materials throughout the disposal chain.[22]

In relation to the third criteria above, while the *EU Ship Recycling Regulation* does not provide a specific definition for 'built structure', this terminology in practice denotes the dry dock method of shipbreaking (refer to Chap. 3 for an examination of distinctions between beaching and dry dock methods).[23] According to the provisions outlined in the *EU Ship Recycling Regulation*, the management of downstream hazardous waste encompasses (a) 'prevention of spillage, particularly within the sea's intertidal zones'[24] and (b) 'processing of dangerous materials and waste produced throughout shipbreaking process exclusively on waterproof surfaces equipped with efficient drainage infrastructure'.[25]

The *EU Ship Recycling Regulation*'s objective is on implementing 'off-the-beach' shipbreaking approach combined with comprehensive downstream waste handling practices. This legislation aims to 'prevent, reduce or eliminate adverse effects on human health and the environment caused by the shipbreaking operation and maintenance of ships flying the flag of a Member State'. Nevertheless, a significant issue is the regulation's failure to offer explicit guidance regarding the interpretation of its 'off-the-beach' provisions or establish clear procedures for shipbreaking facilities to comply with these standards without mandating a funding mechanism from shipowners. This ambiguity in regulatory requirements, as discussed in subsequent sections, may potentially deter EU shipowners to sell ships to beaching-based shipbreaking facilities in South Asia.

The *EU Ship Recycling Regulation*'s off-the-beach shipbreaking approach is questionable for its extraterritorial application. While the *EU Ship Recycling Regulation* lacks international treaty status, it seeks to impose European standards across global

[21] Similar to the *Hong Kong Convention*, the *EU Ship Recycling Regulation* provides that New Vessels flying the flag of an EU Member State are required to have an inventory of hazardous materials on board from 31 December 2018. All EU flagged vessels must have a Ready for Recycling Certificate and cannot go to any yard other than those enlisted in the European List of Ship Recycling Facilities (EU List). For commercial operation and flying the flag of an EU Member State, the certified inventory of hazardous materials is required from 31 December 2020. Any non-EU flagged vessels calling at a port or anchorage of an EU Member State shall have a certified inventory of hazardous materials from 31 December 2020; see Carola Glinski, 'The Public–Private Governance Regime on Sustainable Ship Recycling: An In-depth Analysis' (July 2022) 31 (2) *Review of European, Comparative and International Environmental Law* 268–281.

[22] The *EU Ship Recycling Regulation*, art 13(1)(c).

[23] Dry dock refers to break ships in a built structure and store wastes in a secured storage.

[24] The *EU Ship Recycling Regulation*, art 13(1)(f).

[25] The *EU Ship Recycling Regulation*, art 13(1)(g)(i).

boundaries, requiring all nations outside the EU adhere to its self-created regulatory requirements. Failure to comply renders shipbreaking facilities in non-European territories ineligible to acquire ships from the EU shipowners. Additional requirement is the 'listing approach' referring to shipbreaking facilities operating beyond European borders must have approval the EU.[26] Prior to such evaluation, non-EU facilities must submit applications to the European Commission, demonstrating adherence to regulatory standards through documentation and certification from an independent assessor who has conducted on-site evaluations.[27] The following sections discuss the complications arising from these requirements.

Listing Approach

European Union's compulsory listing of shipbreaking facilities started from 1st January 2019, from when a shipbreaking facility located outside of the European Union must receive prior approval from the European Commission to break an EU-flagged ships over 500 GT (gross tonnage—a measure of a ship's overall internal volume).[28]

In July 2023, the European Commission published a list containing one US-based shipbreaking facility, nine from Turkey and thirty-eight shipbreaking facilities from various EU States, Norwegian, and the UK,[29] but no shipbreaking facility from South Asia.[30] Until 28 October 2021, however, 28 (Twenty-eight) Indian shipbreaking companies had originally applied for EU approval but had been denied as their applications did not comply with the EU's 'off-the-beach' shipbreaking standard. Since Bangladeshi and Pakistani shipbreaking facilities rely heavily on beaching method for breaking ships, no shipbreaking facility from these jurisdictions could file an application to be listed by the EU Commission.[31]

---

[26] The *EU Ship Recycling Regulation*, art 15 (2)(a).

[27] Ibid.

[28] The *EU Ship Recycling Regulation*, art 6(2)(a), arts 32 and 16.

[29] *The European List of Ship Recycling Facilities Pursuant to Regulation* (EU) No. 1257/2013 OJL 190 (28 July 2023) https://eur-lex.europa.eu/legal-content/EN/TXT/?uri=uriserv%3AOJ.L_.2023.190.01.0013.01.ENG

[30] *Decision No 2023/1562 of the EU Commission Implementing Amending Implementing Decision (EU) 2023/1562 establishing the European List of Ship Recycling Facilities*, EU 1257/2013 OJL 190(28 July 2023).

[31] List of ship recycling facilities located in third countries that have applied for inclusion in the European List of ship recycling facilities pursuant to Article 15 of the Ship Recycling Regulation 1257/2013. https://environment.ec.europa.eu/system/files/2021-11/List%20of%20applicant%20yards%20located%20in%20third%20countries%20October%202021.pdf

Flag State Approach

The *EU Ship Recycling Regulation*'s flag State approach does not coordinate with the EU's listing and 'off-the-beach' shipbreaking approaches. The reason is, the *EU Ship Recycling Regulation* applies only to EU flagships which aligns with its aim that the *EU Ship Recycling Regulation* is to monitor the operation and maintenance of ships flying the flag of a Member State.[32] This leaves for ships flying the flag of a non-EU country to escape the regulatory requirements established by the *EU Ship Recycling Regulation.* In other words, EU shipowners can still use the reflagging practice and in consequence, circumvent the regulatory requirements introduced by *EU Ship Recycling Regulation* by reflagging their ships to non-EU owners on international waters. In consequence, it is highly likely to see in the future that the *EU Ship Recycling Regulation* would need further changes. It means, unless the *EU Ship Recycling Regulation* is amended aiming at addressing the issue of reflagging, it is possible that shipbreaking in South Asia will receive more EU origin ships.

Lessons Learned from the EU Ship Recycling Regulation

From the above discussion, three important lessons can be learnt for global shipbreaking regulation. First, the *EU Ship Recycling Regulation* departs from the *Hong Kong Convention*'s non-binding approach. As discussed further below, the *Hong Kong Convention*'s non-binding approach refers to encouraging South Asian shipbreaking facilities to improve their standards gradually rather than banning ships' sale to South Asia's shipbreaking facilities. The *Hong Kong Convention* does not prohibit beaching practices and have a mandatory listing of standard. The *EU Ship Recycling Regulation*'s, on the other hand, prohibits EU shipowners selling ships to South Asia unless they are listed by the EU Commission.

Consequently, a question of dual standards arises as the *Hong Kong Convention*'s voluntary mechanism is to facilitate the improvement of standards and obtain an official certificate of compliance from private entities, such as Nippon Kaiji Kyokai (Class NK) instead of total restriction.[33] More than 75 shipbreaking faculties have already received the certificate of compliance from Class NK, which include five shipbreaking facilities located in Bangladesh. Receiving the certificate of compliance demonstrates these facilities have complied with the *Hong Kong Convention's* standards.[34] Lloyd's register, a UK-based entity and Registro Italiano Navale (RINA),

---

[32] The *EU Ship Recycling Regulation*, Preamble para 7.

[33] Nippon Kaiji Kyokai, known as Class NK, is a ship classification society engaged in a growing range of ship related activities and services to contribute to promoting the protection of human life and property at sea and the marine environment. It is based in Japan and was the first company to issue the compliance certificate to a shipbreaking yard in India. Class NK, 'Introduction About ClassNK' (Webpage). https://www.classnk.or.jp/hp/en/about/aboutNK/

[34] Class NK, 'List of Verified Ship Recycling Facilities by Class NK (As end of June 2025)' https://www.classnk.or.jp/hp/en/activities/statutory/shiprecycle/index.html.

an Italian entity have also issued compliance certificates to 33 Indian shipbreaking facilities.[35] Nevertheless, taking a recent deadly explosion into account that killed at least six workers in a shipbreaking yard located in Bangladesh on 7 September 2024, this private assessment practice has faced serious criticism. The shipbreaking yard named M/S SN Corporation received its certificate of compliance from Class NK in 2022, but it has since shown a poor record of deadly accidents leading to deaths and injuries.[36] Citing this accident in a certified facility, Julia Beckner, a senior health and human rights researcher at Human Rights Watch, questioned the role of classification societies, stating that 'the *Hong Kong Convention* and its so-called certificate of compliance, like the one granted to SN Corporation, create the dangerous illusion that these yards are safe and environmentally sustainable'.[37]

The role of classification societies in a voluntary-based enforcement mechanism introduced by the *Hong Kong Convention* demonstrates three issues regarding its transparency and efficiency. Primary reason is that most of the biggest classification societies are commercially linked to shipowners from developed countries. This business link of major classification societies with shipowners raises questions about their independent authority to issue certificates. Because classification societies may not work freely since they work for their owners—shipping industries, the link creates doubt over their independent certification.[38] Second, there is no liability regime on the process of certification of classification societies and for their accountability if their certifications are not effective. These certification societies are private international companies, which may not be recognised to impose limited liability under the laws of a shipbreaking country. As a result, the mandate of the classification societies to act as recognised organisations and certify the standards of Bangladesh, India, or Pakistan is doubtful because of no liability regime to question their process of certification.[39]

The third area of concern is the business-to-business practices of classification societies. Any privately run shipbreaking facility can contact a private classification society and ask for a compliance certificate. This leaves to a concern that a classification society may issue certificate without even inspecting the practical standards of

---

[35] Robin Des Bois, 'The Mystery of the Nameless Boat, Shipbreaking' (Bulletin of Information and Analysis on Ship Demolition No 55 from 1 January 2019 to 11 June 2019). http://www.robindesbois.org/wp-content/uploads/shipbreaking55.pdf; Ship classification is the main object of RINA's business and it is the founding member of the International Association of Classification Societies formed in 1968. RINA, Marine (Web Page) https://www.rina.org/en/business/marine ; Lloyds Register is a limited company registered in England and Wales. They certify shipbreaking facilities. See for a verified list of shipbreaking facilities, Lloyds Register Verified Ship Recycling Facilities (WebPage) https://www.lr.org/en/lloyds-register-verified-ship-recycling-facilities/

[36] Human Rights Watch, *Bangladesh: Ship Explosion Exposes Regulatory Failures- Deadly Accident in a Yard with Hong Kong Convention Certification* (Webpage, 17 September 2024) https://www.hrw.org/news/2024/09/18/bangladesh-ship-explosion-exposes-regulatory-failures .

[37] Ibid.

[38] Glinski (n 21).

[39] Ibid.

a shipbreaking facility.[40] Prior to issuing a certificate of compliance, it is a requirement for a shipbreaking facility to submit an independent environmental assessment report. But many shipbreaking facilities engage the same classification society for both environmental clearance and a certificate of compliance aiming at negating possible impact of a negative environmental clearance issued by a third party on the certificate of compliance.

It is also reported that many common hazardous substances, including asbestos, have been found lying on Indian beaches certified by a classification society, but the certificate issued by the classification society does not reflect the condition.[41] Despite receiving a certificate of compliance with the *Hong Kong Convention* standards by the same classification society, reports often show that the shipbreaking yards in India maintain different standards.[42] Some yards are of low quality because of dangerous beaching practices.[43] These reported concerns raise serious question about the effectiveness of classification societies' certificates.

Compared *EU Ship Recycling Regulation*'s commission level inspection to the *Hong Kong Convention*'s private inspection system, the lesson learnt is that strict approach established by the *EU Ship Recycling Regulation*'s would be more effective. But reality is that the *EU Ship Recycling Regulation*'s 'off-the-beach' and 'listing' approaches are not suitable for global shipbreaking because of the flag State approach. One of the main reasons is that both the *EU Ship Recycling Regulation* and the *Hong Kong Convention* follow the flag State approach and that a change of flag to a non-party State can circumvent their application.[44]

There is a practical reason for European Union's reliance on South Asian shipbreaking sector. European Union shares a 30% of the global shipbreaking annual demand but there is a growing concern as to the capacity of the EU listed facilities. An increased number of stakeholders are asking if the EU listed facilities can cope with the ever-increasing shipbreaking demand in Europe.[45] Shipping companies argue that listed capacity with 300,000 light displace tonnage is not enough to comply with the 2.5 million light displace tonnage supply of the EU flagships.[46] The

---

[40] NGO Shipbreaking Platform, HKC Statement of Compliance (webpage), https://shipbreakingplatform.org/issues-of-interest/the-law/hkc-soc/

[41] Ibid.

[42] Ibid.

[43] Human Rights Watch, 'Trading Lives for Profit: How the Shipping Industry Circumvents Regulations to Scrap Toxic Ships on Bangladesh's Beaches' (Report, 28 September 2023) https://www.hrw.org/report/2023/09/28/trading-lives-profit/how-shipping-industry-circumvents-regulations-scrap-toxic .

[44] See Chapter 5 for detailed discussion on nonparty State's eligibility to sell ships to the potential Member States of the *Hong Kong Convention*.

[45] Michael Schular, 'NGO shipbreaking Platform Slams Shipping Industry Scaremongering to Undermine European Ship Recycling Regulation', *gCaptain* (online at 6 June 2018) https://gcaptain.com/ngo-shipbreaking-platform-slams-shipping-industry-scaremongering-to-undermine-european-ship-recycling-regulation/

[46] NGO Shipbreaking Platform, 'EU must Take Action to End Dumping of Toxic Ships and Support Capacity Building' (Platform News online at 25 March 2025) https://shipbreakingplatform.org/eu-must-take-action-to-end-toxic-ship-dumping/ .

European Commission itself recognised that principal issue the insufficient capacity in the EU Member States to feed annual shipbreaking demand.[47]

Thus, the South Asian shipbreaking industry remains a top choice for EU shipowners. A report stated that around ten ships beached in South Asia in the first quarters of 2019 after transferring their flags to St Kitts, a Caribbean nation. Greek companies from the EU jurisdiction outshined other global companies.[48] In essence, *EU Ship Recycling Regulation*'s 'off-the-beach' approach is not being properly implemented.

The final lesson learnt from the EU is that the compulsory precleaning is not feasible for the global shipbreaking industry. Perhaps, considering associated problems with compulsory precleaning, such as ship's loss of sailing capacity, increasing cost of transboundary movement of ships, lack of capability for towing vessels to travel a long distance, high cost and risks in cleaning ships the *EU Ship Recycling Regulation* remained silent about it.[49] Shipowners will simply carry on reflagging if the global shipbreaking regime adopts the same 'off-the-beach' and 'listing' approaches provided in the *EU Ship Recycling Regulation.* A related issue is also the same threat of criminal prosecution as EU ships for any failure to comply with precleaning requirements, as discussed in section "Analysis of the Proposals Within the EU to Impose Financial Liability on EU Shipowners" of this chapter. Criminal liability is controversial since it is likely to impose liability for practices, such as beaching, which are legal under the *Hong Kong Convention.*[50]

The lessons learned from the *EU Ship Recycling Regulation* in particular leads one to argue that a systemic approach is considered justifiable in regulating shipowner liability by way of a remedy system. Without such a system, only compulsory precleaning and off-the-beach may be inadequate to change behaviour of shipowners. What is required, instead, is a liability framework that considers the liability of shipowners. An objective of such a framework would be to ensure financial guarantee of all shipowners to cover contributions when a worker dies, gets injured, or suffers work-related diseases from shipbreaking. Kristoffer Tedenhag's argument to have insurance policy for shipbreaking corroborates this proposition.[51] Proposing a financial mechanism with the maintenance of mandatory insurance during the process of shipbreaking, Kristoffer Tedenhag concluded that a financial mechanism is preferable to stopping beaching and introducing mandatory precleaning standards

---

[47] European Commission, 'EU Ship Recycling Regulation: Evaluation and List Update' *Directorate-General for Environment* (Webpage, 19 February 2025) https://environment.ec.europa.eu/news/eu-ship-recycling-regulation-evaluation-and-list-update-2025-02-19_en .

[48] Nicola Mulinaris, 'Platform Publishes South Asia Quarterly Update#24,' *NGO Shipbreaking Platform* (Webpage, 13 January 2022) https://shipbreakingplatform.org/tag/quarterly-update/page/3/ .

[49] Det Norske Veritas, 'Technological and Economical Feasibility of Ship Scrapping in Europe' (Research Report N, 'Technological and Economical Feasibility of Ship Scrapping in Europe' (Research Report No. 2000–3527, 2001) 77–78.

[50] See Chapter 5.

[51] Kristoffer Tedenhag, 'Insurance Aspects of Wrecks and Recycling of Ships from an Environmental Sustainability Perspective' (Master's Thesis, Lund University, 2013) 62.

from a cost perspective.[52] The estimated extra charge determined in the study would be from 0.01 USD/LDT to 0.06 USD/LDT for the insurance premium,[53] whereas the cost of precleaning is about 100–200 USD/LDT depending on a vessel's nature.[54]

Comparing the cost of precleaning with insurance, a reasonable approach is to introduce a financial mechanism that would redress the civil liability of shipowners and eventually change unsafe practices in South Asia.[55] A financial mechanism is required to consider the civil liability of shipowners for compensating human loss.[56] Moreover, as discussed in the next section, the mechanism should incorporate appropriate insurance or financial guarantees, such as a ship recycling certificate and ship recycling insurance proposed within the *EU Ship Recycling Regulation*. This leads to the following question: what should be the nature and features of the proposed financial mechanism in the framework?

Analysis of the Proposals Within the EU to Impose Financial Liability on EU Shipowners

The European Commission has theoretically recognised that a financial mechanism in addition to the *EU Ship Recycling Regulation* is the key to resolving the reflagging problem. Some of the other important objectives of an effective financial mechanism are to prevent, reduce, minimise, and, to the extent practicable, eliminate accidents, injuries, and other adverse effects on human health and the environment caused by ship recycling.[57] Art 29 of the *EU Ship Recycling Regulation* requires the European Commission to conduct a feasibility study and report to the European Parliament and the Council.[58] The preamble of the *EU Ship Recycling Regulation* also clearly states that the report should include the following:

> The feasibility of establishing a financial mechanism applicable to all ships calling at a port or anchorage or a member state, irrespective of the flag they are flying, to generate resources that would facilitate the environmentally sound recycling and treatment of ships without creating an incentive to reflag.

---

[52] Ibid 62.

[53] Ibid.

[54] Maria Sarraf et al., 'Ship Breaking and Recycling Industry in Bangladesh and Pakistan,' (Report No. 58275-SAS, World Bank, 2010) 53.

[55] NGO Shipbreaking Platform, 'Make the Polluter Pay: Why we need the EU Ship Recycling Licence' (Position Paper, October 2016). https://www.shipbreakingplatform.org/resources/library/. (NGO Shipbreaking Platform, 2016a, b).

[56] See Chapters 7 and 8.

[57] The *EU Ship Recycling Regulation*, art 1.

[58] Ibid.

The Scope and Nature of a Financial Mechanism Under the EU Ship Recycling Regulation

The European Commission has already reviewed a number of options between 2005 and 2016, but owing to the nature of taxation, lack of insurance objectives, and scope deficiency of the options, the EU Parliament has not accepted them. For a clear analysis of the options, this chapter classifies them into three terms. First, the accumulation of funds from port levies refers to raising a fund from charging a ship for every entry into an EU port. Second, the ship recycling licence introduces a compulsory licensing system, paying a set fee for a ship to seek entry into an EU port. Third, ship recycling insurance ensures that a ship remains for a set period, and the annual premium is fixed because of a ship's size and age. Every ship entering an EU port must have an insurance certificate on board the ship.

From the conceptual basis of introducing a financial mechanism, the options are important because they reinforce the argument for introducing a financial mechanism for regulating the shipbreaking business. However, a major criticism of the approaches is that although they presume that EU shipowners may send ships to South Asia, the approaches do not intend to impose inter-State liability on EU shipowners and provide a remedy system for workers who face deaths, injuries, or shipbreaking work-related diseases in their value chain. Instead, the approaches propose to benefit EU shipowners by returning the amount they pay to financial mechanisms. In that sense, the financial mechanisms are in fact nothing more than a 'payback system' presuming that the EU shipowners are going to lose their profit by selling ships to EU listed facilities. Therefore, the focus of these mechanisms is to compensate for the price gap of a ship between an EU listed shipbreaking yard and a shipbreaking yard in South Asia.

The next sections examine the capital fund, port levy system, ship recycling licence, licencing system, and ship recycling insurance, an annual insurance system. Section "Analysis of the Proposals Within the EU to Impose Financial Liability on EU Shipowners" D identifies the lessons learned from the mechanisms for the global shipbreaking industry.

Capital Funds

Primarily, the European Commission aimed at introducing capital funds from charging a port levy. In general, the proposed approaches, namely, ship recycling funds, ship recycling guarantees, and ship recycling accounts, require a shipowner to make an annual contribution to the fund for each entry into an EU port and, as a ship grows older, to turn the annual contribution into a capital amount. The final capital amount would then be returned to the last shipowner, showing evidence of ship recycling in an EU listed shipbreaking yard.

Studies published prior to 2016 by the European Commission, Greenpeace, NGO Shipbreaking Platform, and the Director General Environment of the EU proposed capital funds with different names. Ecorys' study (2005) named the financial mechanism the 'ship recycling fund' charging from the owners of newly built ships.[59] The Cowi and Milieu (2009) study proposed creating a fund charging every ship visiting EU ports,[60] and the Milieu study (2013), on the other hand, proposed maintaining a 'ship recycling guarantee' by each ship visiting EU ports.[61] Table 6.2 shows the nature of the proposals put forward to the EU Commission before 2016.

Table 6.2 Key features of the financial proposals in the EU before 2016

Terms	*Author*	*Published by*	*Year*	*Names of the Fund*
The Ship recycling fund	Ecorys	Greenpeace[62]	2005	Ship Recycling Fund
Study in relation to options for new initiatives regarding dismantling of ships	Cowi and Milieu	EU Directorate-General Environment[63]	2009	Ship Recycling Fund
Financial mechanisms to ensure responsible ship recycling	Profundo	Shipbreaking Platform[64]	2013	-Ship Recycling Fund; -Ship recycling Account; -Ship recycling insurance or ship recycling life insurance
Financing the environmentally sound recycling and treatment of ships	Milieu	European Parliament (Impact Assessment)[65]	2013	-Ship Recycling Fund; -Ship recycling Account; -Ship recycling Insurance or ship recycling life insurance -Ship recycling guarantee (SRG)

[59] ECORYS Research and Consulting, 'The Ship Recycling Fund: Financing Environmentally Sound Scrapping and Recycling of Sea-going Ships' (Research Report, Greenpeace, 1 February 2005). https://shipbreaking.wordifysites.com/wp-content/uploads/2019/01/ECORYS-survey-on-a-ship-recycling-fund.pdf *(Ecorys Study, 2005).*

[60] COWI and Milieu Environmental Law And Policy, 'Study in Relation to Options For New Initiatives Regarding Dismantling of Ships' (Research Report, The EU Director General of the Department of Environment, August 2009). https://ec.europa.eu/environment/pdf/waste/ships/fund_note.pdf *(COWI and Milieu Study).*

[61] Milieu Environmental Law and Policy, 'Financing the Environmentally Sound Recycling and Treatment of Ships' (Research Report, Impact Assessment Unit, Directorate for Impact Assessment, The EU Parliament, 2013). *(Milieu Study, 2013).*

[62] Ecorys Study, 2005 (n 60).

[63] Cowi and Milieu Study, 2009 (n 61).

[64] Profundo Economic Research, 'Financial Mechanisms To Ensure Responsible Ship Recycling' (Research Paper, NGO shipbreaking Platform, 22 January 2013) https://shipbreakingplatform.org/wp-content/uploads/2018/11/Financial-mechanisms-for-resonsible-ship-recycling-22_01_2013-FINAL.pdf *(Profundo Study, 2013).*

[65] Milieu Study, 2013 (n 62).

Regardless of capital funds' ability to impose liability, capital funds, as a financial liability system, fall short of imposing financial liability on shipowners in the true sense. This is because, as noted above, instead of proposing to compensate the victims, the proposals set mechanisms to pay back the shipowners from the fund subject to evidence of recycling a ship in an EU listed shipbreaking yard.

The capital funds aim to pay an EU shipowner the cost of the price gap for selling a ship to an EU listed shipbreaking yard, presuming that this option has financial consequences for the EU shipowner,[66] because the *EU Ship Recycling Regulation*-compliant ship recycling facility cannot offer a price as high as a South Asian shipbreaking yard. An EU listed shipbreaking yard would pay less than a shipbreaking yard in South Asia by spending a higher maintenance cost than a South Asian shipbreaking yard (see Chap. 3).[67] On the other hand, a South Asian shipbreaking yard can offer a higher price by not complying with environmental and safety standards. An obvious reason not to comply with environmental and safety standards is their local legal system and business model, as discussed in Chap. 3.[68]

Ecorys-Dnv-GL noted that the price difference between an *EU* ship recycling regulation-compliant shipbreaking yard and a non-*EU* ship recycling regulation-compliant shipbreaking yard may put the *EU* ship recycling regulation-compliant shipbreaking yard at a competitive disadvantage.[69] The shipowners therefore may not want to lose profit and continue to sell ships to EU listed shipbreaking yards. The proposed capital funds therefore acknowledge the possible difference in the operation cost of an EU listed shipbreaking yard and a non-EU listed shipbreaking yard.

Moreover, raising funds from port entry has several practical problems. The option raises concerns among shipowners regarding uneven financial burdens on ships calling more regularly to EU ports than other low-frequency ships to EU ports. A further problem is the taxed nature of the port levy, which creates an extra administrative burden for the port.[70] These practical problems led to the proposal of ship recycling licences by the 2016 Ecorys-Dnv-GL study. The European Commission officially published and backed the study.[71]

---

[66] The latest EU study published by the EU Commission in July 2016 has also recommended to introduce a compulsory accumulation of capital system in the form of a ship recycling licence for both EU and non-EU flag ships visiting EU ports. The SLC administrative fee and insurance premium will accumulate a ship recycling fund; see the EU Commission, 'Report From the Commission To the European Parliament and The Council on The Feasibility of a Financial Instrument' (The EU Commission, COM(2017) 420 final, Brussels, 8 August 2017).

[67] ECORYS-DNV-GL-Erasmus University of Rotterdam, Financial Instrument to Facilitate Safe and Sound Ship Recycling' (Research Report, The EU Commission Directorate-General for Environment, June 2016) 34. *(ECORYS-DNV-GL Study, 2016).*

[68] Ibid 34.

[69] Ibid.

[70] Ibid.

[71] The EU Commission, *Report From The Commission To The European Parliament And The Council on The Feasibility Of Financial Instrument That Would Facilitate Safe And Sound Ship Recycling*, COM (2017) 420 final, Brussels, 8 August 2017.

Ship Recycling Licence

A ship recycling licence is also a payback system, but it aims at resolving the problem of uneven financial burden caused by high-frequency and low-frequency entry of ships to EU ports. Unlike capital funds, which aim at creating capital funds by charging a ship for the number of entries into an EU port, the ship recycling licence is designed as an administrative matter[72] to charge shipowners depending on the type, size, and age of the ship.

The ship recycling licence has two parts: the first part covers the administrative cost of issuing the licence, and the second part is a premium that is levied from shipowners annually. The premium depends on the age, size, and type of ship. In the case of a ship recycling licence, a shipowner can also claim the price gap, and it is payable after showing proof of recycling at an EU listed facility. In the case where a shipowner fails to break ship in an EU listed shipbreaking yard, the EU can forfeit the capital amount. The forfeiture of capital is a procedure of an administrative nature and is subject to judicial review. The forfeited amount will pass to a general benefit fund in the area of the ship recycling fund.

The EU Commission backed the ship recycling licence, although the ship recycling licence is not beyond criticism. The Ecorys, the classification society, Det Norske Veritas (Dnv-GL),[73] and Erasmus University School of Law, who prepared the mechanism commissioned by the EU, argue that the mechanism sensitises shipowners to follow the *EU Ship Recycling Regulation*, who tend to circumvent the regulation by reflagging an EU ship to a non-EU flag, or, outside the jurisdiction of the EU, to which the EU law does not apply.

Therefore, the proposals on the desired financial mechanisms aim at bringing about a behavioural change in shipowners by paying them back what they lose by selling ships to the *EU Ship Recycling Regulation*-compliant shipbreaking yard.[74] The environmental groups and academics are also optimistic about the ship recycling licence. According to the NGO Shipbreaking Platform, the most active environmental group for safe shipbreaking, 'the time-based ship recycling licence affects all beneficial owners of a given ship by distributing the responsibilities and costs of sustainable ship recycling throughout the life cycle of the ship'.[75] Devaux and Nicolai argue that the ship recycling licence would strengthen the *EU Ship Recycling Regulation* by internalising the cost of shipbreaking.[76] The European Environmental Bureau has also backed the 2016 study, stating that:

---

[72] Ibid.

[73] Det Norske Veritas is the world's leading classification societies and a recognised advisor for the maritime industry. DNV, About Us (Web Page) https://www.dnv.com/about/index.html.

[74] ECORYS-DNV-GL Study, 2016 (n 68), 34.

[75] NGO Shipbreaking Platform, 2016 (n 56).

[76] Caroline Devaux and Jean-Philippe Nicolai, 'Designing an EU Ship Recycling Licence: A Roadmap' (July 2020) 117 *Marine Policy Journal* 103,826–7 https://doi.org/10.1016/j.marpol.2020.103826 .

> We call on the European Commission to follow-up this report with a legislative proposal. The effective implementation of European environmental policies has been dependent on making 'polluter pay'. If the EU is serious about its commitment to sustainable ship recycling, all shipowners trading in Europe need to be held financially liable.[77]

Despite receiving support from environmental groups and academics, the ship recycling licence did not convince the EU shipowners. The International Chamber of Shipping contends that the proposal is 'unenforceable and unlawful since the owners have to pay the money, which will be repayable to them after many years when the ownership of a ship may also be changed'.[78] The Asian Shipowners Association contends that the licence fee is without service. A charge without service is not acceptable under international law.[79] The International Chamber of Shipping and the European Community Shipowners' Association, representing 80 per cent of the world's commercial ships, rejected the proposal, arguing that this mechanism would undermine the global IMO efforts for safe disposal of end-of-life ships. This finding indicates that the mechanism slows the global process of improving working and environmental conditions in developing nations, where most ship recycling yards are located.[80]

The comments from shipowners have legal value with respect to the objectives of the *Hong Kong Convention* and the *EU Ship Recycling Regulation.* The primary objective of the *EU Ship Recycling Regulation* is to help promote quick ratification of the *Hong Kong Convention* by EU Members. However, the EU maintains a double standard with the financial mechanism. The accumulation of funds from a port levy and ship recycling licence incentivises the EU shipowners to send their ships only to the EU listed shipbreaking yards that have stricter requirements than the *Hong Kong Convention does.* One such requirement is that the *EU Ship Recycling Regulation* does not allow beaching, whereas beaching is allowed under the *Hong Kong Convention.*

Given that the beaching method is not allowed, the beaching yards who meet the *Hong Kong Convention* standard are not eligible to purchase EU ships. These yards may in fact lose one of the biggest ship recycling market shares from the EU owners. The international community can resolve the gap between the *Hong Kong Convention* and the *EU Ship Recycling Regulation* by forming a global regime aimed at imposing liability on the maritime industry and creating a scope for paying workers if they face deaths, injuries, or work-related diseases while breaking ships.

Globally, there is no such mechanism to regulate the transnational transfer of ships for breaking and to address its negative effects on their value chain (for shipbreaking).

---

[77] Cited in NGO Shipbreaking Platform, 'European Commission Report Recommends the Introduction of a Ship Recycling Licence' (Press Release, 6 July 2016). https://www.shipbreakingplatform.org/press-release-european-commission-report.

[78] The Maritime Executive, 'Shipowners Reject Proposal for Ship Recycling Licence', *The Maritime Executive* (online at 7 August 2016). https://www.maritime-executive.com/article/shipowners-reject-proposal-for-ship-recycling-license.

[79] Lee Lang Liang, 'Asian Shipowners' Rejects EU proposal on Paying Ship Recycling Licences' (online, July 2016). *Seatrade Maritime News.* https://www.seatrade-maritime.com/asia/asian-shipowners-association-rejects-eu-proposal-paying-ship-recycling-licenses.

[80] Ibid.

A mechanism to regulate the interstate transfer of ships for breaking would require shipowners to contribute from their business profit to a fund, leading to the provision of financial security for victims. In the context of oil spills, as discussed in Chap. 7, the liability mechanism in the form of insurance plays the same role.

The Ship Recycling Insurance

Like capital funds and ship recycling licences, ship recycling insurance refers to paying back the price gap between EU listed facilities and non-EU listed facilities in South Asia. Importantly, the Milieu study (2013) named this a 'ship recycling liability insurance', and the Profundo study published by the NGO Shipbreaking Platform in 2013 used 'ship recycling life insurance' in place of liability insurance.[81] Under these schemes, every ship is required to carry an insurance certificate issued by an accredited insurance company to enter into an EU port.

Regardless of the importance of insurance, the Profundo study showed concerns about its proposal of a ship recycling life insurance mechanism, mainly since insurance companies may not be interested in insuring old vessels that are prone to more accidents during shipbreaking.[82] To resolve this gap, the Milieu study (2013) argued for liability insurance rather than life insurance. Regarding the charge, both studies proposed a port levy similar to the capital funds discussed above and that every ship is required to carry an insurance certificate issued by an accredited insurance company.[83] To reclaim the contribution from the insurance, a shipowner must show evidence of sound recycling in an EU-approved recycling facility. Both the Milieu study (2013) and the Profundo study (2013) suggest that a private sector company could be the best option for determining the insurance premium.[84] The amount of the insurance premium depends on the future monetary difference between sound and unsound recycling. The threshold to forecast the difference would include the ship type, the timeframe, and the market conditions. In the case of ownership transfer of a ship, the new owner would open new insurance, and the insurance company would determine the premium.[85] However, the proposal for an insurance mechanism for ship recycling could not turn into a policy because of the lack of an insured object.[86] An

---

[81] Milieu, 'Financing the Environmentally Sound Recycling and Treatment Ships', (Research Report, 2013) 14; Profundo Study, 2013 (n 65) 24–25.

[82] Profundo Study, 2013 (n 65) 29.

[83] ECORYS-DNV-GL Study, 2016 (n 68) 34–38.

[84] Milieu Study, 2013 (n 62) 15; Profundo Study, 2013 (n 65) 29.

[85] Profundo Study, 2013 (n 65) 27–28.

[86] Importantly, to implement the insurance mechanism, the Milieu Study (2013) proposed to amend the existing EU Directive 2009/20/EC on the *Insurance of Shipowners for Maritime Claims* that relates to the insurance of shipowners for maritime claims introducing the requirement of liability insurance for the EU as a whole. Under the directive, any ship sailing the flag of EU or ships that are calling at an EU port are required to carry a certificate of insurance with them; ECORYS-DNV-GL Study, 2016 (n 68) 40.

insurable object is the basis of all insurance policies, which, if damaged or destroyed, would result in financial contributions from the policyholder. In that sense, the loss of price for selling a ship to an EU listed facility is not legally acceptable.

Lessons for Global Shipbreaking

Introducing a global mechanism for imposing financial liability on shipowners is a timely approach. It is the first important lesson learned from the three proposed financial mechanisms within the EU. However, success of insurance, as a financial mechanism, depends on having an insured object and unforeseen event. Hull and Machinery Insurance and Protection and Indemnity Liability Insurance are two of the general insurances that exist during the lifetime of a ship.[87] While the insurances have different names, they cover damage to property and the environment or loss of life.[88]

Following the same objectives, the financial accountability as intended under the proposed supplementary financial mechanisms aim at achieving transparency within the EU. In strict sense, the *EU Ship Recycling Regulation* has no provisions suggesting shipowners that they cannot sell ships to South Asian shipbreaking companies, but clearly it is purposefully designed to discourage shipowners to avoid selling ships to South Asian shipbreaking companies. But with the wide use of reflagging, the *EU Ship Recycling Regulation* has largely remained unsuccessful to achieve the goal of transparency. Perhaps, unsurprisingly, the *Hong Kong Convention* would face the same consequence. So that reflagging cannot be used to circumvent the *Hong Kong Convention*, a supplementary global financial mechanism is necessary. In addressing the liability of shipowners for human harm, the ship recycling licence is a reasonable instance. It includes the features to equally distribute liability for the expense of sound shipbreaking to all owners throughout the life cycle of a ship. However, as proposed under the ship recycling licence (for EU) only paying back the profit lost, to shipowners should not be the sole objective. Rather, focus of the mechanism should be on providing service to shipowners.

Providing compensation to workers in the shipbreaking industry may be a service to shipowners and under the global financial liability framework argued in Chap. 9,

---

[87] Hull and Machinery Insurance is an insurance to compensate physical damages of a ship happened in the event of a maritime peril or other covered perils: at Aligned Insurance, Hull and Machinery Insurance Explained. (Web Page), https://www.alignedinsurance.com/hull-and-machinery-insurance/ ; An insurance that covers all other risk and liability of a ship's owner is generally called Protection and Indemnity liability insurance. This may include coverage for damage of third-party risks during transit, oil spill, and subsequent environmental damage: at Insurance Business, 'What is Protection and Indemnity Insurance'. (Web Page) https://www.insurancebusinessmag.com/au/guides/what-is-protection-and-indemnity-insurance-164290.aspx.

[88] Raunek, 'Different Types of Marine Insurance and Marine Insurance Policies'. (Web Page, Marine Insight, 2 October 2019) https://www.marineinsight.com/maritime-law/different-types-of-marine-insurance-marine-insurance-policies/

there should not be any restriction on transferring ships. But ship transfer should be allowed subject to undertaking monetary responsibility. In that sense, the financial liability framework would not be different from the shipbreaking licence, but the financial responsibility under the framework would be to remedy any accidental injuries or deaths during a ship is broken. It means while the EU financial models are to compensate shipowners for their missed profit, the financial liability framework would be to provide adequate compensation to workers. This concept receives support from the financial liability mechanism established under the *International Convention on Civil Liability for Oil Pollution Damage,* 1992 discussed in Chap. 7. The Convention does not allow shipowners to transport oil from one country to another without maintaining appropriate insurance, which provides adequate compensation to both private and public victims of oil spills.[89]

EU Member States, however, have followed other approaches. For instance, the District Court of Rotterdam (Rotterdam District Court) enforced both the *Waste Shipment Regulation* and the *EU Ship Recycling Regulation* in finding shipowners to commit criminal offences by sending ships to South Asian shipbreaking facilities. The next part explains the approaches before and after the entry into force of the *EU Ship Recycling Regulation.* It argues that by imposing criminal liability the District Court of Rotterdam failed to investigate the issues of shipbreaking workers in the developing countries. Rather than imposing criminal liability it missed an opportunity to trigger the debate for an adequate international mechanism.

Imposition of Criminal Liability by the District Court of Rotterdam

As discussed earlier, the *Waste Shipment Regulation* could not stop sending ships to substandard shipbreaking yards because of the common reflagging practice. In this context, the *Seatrade and* Holland *Maas Scheepvart Beheer II BVs* are two exceptional and interesting cases. In deciding these cases, the District Court of Rotterdam imposed heavy criminal fines on two European shipping companies, Seatrade and Holland Maas Scheepvart Beheer II BV.[90] This section examines the cases in detail and identifies their limitations in not directing an inter-State liability framework.

---

[89] *International Convention on Civil Liability for Oil Pollution Damage,* opened for signature 29 November 1969, [1969] UNTS 319 (entered into force 19 June 1975) *(1969 Civil Liability Convention)*; the Convention was replaced by the *1992 Protocol to the International Convention on Civil Liability for Oil Pollution Damage,* opened for signature 27 November 1992, [1992] UKTS 86 (entered into force 30 May 1996) *(1992 Civil Liability Convention).*

[90] *State v Seatrade* [The District Court of Rotterdam, three-judge economic division for criminal cases], Public Prosecutor Office no. 10/994550–15 15 March 2018 reported in (2018) Rechtspraak.nl; *State v Holland Maas Scheepvart Beheer II BV* [Rotterdam District Court, three-judge economic division for criminal cases], Public Prosecutor Office 18 January 2019 reported in (2019) Rechtspraak.nl 1.

The Court in *Seatrade* relied on the *Waste Shipment Regulation* and imposed criminal fines on an EU shipping company, Seatrade, to hide its intention to dismantle ships in India and Bangladesh.[91] In *Holland Maas Scheepvart Beheer II BV*, the District Court of Rotterdam fined another EU shipping company, Holland Maas Scheepvart Beheer II BV, applying the *EU Ship Recycling Regulation.*[92]

Seatrade and Holland Maas Scheepvart Beheer II BV Cases

Facts of the Cases

In 2012, a Dutch shipping company, Seatrade, sent four old ships from the ports of Hamburg and Rotterdam with an intention to break in India and Bangladesh with full trading conditions, but the company did not disclose the intention of breaking the ships.[93] After Greenpeace, an international non-governmental organisation, published the news, the Office of the Public Prosecutor of Rotterdam conducted a thorough investigation to identify the real intention behind selling the four ships. As per Art 2 of the *Waste Shipment Regulation*, the transfer of any 'hazardous waste' from the ports of Europe to non-OECD countries is illegal and subject to adequate evidence to prove the intention of its final disposal. The Office of the Public Prosecutor filed the case to enforce the law, arguing that the Dutch Company, Seatrade, in fact, intended to send ships for final disposal as waste and breached art 2 of the *Waste Shipment Regulation.*

In the related *Holland Maas Scheepvaart II BV* case, the Office of the Public Prosecutor investigated the sale of a ship named HMS Lawrence to an Indian cash buyer company by a Dutch Company, Holland Maas Scheepvaart II BV, a subsidiary of an international shipping company, WEC Lines BV. The Netherlands is a member of the EU, and under art 14 of the *EU Ship Recycling Regulation*, an EU shipowner cannot export an EU ship beyond the EU border. Under art 22, Member States can introduce provisions for penalties for deterring an infringement of art 14 and take steps to ensure their application. The Office of the Dutch Public Prosecutor sought to enforce the law with a criminal fine or sanction on the grounds that it was a criminal offense to export a ship beyond the EU, and in this case, the company engaged the cash buyer with the same objective.

---

[91] Cash buyers are brokers who purchase ships from shipowners for a short period before selling the ships to a suitable shipbreaking facility. They work on behalf of the shipowners to identify a facility that can pay the shipowner the best price. Another advantage is the cash buyers, by becoming owners of ships, hide the identity of original owners of ships. This helps protects shipowners from being exposed: Alexandra Mikelis, 'Seatrade: A New Approach to Violations of Regulations on Ship Recycling in the European Union' *Norton Rose Fullbright* (Webpage, 2018) https://www.nortonrosefulbright.com/nl-nl/knowledge/publications/f686f825/seatrade-a-new-approach-to-violations-of-regulations-on-ship-recycling-in-the-european-union

[92] Ibid.

[93] Ibid.

Arguments of the Shipowners and Prosecutors in Both the Cases

The key claim in both cases was whether there was enough evidence to prove that the sale of the ships violated the laws. The prosecution argued in both cases that they had enough evidence to prove the intention of the shipowners to send ships beyond the EU border. In *Seatrade*, however, the accused Seatrade argued that the ships continued their commercial operation until the last moment, which suggests that the owner did not intend to declare the ships as waste and that it would be illegal to consider the ships as waste.[94] However, with respect to the email communications and examination of crewmembers, the prosecution proved that there were instructions from Seatrade that ships must not contain much fuel and oils on board at their final destination.[95] Eventually, the primary criminal ruling was set aside by the Court of Appeal in the Hauge in 2020, as the case was settled between the Dutch Public Prosecution Service and shipowners paying EUR 30,00,000.[96]

In contrast, in *Holland Maas Scheepvart Beheer II BV*, the company Holland Maas Scheepvart Beheer II BV admitted the intention to send the ship to India but disputed the jurisdiction of the Netherlands court, stating that the ship left Netherlands waters in 2013 when the *EU Ship Recycling Regulation* was not in force. The company lawyers also argued that the ship started its last journey to India from Italy rather than the Netherlands. However, the argument could not succeed since, even though the *EU Ship Recycling Regulation* had not come into force, as an EU Member State court, the District Court of Rotterdam had the power to enforce the EU laws as per art 22 of the *EU Ship Recycling Regulation*, which provides that.

> Member States shall lay down provisions on penalties applicable to infringements of this Regulation and shall take all the measures necessary to ensure that they are applied.

The Court used this power in deciding the case.

Decisions to Pay Criminal Fines and Disqualify Directors

Seatrade

The Court accepted the evidence produced by the prosecutor and ruled that there were enough reasons to define the operational ships as wastes with respect to the *Waste Shipment Regulation*, which considers any material or substance to be wastes subject to a proof of its holder's intention of disposal and ordered payment of a heavy fine of EUR 750,000. The Court also stated that sending ships to India and Bangladesh as wastes was a serious criminal offence that warranted imprisonment

---

[94] Ibid.

[95] Ibid.

[96] NGO Shipbreaking Platform, 'Seatrade Reaches Settlement with Dutch Public Prosecution Service' (Press Release online at 30 April 2024) https://shipbreakingplatform.org/seatrade-reaches-settlement/ .

of the directors; however, considering that it was an offense committed for the first time, the Court waived the prison sentence and alternatively imposed a 12-month suspension of their directorship position in any company.[97]

Holland Maas Scheepvart Beheer II BV

In *Holland Maas Scheepvart Beheer II BV*, the Court also found the shipowner, Holland Maas Scheepvart Beheer II BV, guilty, and ordered it to pay a heavy criminal fine. The Court accepted the evidence provided by the public prosecutor of the Netherlands and found that the ship that finally reached Alang, India, was sold in 2013. An Indian shipbreaking yard broke the ship under conditions that caused serious damage to the environment and the health of workers and exposed the local population to grave danger.[98]

The Court ordered the company to pay a heavy fine of 780,000 EUR. The company subsequently paid a settlement of 2.2 million EUR. Altogether, the company had to pay almost three million EUR—roughly the price obtained from selling the ship. The Court accepted the settlement since the company made a commitment to avoid scrapping vessels on beaches located in South Asia in the future.

Lessons Learned for Undertaking Responsibility by Shipowners

While each of the two cases is important in furthering the discussion on liability of shipowners, the Court did not impose any liability for the negative consequences of shipbreaking either directly or indirectly. The liability imposed by the Court mainly for the decision to break ships in South Asia. Differently, it can be argued that the Courts only found the act of selling ships illegal instead of what happens to workers for breaking theses toxic ships. By not digging deep into the issue of shipbreaking's human rights consequences, the Courts wasted valuable opportunities to instigate a worldwide debate on civil liability of shipowners and encourage the improvement of standards in South Asia (see Chap. 9).

Nevertheless, one of the significant effects of both *Seatrade* and *Holland Maas Scheepvart Beheer II BV* is the naming and shaming against EU shipping companies. The decisions also reveal that in the absence of an international legal liability system for holding beneficial owners accountable, resorting to criminal liability is what appears to be a crucial legal step against the actual owners. *Seatrade* is important because the Court went behind the veil of reflagging and refused reflagging to allow

[97] Ince Maritime, 'The Seatrade Verdict: Has Scrapping Just Got a Lot More Onerous' (online at 2 October 2018). https://www.incegd.com/en/news-insights/seatrade-verdict-has-scrapping-just-got-lot-more-onerous-0.

[98] NGO Shipbreaking Platform, Press Release (n 97).

them to isolate the Seatrade from responsibility for selling four ships (to Bangladesh and the Indian shipbreaking industry). The company owning the ship intended to break the ships in Bangladesh and India, which led the company to be involved directly in the transboundary sale guided the Court to reach the conclusion. The decision, therefore, means that shipowners must exercise greater care when selling ships to the developing nations. And shipowner's decision-making process may lead to criminal liability with further scrutiny. Arguably, that the Court's approach in *Seatrade* will reduce the practice of reflagging as EU shipowners cannot elude liability under the *Waste Shipment Regulation* simply by reflagging.[99] The *Waste Shipment Regulation* would still apply to any transboundary movement of ships intended for breaking, unless a ship is subject to the *EU Ship Recycling Regulation.* For example, although a ship is not being deemed an EU ship in the case of its non-EU ownership following the *EU Ship Recycling Regulation*, the *Waste Shipment Regulation* may still apply if it can be shown that it had a previous EU owner or that shipping company owning this ship was initially formed within the EU.[100]

Imposing criminal liability on shipowners is not beyond question. Shipowners can be criminally liable only if they are caught red-handed. As an example, in *Seatrade*, prosecution's intervention only followed the investigative news published by Greenpeace about the concealment of Seatrade Limited's plan to break the ships in India. It demonstrates that unless Greenpeace's news was in public, the prosecution would not proceed in filling and prosecuting Seatrade Limited. In simple words, Seatrade Limited would get away with it if international environmental groups Greenpeace or media do not audit them. Between 2019 and 2020, several ships did not have to face such a criminal sanction for sending ships to South Asian after reflagging demonstrates this.[101] Second, the decisions do not ultimately establish a powerful tool that would make all ships from the EU accountable. Juan Ignacio and others opine that criminal sanctions will be incapable of recognising the inter-State liability of shipowners to enforce the *EU Ship Recycling Regulation.* Third, *Seatrade* and *Holland Maas* cases did not specifically address restitution for victims to be a priority for the EU.[102] In such cases, the Court fines are paid to State treasuries, whereas workers, the ultimate sufferers for breaking toxic ships receive nothing.

It is not clear what good the decisions do. In addition to ensuing any potential compensation for workers is paltry, both *Seatrade* and *Holland Maas* have couple of beneficial outcomes. These decisions not only provide a limelight effect, that is, in bringing the liability of shipowners to light, but they also introduce a leverage

[99] Mikelis (n 93).

[100] Ibid.

[101] Michael Schular, 'NGO Shipbreaking Platform Counts 142 Ships Sent to South Asian Beaches in First Three Months of 2019', *gCaptain* (Online at 10 April 2019). https://gcaptain.com/shipbreaking-platform-report-first-quarter-2019/

[102] Wictoria Wennberg, 'Responsible Ship Recycling and Corporate Responsibility: Regulatory Aspects and Legal Challenges' (Master Thesis Lund University) 36–37.

effect, inspiring the bargaining position of victims.[103] The decisions also provide a clear message to those owners who have not viewed the debate on accountability for harm caused to workers from shipbreaking seriously.[104] Nonetheless, doubts about its efficacy under the *EU Ship Recycling Regulation* endure too, since the *EU Ship Recycling Regulation* mandates a more stringent approach than the *Hong Kong Convention* upon which it is mostly based.[105] Because, the current disposition is that the *EU Ship Recycling Regulation* aims to prohibit existing shipbreaking practices without imposing restrictions on reflagging practices, success may not be forthcoming.[106]

Lesssons Learned From the EU Approaches and Stimulating the Debate on IMO Leadership in Shipbreaking

Shipbreaking is integral to the marine business: consequently, suggesting an alternative to reflagging does not legally exist. Rather than abolishing the practice of reflagging, a global framework to deal with the responsibility of shipowners is more reasonable. Chapter 9 provides a discussion on the potential features of a global liability regime and insurance on the shipbreaking sector. Indeed, as explored in Chap. 2, if the point of any international shipbreaking mechanism is to anchor shipowner accountability from a global regulatory justice perspective (if not accountability schemes), then it would well behove the IMO to assume stewardship and propose an international shipbreaking mechanism with goals corresponding those delineated in this book. IMO's leadership is important since shipbreaking is an issue of global market that consists of a highly complex global structure jointly with key parties involved in the global maritime industry.[107]

Moreover, IMO's role is to include IMO more in the global governance of shipbreaking. The increased role of the IMO would objectively help to address the shortage of effective governance and legal action in developing countries. There should be a civil liability framework in addition to the *Hong Kong Convention* because the *Hong Kong Convention* to address the problems. One lesson learned from EU proposals is that if there were to be some sort of liability mechanism it

[103] Surya Deva, *Regulating Corporate Human Rights Violations: Harmonising Business* (Routledge, 2012) 6–7, citing August Reinisch, 'The Changing International Framework for Dealing with Nonstate Actors' in Philip Aston (ed), *Non-State Actors and Human Rights* (Oxford University Press 2005) 74.

[104] The Maritime Executive (n 79).

[105] Editorial Team in Ship Recycling, 'Hong Kong Convention vs EU Ship Recycling Regulation: Where We Stand', *Safety4Sea* (online at 2 November 2022) https://safety4sea.com/cm-hong-kong-convention-vs-eu-ship-recycling-regulation-where-we-stand/ .

[106] Ibid.

[107] Zhang Wan et al., 'Ship Scrappage Records Reveal Disturbing Environmental Injustice' (2021) 130 (1) *Marine Policy* 104,542 https://doi.org/10.1016/j.marpol.2021.104542 .

should have some kind of financial guarantees or insurance around financed by the maritime and shipbreaking industry.

Importantly, the Ship Recycling Insurance model that is being proposed in the EU is not useful as it lacks an insured object. The EU Ship Recycling Licence is equally unsatisfactory as it fails to consider what service the shipowner would receive for their money. However, by grouping the different features in one legal framework, licence, and insurance, the IMO is able to fill these gaps. Workers involved in deaths, injuries, or worker related diseases would be compensated by means of licence and insurance for the shipbreaking industry. In other words, insurance can insure the risk an economic loss of workers (insured object), while the licence can serve shipowners by tracking the change in ownership throughout the life cycle of a ship. More lessons from Chap. 7 are drawn in Chap. 9, where the nature and functional system of the mechanism under genetic filter is also sketched.

There is also a need for political backing and support from the IMO Member States in order to move forward with a new global mechanism to introduce financial liability. As historically the IMO does not have the political will or bona fide interests to lead a global turnaround unless its Member States had positively demonstrated strong political will behind a policy reform, evidence that there is a global support is needed to succeed with any legal reform under the IMO. This kind of Member States support is also relevant to shipbreaking.

As the EU is a strong proponent of a financial-based mechanism, the EU Member States can build in even more strongly to this ground of supporting such a global mechanism within the IMO. Buthe and Mattli point to two reasons for the importance of such an EU role.[108] Wherein, the first point states an inter-State policy and then it falls in line with global preferences. Further, a unified stance of the EU members can put an automatic burden on non-State actors to assume responsibility for compensatory harm.[109] The EU is already leading the way having advocated global regulation for some time now. For instance, the EU Commission clearly was instrumental in the adoption of the *Kiev Protocol* introduced in 2003, which holds mining industry owners liable for damages caused by pollution of transboundary watercourses (see Chap. 8) and is a good illustration of how legal reform would be moved forward.[110]

---

[108] Tim Buthe and Walter Mattli, *The New Global Rules: The Privatisation of Regulation in the World Economy* (Princeton University Press, 2011) 10.

[109] AL Newman and E Posner, 'Putting in the EU in its Place: Policy Strategies and the Global Regulatory Context' in *the European Union as a Global Regulator?* (Routledge, 2017) 96–115.

[110] *The Protocol on Civil Liability and Compensation for Damage Caused by the Transboundary Effects of Industrial Accidents on Transboundary Waters to the 1992 Convention on the Protection and Use of Transboundary Watercourses and Use of Transboundary Watercourses and International Lakes and to the 1992 Convention on the Transboundary Effects of Industrial Accidents,* opened for signature 21 May 2003, UN Doc. ECE/MP.WAT/11-ECE/CP.TEIA/9 (not yet in force). *(Kiev Protocol).*

Conclusion

It is uncertain whether the *Hong Kong Convention* promoting maritime industry's business interest will be successful to limit human and environmental harms from breaking ships. This leads to the question of imposing liability on shipowners under a mechanism that includes financial liability in the form of a certificate together with insurance. The shipowner's liability is to compensate the most vulnerable stakeholders involved in the business transactions adequately. By promoting innovative and strict policies (a financial liability framework), the EU can play a positive role as a global leader in the protection of the marine environment. The EU does this by making their own law, which promotes global reforms.[111] The proposed EU financial mechanisms have already stimulated the debate over a liability framework based on financial liability that can lead to global reforms for the shipbreaking industry.

Taking the financial mechanisms proposed for the EU into consideration, the next chapter addresses the research question: What can the shipbreaking industry learn from reform measures in other industries where catastrophic events, worker deaths, injuries and illnesses from unsafe working environments have brought about regulatory changes? To assist in addressing regulatory reforms, the next chapter presents a detailed analysis of liability frameworks adopted in three industries: oil transport, transboundary movement of ships, and offshore oil industries.

Bibliography

Articles/Books/Reports

Alcadia, Juan Ignacio, Francisco Piniella and Emilio Rodriguez-Diaz, '"The Mirror Flags": Ship Registration in Globalised Ship Breaking Industry' (2016) 48 *Transportation Research Part D* 378

Alcaide, Juan Ignacio, Emile Rodriguez-Diaz and Francisco Piniella, 'European Policies on Ship Recycling: A Stakeholder Survey' (2017) 81 *Marine Policy*, 262

Devaux, Caroline and Jean-Philippe Nicolai, 'Designing A EU Ship Recycling Licence: A Roadmap' (2020) 117 *Marine Policy Journal*, 7

Hejj, Christian, Govert E. Bijwaard and Sabine Knapp, 'Ship Inspection Strategies: Effect on Maritime Safety and Environmental Protection' (2011) 16 *Transportation Research Part D* 42

Kissack, R, 'The performance of the European Union in the international Labour Organisation' (2015) 33(6) *Journal of European Integration* 651

Young, Alasdair R., 'The European Union as a Global Regulator? Context and Comparison' (2015) 22(9) *Journal of European Public Policy* 1233

Buthe, Tim and Walter Mattli, *The New Global Rules: The Privatisation of Regulation in the World Economy* (Princeton University Press, 2011)

Galley, Michael, *Shipbreaking: Hazards and Liabilities* (Springer International Publishing, 2014)

Mikelis, Nikos, *The Recycling of Ships* (Global Maritime Services (GMS) Leadership, 2nd ed, 1 October 2019)

---

[111] Ibid.

Puthurcherril, Tony George, *From Shipbreaking to Sustainable Ship Recycling: Evolution of a Legal Regime* (Matinus Nijhoff Publishers, 2010)
Deva, Surya, *Regulating Corporate Human Rights Violations: Harmonising Business* (Routledge, 2012) 6–7, citing August Reinisch, 'The Changing International Framework for Dealing with Nonstate Actors' in Philip Aston (ed), *Non-State Actors and Human Rights* (Oxford University Press 2005) 74
Tedenhag, Kristoffer, 'Insurance Aspects of Wrecks and Recycling of Ships from an Environmental Sustainability Perspective' (Master's Thesis, Lund University, 2013)
ECORYS-DNV-GL-Erasmus University of Rotterdam, Financial Instrument to Facilitate Safe and Sound Ship Recycling' (Research Report, The EU Commission Directorate-General for Environment, June 2016)
Committee Draft Report on the proposal for a regulation of the European Parliament and of the Council on ship recycling, 2012/0055 (COD), (Nov. 12, 2012)
COWI and Milieu Environmental Law And Policy, 'Study in Relation to Options For New Initiatives Regarding Dismantling of Ships' (Research Report, The EU Director General of the Department of Environment, August 2009). https://ec.europa.eu/environment/pdf/waste/ships/fund_note.pdf
Denmark, 'Proposal for an Enforceable Legally Binding System for the Recycling of Ships', Submission to the IMO Maritime Environment and Protection Committee (IMO MEPC 53/3/7)
ECORYS Research and Consulting, 'The Ship Recycling Fund: Financing Environmentally Sound Scrapping and Recycling of Sea-going Ships' (Research Report, Greenpeace, 1 February 2005). https://shipbreaking.wordifysites.com/wp-content/uploads/2019/01/ECORYS-survey-on-a-ship-recycling-fund.pdf
EU Commission, 'Report From the Commission To the European Parliament and The Council on The Feasibility of a Financial Instrument' (The EU Commission, COM(2017) 420 final, Brussels, 8 August 2017)
European Commission, Proposal for a Regulation of the European Parliament and of the Council on Ship Recycling, Executive Summary of Impact Assessment accompanying the Document, Brussels, 23.03.12, SWD (2012) 45 final, COM 2012 118 final
Milieu Environmental Law and Policy, 'Financing the Environmentally Sound Recycling and Treatment of Ships' (Research Report, Impact Assessment Unit, Directorate for Impact Assessment, The EU Parliament, 2013)
Milieu, 'Financing the Environmentally Sound Recycling and Treatment Ships', (Research Report, 2013) 14; Profundo Study, 2013
Pastorelli, Silvia, 'EU Ship Recycling Regulation: What's in it for South Asia' (Research Paper, European Institute for Asian Studies, August 2014) https://www.eias.org/wp-content/uploads/2016/02/EU-Asia-at-a-glance-Pastorelli-EU-Ship-Recycling.pdf
Profundo Economic Research, 'Financial Mechanisms To Ensure Responsible Ship Recycling' (Research Paper, NGO shipbreaking Platform, 22 January 2013) https://shipbreakingplatform.org/wp-content/uploads/2018/11/Financial-mechanisms-for-resonsible-ship-recycling-22_01_2013-FINAL.pdf
Sarraf et al, Maria, 'Ship Breaking and Recycling Industry in Bangladesh and Pakistan,' (Report No. 58275-SAS, World Bank, 2010)
Veritas, Det Norske, 'Technological and Economical Feasibility of Ship Scrapping in Europe' (Research Report N, 'Technological and Economical Feasibility of Ship Scrapping in Europe' (Research Report No. 2000–3527, 2001)

Cases

State v Holland Maas Scheepvart Beheer II BV [Rotterdam District Court, three-judge economic division for criminal cases], Public Prosecutor Office 18 January 2019 reported in (2019) Rechtspraak.nl 1

State v Seatrade [Rotterdam District Court, three-judge economic division for criminal cases], Public Prosecutor Office 10/994550–15, 15 March 2018 reported in (2018) Rechtspraak.nl 1, ECLI:NL:RBROT:2018:2108 https://www.rechtspraak.nl/Organisatie-en-contact/Organisatie/Rechtbanken/Rechtbank-Rotterdam/Nieuws/Documents/English%20translation%20Seatrade.pdf

State v Seatrade [The District Court of Rotterdam, three-judge economic division for criminal cases], Public Prosecutor Office no. 10/994550–15 15 March 2018 reported in (2018) Rechtspraak.nl

Stitching Greenpeace Nederland v The Minister of Housing, Spatial Planning and The Environment (Council of State, Case No. 2200606331/1, 21 February 2007

The Clemenceau Case (2005) (Council of State, Case Number 288801, 15 February 2006)

The Sandrien Case (Council of State, Case Number 200105168/2, 19 June 2002)

Treaties

1992 Protocol to the International Convention on Civil Liability for Oil Pollution Damage, opened for signature 27 November 1992, [1992] UKTS 86 (entered into force 30 May 1996) *(1992 Civil Liability Convention)*

Decision No 2023/1562 of the EU Commission Implementing Amending Implementing Decision (EU) 2023/1562 establishing the European List of Ship Recycling Facilities, EU 1257/2013 OJL 190(28 July 2023)

International Convention on Civil Liability for Oil Pollution Damage, opened for signature 29 November 1969, [1969] UNTS 319 (entered into force 19 June 1975)

Regulation (EC) No 1013/2006 of the European Parliament and of the Council of 14 June 2006 on Shipments of Waste OJ (L 190) 1

Regulation (EU) No. 1257/2013 of the European Parliament and of the Council of 20 November 2013 on Ship Recycling and Amending Regulation (EC) No. 1013/2016 and Directive 2009/16/EC, 2013, OJ (L 330) 1

The International Convention for the Safe and Environmentally Sound Recycling of Ships, opened for signature September 2009, IMO Doc. SR/CONF/45 (19 May 2009) (not yet in force)

The Protocol on Civil Liability and Compensation for Damage Caused by the Transboundary Effects of Industrial Accidents on Transboundary Waters to the 1992 Convention on the Protection and Use of Transboundary Watercourses and Use of Transboundary Watercourses and International Lakes and to the 1992 Convention on the Transboundary Effects of Industrial Accidents, opened for signature 21 May 2003, UN Doc. ECE/MP.WAT/11-ECE/CP.TEIA/9 (not yet in force)

Others

Aligned Insurance, Hull and Machinery Insurance Explained. (Web Page), https://www.alignedinsurance.com/hull-and-machinery-insurance/

Azoulay, David and Nathaniel Eisen, 'Legality of the EU Commission Proposal on Ship Recycling' (Research Report No 1101, Centre of International Environmental Law, December 2012) 3 https://www.shipbreakingplatform.org/wp-content/uploads/2020/09/CIEL-Legality-EU-Proposals-on-Ship-Recycling-2020.pdf

Blanco, Soledad, 'Recycling for EU Flag Ship Owners' (YouTube, 16 March 2012, 3.02–3.10). http://www.youtube.com/watch?v=nxk_c0Abhos

Bois, Robin Des, 'The Mystery of the Nameless Boat, Shipbreaking' (Bulletin of Information and Analysis on Ship Demolition No 55 from 1 January 2019 to 11 June 2019). http://www.robindesbois.org/wp-content/uploads/shipbreaking55.pdf

Class NK, 'Introduction About ClassNK' (Webpage) https://www.classnk.or.jp/hp/en/about/aboutNK/

DNV, About Us (Web Page) https://www.dnv.com/about/index.html

DNV-GL, 'The EU Ship Recycling Regulation-Coming into General Application on 31 December 2018' (Web Page, 20 December 2018) https://www.dnvgl.com/news/the-eu-ship-recycling-regulation-coming-into-general-application-on-31-december-2018-135690

Human Rights Watch, *Bangladesh: Ship Explosion Exposes Regulatory Failures- Deadly Accident in a Yard with Hong Kong Convention Certification* (Webpage, 17 September 2024) https://www.hrw.org/news/2024/09/18/bangladesh-ship-explosion-exposes-regulatory-failures

Ince Maritime, 'The Seatrade Verdict: Has Scrapping Just Got A Lot More Onerous' (online at 2 October 2018). https://www.incegd.com/en/news-insights/seatrade-verdict-has-scrapping-just-got-lot-more-onerous-0

Insurance Business, 'What is Protection and Indemnity Insurance' (Web Page) https://www.insurancebusinessmag.com/au/guides/what-is-protection-and-indemnity-insurance-164290.aspx

Liang, Lee Lang, 'Asian Shipowners' Rejects EU proposal on Paying Ship Recycling Licences' (online, July 2016). *Seatrade Maritime News*. https://www.seatrade-maritime.com/asia/asian-shipowners-association-rejects-eu-proposal-paying-ship-recycling-licenses

Lloyds Register Verified Ship Recycling Facilities (WebPage) https://www.lr.org/en/lloyds-register-verified-ship-recycling-facilities/

News Agencies, 'European Companies Dumping Toxic Ships on Bangladesh beaches' *ALJAZEERA* (online, 27 Sep 2023) https://www.aljazeera.com/news/2023/9/28/european-companies-dumping-toxic-ships-on-bangladesh-beaches-hrw-says

NGO Shipbreaking Platform, 'Another Dutch Ship Owner Faces Enormous Fine for Having Beached a Vessel' (Press Release, 20 January 2019). https://shipbreakingplatform.org/press-release-dutch-ship-owner-holland-maas-fined/

NGO Shipbreaking Platform, 'European Commission Report Recommends the Introduction of a Ship Recycling Licence' (Press Release, 6 July 2016). https://www.shipbreakingplatform.org/press-release-european-commission-report-

NGO Shipbreaking Platform, 'Make the Polluter Pay: Why we need the EU Ship Recycling Licence' (Position Paper, October 2016). https://www.shipbreakingplatform.org/resources/library/

NGO Shipbreaking Platform, 'Seatrade Convicted For Trafficking Toxic' (Press Release, 15 March 2018). shipshttps://www.shipbreakingplatform.or/press-release-seatrade-convicted

NGO Shipbreaking Platform, HKC Statement of Compliance (webpage), https://shipbreakingplatform.org/issues-of-interest/the-law/hkc-soc/

Raunek, 'Different Types of Marine Insurance and Marine Insurance Policies'. (Web Page, Marine Insight, 2 October 2019) https://www.marineinsight.com/maritime-law/different-types-of-marine-insurance-marine-insurance-policies/

RINA, Marine (Web Page) https://www.rina.org/en/business/marine

Rose, Norton, 'Seatrade: A New Approach to Violations of Regulations on Ship Recycling in the European Union?' (Web Page, May 2018)

https://www.nortonrosefulbright.com/en/knowledge/publications/f686f825/seatrade-a-new-approach-to-violations-of-regulations-on-ship-recycling-in-the-european-union

Schular, Michael, 'NGO Shipbreaking Platform Counts 142 Ships Sent to South Asian Beaches in First Three Months of 2019', *gCaptain* (Online at 10 April 2019). https://gcaptain.com/shipbreaking-platform-report-first-quarter-2019/

Schular, Michael, 'NGO shipbreaking Platform Slams Shipping Industry Scaremongering to Undermine European Ship Recycling Regulation', *gCaptain* (online at 6 June 2018) https://gcaptain.com/ngo-shipbreaking-platform-slams-shipping-industry-scaremongering-to-undermine-european-ship-recycling-regulation/

The European List of Ship Recycling Facilities Pursuant to Regulation (EU) No. 1257/2013 OJL 190 (28 July 2023) https://eur-lex.europa.eu/legal-content/EN/TXT/?uri=uriserv%3AOJ.L_.2023.190.01.0013.01.ENG

The Maritime Executive, 'Another Dutch Shipowner Fined for Beaching a Vessel' (online at 21 January 2019). https://www.maritime-executive.com/article/another-dutch-shipowner-fined-for-beaching-a-vessel

The Maritime Executive, 'Shipowners Reject Proposal for Ship Recycling Licence', *The Maritime Executive* (online at 7 August 2016). https://www.maritime-executive.com/article/shipowners-reject-proposal-for-ship-recycling-license

World Maritime News, 'PHP Shipbreaking and Recycling Industries Wins HKC Compliance Statement', *World Maritime News* (online at 16 January 2020). https://www.offshore-energy.biz/php-ship-breaking-and-recycling-industries-wins-hkc-compliance-statement/

Chapter 7
Lessons Learned from the Case Studies of Global Oil, Shipping, and Oil Rig Industries

Abstract This chapter explores necessary legal reforms in the shipbreaking industry. Following three case studies, it examines post-incident regulatory changes that aimed at improving business practices and minimising harm. The examination focuses on three key regulatory reforms relevant to the shipbreaking industry. First, the chapter evaluates regulatory changes following major oil spill events and the effectiveness of industry-specific civil liability mechanisms globally. Second, it proposes an insurance-led enforcement mechanism, inspired by oil rig incidents, to reform the shipbreaking industry. Third, it analyses a ship-specific certificate system introduced after a catastrophic event in the UK maritime industry and evaluates the importance of such a system for the shipbreaking industry.

Keywords Oil spill · Legal reform · Regulatory changes · International Maritime Organisation · Protocol · Treaty · Accident · Liability and compensation system · Exclusion of liability · Compulsory insurance

Introduction

This chapter assesses the legal reforms necessary for shipbreaking sector. Drawing on three case studies, it evaluates post-incident regulatory changes, particularly those that have introduced compensation mechanisms, as well as other reforms aimed at enhancing industry practices and reducing harm to individuals.[1] The analysis in this chapter reviews three specific regulatory changes and identifies lessons learnt relevant to the proposed shipbreaking liability certificate (SLC), which is discussed as a potential international civil liability framework in the book.

The chapter is divided into four parts. Section "Case Studies on the International Oil Spill Legal Regime" reviews a series of major oil spill disasters, namely, the Torrey Canyon in 1967; Amoco Cadiz in 1978; Erika in 1999 and Prestige in 2002. It

[1] However, although the regulatory mechanisms do not focus on the problems with business practices within the industries, the approaches have an indirect impact to resolve the problems within the business practices.

M. Z. Ali, *Worker Injustices in the South Asian Shipbreaking Industry*, International Law in Asia, https://doi.org/10.1007/978-981-95-8325-6_7

focuses on the subsequent legal responses regarding civil liability and compensation and examines the elements that have contributed to the success of these mechanisms within the global maritime industry.

Section "Piper Alpha Incident: Insurance-Led Enforcement Mechanism" investigates the Piper Alpha, a significant oilrig accident that led to the adoption of the principle 'high risk results in high insurance premium,' aimed at reinforcing existing safety measures in the UK's oil and gas exploration sector. This part maintains that such an insurance-based enforcement system is suitable for shipbreaking in South Asia, particularly as national and international regulations in this context are insufficient to compel shipowners to compensate human harms in the shipbreaking sector.

Section "Plimsoll Line Incident and Importance of a Load Lines Certificate" examines the Plimsoll Line case from 1871, which was instrumental in establishing a mandatory Load Linces Certificate under the *International Convention for the Safe and Environmentally Sound Disposal of Ships* (*Hong Kong Convention*).[2] Both this part and Chap. 9 of the book advocate for the introduction of a similar certification process specific to shipbreaking industry. Section "Conclusion" concludes this chapter by recommending that the shipbreaking regulatory framework should adopt a civil liability model, drawing insights from the approaches to civil liability and compensation discussed in this chapter. Table 7.1 summarises the major approaches of the mechanisms discussed in the chapter.

Case Studies on the International Oil Spill Legal Regime

The regime governing oil spills is a complex web of laws and, therefore, the next section "Evolution of the Regime" explains the regime briefly before discussing the mechanism in section "Oil Spill Liability and Compensation System".

Evolution of the Regime

Oil spill incidents led to substantial legal developments (civil liability regime) with respect to compensation payment to victim States and private entities between 1967 and 2005. The legal developments followed a recognition within the maritime and oil industry that oil spill accidents are unavoidable as long as oil is transported by sea.[3] Both oil and shipping industries supported the legal changes acknowledging the

---

[2] *The International Convention for the Safe and Environmentally Sound Disposal of Ships*, opened for signature 1 September 2009, IMO Doc. SR/CONF/45 (19 May 2009) (not yet in force) (*The Hong Kong Convention*).

[3] Petrissa Eckle, Peter Burgherr, and Edouard Michaux, 'Risk of Large Oil Spills: A Statistical Analysis in the Aftermath of Deepwater Horizon' (2012) 46 (23) *Environmental Science and Technology* 13,002–13,008.

Table 7.1 The measures used in other global industries

Case studies	Principles	Approach details	Measures	Region/Country	Discussion
Torrey Canyon, Amoco Cadiz, Prestige and Eika Oil Spill	The International Oil Spill Regime	Shipowners and Oil industries pay compensation to victims	Oil Spill Insurance	International	section "Case Studies on the International Oil Spill Legal Regime"
Piper Alpha	The UK Offshore Act	As Low as Reasonably Practicable Practices	Goal Setting of protective measures	The UK	section "Piper Alpha Incident: Insurance-Led Enforcement Mechanism"
Plimsoll Line Incident	The International Load Lines Convention	International Load Lines Certificate	Restriction to overload a ship	International	section "Plimsoll Line Incident and Importance of a Load Lines Certificate"

fact that with ongoing maritime oil transfers, such incidents cannot be entirely eradicated.[4] But the case is different in shipbreaking sector. While shipbreaking sector is connected to maritime industry (as the end of life) and oil industry (for carrying oil during a ship's operational life), this sector has yet to consider civil liability regime for shipowners and shipbreaking industries within which compensation can be paid to victims of shipbreaking. Therefore, learning lessons for global shipbreaking sector, the paragraphs below highlight the legal developments in relation to oil spill incidents, which occurred in three stages.

The preliminary phase began with the Torrey Canyon incident in 1967, which resulted in regulatory reform whereby the shipping industry assumed corporate responsibility for oil spills. All started when the Liberian-flagged super tanker Torrey Canyon ran aground near the British coast carrying 120,000 tons of crude oil. The resulting spill contaminated vast transboundary coastal areas in both the UK and France. This raised issues about the principle and procedure for these nations to seek compensation from shipping companies whose ships caused the significant oil spillage.[5] The legal frameworks existed during the time offered little support to claim compensation for the environment pollution, exposing complexities in maritime business structure. The involvement of multiple private parties further complicated the determination of appropriate jurisdiction or laws applicable to the affected governments' claims.[6]

In response to this legal uncertainty, both the shipping and oil industries assumed responsibility through two voluntary accords, which later formed the basis for two very successful international conventions.[7] Initially, shipping industries introduced a voluntary scheme, namely, the '*Tanker Owners Voluntary Agreement Concerning Liability for Oil Pollution*,' setting a standard for compensation.[8] The IMO (formerly known as the Intergovernmental Maritime Consultative Organisation (IMCO))[9]

---

[4] Alan Boyle, 'International Law and Liability for Catastrophic Environmental Damage' (2011) 105 *Proceedings of the American Society of International Law* 423–427.

[5] Pham Van Tan, 'Compulsory Civil Liability Insurance, Financial Security: An Integral Component Compensation for Ship-Source Oil Pollution Damage (2021) 33 (2) *International Journal of Maritime History* 435–441.

[6] The super tanker *Torrey Canyon* flying the flag of Liberia ran aground near the coast of Great Britain containing 120,000 tons of crude oil in 1967. In case of *Torrey Canyon*, the ship was owned by a Bermudan corporation called Barracuda that in fact was a subsidiary company of the Union Oil Company of California and before the final journey the ship was chartered to British Petroleum, a UK oil company: at Colin De La Rue, Charles Anderson, and Jonahan Hare, *Shipping and the Environment: Law and Practice* (Informa Law from Routledge, 2022).

[7] Pauline Marchand, 'The International Law Regarding Ship-Source Pollution Liability and Compensation: Evolution and Current Challenges' (2017) 1 *International Oil Spill Conference Proceedings* 193–210.

[8] *Tanker Owners Voluntary Agreement Concerning Liability for Oil Pollution* (signed 7 January 1969) [1969] ILM 8(3) (entered into force 6 October 1969).

[9] It is a special arm of the United Nations (UN). In 1948, the UN Member States adopted the *Convention on the Inter-Governmental Maritime Consultative Organisation* (IMCO) that entered into force in 1958. Primarily known as the Inter-Governmental Maritime Consultative Organisation (IMCO), was changed to IMO in 1982. Its main objective is to provide mechanisms for inter-State

adopted the *International Convention on Civil Liability for Oil Pollution Damage* in 1969 (*International Civil Liability Convention*),[10] following the industry-wide support for the *Tanker Owners Voluntary Agreement Concerning Liability for Oil Pollution* schemes. The *International Civil Liability Convention* largely incorporated the features of the private *Tanker Owners Voluntary Agreement Concerning Liability for Oil Pollution* agreement, such as strict liability for shipowners, limitation of liability, and requirements to maintain liability insurance for transnational oil shipments.

As a key stakeholder in global oil transportation, the oil industry also addressed the issue of financial liability and compensation. In 1971, it implemented a voluntary scheme, namely, *Contract Regarding a Supplement to Tanker Liability for Oil Pollution* and agreed to share the financial burden of shipowners.[11] This was followed by another IMO-led instrument, namely, the *International Convention on the Establishment of an International Fund for Compensation for Oil Pollution Damage* in 1971 (*1971 Fund Convention*),[12] which supplemented the *International Civil Liability Convention*, 1969, increasing the amount of compensation for victims.

The second phase was driven by the Amoco Cadiz spill in 1978 off the French coast, which required the IMO to confront new challenges concerning extensive compensation claims after accidents involving even larger oil tankers.[13] This led to amendments in both the *International Civil Liability Convention, 1969,* and the *1971 Fund Convention*, raising compensation ceilings and enabling response to the approximately USD two billion cleanup costs following the Amoco Cadiz incident.[14]

---

co-operation for following its regulations and practices affecting inter-State shipping. More so, the IMO aims to motivate Member States to adopt the best standards of practice not only for ensuring maritime safety and navigational efficiency, but for restricting marine pollution from ships: at The International Maritime Organisation, *Brief History of IMO* (Web Page) http://www.imo.org/en/About/HistoryOfIMO/Pages/Default.aspx.

[10] *International Convention on Civil Liability for Oil Pollution Damage*, opened for signature 29 November 1969, UNTS 973 (entered into force 19 June 1975) replaced by the *1992 Protocol to the International Convention on Civil Liability for Oil Pollution Damage*, opened for signature 27 November 1992, UNTS 1956 (entered into force 30 May 1996).

[11] *Contract Regarding a Supplement to Tanker Liability for Oil Pollution*, signed 14 January 1971, [1971] ILM 10(1) (entered into force 15 October 1977).

[12] *International Convention on the Establishment of An International Fund for Compensation for Oil Pollution Damage*, opened for signature 18 December 1971, [1971] ILM 284 (entered into force 16 October 1978) *(1971 Fund Convention)*. This *1971 Fund Convention* was superseded by the *Protocol of 1992* to the *International Convention on the Establishment of An International Fund for Compensation for Oil Pollution Damage*, opened for signature 27 November 1992, [1992] UKTS 87 (entered into force 24 May 2002) *(1992 Fund Convention)*.

[13] More than two billion USD of cleaning up challenged the earlier legal limit of compensation. The *Amoco Cadiz* ship had run aground in the territorial waters of France, discharging 230,000 tons of crude oil into the seawater on March 16, 1978, near the Brittany beach again within the territorial scope of the *Torrey Canyon*: at Michael Faure and Wang Hui, 'Economic Analysis of Compensation for Oil Pollution Damage' (2006) 37 *Journal of Maritime Law and Commerce* 179–205.

[14] Mans Jacobson, 'The International Regime of Compensation for Oil Pollution Damage and the Policy of the International Oil Pollution Compensation Funds as to the Admissibility of Claims' (2002) 1 (1) *World Maritime University Journal of Maritime Affairs* 59- 69.

Nonetheless, subsequent incidents, such as the 1999 Erika oil spill off the coast of Brittany in France,[15] and the 2002 Prestige incident near Spain, demonstrated that even these enhanced limits were not enough.

Consequently, aiming at covering more compensation amount, parties to the *International Civil Liability Convention, 1969* and *1971 Fund Convention* introduced more amendments: the *International Civil Liability Convention, 1969,* converted into the *1992 Convention on Civil Liability* and the *1971 Fund Convention* evolved into the *1992 Fund Convention.*[16] Additionally, in 2003, signatories to the *1992 Fund Convention* introduced the *2003 Protocol Establishing an International Oil Pollution Compensation Supplementary Fund Supplementary Fund Protocol* (*Supplementary Fund Protocol*), which elevated liability limits and broadened the scope of contributors to include parties such as shipbuilders.[17]

The *Supplementary Fund Protocol* entered into force in 2005,[18] raising the maximum compensation available to USD 1038 million. Under the *Supplementary Fund Protocol,* amounts exceeding the ceiling established by the *1992 Convention on Civil Liability* and the *1992 Fund Convention* are covered by contributions from the concerned oil industry, without increasing the financial liability of shipowners. However, this arrangement placed an additional liability on oil industry participants whenever spill-related damages surpassed the *1992 Convention on Civil Liability* and the *1992 Fund Convention* caps.

The third phase involved efforts to balance this financial responsibility between shipowners and oil companies. The International Group of Protection and Indemnity (P&I) clubs[19] implemented two separate agreements: the *Small Tanker Oil Pollution Indemnification Agreement* (STOPIA) and *the Tanker Oil Pollution Indemnification*

---

[15] On 13th December 1999, a Maltese single hull oil tanker, the *Erika* broke into two parts 45 nautical miles off the coast of Brittany in France. The incident caused to spill approximately 20,000 tonnes of heavy fuel oil. That was a massive disaster affecting approximately 400 kms of shoreline. France, being the public victim, claimed for the cleaning up of the coastal environment cost. Private loss was also enormous. It hit hard the fisheries and tourism sector, in particular around the affected area. The total value of claims was USD 521.18 million, but claimants received only USD 188.3 million under the Conventions: at Jason Chuah, 'The Third EU Maritime Safety Package Objectives and Challenges' (2009) 15 *Journal of International Maritime Law* 271-290.

[16] *International Convention on the Establishment of An International Fund for Compensation for Oil Pollution Damage*, opened for signature 27 November 1992, [1992] UKTS 87 (entered into force 24 May 2002) *(1992 Fund Convention)*; *1992 Protocol to the International Convention on Civil Liability for Oil Pollution Damage*, opened for signature 27 November 1992, UNTS 1956 (entered into force 30 May 1996).

[17] The *2003 Protocol Establishing an International Oil Pollution Compensation Supplementary Fund*, opened for signature 16 May 2003, [2003] 92FUND/A.8/4, Annex I (entered into force 3 May 2005) *(2003 Supplementary Fund Convention).*

[18] The requirement for entry into force was achieved in December 2004 when eight states receiving 450 million tons of contributing oil ratified the protocol: at Art 21 of the *2003 Supplementary Fund Protocol.*

[19] Oil spill incidents and their compensation have a close connection with Insurance industries. One of the major insurance providers in marine transport is the International Group of Protection and Indemnity (P&I) clubs. The club has thirteen principal underwriting member clubs and mutual insurers. Together, they provide a cover of liability (protection and indemnity) to 90% of the world

Agreement (TOPIA).[20] STOPIA increased the liability threshold for shipowners of smaller vessels under the *1992 Convention on Civil Liability* from 5000 to 29,548 gross tonnage. This eventually led to minimise the burden on oil industries covering larger ships. In the meantime, TOPIA established a framework for cost-sharing by which shipowners and oil industry actors split compensation obligations equally (50%) to indemnify the *Supplementary Fund Protocol*.[21] For example, if under the *Supplementary Fund Protocol*, an oil industry pays an extra two million USD, TOPIA stipulated that a shipowner is to reimburse USD one million to the concerned oil industry. The IMO accepted all the voluntary agreements in 2005 leading to their entry into force on 20 February 2006.[22]

Between 1969 and 2006, oil spill regime experienced significant changes which shifted responsibility onto non-State actors, particularly oil and shipping companies, by requiring them to provide compensation for resulting harm. Despite this evolution, the central aim remained the provision of prompt and adequate compensation to affected parties through an international civil liability framework. This was possible because the industries undertook responsibility for the compensatory harm.[23] The next section explains the oil spill liability and compensation system in detail.

ocean-going vessels: at Mans Jacobsson, 'Liability Regimes in Contemporary Maritime Law' in *Ship Source Pollution—Oil and Hazardous and Noxious Substances* (Routledge, 2020) 3–18.

[20] International Oil Pollution Convention Fund, *Small Tanker Oil Pollution Indemnification Agreement* (as amended 2017), opened for signature 28 February 2005, [2005] ILM 92FUND/A.ES.10/13 (entered into force 20 February 2006); *The Tanker Oil Pollution Indemnification Agreement* (as amended 2017), opened for signature 28 February 2005, [2005] ILM SUPPFUND/A/ES.2/7 (entered into force 20 February 2006).

[21] International Oil Pollution Convention Fund, *Small Tanker Oil Pollution Indemnification Agreement* (as amended 2017), opened for signature 28 February 2005, [2005] ILM 92FUND/A.ES.10/13 (entered into force 20 February 2006); *The Tanker Oil Pollution Indemnification Agreement* (as amended 2017), opened for signature 28 February 2005, [2005] ILM SUPPFUND/A/ES.2/7 (entered into force 20 February 2006).

[22] The basis of these two agreements is not to exceed the burden of either of the two industries for more than 60%. Reviews should be done after the first ten years that should follow further review in every five years: at Explanatory Note, The International Regime for Compensation for Oil Pollution Damage (The Secretariat of the International Oil Pollution Compensation Funds, January 2012) https://www.iopcFund.org/npdf/genE.pdf.

[23] Marko Pavliha and Mitja Grvec, 'The 2003 Supplementary Fund Protocol: An Important Improvement to the International Compensation System for Oil Pollution Damage' (2008) 58(1–2) *Zbornik PFZ* 307, 330.

Oil Spill Liability and Compensation System

The oil spill liability and compensation system established by the IMO parties is an appropriate example of how the corporate liability principle is being implemented.[24] Until 2020, USD 1038.85 million in compensation payments demonstrates the system's ability to address the concerns raised following the oil spill disasters.[25] The success is largely because of its salient features, such as strict liability of shipowners, liability of registered shipowners, limitation of shipowners' liability, and compulsory insurance or financial security.

This liability regime has three components. The first component is the *1992 Convention on Civil Liability*, which sets out the main criteria that must be satisfied for fault to be ascribed to a responsible party. The second component is represented by the *1992 Fund Convention*, and the third is by the compensation based on the *2003 Supplementary Fund Protocol*. This protocol supplements the *1992 Convention on Civil Liability* limit for the purpose of providing sufficient compensation to victims of an oil pollution incident where the liability is limited. The following section highlights the key features of the overall liability and compensation system.

Key Features of the 1992 Convention on Civil Liability

According to the *1992 Convention on Civil Liability*, subject to a few exceptions, a shipowner is strictly liable to pay compensation for an oil spill and its negative consequences to both environment and public health. However, the liability is limited to a certain amount over which a victim cannot claim any compensation. Shipowners with respect to pay the compensation are required to maintain insurance or any other suitable financial guarantee. These features are discussed below.

Liability of Shipowners

Shipowners must bear the liability to pay compensation, which is confirmed under the 1992 *Convention on Civil Liability*. Article 3 (1) of the *1992 Convention on Civil Liability* provides that shipowners of a State Party shall be liable for pollution damage caused within the territory of another Member State.[26] In accordance with the Convention, owner of a ship means the Party registered as an owner or, in the

---

[24] Yuan Yang, Liability and Compensation for Oil Spill Accidents' (Summer 2017) 57 (2) *Natural Resources Journal* 465–492.

[25] International Chamber of Shipping and International Group of P&I Associations, Submission No IOPC/APRIL17/4/6 to the International Oil Pollution Compensation Funds, April 2017 sessions, 2.

[26] International Oil Pollution Compensation Fund, *Decision Identification No 001676, Nefterudovoz-57 M incident*, 28th sess, Agenda Item 5, IOPC Doc 92FUND/EXC.28/8 (22 March 2005).

absence of registration, the party owning the ship.[27] The definition of a shipowner also includes a person who is in control of the ship or who has an indirect interest in the ship.[28] Whether or not the owner is actively engaged in the operation of that ship is not relevant under the Convention. One of the objectives of the *1992 Convention on Civil Liability* is to provide compensation to victims of incidents involving oil spills during the maritime transport of oil. Because of this, the Convention does not apply to oil spill done by ships other than oil tankers (a ship that is used as any sea-going vessel and seaborne craft of any type that is constructed or adapted for the carriage of oil in bulk as cargo) and.[29] Oil is defined as 'any persistent hydrocarbon mineral oil including crude oil, fuel oil, heavy diesel oil and lubricating oil, whether carried on board a ship as cargo or in the bunkers of such a ship'.[30]

The *1992 Convention on Civil Liability* also adopts the principle of strict liability for convenient access to compensation. Because of the strict liability, victims are not required to go through the difficult process to investigate and find fault of shipowners in the case of an oil spill. It means unless there is an 'act of war', 'insurrection or a natural phenomenon', or the oil spill was caused by 'an act or omission done with intent to cause damage by a third party', victims have the right to claim compensation directly from the responsible shipowners or insurance companies.[31] The question of employing joint and several liability of shipowners will arise if more than one ship is involved in causing pollution-related damage. But that is not possible in cases if the damage can reasonably be separated.[32]

Balance is also achieved in the *1992 Convention on Civil Liability*. While shipowners have strict liability, the *1992 Convention on Civil Liability* places a limit on the liability of shipowners. Accordingly, shipowners do not have to pay compensation beyond a certain limit.

Exclusion or Limitation of Liability

The *1992 Convention on Civil Liability* limits the financial liability in accordance with the tonnage of a ship.[33] But a shipowner will lose their right to pay limited

[27] *1992 Convention on Civil Liability*, art 1(3).

[28] Jose Juste-Ruiz, 'Compensation for Pollution Damage Caused by Oil Tanker Accidents: From Erika to Prestige' (2010) 1 (1) *Aegean Review of the Law of the Sea and Maritime Law* 37–60.

[29] Astrid Kalkbrenner, 'Compensating for Catastrophic Harm: Civil Liability Regimes and Compensation Fund' (PhD Thesis, The University of Calgary, 2015) 212; *1992 Convention on Civil Liability*, art 1(1).

[30] Ibid art 1 (5).

[31] Ibid arts 3(2) (a)-(c).

[32] Ibid art 4.

[33] For a ship not exceeding 5000 units of gross tonnage, the *1992 Convention on Civil Liability* limit is 4510,000 units of account (Special Drawing Rights). For a ship between 5000 units of gross tonnage and 140,000 units of tonnage, the *1992 Convention on Civil Liability* limit is 4,510,000 Special Drawing Rights (SDR) plus 631 SDR for each extra unit of tonnage. For a ship carrying

compensation if it is proved that they have involvement in the oil spill through their knowledge or intention.[34]

In the event of an oil spill, the shipowner has to create a fund representing the total sum in accordance with the limit of liability in a court of law or other specified place of any State Party. In relation to the establishment of the fund, direct deposits to court, bank guarantees or other securities acceptable under the law of the State Parties are deemed sufficient.[35]

Compulsory Insurance

Shipowners must have insurance. A ship carrying more than 2000 tons of bulk oil as cargo falls into this mandatory insurance policy. Other financial security, including a bank guarantee or a letter or certificate issued by an international financial institution, is also acceptable, provided that the amount covered by the insurance or other financial security is in accordance with the limit of liability prescribed in art 5 (1) of the *1992 Convention on Civil Liability*.[36]

Security to receive compensation in case of an oil spill has been the heart of the overall mechanism of the *1992 Convention on Civil Liability*. During preliminary meetings on the introduction of the *Convention on Civil Liability*, 1969, State Parties unanimously opposed making insurance obligatory, but representatives of the US and France insisted that this was necessary for the enforcement of strict liability on shipowners.[37]

Direct Claim of Compensation

Along with insurance, an innovative approach of the *1992 Convention on Civil Liability* is to allow victims to claim compensation from the insurer directly.[38] Every shipowner covered under the Convention needs to prove financial security with respect to the direct claim of a victim. Art 7 (2) of the *1992 Civil Liability Convention* provides the following:

> The owner of a ship registered in a contracting state and carrying more than 2000 tons of oil in bulk as cargo shall be required to maintain insurance or other financial security, such as the guarantee of a bank or a certificate delivered by an international compensation fund,

---

14,000 units of gross tonnage or over, the *1992 Convention on Civil Liability* limit is 89,770.000 SDR.

[34] Ibid art 5(2).

[35] Ibid.

[36] Ibid art 7(1).

[37] Kalkbrenner (n 32) 216.

[38] *1992 Convention on Civil Liability*, art 7(8).

> in the sums fixed by applying the limits of liability prescribed in Article 5, paragraph 1, to cover his liability.[39]

As a proof of insurance or other financial security, every shipowner covered under the *1992 Civil Liability Convention* has to maintain a civil liability certificate (CLC) and demonstrate enforceability. The flag state of a shipowner issues the certificate of the ship after the shipowner provides proof of insurance.[40] Art 7(2) of the *1992 Civil Liability Convention* provides the following:

> With respect to a ship registered in a contracting state, a certificate attesting to insurance or other financial security should be issued or certified by the appropriate state of the ship's registry.

An insurance or financial security provider cannot deny a claim that the concerned shipowner breached his or her insurance contract with the insurer or financial security provider.[41] This means that the breach of contractual terms of an insurance agreement is not allowed as a defence against direct action.

The direct claim system is a deviation from the traditional marine insurance of indemnity, wherein the third-party victim has no right to claim from the insurer. Traditionally, marine insurance is an agreement between insurers and insurers and depends on the terms of the insurance agreement. In the context of an oil spill accident, the insurer or financial security provider takes the position of the shipowner in legal action and can take all the defences that are applied to a shipowner except for the defence of bankruptcy or winding up of the shipowner.

Rules of the Second Pillar of the Regime Under the *1992 Fund Convention*

The *1992 Fund Convention* has included two important objectives. The first objective is to provide full compensation, and the second objective is to share compensation between the shipping and oil industries.[42] Art 2 of the *1992 Fund Convention* formed the International Oil Pollution Compensation Fund (IOPCF) and endorsed it with the duty to decide on the claims in relation to substitution and addition if the claims were not covered under the *1992 Convention on Civil Liability*. Substitution applies when the shipowner is not responsible for providing compensation due to legal exemptions under the *1992 Convention on Civil Liability* regime, for example, in the case of the application of a force majeure or when it is not possible to identify a ship.[43] The IOPCF also provides an upper limit on compensation and supplements the limit prescribed in the *1992 Convention on Civil Liability*.[44]

---

[39] Ibid art 7(1).

[40] Ibid, art 7(2).

[41] Ibid art 7(8).

[42] Kalkbrenner (n 32) 218.

[43] Ibid.

[44] Ibid.

The *1992 Fund Convention* also has a liability limit similar to that of the *1992 Convention on Civil Liability*. The maximum amount of liability under the *1992 Fund Convention* is 203,000,000 units of account, which is equivalent to USD 286,130,292.18, including any amount paid under the *1992 Convention on Civil Liability*.[45] A victim can claim this even if the damage is the consequence of a natural disaster of exceptional, inevitable, and irresistible character.[46]

The *1992 Fund Convention* has also conferred subrogation rights to the IOPCF. This means that the IOPCF has the right to claim compensation from a shipowner or shipowner's guarantor or insurer after compensation has been paid from the fund to the victim.[47] The *1992 Fund Convention* also confers the subrogation right to a State Party or agency that has paid compensation for pollution damage to private victims following its State law. In such a case, a State or agency can exercise the same rights as a victim.[48]

The contribution to the fund is to ensure the redistribution of liability and costs of paying adequate compensation. The fund is created from the contributions of private oil importers. Importers of oil must make primary and annual contributions via the port, terminal or installation facilities of a State Party. Any person who has received more than 150,000 tonnes of oil by shipping and used any port or terminal or installation of a State Party of the *1992 Fund Convention* in a calendar year must contribute to the fund.[49]

The Third Pillar of the Compensation System Under the 2003 Supplementary Fund Protocol

The *Supplementary Fund Protocol* provides third-tier compensation to victims in addition to the amount paid under the *1992 Convention on Civil Liability* and the *1992 Fund Convention*. Table 7.2 below shows the limit set in each of the pillars, and the highest is USD 1038 million. The three tiers are thus linked to each other. However, it is optional for parties to the *1992 Fund Convention* to join the *Supplementary Fund Protocol*, but without becoming parties to the *1992 Convention on Civil Liability* and *Fund Conventions*, a State cannot join the *Supplementary Fund Protocol*.[50]

The *1992 Fund Convention* has developed a pro-rata system of compensation payments when the amount of compensation exceeds the legal limit. The aim of the pro-rata system is to reduce the actual compensation amount to the legal limit

---

[45] Ibid art 4(4) (a).

[46] Ibid art 4(4) (b).

[47] See art 9(1) of the *1992 Fund Convention*. A Guarantor is a person who provides insurance or other financial security to cover an owner's liability under art 7(1) of the *1992 Convention on Civil Liability*: at *1992 Fund Convention*, art 1(7).

[48] *1992 Fund Convention*, art 9(3).

[49] *1992 Fund Convention*, arts 12(2) (a)-(b); Under Art 1(3), 'contributing oil includes coastal deliveries of oil which are then reshipped by coastal transport'. The same oil can be counted several times: at art. 10.

[50] Ibid.

Table 7.2 Limitations on liability under the civil liability regime of oil spill between 1969 and 2003

Tanker Size (gross tonnage)	*1969 Civil Liability Convention* as amended (in million)	*1992 Civil Liability Convention* as amended (post 2003) (in million)	*1992 Fund Convention* (post 2003) (in million)	*2003 Supplementary Fund Protocol* (in million)
5000	$0.92	$6.24	$281	$1038
10,000	$1.84	$10.61	$281	$1038
50,000	$9.20	$45.53	$281	$1038
100,000	$18.40	$89.18	$281	$1038
140,000	$19.37	$124.06	$281	$1038
150,000	$19.37	$124.21	$281	$1038
200,000	$19.37	$124.21	$281	$1038

The original figures are SDR = Special Drawing Right, and the exchange rate is 1 SDR = $ 1.39 as of 17.02.2021. The unit of account is defined by the International Monetary Fund.
Source The *United Nations Conference on Trade and Development Report 2017.*

proportionately. When the claim amount is higher than the limit of the *1992 Fund Convention*, the victims receive compensation proportionate to the limit in lieu of their original claim amount.

However, following the pro-rata system after *the Prestige* incident caused widespread criticism, which reduced the claims of Portugal, France, and Spain. Taking the reduction into account, the *Supplementary Fund Protocol* aims to change this pro-rata system, yet still with a limit.[51] As per art 4 of the *Supplementary Fund Protocol*, subject to becoming a party to the *Protocol* and the *Fund Convention*, a State party or victim has to establish their claim meeting the requirements of the *1992 Convention on Civil Liability* and the *1992 Fund Convention.*

The assembly of the IOPCF then makes a temporary or final order of approval on that claim. The *Supplementary Fund Protocol* then intervenes if the shipowner or his insurer and the *1992 Fund Conventions* are insufficient to meet the valid demand of a claimant.

Support from the *Supplementary Fund Protocol* is mandatory if the total damage exceeds the limit or if there is a risk of exceeding the limit of the *1992 Convention on Civil Liability* and the *1992 Fund Convention*, which is currently USD 281 million. After meeting the criteria, the *Supplementary Fund Protocol* is responsible for paying the difference in amount between the limit of the *Supplementary Fund Protocol* (approximately USD 1038 million) and the earlier conventions (which is USD 281 million under the *1992 Convention on Civil Liability* and *Fund Conventions*) to the victims.

The *Supplementary Fund Protocol* was against the basic principle of sharing responsibility between the shipping and oil industries. Only oil industries had

[51] Ibid.

to contribute to the supplementary fund under the *Supplementary Fund Protocol* (*Protocol*). The *Protocol* does not shift any burden of the increased amount to shipowners. This finding calls into question the shared responsibility theory of the whole compensation system. The *Small Tanker Oil Pollution Indemnification Agreement* (STOPIA) and *the Tanker Oil Pollution Indemnification Agreement* (TOPIA) finally resolved the issue, and shipowners are now required to cover larger ships (29,548 gross tonnage) and contribute 50% to the supplementary fund, as discussed above.

Lessons Learned for the Shipbreaking Industry

With respect to oil spill incidents, the above principles establish an effective system for addressing liability and paying compensation to victims. An important aspect of the three pillars of the oil spill regime is its effectiveness in preventing further accidents. The regime has a positive effect on the prevention of accidents. Kalkbrenner claims that the primary purpose of the *1992 Convention on Civil Liability* is to provide adequate compensation that has an indirect effect on prevention.[52]

As discussed in Chap. 9, the civil liability framework proposed for shipbreaking can also have an indirect effect on prevention. Oil industries prefer transporting oil via good shipping companies to save their funding expenditures and take less risk to contribute to the funds created after the *1992 Fund Convention* and the *Supplementary Fund Protocol*. This tendency of the oil industry eventually works to prevent more accidents.[53] The successful implementation of the SLC framework discussed in Chap. 9 may guide shipbreaking yards to improve their standards gradually. This would help indirectly reduce shipbreaking-related deaths, injuries, and diseases.

Prevention requires every party to act together. The regime binds both the oil and shipping industries, which are the main stakeholders. This is an implied way of controlling unsafe shipping practices. Financial security also acts to prevent accidents. It ensures the victims that their claim will be paid. Importantly, although a shipowner's liability to pay compensation is limited, the reckless or negligent behaviour of a shipowner contributing to an incident can turn the limited liability to an unlimited liability. This change in liability means that there is every possibility to claim full compensation in law, which results in taking care in oil transport and has an indirect effect on prevention.[54]

A different view is that there is no mechanism for direct compensation for environmental damage. The regime has no role in upgrading an already damaged environment. The regime does not compensate unless it is related to economic loss (fishery, tourism, or scientific research). Nevertheless, economic loss is linked to environmental damage. For example, water pollution causes death in fish, which eventually affects the fishing community. In that sense, environmental damage is intricately

[52] Kalkbrenner (n 32) 23.

[53] Ibid.

[54] Ibid.

linked to economic loss, so the regime indirectly compensates for environmental damage.[55] Although the regime does not consider cleaning the environment and restoring it to its original condition, it supports cleaning up costs, and it rests with the quality of each state in terms of how much it can be cleaned and restored before successfully claiming and receiving compensation.

Historical comparison is used to assess the success of a regime. Jihong Chen and others claim that despite increasing oil transport by sea, the rate of accidents has decreased through the development of the regime since 1969.[56] Until 2020, one hundred and twenty states had become parties to the *1992 Civil Liability Convention,* and this increased number of state ratifications signals the success of the regime.[57] Importantly, other specific areas, such as transboundary pollution and the carriage of hazardous and noxious substances by the sea, use the Conventions as guiding principles for developing a liability and compensation framework.[58]

The most important lesson learned from the oil spill regime is the importance of establishing a special liability and compensation mechanism that considers the features of a particular industry. Such a mechanism would prevent future accidents in dangerous industries, such as shipbreaking, by establishing the responsibility for both shipping and shipbreaking companies. Both should contribute to compensation so that prevention and compensation work hand-in-hand.

The oil spill regime is a model of the corporate liability principle discussed in Chap. 2.[59] Such a victim-oriented approach rooted in the corporate liability principle is required under the shipbreaking regime. Shipping companies may not support a similar regime due to the extent of the business compared with the oil spill regime. An oil spill could develop into legal action from industry because of the global nature of the business. In the case of an oil spill, the centre of focus is compensation; because of State Parties' proactive role in safeguarding victims of oil pollution, industries agree to take responsibility.[60] On the other hand, the shipbreaking industry operates in a few countries of South Asia, and shipbreaking problems are assumed to be problems faced by nations in the shipbreaking industry. Perhaps, for this reason, most powerful shipping countries are not concerned about this, and they do not create any pressure on the shipping industry to introduce compensation for victims, even though the extent of loss is much more visible in shipbreaking incidents than in oil spill incidents through the lens of human rights.

---

[55] Kalkbrenner (n 32) 41.

[56] Weipan Zhang et al., 'Governance of Global Vessel-Source Marine Oil Spills: Characteristics and Refreshed Strategies' (2021) 213 *Ocean and Coastal Management* 105,874 https://doi.org/10.1016/j.jclepro.2017.12.238.

[57] IOPC Funds, 'State Parties to both the 1992 Civil Liability Convention and the 1992 Fund Convention' (Webpage) www.iopcfunds.org

[58] Pauline Marchand, 'The International Law Regarding Ship-Source Pollution Liability and Compensation: Evolution and Current Challenges' (Conference Paper, International Oil Spill Conference, 17 May 2017) 1–2.

[59] Kalkbrenner, (n 32) 231.

[60] Pavliha and Grvec (n 25) 330.

The comparison between oil spill incidents and shipbreaking incidents highlights the similar nature of adverse consequences. There are several similarities, but their legal standards differ significantly. For example, shipbreaking incidents cause human deaths and injuries in the shipbreaking process along with damage to the coastal environment, but they do not spark any liability or compensation regimes. The environment and shipbreaking workers directly become victims of the business activities of nonstate parties, including shipowners, who generally act beyond the jurisdictions of countries where incidents occur. On the other hand, while incidents have caused losses, mainly to natural habitats and tourism in surrounding areas, oil spill incidents have triggered a comprehensive legal framework for liability and compensation.

The issue of benefit is the key to both shipbreaking and the maritime industry. Enjoying benefits while perpetuating injustice should not be acceptable unless it is backed by a liability and insurance regime. The question is, as the shipbreaking yards and shipowners are not compliant with the proposed standards provided in the *Hong Kong Convention*, who would blow the whistle to enforce the standards. An enforcement mechanism led by the insurance industry would be the best option. This would create indirect pressure on shipowners and shipbreaking yards, with a risk of paying a high insurance premium if their standards are not enough to provide adequate safety for workers. The *Piper Alpha* incident discussed in the following section is a good example to illustrate this in facilitating the improvement of standards in the very risky offshore oil industry.

Piper Alpha Incident: Insurance-Led Enforcement Mechanism

The Incident

Piper Alpha, a North Sea oil production platform, was destroyed by an explosion caused by a gas leak on 6 July 1988, killing 167 workers, which was over 50 per cent of the crew. This incident led to regulatory changes worldwide with respect to managing risks in relation to practical circumstances.[61] Most importantly, an important change triggered by the incident was the inspection policy—the procedure of monitoring the safety standards by the insurance industry.

The Piper Alpha incident was primarily due to shoddy industry practices.[62] It was an offshore rig under maintenance. Because of misunderstanding between the night and day shift employees the night workers, in the absence of knowledge of the ongoing maintenance, turn on machineries contained a valve that had already

[61] Rhona Flin, 'Decision Making in Crises: The Piper Alpha Disaster' (2001) *Managing Crises: Threats, Dilemmas, Opportunities* 103–118.

[62] Victor D. Briz Narvaez, Analysing the Root Causes of the Piper Alpha Incident: Lessons for Safety in Hazardous Industries' *HSE Pills* (Linkedin, 13 July 2023) https://www.linkedin.com/pulse/hse-pill-3-analyzing-root-causes-piper-alpha-incident-v%C3%ADctor-briz/.

been taken off. The blind flange therefore broke down with loss of containment across Piper Alpha,[63] leading to the explosion, which cost lives of 167 people. And a considerable among of crude oil was released into the seawater.[64] The deaths and environmental damage to the coastal environment largely influenced the development of policy, resulting in more stringent inspection and safety assessments conducted by insurance industry.

Post-Incident Legislative Developments

Following the Piper Alpha explosion, the government of the United Kingdom passed two laws: *the Offshore Safety Act 1992* and the *Offshore Safety (Protection against Victimisation) Act 1992*. These laws tightened safety requirements for offshore industries but instead had left it up to the industry on a case-by-case basis to determine how unsafe conditions could be addressed. It was at that point that the insurance industries took over by enforcing a 'safety case', which refers to a structured and well-reasoned argument, backed by a robust body of evidence, which demonstrates that a system is acceptably safe to operate within a specific application and environment.[65]

The Piper Alpha incident had a heavy blow on the business of insurance industries. Providing compensation for twelve different losses, including liabilities for deaths and injuries, they faced significant business losses.[66] The loss was around USD 1500 million.[67] In light of this loss, risks were reassessed by insurers, with a closer eye being kept on whether the offshore structures were following the *Offshore Safety Act* of 1992.

Insurance premiums were also raised by several insurers for offshore oil rig companies which did not maintain the structure as per their recommended standards. This took place when the underwriters reported that the loss was worse than they had expected. Some insurers experienced loss more than their catastrophic reinsurance protections, which made the insurance more expensive, and the price increased by 40%. Leading energy underwriters, such as Lloyds, had been attempting to drive market change by ratcheting up the premium.[68] But did this heightened scrutiny lead to better industry practices? According to Dominick Hoare, a joint active underwriter

---

[63] L.W.D. Cullen, 'The Public Inquiry into the Piper Alpha Disaster' (1993) 1 and 2 (Report to Parliament by the Secretary of State for Energy by Command of Her Majesty, November 1990) *Tech Rep. Her Majesty's Government, London.*

[64] David A Alexandar, 'Psychiatric Intervention after the Piper Alpha Disaster (1991) 84 (1) *Journal of the Royal Society of Medicine* 8–11, 8.

[65] Michael P. Broadribb, 'What Have We Really Learned? Twenty-Five Years after Piper Alpha' *Process Safety Progress* (2015) 34 (1) 16–23.

[66] Hales K., Insurance—Piper Alpha "et al." (1995) 13 (2–3) *Energy Exploration and Exploitation* 253–260.

[67] Ibid 257.

[68] R. T. Canaway, 'Business Interruption Insurance for North Sea Oil and Gas Production Fields' (Conference Paper, SPE Offshore Europe, September 1989) https://doi.org/10.2118/19220-MS.

at Munich Re Underwriting, Piper Alpha showed how inadequate some exposure monitoring was at that time. He added that 'life has changed dramatically since'.[69] The observation indicates the role played by Piper Alpha as a catalyst for changing the insurance industry's approach to risk assessment. After the incident, every installation needs to demonstrate how they are implementing a suitable approach to the management of risk to main offshore complex.

Lessons Learned for the Global Shipbreaking Industry

After Piper Alpha and subsequent legal developments, industry practice has changed—largely as a result of the insurance industries' risk analysis. Piper Alpha showed that rigorous enforcement by the insurance industry can lead positive changes to industry practices. In fact, 'high risk leads to high premium for the insurance' was the principle that forced the industries to implement the *Offshore Safety Act 1992* and the *Offshore Safety (Protection against Victimisation) Act 1992*. This principle is applicable to the shipbreaking sector because it has the effect of forcing shipowners to raise standards. This means that if there is liability insurance for shipbreaking and workers in shipbreaking start to bring claims, the insurance provider will respond to this risk, making it more expensive to cover shipbreaking risks and resulting in changes in the shipbreaking industry.

One distinction between the regulatory trajectory of other incidents discussed in this chapter and Piper Alpha is that the former resulted first in the creation of national laws and second to an improvement in the global offshore oil extraction industry; however, an international framework would first need to be in place for the global shipbreaking industry.[70] However, Piper Alpha is an important example relevant to shipbreaking. It shows that insurance industries can effectively contribute to global regulatory changes by being able to influence risk assessment policy on a global level. The subsequent section also considers an example, namely, the Plimsoll Line incident, which provided a similar case for global reform, after the United Kingdom had put in place an effective certificate system for tracking all shipowners in relation to the enforcement of standards, which eventually facilitated controlling the risks from overloading their ships internationally.

[69] Lloyd's, '1988 The Piper Alpha Explosion' *Piper Alpha* (Web Page) https://www.lloyds.com/about-lloyds/history/catastophes-and-claims/piper-alpha

[70] Woolfson C., 'Preventable Disaster in the Offshore Oil Industry: From Piper Alpha to Deepwater Horizon' (2012) 22 (4) *New Solutions: A Journal of Environmental and Occupational Health Policy* 497–524.

Plimsoll Line Incident and Importance of a Load Lines Certificate

Overloading cargo ships was a major problem leading to periodic maritime disasters of the nineteenth century. Aiming at preventing such incidents, the International Maritime Organisation (IMO) implemented the Load Lines Certificate, which is compulsory for all ships to sail on international waters.

The 'Bridlington Gale' (gale) is a historic case of a maritime accident which influenced the establishment of the Load Lines Certificate. This happened on Friday, 10th February in 1871 at Bridlington, when a gale drove wrecked ships away that had sheltered there, with the loss of about 70 seamen. The storm (gale) wrecked as many as 23 coal carrying ships, a lot of them carrying too much load. Overloading and poor maintenance were the primary causes of shipwrecks and loss of life in those days.[71]

The incident is named after Samuel Plimsoll, a British Member of Parliament, who fought for reforming the shipping laws in the UK in the immediate aftermath of the tragedy. As he wanted to protect against danger of overload, he proposed using the marking on the ship's sides for communicating the safe load on-board. His goal was to prevent ships from sailing with overloaded cargoes and reduce the risk to life for boatmen by introducing a mark onto the hull of the ships. Plimsoll supported his efforts with the publication of his book, 'Our Seaman', one year after the Bridlington Gale, which further mobilized public opinion around the country.[72] In response, the UK government established a Royal Commission to investigate the state of commercial shipping.[73] Plimsoll's suggestions were accepted by the Commission and developed into legislative proposal in the form of a bill.[74]

Regulatory Developments Following the Incident

The UK parliament passed the *Merchant Shipping Act* in 1876, requiring a load line to be drawn on the hull of all seagoing vessels.[75] The *Merchant Shipping Act* required shipowners to draw a mark onto the hulls of their ships with the objective of ensuring that they were not overloaded. The implementation of a requirement that cargo be stowed below this line was a major improvement to British laws concerning safety

71 Jim Rice, Bridlington's Great Gale–the Tragedy that Drew a Line in Shipping History (News Release, *Lifeboats*, 4 February 2022) https://rnli.org/news-and-media/2022/february/04/bridlingtons-great-gale-the-tragedy-that-drew-a-line-in-shipping-history.

72 Samuel Plimsoll, 'Our Seaman; An Appeal' (Virtue and Co., London, 1873).

73 Harry Leach et al., *Report of the Royal Commission on the Merchant Marine Practices and Conditions*, Pro MT/9 36 M.5489/1873.

74 Ibid 78.

75 *The Merchant Shipping Act 1876 (UK)*, came into force in November 1876.

at sea. Honouring Samuel Plimsoll's role in the development of this measure, this mark is referred to as Plimsoll Line.

The Plimsoll line (also known as a load line or international load line) is a visual indicator affixed to the side of ocean-going vessels that divides the hull into few sections, and each section is identified by a symbol that indicates maximum depth to which the vessel can be safely immersed when loaded with cargo. Eventually, this practice was adopted internationally, and other major shipping companies such as Lloyd's of London copied the process.[76] Commercial insurers also stipulated a ship's compliance with load line laws as a condition of coverage.

The generally accepted principles of the Plimsoll line were incorporated in 1930 into the first *International Load Lines Convention*, based on the UK *Merchant Shipping Act* and making it applicable internationally.[77] The Convention was amended in 1966 to introduce criteria concerning the freeboard of ships (i.e., the distance from waterline to the freeboard deck),[78] redistribution and flooding for the subdivision and damage stability calculations to take into account local and seasonal conditions of travelling areas. With respect to the subdivision and damage stability calculations, the *1966 Load Lines Convention* considers the possible dangers in different zones and different seasons.[79]

The *1966 Load Lines Convention*'s main objective is to require adequate freeboard and reserve buoyancy (volume of ship above the waterline) to ensure adequate stability and to limit stress to the hull amidships by seaway and other conditions.[80] Preamble to the *1966 Load Lines Convention* states that its purpose is to fix the maximum draught to which international ships may be loaded and maintain a reasonable balance between the manning of ships in relation to their size and the number of passengers and crew to be carried.

The *1966 Load Lines Convention* therefore requires all cargo vessels be issued with an international Load Line certificate. According to art 3, 'No vessel of a Member State shall undertake international voyages unless the space regulations of this Convention have been fulfilled'. The Convention, however, does not apply to warships and other ships owned or operated by Contracting State and used, for the time being, only on government non-commercial service, fishing vessels, ships not propelled by mechanical means or ships of less than 150 gross tonnage.[81] It is the responsibility of each port State through its existing port state control (PSC) system

---

[76] Analyn N Youmang et al., 'Acquisition of Applied Load to Cargo Vessels Using Plimsoll Line and Buoyant Force Detection Using Technology with SMS Notification' (Conference Paper, IEEE 5th Eurasia Conference on IOT, Communication and Engineering, 27 October 2023) 145–148.

[77] *International Load Line Convention 1930*, opened for signature 5 July 1930, UNTS 858 (entered into force 1 January 1931) superseded by *1966 International Convention on Load Lines* opened for signature 05 April 1966, 640 UNTS 133 (entered into force 21 July 1968) as between contracting parties to later convention, to that extent their provisions conflict.

[78] Ibid.

[79] *Regulation of the 1966 Load Lines Convention,* Annex 1, regs 27(3) and 27(3) to 27(10).

[80] Ibid.

[81] *1966 International Convention on Load Lines*, arts 4 and 5.

to enforce compliance by ensuring that such ships have a valid load line certificate, in line with international safety, security, and environmental standards, whether they are owned by someone or not. The Paris Memorandum of Understanding, an organisation that consists of 27 participating maritime administrations, specifies that shipowners are responsible for complying with the Convention.[82] Otherwise, port authorities may deny entry or detain a ship until the non-compliance is rectified.[83]

Lessons Learned for the Shipbreaking Industry

From the above discussion, three relevant lessons can be learnt to support the proposed SLC framework (see Chap. 9).

First, the certification system established by the Load Line certificate is applied to all ships irrespective of who owns the ship, is highly relevant to shipbreaking industry.[84] The load line certificate is one of the most widely known systems of voluntary regulation that is ever contemplated in the maritime world, and over 140 countries are contracting States to the Convention.[85] Similarly, the establishment of a shipbreaking liability certificate, valid throughout the lifecycle of ships, from the design phase to demolition, could serve to make shipping and shipbreaking companies responsible for the procurement of an adequate insurance certificate and track the owners involved in operating and breaking a ship.[86] Chapter 9 suggests this as a global standard and argues that the IMO should actively encourage its adoption to implement the regulatory requirements contained in the *Hong Kong Convention*.

Second, the *1966 Load Lines Convention*'s history demonstrates that the effective political will and active participation of the shipping industries are essential for the success of the ideas developed in Chap. 9. The development of the Plimsoll line is a good example of the confluence of three main forces: national law (especially in the UK), industry-wide acceptance, and international action by the IMO to introduce the *1930 and 1966 Load Lines Conventions*. This emphasises the need for States and shipping companies to work together with the insurance industry and leading shipping nations to develop workable and meaningful international standards. such as shipping companies, insurance companies and large shipping States.

Third, the IMO must take responsibility to introduce the shipbreaking liability certificate. Given that shipbreaking activities are inherently connected with the shipping industry, the IMO should oversee creating awareness among shipowners,

---

[82] Paris MoU, on Port State Control, 'Organisation' (Web Page) parismou.org/about-us/organisation.

[83] See *Paris Memorandum of Understanding on Port State Control*, adopted 26 January 1982, IMO Res A.1052(27) (entered into force 1 July 1982), ss 3(4), 3(6) and 3(8).

[84] It is one of the widely ratified of all the IMO conventions: at Phillip Alman et al., 'The International Load Lines Convention: Crossroad to the Future' (October 1992) 29(4) *Marine Technology* 233, 234.

[85] Ibid.

[86] See Chapter 9.

insurers, and major shipbreaking countries to get general recognition of the new certificate system in relation to shipbreaking. The legal evolution of shipbreaking follows a different course from the Load Lines Convention. In the latter case, it was industry adoption of good national practice which then drove international legal reform. In shipbreaking, however, legal change is impeded by fierce competition between shipbreaking States. Because of regime competition among shipbreaking States, it is unlikely that any one State would act unilaterally and implement a shipbreaking liability certificate and insurance regime to the disadvantage of its domestic industry, without an overriding international policy.

Conclusion

A similar framework is required for end-of-life ships to the liability and compensation mechanism used in the oil transport business so that developing countries continue purchasing ships for breaking; and at the same time, shipowners remain responsible for paying compensation to workers to break ships. The framework would be an additional international mechanism to the *Hong Kong Convention* that aims at compensating workers to ensure better legal protection with the IMO's leadership. Particularly, the legal framework needs to aim at compensation and impose obligations on all stakeholders—the original owner of a ship, cash buyers, open registry countries and shipbreaking companies—to ensure justice to victim workers, the most vulnerable party to the industry.[87] The underlying reason to argue for an international compensatory framework is the dangerous character of the business and lack of an adequate mechanism in the *Hong Kong Convention* and domestic laws of South Asian countries to regulate unsafe practices, as discussed in Chaps. 4 and 5.

The oil spill events discussed in section "Case Studies on the International Oil Spill Legal Regime" of this chapter show that despite the environmental and human rights consequences of the oil spill incidents, the regulatory changes were not to stop the business. The international community and shipping companies introduced special mechanisms for liability and compensation to continue with their businesses.[88] In comparison with shipbreaking, although the death and injury rates of oil incidents are lower, laws on liability and compensation have developed, distributing liability for incidents to international companies that have a greater share of their business and profit.[89]

Learning lessons from the steps taken by the insurers after the incident, section "Piper Alpha Incident: Insurance-Led Enforcement Mechanism" of this chapter argued that unless insurers put pressure on shipowners to comply with existing

[87] Mohammad Zulfikar Ali, 'Injustice to Workers in the Shipbreaking Industry in South Asia: A Quest for a Civil Liability Framework in International Law' (PhD Thesis, Curtin University, 2022) 229.

[88] Ibid.

[89] Ibid.

regulatory and voluntary standards, this risky shipbreaking industry would remain non-compliant and risky for workers.

Section “Plimsoll Line Incident and Importance of a Load Lines Certificate” discussed that the regulatory changes after the Plimsoll line incident also did not aim to stop the business of carrying cargos by minimising risk. Load line certificates allow the shipping industry to use larger ships but within a limit. Learning from the Load Lines Certificate, a shipbreaking certificate should provide scope to a shipowner so that a shipowner can sell ships to the highest bidder, but liability and compensation frameworks must supplement the shipbreaking certificate. In addition to shipping companies, the shipbreaking industry must also show a shipbreaking certificate to be eligible for purchasing a ship. The global regulatory mechanism proposed in Chap. 9 requires an in-depth analysis of other global events that have triggered reforms in existing laws and regulations.[90]

The next chapter addresses the following question: What are the salient features of a new international framework that can lead to changes in workers’ compensatory regime in the South Asian shipbreaking industry—exploring liability protocols in relation to inter-State waste trade and the inter-State effects of industrial accidents on transboundaries.

Bibliography

Articles/Books/Reports

Adshead, Julie ‘The Application and Development of the Polluter-Pays Principle Across Jurisdictions in Liability for Marine Oil Pollution: The Tales of the ‘Erika’ and the ‘Prestige’ (2018) 30 *Journal of Environmental Law* 425

Chen, Jihong et al, ‘Oil Spills from Global Tankers: Status Review and Future Governance’ (2019) 227 *Journal of Cleaner Production* 31

Pavliha, Marko and Mitja Grvec, ‘The 2003 Supplementary Fund Protocol: An Important Improvement to the International Compensation System for Oil Pollution Damage’ (2008) 58(1–2) *Zbornik PFZ* 307

Rosenthal, Linda and Carol Raper, ‘Amoco Cadiz and Limitation of Liability for Oil Spill Pollution: Domestic and International Solution’ (Fall 1985) 5(1) *Virginia Journal of Natural Resources Law* 259

Somers, Eduard and Gwendoline Gonsaeles, ‘The Consequences of the Sinking of the M/S Erika in European Waters: Towards a Total Loss for International Shipping Law’ (2010) 41(1) *Journal of Maritime Law and Commerce* 57

Southwards, Eve C. and A.J. Southwards, ‘Recolonisation of Rocky Shores in Cornwell After the Use of Toxic Dispersants to Clean Up the Torrey Canyon Spill’ (1978) 35(5) *Journal of the Fisheries Research Board of Canada* 682

Tan, Pham Van, ‘A Study of Compulsory Insurance for Civil Liability for Oil Pollution Damage Caused by Ships: What are the Rules for Small Ships that Have No Formal Obligations Under the Convention’ (2021) 13 (2) *Australian Journal of Maritime and Ocean Affairs* 113

---

[90] Ibid.

Wetterstein, Peter, 'Environmental Impairment Liability after the Erika and Prestige Accidents' (2004) 46 *Scandinavian Study of Law* 230

Wu, Chao 'Liability and Compensation for Oil Pollution Damage: Some Current Threats to the International Convention System' (2002) 7 *Spill Science and Technology Bulletin* 105

Zhu, Ling, Ming Zhao Zhang, 'Insuring against Marine Pollution Liability: An International Perspective' (2015) 46, *Journal of Maritime Law and Commerce* 373

Beck, Matthias and Lynn T Drennan, 'Offshore Risk Management: Myths, Worker Experience and Reality' (Conference Paper, Qualitative Evidence-based Practice Conference, 15–17 May 2017) 1

K Hales, 'Insurance- Piper Alpha "et al"' (1995) 13(2/3) *Special Edition: New Zealand Petroleum Conference: Selected Papers* 253

Marchand, Pauline, 'The International Law Regarding Ship-Source Pollution Liability and Compensation: Evolution and Current Challenges' (Conference Paper, International Oil Spill Conference, 17 May 2017)

M'Gonigle, R Michael & Mark W Zacher, *Pollution, Politics, and International Law – Tankers at Sea* (Berkeley, Los Angeles: University of California Press, 1979)

Rue, Colin De La and Charles B Anderson, *Shipping and the Environment* (Taylor and Francis Ltd., 2nd Edition, 2009)

Aldosari, Khalid R., 'The Applicability of the International and Regional Efforts to Prevent Oil Pollution; Comparative Analysis Between the Arabian Gulf Region and the North Sea' in Angela Carpenter, Tafsir Martin Johansson, and James Anderson Skinner (eds) *Sustainability in the Maritime Domain: Strategies for Sustainability* 199

Michele M. Comenale Pinto, *The Mechanism of Funds for the Compensation of Maritime Environmental Damage, International Law of the Sea: Current Trends and Controversial Issues* in Cura di Angela Del Vecchio (ed) (Eleven International Publishing, 2013) 262

Kalkbrenner, Astrid, 'Compensating for Catastrophic Harm: Civil Liability Regimes and Compensation Fund' (PhD Thesis, The University of Calgary, 2015) 187

International Oil Pollution Compensations Funds, *Annual Report* (Final Report, 2020) 6–7.

International Chamber of Shipping and International Group of P&I Associations, Submission No IOPC/APRIL17/4/6 to the International Oil Pollution Compensation Funds, April 2017 sessions, 2

Leach, Harry et al, *Report of the Royal Commission on the Merchant Marine Practices and Conditions*, Pro MT/9 36 M.5489/1873

North Atlantic Space Administration, 'The Case for Safety: The North Sea Piper Alpha Disaster' (System Failure Case Study No 7 (4), May 2013)

Petrie, J.R., *Piper Alpha Technical Investigation Interim Report,* London Department of Energy, Director of Safety, Petroleum Engineering Division Doc no. 643/4/10/1 (September 1988)

Legislation

The Merchant Shipping Act 1876 (UK) came into force in November 1876

Treaties

Tanker Owners Voluntary Agreement Concerning Liability for Oil Pollution, signed 7 January 1969, [1969] ILM 8(3) (entered into force 6 October 1969)

Contract Regarding a Supplement to Tanker Liability for Oil Pollution, signed 14 January 1971, [1971] ILM 10(1) (entered into force 15 October 1977)

International Convention on Civil Liability for Oil Pollution Damage, opened for signature 29 November 1969, [1969] UNTS 319 (entered into force 19 June 1975) *(1969 Civil Liability Convention)*

1992 Protocol to the International Convention on Civil Liability for Oil Pollution Damage, opened for signature 27 November 1992, [1992] UKTS 86 (entered into force 30 May 1996) *(1992 Civil Liability Convention)*

International Convention on the Establishment of An International Fund for Compensation for Oil Pollution Damage, opened for signature 18 December 1971, [1971] ILM 284 (entered into force 16 October 1978) *(1971 Fund Convention).*

This *1971 Fund Convention* was superseded by the *Protocol of 1992* to the *International Convention on the Establishment of An International Fund for Compensation for Oil Pollution Damage*, opened for signature 27 November 1992, [1992] UKTS 87 (entered into force 24 May 2002) *(1992 Fund Convention)*

The *2003 Protocol Establishing an International Oil Pollution Compensation Supplementary Fund*, opened for signature 16 May 2003, [2003] 92FUND/A.8/4, Annex I (entered into force 3 May 2005) *(2003 Supplementary Fund Convention).*

International Load Line Convention 1930, opened for signature 5 July 1930, UNTS 858 (entered into force 1 January 1931) superseded by *1966 International Convention on Load Lines* opened for signature 05 April 1966, 640 UNTS 133 (entered into force 21 July 1968) as between contracting parties to later convention, to that extent their provisions conflict)

International Convention on Civil Liability for Oil Pollution Damage, opened for signature 29 November 1969, UNTS 973 (entered into force 19 June 1975) replaced by *the 1992 Protocol to the International Convention on Civil Liability for Oil Pollution Damage*, opened for signature 27 November 1992, UNTS 1956 (entered into force 30 May 1996.

International Oil Pollution Compensation Fund, *Decision Identification No 001676, Nefterudovoz-57 M incident*, 28th sess, Agenda Item 5, IOPC Doc 92FUND/EXC.28/8 (22 March 2005)

International Oil Pollution Convention Fund, *Small Tanker Oil Pollution Indemnification Agreement* (as amended 2017), opened for signature 28 February 2005, [2005] ILM 92FUND/A.ES.10/13 (entered into force 20 February 2006)

Paris Memorandum of Understanding on Port State Control, adopted 26 January 1982, IMO Res A.1052(27), entered into force 1 July 1982

The Tanker Oil Pollution Indemnification Agreement (as amended 2017), opened for signature 28 February 2005, [2005] ILM SUPPFUND/A/ES.2/7 (entered into force 20 February 2006)

Others

Explanatory Note, The International Regime for Compensation for Oil Pollution Damage (The Secretariat of the International Oil Pollution Compensation Funds, January 2012) https://www.iopcFund.org/npdf/genE.pdf

Gard, *Load lines* (Web Page, Insight 209, 16 January 2013) https://www.gard.no/web/updates/content/20734108/load-lines#:~:text=The%20purpose%20of%20the%20load,as%20a%20result%20of%20overloading.

Gray, William, Bridlington RNLI Remember The Great Gale of 1871, 150 Years On (News Release, *Lifeboat*, 26 January 2021) https://rnli.org/news-and-media/2021/january/26/bridlington-rnli-remember-the-great-gale-of-1871-150-years-on

International Tanker Owners Pollution Foundation, *Torrey Canyon, United Kingdom, 1967* (Web Page, 23 May 2014) , https://www.itopf.org/in-action/case-studies/case-study/torrey-canyon-united-kingdom-1967/

INTLERG, 'Do You Know What Plimsoll Lines on Ships Are?' (Web Page, 30 November 2019) https://intlreg.org/2019/11/30/do-you-know-what-plimsoll-lines-on-ships-are/

IOPC Funds, 'State Parties to both the 1992 Civil Liability Convention and the 1992 Fund Convention' (Webpage) www.iopcfunds.org

Lloyd's, '1988 The Piper Alpha Explosion' *Piper Alpha* (Web Page) https://www.lloyds.com/about-lloyds/history/catastophes-and-claims/piper-alpha

Menon, Catherine, Richard Hawkins, and John McDermid, 'Defence Standard 00–56 Issue 4: Towards Evidence-Based Safety Standards'(Web Page) https://www-users.cs.york.ac.uk/rdh2/papers/SSS09%20 Paper%20final.pdf

Ministry of Defence, Defence Standard 00–56: Safety Management Requirements for Defence System (Issue no. 4, 1 June 2007) https://www.skybrary.aero/bookshelf/books/344.pdf

Paris MoU, on Port State Control, 'Organisation' (Web Page) parismou.org/about-us/organisation

The International Maritime Organisation, *Brief History of IMO* (Web Page) http://www.imo.org/en/About/HistoryOfIMO/Pages/Default.aspx

Chapter 8
Lessons Learned from the Case Studies of International Mining and Waste Trade Industries

Abstract This chapter addresses the question: What are the key features of a new international framework that can improve the compensatory regime for workers in the South Asian shipbreaking industry? In determining key features, it examines lessons from the civil liability protocols following the Koko and Baia Mare disasters. The liability protocols shifted responsibility from host States of the incidents to the industry in control, making the examination relevant to the shipbreaking industry. Importantly, these protocols provide valuable guidance to shipbreaking industry that implement the civil liability principle and supplement existing international legal frameworks regulating the industry.

Keywords Shifting liability · Industry in control · Regulation of industry · Basel protocol · Kiev protocol · Waste trade · Good neighbourliness principle · Transboundary movement of wates · Industry-specific liability mechanism · Strict liability · Direct claim

Introduction

The Koko and Baia Mare incidents and their post-incident civil liability protocols offer a good model for the shipbreaking industry by introducing unique liability protocols to supplement their pre-existing special Conventions, which mainly follow a preventive model. The two civil liability protocols examined in this chapter are the *Basel Protocol on Liability and Compensation for Damage resulting from the transboundary Movements of Hazardous Wastes and Their Disposal (Basel Protocol), 1999,* and *the Protocol on Civil Liability and Compensation for Damage Caused by the Transboundary Effects of Industrial Accidents on Transboundary Waters to the 1992 Convention on the Protection and Use of Transboundary Watercourses and Use*

M. Z. Ali, *Worker Injustices in the South Asian Shipbreaking Industry*, International Law in Asia, https://doi.org/10.1007/978-981-95-8325-6_8

of Transboundary Watercourses and International Lakes and to the 1992 Convention on the Transboundary Effects of Industrial Accidents, 2003 (Kiev Protocol).[1] Although the *Basel* and *Kiev Protocols* have not yet entered into force, owing to an inadequate number of ratifications,[2] the shipbreaking industry can learn lessons from their innovative approaches, which include specific mechanisms for compensation and liability, including recoverable damage, limitation of liability, direct claim, insurance and enforcement mechanisms. The lessons learned from the specific mechanisms for compensation and liability are then used to develop the criteria for shipbreaking liability and compensation and design the shipbreaking liability certificate (SLC), a global civil liability framework for shipbreaking industry in Chap. 9, which would similarly supplement the *Hong Kong Convention.*[3]

This chapter has four parts. In sections "Lessons Learned from Koko" and "The Baia Mare Incident and its Post Legal Reforms: A Lesson for the Shipbreaking Industry", the concerned incidents and regulatory changes are reviewed first, followed by an analysis under the heading 'Lessons for the Global Shipbreaking Industry'. This chapter will make concluding remarks in section "Conclusion". Chapter 9 will apply the lessons learned, undertaking a critical examination of the SLC framework.

---

[1] *Basel Protocol on Liability and Compensation for Damage Resulting from the transboundary Movements of Hazardous Wastes and Their Disposal* opened for signature 10 December 1999, UN Doc. UNEP/CHW.1/WG/1/9/2 (not yet in force). *(the Basel Protocol)*; *the Protocol on Civil Liability and Compensation for Damage Caused by the Transboundary Effects of Industrial Accidents on Transboundary Waters to the 1992 Convention on the Protection and Use of Transboundary Watercourses and Use of Transboundary Watercourses and International Lakes and to the 1992 Convention on the Transboundary Effects of Industrial Accidents,* opened for signature 21 May 2003, UN Doc. ECE/MP.WAT/11-ECE/CP.TEIA/9 (not yet in force). *(Kiev Protocol).*

[2] Art 29 of the *Basel Liability Protocol* provides that 'the protocol shall enter into force on the nineteenth day after the date of deposit of the twentieth instrument of ratification, acceptance, formal confirmation, approval or accession'. The requirement has not yet been met because up to 27 April 2021 only 12 States acceded into the *Basel Liability Protocol*: at United Nations Treaty Collection, 'Depository' (Web Page) https://treaties.un.org/Pages/ViewDetails.aspx?src=TREATY&mtdsg_no=XXVII-3-b&Chapter=27&clang=_en; Art 29 of the Kiev Protocol provides that the protocol shall enter into force on the nineteenth day after the date of deposit of the sixteenth instrument of ratification, acceptance, formal confirmation, approval or accession. The requirement has not yet been met since up to 27 April 2021 only Hungary has ratified the *Kiev Protocol*: at United Nations Treaty Collection, 'Depository' (Web Page), https://treaties.un.org/Pages/ViewDetails.aspx?src=TREATY&mtdsg_no=XXVII-16&Chapter=27&clang=_en.

[3] *The Hong Kong International Convention for the Safe and Environmentally Sound Recycling of Ships*, opened for Signature 1 September 2009, IMO Doc. SR/CONF45 (entered into force 26 June 2025). *(Hong Kong Convention).*

Lessons Learned from Koko

Private traders collected and dumped several thousand tons of toxic waste in the Nigerian village of Koko, from various European locations, notably Italy.[4] The total tonnage of the hazardous waste so dumped was approximately 3800 tons. Five vessels conveyed the waste to Koko between 1987 and 1988. Because of the lack of appropriate waste management, the dumping led to the death and severe injury of thousands of local people handling toxic material during the removal of the waste (Koko incident).[5]

What became very clear after the incident that there was no effective regulatory mechanism capable of redressing the environmental and human harms done by cross border waste movement, other than the international environmental concept of 'good neighbourliness' or *sic utere tuo, ut alienum non laedas*. This means (inter alia) that each country has an obligation not to take action which is harmful to other States.[6] While it was a well-founded principle of customary international law, this could not play a role to regulate such transboundary movement of waste or to compensate the victims of the incident without adequate process and legal procedure.[7] The Koko incident made the international community acknowledged that a liability regime was necessary to regulate the transboundary movement of hazardous wastes.[8]

Basel Convention to Basel Protocol–Evolution of a Legal Regime of Liability and Compensation

Nigeria, at first, campaigned for a global solution to the control of hazardous waste movements. International collaboration came only after Nigeria's leadership, but it took much time and effort. However, realising the urgency of an industry-specific mechanism to regulate increasing waste trade led the international community to adopt the *Basel Convention on the Control of Transboundary Movements of*

---

[4] An Italian waste trading company, Messrs S.I Ecomar in collaboration with an Italian businessperson, Gianfrance Rafaellin, who lived in Nigeria, dumped the wastes: at S. Gozie Ogbodo, 'Environmental Protection in Nigeria: Two Decades after the Koko Incident' (2009) 15 *Annual Survey of International and Comparative Law* 1, 2–3.

[5] Ibid. 16–17.

[6] *Trail Smelter Arbitration (The United States v Canada) (Award)* (Trail Smelter Arbitral Tribunal Decision, 16 April 1938 and 11 March 1941) and re-established under Principle 21 of the *Declaration of the United Nations Conference on the Human Environment*: at United Nations Environmental Program, *the Declaration of the United Nations Conference on the Human Environment,* 11 ILM 1416 (16 June 972) online: UNEP website http:www.unep.org/Documents/Default.asp?DocumentID=97&ArticleID=1503

[7] See discussion on the problem with the application of customary international law: at Patricia Birnie & Alan Boyle, *International Law and the Environment*. (Oxford University Press, 2nd ed, 2002) 16–17.

[8] Ibid.

Hazardous Wastes and Their Disposal (*Basel Convention*) on 22 March 1989 at a conference held in Basel, Switzerland.[9]

On 5 May 1992, the *Basel Convention* entered into force following twentieth ratification. The *Basel Convention* does not restrict the trade in waste between nations per se. Rather, it permits each contractual party to restrict the transboundary movement of waste using national, bilateral or multilateral means.[10] Balancing the demands and concerns of industrialised nations, the *Basel Convention* provided a strong base for controlling the movement of wastes.[11]

The *Basel Convention* allows the trade of hazardous waste, however the industrialised countries commit to help the developing countries improve their waste management. But, unlike the *International Convention on the Establishment of An International Fund for Compensation for Oil Pollution Damage*, 1992 (*1992 Civil Liability Convention*) discussed in Chap. 7,[12] the *Basel Convention* did not include a comprehensive compensation regime. This inadequacy might underscore a fundamental difference inherent in international laws that are mostly driven by industrialised and developing countries. The United Nations Environmental Program, a specialised UN agency, adopted the *Basel Convention* to accommodate the requirements of developing countries, which decision makers perceived as having been left out after Koko crisis, while the shipping nations enacted the *1992 Civil Liability* and *Fund Conventions* to solve their problems after oil spill incidents.[13] It is open to speculation whether this is the reason why the *Basel Convention* left the potential victims to have no mechanism for their compensation.[14] However, the *Basel Convention* includes art 12, which permits a new protocol to be formulated specific to the issue of liability and compensation. Article 12 provides that:

> States should cooperate in adopting, as soon as possible, a protocol setting out appropriate rules and procedures in the field of liability and compensation for damage resulting from the transboundary movement and disposal of hazardous wastes and other wastes.

The importance of compensating victims in developing countries within a financial mechanism is demonstrated under art 12.[15] Following art 12, the parties to the

---

[9] *Basel Convention on the Control of Trans-boundary Movements of Hazardous Wastes and their Disposal*, opened for signature 22 March 1989, 1673 UNTS 126 (entered into force 5 May 1992) (*The Basel Convention*).

[10] Kathleen Howard, 'The Basel Convention: Control of Transboundary Movements of Hazardous Wastes and Their Disposal' (1990–1991) 14 *Hastings International and Comparative Law* 223.

[11] Ibid.

[12] *International Convention on Civil Liability for Oil Pollution Damage*, opened for signature 27 November 1992, UNTS 1956 (entered into force 30 May 1996).

[13] See Chap. 7.

[14] Peter Lawrence, 'Negotiation of a Protocol on Liability and Compensation for Damage Resulting from Transboundary Movements of Hazardous Wastes and their Disposal' (1998) 7(3) *Review of European, Comparative and International Environmental Law (RECIEL)* 249, 249.

[15] Almaz Omanova, 'International Practice of Compensation for Damage Caused by Environmental Violations in the Management of Tailing Storage Facilities and Waste Dumps' (April 2025) 8 (1) *Grassroots Journal of Natural Resources* 964–988. http://dx.doi.org/10.33002/nr2581.6853.080141 .

Basel Convention adopted the *Basel Protocol* in 1999 at their fifth Conference of the Parties (COPs), with the objective of compensating those impacted by an incident similar to Koko. The *Basel Protocol* acknowledges that the generation and disposal of hazardous waste are a threat to human health, property, and the environment.[16] In essence, the *Basel Protocol* apportions liability for damage suffered during the movement or management of such waste following the features below.

Liability Under the *Basel Protocol, 1999*

Objectives of the Basel Protocol

The primary aim of the *Basel Protocol* is to develop international and domestic legal instruments to assign liability and ensure adequate indemnity.[17] Article 1 of the *Basel Protocol* explicitly provides that the instrument is a major step towards the objective of securing adequate and prompt compensation for victims.

Who is Responsible?

The *Basel Protocol* imposes strict liability on a person who has 'operational control over such waste'.[18] This is a major legal shift since the international transfer of waste generally involves the actions of multiple parties, including private importers, exporters and affected Staes. The notifier is the person or company that informs its government to receive prior consent, to ship waste across borders. When the importer ultimately receives and deposes of the waste, it becomes the disposer. It might even be the exporting or importing State or a company. The difference between being a notifier or not depends on the interest of the entity to ship or receive the waste, if that intention is present they must, by law, notify the states of the specific governments about the transfer.[19]

If both the exporting and importing States are *Basel Convention* parties, the liability for compensation remains with the notifier until the disposer, as the importer, has assumed control over the waste.[20] The notifier's liability transfers to a disposer upon the disposer taking possession of the wastes.

In addition to the absolute liability of the notifier or disposer, all of the parties involved may be found responsible if their deliberate, reckless, or negligent acts, or their untimely application of the rules of the Convention causes or contributes to

[16] See Preamble of the *Basel Protocol* [4].

[17] Ibid. [1] and [6].

[18] The *Basel Protocol*, art 22.

[19] The *Basel Convention*, art 6.

[20] The *Basel Protocol*, art 4.

the damage.[21] If there was no notice and if they had operational control before the disposer, then both the exporting and importing State can be liable.[22]

Subject to the conditions listed under the *Basel Protocol*, such waste would have to be listed as hazardous wastes under the *Basel Convention* and the laws of the country concerned would have formally recognise such as hazardous.[23]

Liability Principle

The liability of a responsible person to provide compensation is strict.[24] A victim does not need to prove any fault from the responsible person if the fact proves to be a damage caused by the transboundary movement of wastes. As per art 4, the primary duty of a person in control of wastes is to ensure safety during loading, packaging, transit, unloading, and disposing of the wastes to prevent pollution. Despite taking proper measurers, the enforcement of liability is still possible in the case of a person's failure to limit economic loss.

Recoverable Damages

The *Basel Protocol* does not include all types of damage. The extent of damage within the *Basel Protocol* is economic rather than the cost of environmental damage having long-term adverse effects. According to art 2(2)(c), claimable damages only include damage to personal injury and property, 'loss of income deriving from an economic interest in use of the impaired environment, costs of reinstatement of impaired environment, and costs of specific measures taken to prevent, minimise, or mitigate damage, or to effect environmental clean-up'.

Limitation of Liability: Weight Matters

The strict liability for compensating for the damage claim under the *Basel Protocol* has a maximum limit. Subject to the determination of the limit by the domestic law of each contracting Party, the limitation mainly depends on the weight of wastes.[25] The maximum amount is thirty million units of account on the basis of the amount of the

---

[21] Ibid. art 5.

[22] Ibid. art 4(1).

[23] Ibid. art 3.

[24] Ibid. art 4(1).

[25] For a weight below 5 tonnes, the amount is one million, or for a weight between 5 and 25 tonnes, the amount is two million, or for a weight between 25 and 50 tonnes, the amount is four million units of account. For any shipment between 50 and1000 tonnes, the amount is six million or 10 million when the shipment is between 1000 tonnes and 10,000 tonnes. An additional 1000 units of account for every additional tonne of waste up to a maximum amount of 30 million units of account: at *Basel Protocol*, art 12 and Annex II.

wastes. However, the minimum limit differs among notifiers, exporters, or importers and disposers. It cannot be less than two million USD for a claim against a disposer and one million USD in case of a claim against a notifier, exporter, or importer.[26] The limitation of liability is not applicable when the cause of the damage is not compliant with the *Basel Convention* requirements or when someone has intended or showed negligence in inflicting the damage.[27]

Financial Security

Insurance plays a vital role in providing adequate compensation when the assets of a responsible entity fall short. The *Basel Protocol*'s primary aim is to provide adequate compensation; therefore, a prospective entity wishing to trade waste has two mandatory obligations: first, the trader has to cover the minimum liability amount specified in Annex II, and second, it is required to confirm that its insolvency is not going to affect a higher compensation claim. The *Basel Protocol* even accepts insurance or bonds or any other form of financial guarantee, such as financial security,[28] for an amount not less than the minimum limits specified in paragraph 2 of Annex B. One exception to this criterion is that the State-owned companies can fulfil the obligation through self-insurance without invoking any financial security. Importantly the parties are required to deliver a document of coverage to the competent authorities to guarantee the compensation.

Direct Claim

The *Basel Protocol* allows victims to claim compensation directly from the insurer or financial guarantor. The insurer can later obtain the amount indemnified from the person liable.[29] Co-payment or deductibles between the insurer or guarantor and the insured are permissible to provide maximum protection to victims, but failure from the insured to pay deductibles or co-payments cannot be an excuse to delay such claims. Victims can also claim compensation for the damage 'in the court of a contracting party where the damage is the consequence of the incident occurred, or the defendant has a habitual residence or has his principal office of the business'.[30]

The *Basel Protocol* is yet to enter into force, but it has introduced a new tool for victims in identical industries. Waste transfer is difficult to manage by a specific mechanism because of the involvement of several international parities,[31] but the features of the *Basel Protocol* create a good foundation for adequate and prompt

---

[26] Ibid.

[27] Ibid. art 5 and 12(1).

[28] Ibid. art 14.

[29] Ibid. art 14(4).

[30] Ibid. art 17.

[31] Lawrence (n 14) 254.

compensation claims for victims involved in the transboundary transfer of wastes. Shipbreaking is a type of waste transfer. The *Basel Protocol* has therefore provided some important lessons for the shipbreaking industry.

Lessons Learned from the Koko

The *Basel Protocol* not only eyes on business matters, but it also deals with responsibility for human and environmental harm. To that end, the Koko incident and the *Basel Protocol* show that regulatory restrictions with compensation frameworks work better than completely banning the same industry. What the incident teaches is that an international legal framework should keep businesses running while focusing on helping the victims—it is the same principle of balancing economic needs with social protection. As per the *Basel Protocol*, the parties who promote hazardous business can be made accountable regarding their actions.[32]

According to the *Basel Convention*, countries can transfer waste across borders with proper rules, and the *Basel Protocol* helps regulating the process with a compensatory approach. On the other hand, the *Hong Kong Convention* allows trading with old ships as a special form of waste trade but does not have a liability and compensatory framework to compensate victims.[33] This lesson is important for shipbreaking since the *Hong Kong Convention* only focuses on continuing the shipbreaking business in South Asia, but it does not make shipowners liable to pay compensation even though they promote this business in the region.[34] This shows a basic difference between international waste laws and shipbreaking laws. Shipbreaking is surely a unique type of waste movement from rich countries to poor nations. Moreover, this process transfers environmental problems along with old ships. The lessons from the *Basel Protocol* about liability and compensation for shipbreaking can contribute to the *Basel Protocol* proposed in Chap. 9.

This SLC framework, being a legal means to provide compensation is vital for developing countries. Developing countries do not have the capacity to manage such dangerous industries including shipbreaking that kill and injure workers. Further, the industry itself poses serious risks that these nations cannot handle properly, which reinforces the necessity of the SLC. But the contribution amount from the shipowners should have a fixed limit. This is important so that industries and insurers know their financial liability beforehand, and this limit should follow the pattern of waste quantity stored in a ship, similar to the *Basel Protocol.*

---

[32] Both developed and developing countries have shares in the trade. Developed countries must transfer the waste mainly because of the cost involved in their countries to dispose them. They also do not have adequate disposal facilities relative to the amount of waste they produce.

[33] See Chap. 5.

[34] Michael Galley, *Shipbreaking: Hazards and Liabilities* (Springer International Publishing, 2014) 1–2.

As per the *Basel Protocol*, victims can directly claim compensation form the insurance company.[35] This is the second lesson learned for shipbreaking. Following this approach for shipbreaking, victims should have the ability to claim directly from insurance companies or financial guarantors of responsible parties (shipowners). As most ships come from developed countries without any prior notification, a direct claim could be useful for making these entities directly accountable.[36] The principle recognises that waste trade itself involves multiple parties in international waste trade. In shipbreaking, shipowners change their flags to avoid cleaning requirements before breaking ships. This helps them circumvent legal obligations for proper waste removal. As mentioned in Chap. 3, they use cash buyers to hide their real identity. Using the direct claim approach, cash buyers and final flag States cannot escape the liability regarding compensation payments to shipbreaking victims. This principle is crucial for ensuring victims are paid their proper compensation.

The third lesson is that better disposal standards need proper notification so that government in developed countries knows about their waste transfers. Further, notification system helps developing countries dispose of waste properly and gain benefit from the waste trade. The *Basel Convention* recognises the problems that developing countries face and focus on improving their standards through a notification system.[37] The *Basel Protocol* requires the exporting country to notify and track waste transfers. This notification system helps monitor disposal standards when private importers handle the waste leading to support improving standards in developing countries. This lesson is important for shipbreaking because shipbreaking countries have limited capacity to improve standards alone without assistance from major shipping nations. The SLC framework proposed in Chap. 9 can work as a financial mechanism to compensate workers properly and further require developed nations to support developing countries in improving shipbreaking standards. The SLC framework would ensure adequate compensation payment in one hand and ensure international cooperation for better industry practices on the other.

Last, the Koko incident importantly teaches that when private companies from a country causes harm, that country's government must take responsibility for their actions. Moreover, the State cannot escape liability simply because the wrongdoing was done by private enterprises. Many global problems remain unresolved because of reluctance of States to accept responsibility. But with respect to State responsibility, Koko incident demonstrates that global solutions are difficult to manage unless the corresponding States take responsibility, considering the same negative effects of the problems.[38] With respect to shipbreaking, major shipping nations rarely speak against their private shipowners regarding sending ships for breaking in South Asia. This is

---

[35] *Basel Protocol*, art 14(4).

[36] Mohammad Zulfikar Ali, 'Injustice to Workers in the Shipbreaking Industry in South Asia: A Quest for a Civil Liability Framework in International Law' (PhD Thesis, Curtin University, 2022) 246–247.

[37] See Chap. 9.

[38] Venessa S.W. Tsang, 'Establishing State Responsibility in Mitigating Climate Change under Customary International Law' (Graduate Thesis, Columbia University) 1.

why; the lesson is important for shipbreaking. Leaning this lesson, major shipping nations must take responsibility and further push the IMO to adopt a shipbreaking liability protocol.

As discussed in the following Part, support from developed nations is the principle established after the *Baia Mare* gold mining spill incident. Preceding the incident, the European Union Member States pushed the international community and introduced the *Kiev Protocol*, a global liability mechanism. The next part looks at the *Kiev Protocol* that international community adopted after the *Baia Mare* gold mining spill incident. Similar to the *Basel Protocol*, the *Kiev Proto*col supplemented existing convention mechanisms for supporting victims.

The Baia Mare Incident and Its Post Legal Reforms: A Lesson for the Shipbreaking Industry

The Incident

Mining accidents cause serious damage to cross-border water resources. Profits generated by mining is huge but industrial accidents can create heavy financial losses for the country and nearby nations threatening the plants and animals living in different regions. Moreover, citizens affected by these accidents also face serious financial consequences. But because, there was no special law with a mechanism to compensate victims, it was challenging for victims' compensation. The Baia Mare incident was the first incident to highlight this deficiency in transboundary water laws (mentioned below).

In late January 2000, Northwestern Romania experienced the Baia Mare incident when a mining waste dam burst causing significant environmental damage. In such a dam, soil barriers are made to hold waste materials following extraction activities after valuable materials are removed. In Baia Mare, the bursting of the dam released 100,000 cubic meters of cyanide-contaminated water into the Lapos and Somes (Szamos) rivers. As the two transboundary rivers flow across borders, the cyanide flowed through three European countries. As per reports, the cyanide release caused major damage to aquatic life in rivers in three countries, Hungary, Yugoslavia, and Romania. In consequence, Aurul, which was a joint venture company between Australia's Esmeralda Exploration and the Romania's government, was running the facility had to pay compensation to the victims.[39]

[39] The joint venture between an Australian mining company, Esmeralda Exploration Limited and a Romanian Company Romanian Compania Nationala a Metalelor Pretiosasis si Neferoase (REMIN), was formed to re-process an abandoned tailings pond for extracting gold, silver, and other metals. The location of the gold mining industry was by the town of Baia Mare in Romania. The incident was named after the place of occurrence. At around 20.00 GMT, on 30 January 2000, the tailings pond overflowed near the city of Baia Mare: at.

Legal Gaps

In the first instance, *the Convention on the Protection and Use of Transboundary Watercourses and International Lakes*, and *the Convention on the Transboundary Effects of Industrial Accidents (the 1992 Helsinki Conventions)* created frameworks to prevent and reducc cross-border impacts from mining accidents. Moreover, these conventions focus on protecting shared water bodies and managing industrial accidents that affect neighbouring countries.[40] The United Nations Economic Commission of Europe (UNECE), a specialised organisation of the United Nations, adopted both conventions in March 1992 in Helsinki, Finland. The *1992 Helsinki Conventions*' primary objective is to integrate international cooperation with domestic measures through enforcement mechanisms. These mechanisms further established basic standards for notification, collaboration, loss mitigation, public information access, and data sharing.[41] However, following the Baia Mare disaster, global stakeholders recognised that the pre-existing *1992 Helsinki Conventions* had the deficiencies of not having a proper compensatory mechanism, which needed improvement. The *1992 Helsinki Conventions* addressed cross-border industrial accident effects, but they did not establish liability provisions or compensation requirements for private parties.[42] The Baia Mare incident showed that international operators of the mining industry had no responsibility for causing detrimental human and environmental consequences. This gap is similar to shipbreaking sector, which also has no mechanism to compensate workers for their loss. Opposite to shipbreaking, the legal regime evolved after the Baia Mare incident reflected the changing social needs triggered by judicial interpretations.

Evolution of a Legal Regime

The Baia Mare incident showed systematic problems in the *1992 Helsinki Conventions*. Following the Baia Mare incident, Hungary struggled to claim compensation-imposing liability on Aurul. Hungary's difficulty exposed the legal gap in the *1992*

Solveig Argeseanu Cunningham, Incident, Accident, Catastrophe: Cyanide on the Danube' (2005) 29 (2) *Disasters* 99–128.

[40] *The Convention on the Protection and Use of Transboundary Watercourses, and International Lakes*, signed 17 March 1992, 1936 UNTS 269 (entered into force 6 October 1996); *the Convention on the Transboundary Effects of Industrial Accidents*, signed 18 March 1992, 2105 UNTS 457 (entered into force 18 April 2000) *(The 1992 Helsinki Conventions)*.

[41] Forenc Laszlo, Lessons Learned from the Cyanide and Heavy Metal Accidental Water Pollution in the Tisa River Basin in the Year 2000' in *Management of Intentional and Accidental Water Pollution* (Springer Netherlands, 2006) 43–50.

[42] Ibid.

Helsinki Conventions. Before filing a legal proceeding, Hungary offered Aurul a settlement deal, but the operator refused to take responsibility and rejected the offer.[43]

The Hungarian State later filed a suit at Budapest's Capital Court in April 2001. The legal proceeding was regarding USD 143 million compensation claim from the operator, Aurul.[44] Individuals, including anglers, also filed legal proceedings against Aurul. But the Court suspended private cases until the court passed any final decision in the case filed by Hungary. In 2005, the Capital Court finally decided that the defendant company had no legal responsibility for damages.[45] This happened because there was no legal mechanism to claim compensation at that time. This ruling intensified a debate in the EU about making separate laws for liability and compensation in addition to *the 1992 Helsinki Conventions*. The international community soon responded following a call from the EU to address the problem introducing the *Kiev Protocol* to *the 1992 Helsinki Conventions*.[46]

The United Nations Economic Commission of Europe (UNECE), a special arm of the United Nations, formally adopted the *Kiev Protocol* on 21 May 2003. The adoption took place at the Ministerial Conference, 'Environment for Europe' in Kiev, Ukraine.[47] Twenty-two State Parties including Romania, Hungary, and Yugoslavia supported the *Kiev Protocol* during the Second Joint Special Session of the Meeting of the Parties to *the 1992 Helsinki Conventions*.

As per status, the *Kiev Protocol* has not yet entered into force. It has not yet received enough ratification. Compared between the *Hong Kong Convention* and pre-existing *1992 Helsinki Conventions*, the *Kiev Protocol* provides a foundation to argue for a supplementary international framework for the shipbreaking industry. This is to resolve the gap in the *Hong Kong Convention*, which does not have a liability and compensation mechanism for the shipbreaking industry. The next section examines the *Kiev Protocol*'s regulatory framework and structure. The *Kiev Protocol* resembles the principles of strict liability, channelling liability on polluters, and proof of financial security similar to the *Basel Protocol* as discussed previously but differs

---

[43] Hungary argued that on September 2000 they were ready to settle with the Australian mining company. The firm denied: at Istvan Egresi, 'The Curse of the Gold: Discourses Surrounding the Project of the Largest Pit-Mine Europe' (2011) 5 (2) *Journal of Studies and Research in Human Geography* 57–68.

[44] Simon Mann, 'Angry Hungary Demands Compensation' *Sydney (Australia) Morning Herald* (10 February 2000) 8.

[45] *Hungary v Aurul* (Hungarian Capital Court, case no. 4.P. 23.771/2001 137) Decision dated 8 May 2006; M. G. Faure and G. Betlem, 'Applying National Liability Law to Transboundary Pollution: Some Lessons from Europe and the United States' in M. Faure and Y. Song (eds), *China and International Environmental Liability, Legal Remedies for Transboundary Pollution* (Edward Elgar, 2008) 129–191.

[46] Ibid.

[47] United Nations Economic Commission of Europe, *Draft Decision by the Parties to the UNECE Conventions on the Protection and use of Transboundary Watercourses and International Lakes and the Transboundary Effects of Industrial Accidents Regarding the Protocol on Civil Liability and Compensation for Damage Caused by the Transboundary Effects of Industrial Accidents on Transboundary Waters*, Environment for Europe, 5th Ministerial Conference, UN Doc. ECE/MP.WAT/2003/2 CP.TEIA/2003/4 (21–23 May 2003).

that it defines a person who is financially responsible for the harm and compensation payments.

Goal and Salient Features of the Kiev Protocol, 2003

The *Kiev Protocol* outlines an important objective in its Preamble, which is to provide third-party liability for adequate and prompt compensation.[48] Article 1 of the *Kiev Protocol* provides that the objective of the *Kiev Protocol* is to 'ensure adequate and prompt compensation for damage caused by the transboundary effects of industrial accidents on transboundary waters'.[49] Unlike the oil spill legal regime discussed in Chap. 7, which aims to build an equitable system of loss distribution, the *Kiev Protocol*'s aim is to introduce civil liability to companies that can 'contribute to the practical application of safety measures and hazardous activities and thus help to prevent industrial accidents and limit their adverse effect on people and environment'.[50] Following the objectives of that link both to compensation and prevention, the *Kiev Protocol* includes the following features for imposing responsibility on responsible parties and paying compensation.

Who Bears the Liability

The *Kiev Protocol* acknowledges 'the risk of damage to human health, property, and the environment caused by transboundary effects of industrial accidents[51] and imposes liability on the operator of an industry'.[52] On proof of industrial accident and damage, unless otherwise provided in art 4 and 5 of the *Kiev Protocol*, the operator of an industrial installation is liable.[53]The section, 'Immunities, Exonerations, and Defences to Operators' below discusses the exceptions to the operator's liability rule. Imposing liability on the operator has dual functions. It is direct and accessible for the victims to impose liability on a particular person, and the victims find it easy since it does not require finding proof of a fault. The nature of the damage may find one or more operators liable. The *Kiev Protocol* addresses the issue by imposing joint and

[48] Preamble of the *Kiev Protocol*, [3] and [6].

[49] The *Kiev Protocol*, art 1.

[50] Ibid. 5.

[51] Preamble of the *Kiev Protocol* [5].

[52] Phani Dascalopoulou-Livada and Alexandros Kolliopoulos, 'The 2003 Kiev Protocol on Civil Liability and Compensation for Damage Caused by the Transboundary Effects of Industrial Accidents on Transboundary Waters', in the *UNECE Convention on the Use and protection of Transboundary Watercourses and Lakes Its Contribution to International Water Cooperation Series* (Brill Online Publication, 2015). https://brill.com/view/book/edcoll/9789004291584/B9789004291584-s024.xml.

[53] The *Kiev Protocol*, art 4(1).

individual liability on the operators in case the share of damage is not reasonably separable.

Scope of *Liability*

The liability of an operator is restricted by the damage caused by an industrial accident.[54] Article 4 of the *Kiev Protocol* imposes 'the liability in the event of any damage caused by an industrial accident in the course of a hazardous activity'. The victim does not require proving any fault from the operator if the fact proves to be transboundary damage caused by an industrial operation.[55]

The foreseeability of damage has a special place in the *Kiev Protocol*. The classic exoneration clauses, including force majeure or intervention of third parties, are in place in the *Kiev Protocol*, but if a victim can show that the damage was foreseeable, an operator cannot escape the liability using the exoneration clauses. Whereas strict liability is the basis of shifting liability on the operator, the *Kiev Protocol* also includes the scope to impose fault liability upon the operator. Based on knowledge of the person liable, it is an area to be addressed by the domestic law of the parties to the *Kiev Protocol*.[56]

Immunities, Exonerations, and Defences to Operators

The degree to which an operator can escape depends on the facts and circumstances of each case. As mentioned above, operators have strict liability for any transboundary damage caused by industrial accidents, but in the presence of some facts and circumstances, the operators may evade responsibility—for example, where an operator can show that the damage was the result of the victim's fault. Conversely, escaping liability is not absolute, given that it depends on surrounding circumstances during the time of occurrence. Art 4(3) states that 'the compensation may be reduced or disallowed having regard to all the circumstances'.

Recoverable Damages

A victim can only claim compensation for economic loss to property and person under the *Kiev Protocol*. Pursuant to art 2(d) of the *Kiev Protocol*, a victim can claim damage if it causes him (i) 'loss of life, or personal injury'; (ii) 'loss of, or damage to, property other than property' belonging to the person liable under the Protocol; and

---

[54] Ibid. art 4.

[55] United Nations Economic Commission for Europe (UNECE), 'Background Document for the UNECE Workshop to be Held in Budapest, on 21–22 May 2007' (Background Report, 11 April 2007) 32.

[56] The *Kiev Protocol*, art 4.

(iii) 'loss of income' directly because a victim has lost his or her legally protected interest in any use of the transboundary waters for economic purposes.

More so, according to art 2(d) of the *Kiev Protocol*, a victim can claim compensation for damage if his or her loss is the consequence of damage to transboundary waters that can even include 'savings and costs', such as the 'cost of measures of reinstatement of impaired transboundary waters, limited to the costs of measures actually taken or to be undertaken', and 'the cost of response measures, including any loss or damage caused by such measures, to the extent that the damage was caused by the transboundary effects of an industrial accident on transboundary waters'.

Limitation of Liability

Subject to further improvement, the amount of strict liability is fixed under the *Kiev Protocol*. Annex II of the *Kiev Protocol* provides the mechanism to determine the maximum liability. There are three categories; A, B, and C in Annex II and the amount applicable in each category depends on the type and amount of hazardous substances.[57] The maximum liability amount is between 10 and 40 million units of account. The limitation is not applicable when damage is the consequence of the fault of an operator.[58] The *Kiev Protocol* also allows the minimum limits of liability. The amount ranges between 2.5 and 10 million units within the A, B, and C groups. The minimum liability scheme provides justification for the claim addressing the nature of the industrial installation or the hazardous substances involved in an incident and the difficulty in determining the liability of the operator.

Insurance to Provide *Financial Security*

Insurance plays a vital role in two ways: how to provide adequate compensation when the assets of the operator fall short and how to ensure prompt compensation. Concerning adequate compensation, art 11 of the *Kiev Protocol* provides that the operators have two mandatory obligations. First, an operator must cover the minimum liability amount specified in Annex II, and second, an operator must confirm that an operator's insolvency will not affect higher compensation claims. State-owned companies can fulfil the obligation of insurance by self-insurance without invoking any financial security. To fulfil their duties, they must have coverage by insurance or financial security, including bonds or any financial guarantee so that their assets do not fall short of meeting a compensation claim.

With respect to prompt compensation, the *Kiev Protocol* allows victims to claim compensation directly from the insurer or any person providing a financial guarantee. Following the legal claim from a victim, 'the insurer or guarantor shall have the right

[57] *Annex II Limits of Liability and Minimum Limits of Financial Securities* to the *Kiev Protocol*, Part I and II.

[58] The *Kiev Protocol*, art 5 provides fault-based liability is unlimited.

of recourse from the person liable under art 4 to be joined in the proceedings'. In addition, co-payment or deductibles between the insurer or guarantor and insured are acceptable under art 11 to provide the highest safeguard to the victims. However, the insurer or financial provider cannot delay any claim by taking the defence that the insured has failed to pay deductibles or copayments.

Enforcement Mechanism

Two options are open to the victims for enforcing the mechanism. The first route is to file a case. For legal proceedings, the place of suit is the place of occurrence, damage, or the country of residence of the defendant. If the defendant is a company or another legal person, the victim must file a case in its principal office or its statutory seat or central location. Notably, Hungary, after the *Baia Mare* incident, filed the case in its Capital Court as the place of residence of the defendant.[59] The second route is to agree with the operator to settle the dispute in arbitration as per the *Permanent Court of Arbitration Optional Rules for the Arbitration of Disputes Relating to Natural Resources and the Environment*. These innovative approaches are especially crucial for any industry-specific liability and compensation mechanism. Considered more in Section 'E' below, the legal and innovative features of the *Kiev Protocol* provide essential lessons for the shipbreaking industry.

The *Kiev Protocol* has yet to be enforced because of a lack of adequate ratification from a sufficient number of states. An underlying reason for this is that the Protocol has not made all profitable entities responsible other than the operators of the industries. For example, in the case of the gold mining industry in *Baia Mare*, beneficial entities include the gold user, gold seller, dam construction company, and cyanide producer. They are the beneficial parties from gold mining, but the *Kiev Protocol* has not addressed their contribution to damage. Phani argues that one of the main impediments to the success of this *Kiev Protocol* is the uncertainty over the amount of such transboundary damage caused by industrial accidents. This obligation causes the insurance premium to increase.[60] Despite these limitations, the *Kiev Protocol* is an excellent starting point for solving complex transboundary problems. The operator of an industrial installation is liable for damage, which is subject to the damage that results from an event resulting from an industrial accident. An industrial accident is closely linked to hazardous activity. This means an event resulting from an uncontrolled development in the course of hazardous activity during manufacture, use, storage, handling or disposal, and transportation onsite or offsite via pipelines from an installation. As per the definition, it is possible to make companies liable for both the production and transportation of waste via pipelines. Hazardous activity is related to the use of hazardous substances beyond the prescribed limit provided

[59] The *Kiev Protocol*, art 13(1).

[60] Dascalopoulou-Livada and Kolliopoulos (n 51) 334.

by Annex I and is sufficient to cause transboundary damage to transboundary waters and their water uses in the case of an industrial accident.[61]

There is little difference in defining responsible parties in both shipbreaking and other inter-State industries. In both cases, the responsible parties are international in character and remain out of reach of existing international mechanisms owing to legal gaps (as discussed previously). This characteristic of the two industries allows the learning of essential lessons from the Baia Mare incident and its legal development in terms of liability and compensation for shipbreaking industries.

Lessons Learned from the Baia Mare Incident

The 'beneficiary pays' concept holds significant practical importance for the shipbreaking sector. In the *Kiev Protocol*'s civil liability framework, this principle serves as cornerstone by utilising proven mechanisms such as strict liability, responsibility transfer, and financial guarantees.[62] A core element of the *Kiev Protocol* involves the operator's strict liability. This represents an innovative tool to implementing corporate responsibility principles and carries substantial relevance for South Asian shipbreaking sector.

The *Kiev Protocol* emphasises liability and compensation matters. In contrast, the *Hong Kong Convention* applied to shipbreaking sector offers no liability or compensation framework. Therefore, the distinctive characteristics of the *Kiev Protocol* become essential when advocating for such a structure in shipbreaking. Furthermore, the *Kiev Protocol* advocates for civil liability rather than environmental liability alone. Civil liability encompasses both environmental and financial responsibility, while environmental liability has a narrower scope. In shipbreaking sector, workers face direct harm due to hazardous materials embedded in a ship's structure. Considering the features of South Asia's shipbreaking sector, an international framework should prioritise establishing accountability for worker fatalities and injuries. The Court of Appeal of England and Wales has determined that entities bear a duty of care and must provide compensation when creating profit-driven danger.[63]

The principle that responsibility should accompany danger also applies to the shipbreaking sector. Despite understanding the human cost in South Asian shipbreaking operations, shipping companies have consistently avoided accountability. The Baia Mare incident demonstrates how liability can extend to industries even when accidents are not directly their fault. Aurul constructed a tailings dam using a zero-leak system to prevent spillage. When facing legal action, the company argued that adverse weather caused the damage, but this defence proved inadequate. Investigation, on the other hand, revealed that while conditions were severe, they were

[61] The *Kiev Protocol*, art 2(e).

[62] Dascalopoulou-Livada Kolliopoulos (n 51), 336.

[63] *Hamida Begum (on behalf of MD Khalil Mollah) v Maran (UK) Limited* [2021] EWCA Civ 326.

foreseeable occurrences happening approximately every twenty-five years.[64] In this context, the Baia Mare incident highlighted how foreseeability or awareness of potential accidents determines operator responsibility. The reasoning applies equally to shipbreaking, as shipping companies understand the poor conditions in South Asian shipbreaking facilities, for which they must acknowledge accidents and pollution are predictable rather than extraordinary events.

The financial security framework with maximum limits offers valuable insights for the shipbreaking sector. Since South Asia handles a substantial portion of global shipbreaking activities, implementing a financial security system with minimum and maximum thresholds would suit the industry. This approach would inform shipowners about their maximum liability and contributions to the system.

Similar to the *Koko incident* and other cases examined in Chap. 7, it is demonstrated that there is a need for a supplementary protocol to the *Hong Kong Convention.* As discussed in this chapter, the *1992 Helsinki Conventions* were established to address transboundary damage from industrial accidents while allowing continued industrial operations. With continuity of business in mind, these conventions aim to maintain industrial activities under regulatory requirements including notification, emergency response, mitigation, and cooperation during catastrophic events. But the *1992 Helsinki Conventions* contain no provisions for civil liability regarding environmental pollution or victim compensation. Although domestic legislation addressed these areas, national laws and institutions achieved limited success in enforcing liability and compensation due to the international nature of the businesses.[65] This is the reason why Hungary could not enforce liability or secure compensation for private victims under domestic law against Aurul. This argument aligns with arguments made by Stephen Sec and others. Using Baia Mare as evidence, their research criticised Romanian mining laws that prioritised mining investment over industrial liability.[66] Similarly, South Asian domestic laws follow comparable approaches that inadequately address liability for beneficial entities or ship sellers regarding the human costs in breaking their ships.[67](see Chaps. 4 and 5).

At the international level, *the Hong Kong Convention* also lacks liability and compensation mechanisms (see Chap. 5). Instead, it promotes shipbreaking activities, similar to how the *1992 Helsinki Conventions* supported mining industries. However, the *Kiev Protocol* supplements the *1992 Helsinki Conventions* and ensures liability and compensation payment. The United Nations Economic Commission for Europe developed the *Kiev Protocol* as a separate law on liability and compensation, yet no comparable mechanism exists to supplement the *Hong Kong Convention* for shipbreaking operation.

---

[64] The European Union Commission, 'Report of the Baia Mare Taskforce' (Investigation Report, December 2000) http://viso.jrc.ec.europa.eu/pecomines_ext/docs/bmtf_report.pdf

[65] Justine Bendel, *Litigating the Environment: Process and Procedure before International Courts and Tribunals* (Edward Elgar Publishing, 2023) 5–6.

[66] Stephen Stec et al., 'Transboundary Environmental Governance and the Baia Mare Cyanide Spill' (2001) 27(4) *Review of Central and East European Law* 671, 671.

[67] See Chap. 3.

The *Kiev Protocol*'s enforcement structure provides the final lesson for the shipbreaking industry. Regarding liability and compensation assurance, domestic laws should hold special significance within international law. Notably, victims can pursue compensation cases in their domestic courts. When seeking additional rights, the procedural importance of national law remains crucial since national judicial institutions readily accept these proceedings. With respect to national law's procedural importance, the *Kiev Protocol* includes three features acknowledges the importance of domestic laws in three ways. First, domestic laws apply when the *Kiev Protocol* remains silent on substantive and procedural issues.[68] Second, it permits additional rights and protective measures beyond the *Kiev Protocol* despite 'matters of substance regulated by the *Kiev Protocol*'.[69] Third, most significantly, domestic law may supersede the Kiev Protocol when victims approach the court.[70]

Conclusion

This chapter has extracted important lessons from case studies in international mining and waste trade sectors, examining the Baia Mare and Koko incidents. Both cases reveal that legal reforms followed similar approaches—establishes separate liability and compensation frameworks to supplement existing conventions. This occurred because the international community recognised the importance of separate financial mechanisms, which the existing conventions lack. This indicates that successful policy changes for the shipbreaking sector require support from major shipping companies and their respective governments with clear objectives, while maintaining current maritime industry profit structures alongside proper enforcement mechanisms.

The *Basel* and *Kiev Protocols* await enforcement because of insufficient ratification. Nevertheless, they represent important initiatives for addressing global waste trade problems and transboundary damage to waterways from industrial activities. These incidents and their subsequent legal frameworks regarding liability and compensation provide excellent examples and analogies for international shipbreaking operations.

Bibliography

Articles/Books/Reports

Balkau, Fritz, 'Learning from Baia Mare' (2005) 3 *Environment and Poverty Times*, 1

[68] The *Kiev Protocol*, art 16 (1).

[69] Ibid. art 17.

[70] Ibid. art 16(2).

Dascalopoulou-Livada, Phani and Alexandros Kolliopoulos, 'The 2003 Kiev Protocol on Civil Liability and Compensation for Damage Caused by the Transboundary Effects of Industrial Accidents on Transboundary Waters, in the UNECE Convention on the Use and protection of Transboundary Watercourses and Lakes Its Contribution to International Water Cooperation Series' (Brill Online Publication, 2015). https://brill.com/view/book/edcoll/9789004291584/B9789004291584-s024.xml

Lawrence, Peter, 'Negotiation of a Protocol on Liability and Compensation for Damage Resulting from Transboundary Movements of Hazardous Wastes and their Disposal' (1998) 7(3) *Review of European, Comparative and International Environmental Law (RECIEL)* 249

Liu, Sylvia F., 'The Koko Incident: Developing International Norms for the Transboundary Movement of Hazardous Waste' (1992) 8 *Journal of Natural Resources and Environment Law* 148

Lucas, Cadric, '*Baia Mare* and Baia Borsa Accidents: Cases of Severe Transboundary Water Pollution' (2001) 31(2) *Environmental Policy and Law* 108

Stec, Stephen et al, 'Transboundary Environmental Governance and the Baia Mare Cyanide Spill' (2001) 27(4) *Review of Central and East European Law* 671

Ayobayo, Babade James, 'The Koko Incident- Law of the Sea and Environmental Protection' (Seminar Paper, University of Lagos, November 2014) 14–15

Birnie, Patricia and Alan Boyle, *International Law and the Environment*. (Oxford University Press, 2nd ed, 2002)

Galley, Michael, *Shipbreaking: Hazards and Liabilities* (Springer International Publishing, 2014)

Springer, Allan L., *Cases of Conflict-Transboundary Disputes and Development of International Environmental Law* (University of Toronto Press, 2016) 99

Onyerikam, Ifeokma M., 'Achieving Compliance with the Basel Convention on Transboundary Movement of Hazardous Waste' (LLM Thesis, University of Alberta, 2007) 13–15

United Nations Economic Commission for Europe (UNECE), 'Background Document for the UNECE Workshop to be Held in Budapest, on 21–22 May 2007' (Background Report, 11 April 2007) 32.

Treaties

Basel Protocol on Liability and Compensation for Damage Resulting from the transboundary Movements of Hazardous Wastes and Their Disposal opened for signature 10 December 1999, UN Doc. UNEP/CHW.1/WG/1/9/2 (not yet in force)

Convention on the Protection and Use of Transboundary Watercourses, and International Lakes, signed 17 March 1992, 1936 UNTS 269 (entered into force 6 October 1996)

Convention on the Transboundary Effects of Industrial Accidents, signed 18 March 1992, 2105 UNTS 457 (entered into force 18 April 2000)

Declaration of the United Nations Conference on the Human Environment: at United Nations Environmental Program, *the Declaration of the United Nations Conference on the Human Environment,* 11 ILM 1416 (16 June 972) online: UNEP website http:www.unep.org/Documents/Default.asp?DocumentID=97&ArticleID=1503

International Convention on Civil Liability for Oil Pollution Damage, opened for signature 27 November 1992, UNTS 1956 (entered into force 30 May 1996)

Protocol on Civil Liability and Compensation for Damage Caused by the Transboundary Effects of Industrial Accidents on Transboundary Waters to the 1992 Convention on the Protection and Use of Transboundary Watercourses and Use of Transboundary Watercourses and International Lakes and to the 1992 Convention on the Transboundary Effects of Industrial Accidents, opened for signature 21 May 2003, UN Doc. ECE/MP.WAT/11-ECE/CP.TEIA/9 (not yet in force)

The Basel Convention on the Control of Trans-boundary Movements of Hazardous Wastes and their Disposal, opened for signature 22 March 1989, 1673 UNTS 126 (entered into force 5 May 1992)

The Hong Kong International Convention for the Safe and Environmentally Sound Recycling of Ships, opened for Signature 1 September 2009, IMO Doc. SR/CONF45 (not yet in force)
United Nations Economic Commission of Europe, *Draft Decision by the Parties to the UNECE Conventions on the Protection and use of Transboundary Watercourses and International Lakes and the Transboundary Effects of Industrial Accidents Regarding the Protocol on Civil Liability and Compensation for Damage Caused by the Transboundary Effects of Industrial Accidents on Transboundary Waters*, Environment for Europe, 5th Ministerial Conference, UN Doc. ECE/MP.WAT/2003/2 CP.TEIA/2003/4 (21–23 May 2003)

Cases

Hamida Begum (on behalf of MD Khalil Mollah) v Maran (UK) Limited [2021] EWCA Civ 326
Hungary v Aurul (Hungarian Capital Court, case no. 4.P. 23.771/2001 137) Decision dated 8 May 2006
Trail Smelter Arbitration (The United States v Canada) (Award) (Trail Smelter Arbitral Tribunal Decision, 16 April 1938 and 11 March 1941)

Others

Reliefweb, 'Hungarian Government Demands Compensation from "Aurul"' (Press Release, 14 March 2001) https://reliefweb.int/report/hungary/hungarian-government-demands-compensation-aurul
Reliefweb, 'Hungary Files Suit for Cyanide Leakage' (Press Release, 30 April 2001) , https://reliefweb.int/report/hungary/hungary-files-suite-cyanide-leakage
The European Union Commission, 'Report of the Baia Mare Taskforce' (Investigation Report, December 2000) http://viso.jrc.ec.europa.eu/pecomines_ext/docs/bmtf_report.pdf
United Nations Treaty Collection, 'Depository' (Web Page) https://treaties.un.org/Pages/ViewDetails.aspx?src=TREATY&mtdsg_no=XXVII-3-b&Chapter=27&clang=_en

Chapter 9
Proposal for a Shipbreaking Liability Certificate and Shipbreaking Insurance

Abstract The Chapter introduces and explains a global civil liability (shipbreaking liability certificate or SLC) framework, addressing the main research question: what liability framework is required to make the maritime industry accountable for the harm to human life and health (workers' deaths, physical injuries, and work-related diseases) in major shipbreaking countries? The SLC framework proposed in this chapter is necessarily an international compensatory legal framework filling in the gaps of having only preventive mechanism in the *Hong Kong Convention*.

An underlying feature of the SLC framework is a requirement for overlapping (or concurrent) insurance during the shipbreaking process and, therefore, joint liability (i.e., sharing of costs between the last shipowner and the shipbreaking facility) for any worker compensation claim that arises during the breaking of the ship. The overlapping insurance is aimed to be achieved by the dual SLCs (i.e., the SLC held by the last shipowner and the SLC held by the shipbreaking yard) in place during the shipbreaking process. The proposed SLC is thereby to practically follow the 'cradle to grave' (or a 'shipyard to shipbreaking yard') approach for all shipowners involved in the shipbreaking business chain and make them accountable for the human harms in breaking ships.

Keywords Shipbreaking liability certificate · Sharing cost · Joint liability · Direct claim · Financial security · Commercial life of a ship · Shipbreaking yard · Direct compensation claim · Strict liability · Cash buyers · Short-term owners

Introduction

This chapter draws on the lessons from the findings presented in Chaps. 2 to 8, particularly from the compulsory 'Load Lines Certificate', a case study discussed in Chap. 7, section "Plimsoll Line Incident and Importance of a Load Lines Certificate". It proposes a global civil liability framework (shipbreaking liability certificate or SLC) illustrated in Fig. 9.1 below for the shipbreaking industry. The global

M. Z. Ali, *Worker Injustices in the South Asian Shipbreaking Industry*, International Law in Asia, https://doi.org/10.1007/978-981-95-8325-6_9

civil liability framework is based on the introduction of a compulsory shipbreaking liability certificate (SLC) for all commercial ships sailing on international waters:

1. to apply throughout the operating life and the shipbreaking process for the ship;
2. to be renewed annually and at any transfer of ownership for the ship; and
3. to be issued and administered by the International Maritime Organisation (IMO).

The SLC framework is based on obtaining two separate SLCs (the dual-SLC system) for a ship by a shipowner and a shipbreaking facility. According to Fig. 9.1, the International Maritime Organisation (IMO) would need to issue a SLC for a ship's commercial operation (SLC for a shipowner), which remains in place until a shipbreaking facility completes their shipbreaking process (SLC for a shipbreaking facility). The shipbreaking facility, being the last owner of a ship, would be required to renew the SLC and thus maintain shipbreaking liability insurance for the ship. The IMO can renew the SLC only if the commercial owner of a ship, including a shipbreaking facility shows evidence of active shipbreaking liability insurance from approved maritime insurance companies.

The SLC framework requires all parties to maintain insurance coverage during shipbreaking, creating equal financial responsibility when workers get injured during shipbreaking operations. Both the owner of an old ship and shipbreaking facility will maintain insurance coverage at the same time. The dual insurance coverage (i.e., the SLC held by the last shipowner and the SLC held by the shipbreaking yard) would ensure that both parties are jointly responsible for compensating affected workers. A consequence of maintaining such dual SLCs is to consider a valid claim for injury or death that may occur during shipbreaking, when both insurances would jointly be liable to pay compensation to shipbreaking workers through their corresponding insurances. In essence, under the dual-SLC system, the accountability of all responsible parties involved in a ship is inter-connected from the 'cradle to grave' (or

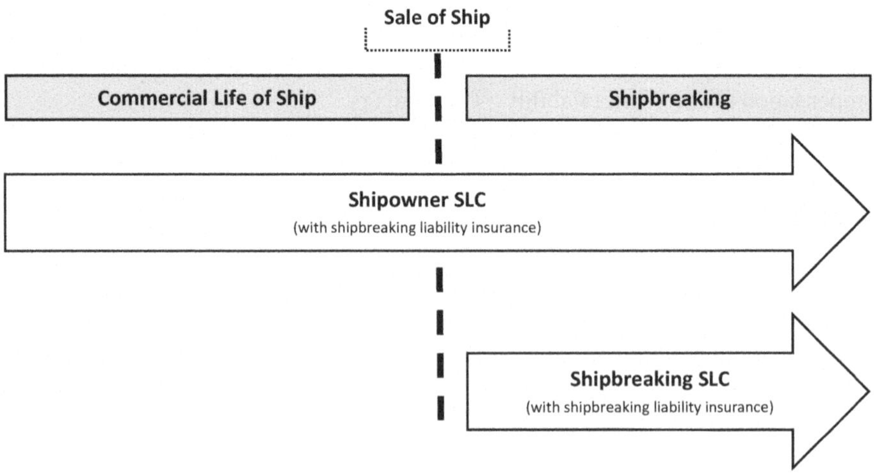

Fig. 9.1 The proposed SLC system

'shipyard to shipbreaking facility'). With this approach, it may not be possible for all shipowners involved in the shipbreaking business chain to escape their liability for breaking ships.

The SLC framework would aim to fill regulatory gaps left by the *Hong Kong Convention*, creating a global legal framework (see Chap. 5 for the discussion on the gaps).[1] The proposed SLC framework explained in this chapter answers the principal research question: What legal and liability framework is required to make the maritime industry accountable for the harm to human life and health (workers' deaths, physical injuries, and work-related diseases) in major shipbreaking countries?

This chapter is divided into six parts. Section "Shipbreaking Liability Certificate (SLC) Framework" explains the fundamental characteristics of the proposed SLC framework, which includes shared liability to pay compensation. This part also examines the use of a third-party verification system and discusses possible premium reductions for compliant parties.

Section "Establishing the Baselines for the Shipbreaking Insurance and SLC Administrative Fee" presents a methodology for calculating administrative fees and insurance premiums and further provides methods for estimating compensation payouts. Also, the international compensation standard proposed in this part aligns with the ILO's *Employment Injury Benefit Convention*, which promotes continued financial support for injured workers and their families. This further ensures sustained assistance for those affected by workplace injuries.[2] Furthermore, this part compares compensation pay standards between countries that export ships and countries that import ships. Section "Enforcement Measures" proposes enforcement methods following which workers can file claims directly with insurance companies or through a Worker Advocate. Section "Conclusion" concludes the Chapter by summarising the key recommendations and implications for reforming shipbreaking laws with a focus on liability.

Shipbreaking Liability Certificate (SLC) Framework

The SLC system encompasses two distinct classifications: a commercial owner of a ship, who must have a shipowner SLC and a shipbreaking liability insurance, and a shipbreaking facility, which must have second SLC and shipbreaking liability insurance. In defining a shipowner, the proposed SLC would need to include a commercial ship's owner (long-term owner), short-term owners that include cash buyers and flag-of-convenience countries. Cash buyers or flag-of-convenience countries acquire ownership of a ship through ownership transfers from original owners who operate

[1] *The Hong Kong International Convention for the Safe and Environmentally Sound Recycling of Ships*, opened for Signature 1 September 2009, IMO Doc. SR/CONF45 (not yet in force). (*Hong Kong Convention*).

[2] *Employment Injury Benefits Convention, 1964* (amended in 1980), adopted on 17 June 1964, ILO Convention no. 121, entered into force 28 July 1967 (*Employment Injury Benefits Convention*).

ships commercially over an extended period or from cash buyers when ships change hands multiple times before reaching a shipbreaking facility (see Chaps. 3 and 5). In the same way, a shipbreaking facility obtains ownership of a ship through transfer of title from cash buyers, flag-of-convenience countries or directly from original owners, maintaining ownership until completion of shipbreaking.

Unless the SLC resolves the three problems identified below, it will not be a truly comprehensive framework for worker compensation that accords with the requirements of rectificatory justice. The problems are:

1. the lack of international or national instruments to compensate workers in the South Asian shipbreaking industry;
2. the inability of existing preventive mechanisms in the international and national shipbreaking legal regime to improve occupational health and safety conditions and thereby reduce rates of work-related deaths, injuries, and diseases; and
3. the lack of transparency in the international transfer of ships for breaking and, specifically, the failure of the IMO to effectively supervise these transfers.

In addition to resolving the problems, it is important for the SLC to meet certain goals explained below.

Goals of the SLC Framework

The SLC should meet the following goals. They are to:

- provide a means for prompt and adequate compensation to shipbreaking workers for serious economic losses that workers (or their families) incur because of deaths, injuries, and work-related diseases.
- implement appropriate and effective procedures for workers to claim compensation, for claims to be determined, and for compensation payments to be administered.
- improve transparency in the employment of shipbreaking workers to support workers' ability to claim compensation for deaths, injuries, and work-related diseases suffered during shipbreaking work.
- create a legal framework for worker compensation based on ship-specific insurance as a financial guarantee for payment compensation and strict and limited liability for shipowners, following approaches used in the maritime, mining and waste trade industries.
- implement prompt and effective enforcement measures to ensure compliance by all shipowners, including short-term owners (cash buyers) and shipbreaking yards.

The following sections discuss in detail how the proposed SLC can meet these goals.

Two Points of Intervention Under the SLC Framework and Method of Financial Contribution to the Shipbreaking Insurance and the SLC Administrative Fee

The objective of the proposed Shipbreaking Liability Certificate (SLC) is to establish mandatory insurance coverage throughout a ship's operational life span as prerequisite for securing the required SLC certification from the International Maritime Organisation. A key objective of this certification system involves maintaining dual insurance policies and certificates. Of these two certificates, one is during a ship's commercial operation, and the other is to cover shipbreaking activities throughout a ship's final days at a shipbreaking facility. The SLC would therefore intervene in two critical phases: (a) for the period of its commercial operation and (b) at the transitional phase preceding the ship's complete demolition at a shipbreaking facility. To that end, the intervention under the SLC system would be at two points. Initially, it would intervene during the IMO's certificate issuance process. The proposed SLC incorporates two fundamental elements applicable to all commercial ships: (1) an official certificate (the SLC) administered by the IMO and (2) shipbreaking liability insurance provided by a maritime insurance company. Shipowners must submit applications to the IMO, confirming compliance with established safety and environmental standards mandated by the *Hong Kong Convention* for a safe shipbreaking process before a ship commences its commercial operation.

The SLC requirement is for both new and existing ships. All existing ships that are already in commercial operation must also file an application to the IMO for a SLC. These additional requirements supplement existing commercial operation of ships, creating distinct provisions within the SLC framework.[3] It aims to ensure active IMO participation in shipbreaking industry oversight. While alternative mechanisms could assign the responsibility to flag States, such arrangement risks inadequate supervision, making IMO involvement more appropriate than flag State oversight. But the question arises what needs to be demonstrated by a shipowner.

Maintaining a ship's inventory of hazardous materials issued by an internationally recognised institution would be the primary requirement in obtaining the SLC from the IMO. Following certificate issuance, the IMO (or designated representatives) must ensure ongoing administrative maintenance, including detail updates of a ship and payment processing. During commercial operations, the IMO would not need to issue or renew certificates unless ships demonstrate valid shipbreaking insurance certificates from international maritime insurance companies, maintained through annual premium payments.

Subsequently, prior to ship acquisition for breaking, a shipbreaking facility must establish shipbreaking insurance coverage and apply for new ship-specific certificates. The proposed certification for breaking contains two core components for any facility intending to purchase and break ships: (1) an IMO-issued and administered

[3] International Maritime Organisation, Registration of Ships and Fraudulent Registration (Web Page) https://www.imo.org/en/OurWork/Legal/Pages/Registration-of-ships-and-fraudulent-registration-matters.aspx

ship certificate and (2) shipbreaking liability insurance for breaking the ship issued by a maritime insurance company. The proposed SLC framework for shipbreaking operations requires facilities to establish new insurance and certification arrangements, maintaining them until complete shipbreaking alongside the existing SLC and shipbreaking insurance of a shipowner. But the SLC for shipowner and shipbreaking facility would be different in nature. Continuing insurance and certification until the ship's final day would require one-time premium payments from shipbreaking facilities, while commercial owners would make ongoing annual payments until a ship is completely broken. But should shipbreaking facilities maintain ownership beyond one-year, additional payments apply only to extended period. During commercial operations, the SLC is to include dual payment (SLC charge), paid annually by owners: (1) a smaller portion (30% of annual payment) covering administrative costs for the SLC establishment and management, paid to the IMO, and (2) a larger portion (70% of annual payment) covering insurance premiums to maintain coverage, paid to insurers until a ship's final day.

Shipbreaking liability certificate for shipbreaking operation would also involve dual payments made by facilities solely during breaking periods. Similar to commercial operations, the SLC for shipbreaking operations would include (1) a smaller administrative component (30% of the annual payment) covering administrative costs for the SLC establishment and management, paid to the IMO, and (2) a larger component (70% of annual payment) covering insurance premiums paid to insurers until a ship's final day.

Cost calculations for insurance premiums (70%) and administrative fees (30%) utilise common shipbreaking market characteristics, which include annual average volumes of shipbreaking and fatalities and injuries occurring at global shipbreaking facilities. See further below*: determination of costs for insurance premiums* for both commercial and shipbreaking operations.

Maintaining dual SLCs and insurances (for both commercial and shipbreaking operations) until the final day of a ship serves two specific purposes. First, it establishes shared compensation mechanisms for injured or deceased workers and deceased workers' families. Second, it ensures shared compensation responsibilities between all owners and shipbreaking facilities, which eventually establishes reasonable expectations that shipbreaking workers can receive compensation from both insurers.

An alternative approach involves merging the shipbreaking insurance policy for commercial operation of a shipowner with shipbreaking operation policies rather than maintaining separate coverage. Unlike joint policies, merged policies create single dismantling liability insurance coverage across a ship's operational life span. But under the merged policies, shipbreaking facilities must notify insurers of their intention of shipbreaking and establish shipbreaking insurance. This notification would then assist to adjust premiums, with all parties acting in good faith and policies responding only after facilities signal shipbreaking intentions.

With respect to cash buyers or open registry countries maintaining temporary ownership, the SLC framework requires IMO notification regarding ship purchases and sales while continuing SLC of the previous owner, paying prescribed administrative fees and insurance premiums for intended ownership periods. Maintaining SLC becomes integral to formal ownership transfer requirements imposed by the IMO, contrasting with current flag State requirements.[4]

Under the proposed SLC, the IMO would require applicants to specify whether (1) applicants (cash buyers or open registry countries) will operate ships commercially or (2) applicants will sell ships for breaking. The first option applies to standard certification charge requirements with ongoing annual insurance and administrative fee payments similar to commercial operations, while the second option requires single administrative fee and insurance premium payment similar to shipbreaking operations.

The declaration to the IMO under the SLC framework would serve as express intention indicators. Intention declaration may indicate either shipbreaking intentions or owner's intentions regarding ship's final journey for breaking. Legal consequences for non-disclosure would lead to cash buyers or open registry countries to annual administrative fees and insurance premiums similar to commercial operator's SLC charge scheme. Additionally, failure to make annual payments would result in IMO refusal to process subsequent ownership transfer applications.

The proposed SLC acknowledges enforcement-related difficulties regarding ownership transfer arrangements, as cash buyers, open registry countries, or shipbreaking facilities might circumvent recommended ownership transfer applications. Attempting to resolve such a problem, as considered further in Section F below, the 'Liability of Last Active Insurance Policy' can be introduced, meaning that the last active insurer of the original owner will pay compensation in the event of a death, injury, or disease faced by a worker in a shipbreaking facility. Figure 9.2 shows the process flow of the SLC, and Fig. 9.3 shows the proposed SLC framework.

Determination of Costs for the SLC Administrative Fee and Insurance Premium

Independent surveyors employed by shipowners can determine their cost of insurance and the SLC administrative fee. Such an engagement can be both for ships in commercial operation or shipbreaking operation.

The well-known port state control (PSC) mechanism of the Paris Memorandum of Understanding for commercial ships can police the SLC mechanism (see Chapter 7). Officers present at different ports can have the responsibility to ensure that ships

---

[4] It is the duty of all flag Member States to monitor the change of ownership: at arts 91 and 92 of the *United Nations Convention on the Law of the Seas*, adopted on 10 December 1982, 1982 UNTS 397, entered into force on 1 November 1994; However, this mechanism is not effectively working which has led the IMO to interfere into the process: at See International Maritime Organisation, 'Registration of Ships and Fraudulent Registration Matters' (Webpage) Registration of ships and fraudulent registration matters (imo.org).

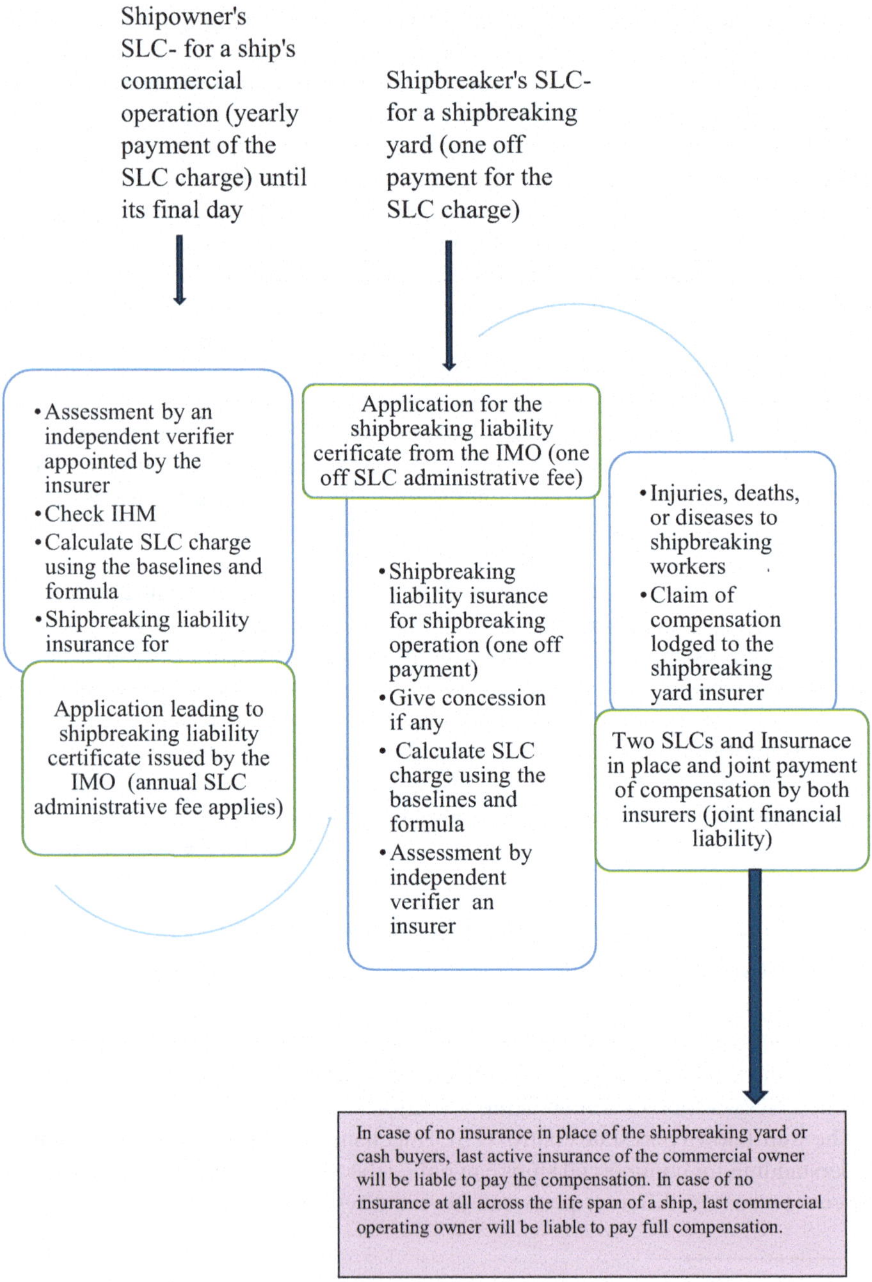

Fig. 9.2 Process flow of the two SLCs and insurance leading to compensation payments

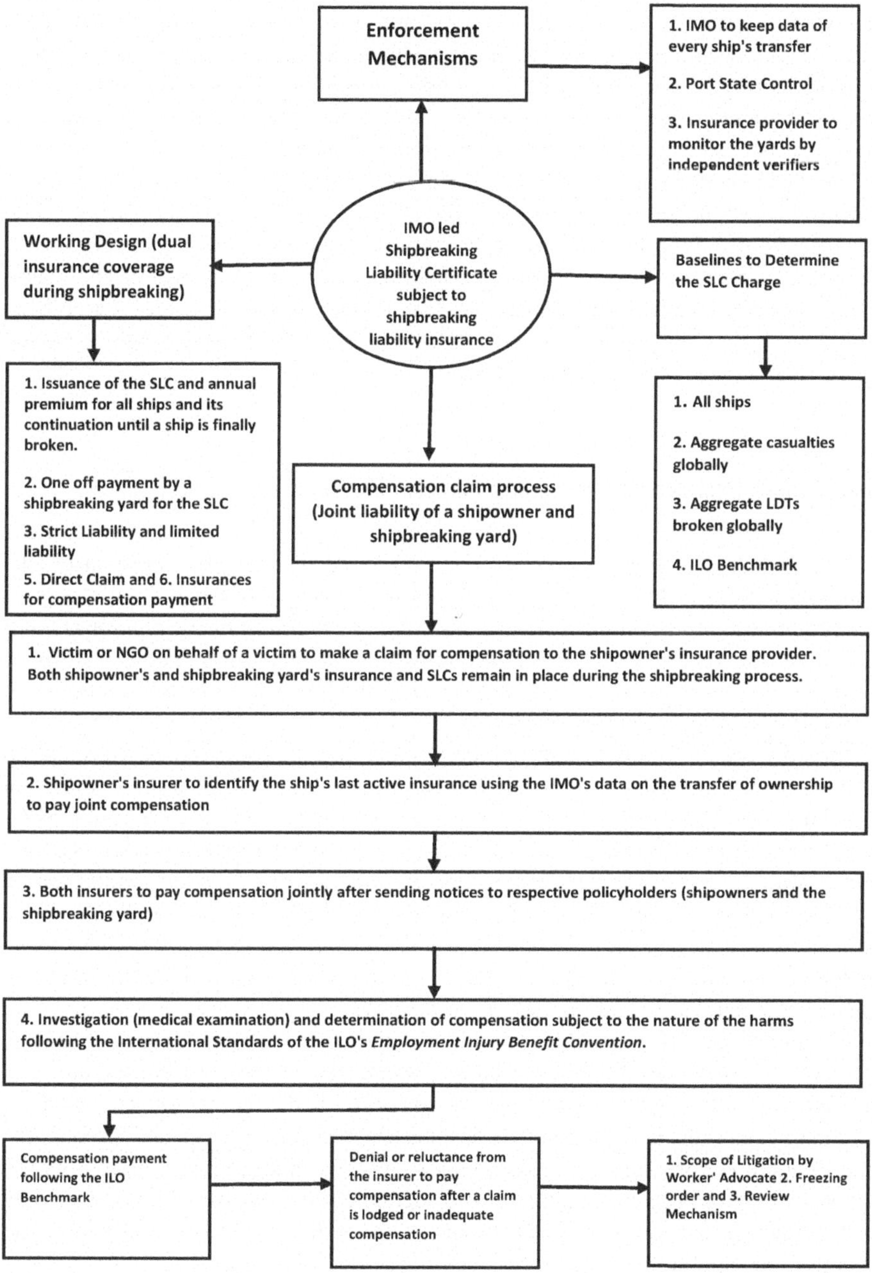

Fig. 9.3 The proposed framework

are complying with SLC standards. In relation to the enforcement of the SLC standards for shipbreaking facilities, an independent verifier can inspect whether a shipbreaking facility is complying with environmental and safety standards set out in the *Hong Kong Convention*, as shown in Table 9.1. The section entitled *'Enforcement Measures'* below discusses the enforcement mechanism.

The SLC model can capture the features of both temporary and permanent shipowners, where the former includes the cash buyers and open registries, while the latter are the shipping companies. Premium calculations may vary according to the nature of a shipowner. Temporary owners may be assessed based on the length of time they hold the property, which may lead to daily or monthly rates. Or perhaps premiums could be on the same yearly basis, and anything unused would be passed on to the new owner when the ship is sold.

Last Active Insurance to Compensate Victims

With respect to the issue of compensation payment in insurance lapse cases, the proposed SLC must have a safety net. Insurance lapses may happen when a shipbreaking facility does not insure a ship upon a ship purchase, or the previous owner had let the insurance lapse leading to a reluctance from a shipbreaking facility to reacquire SLC and insurance. In such cases, it is the last active insurance which will be responsible to pay compensation.

The concept of 'last active insurance' means that the most recent owner of an insured ship is financially responsible for the payment of compensation. In the event of a claim (for loss of life, injury or occupational illness) brought under the SLC-supported scheme, where it is established that a ship did not have insurance at the time of breaking, the last insurance of the ship, if there is any, shall pay the compensation due. That leaves the last owner of a ship to have had valid insurance on whom the responsibility to insure the end-of-use would fall—in case any of the buyers (including a cash buyer or an open registry country or shipbreaking facility) had failed to maintain shipbreaking liability insurance.

The role of the IMO would be important with respect to registering the SLC and insurance. The IMO would need to establish a centralised register for certification and insurance records of every ship within the proposed SLC framework. The database would allow workers to track down the last known insurance provider. Consequently, if an incident occurs during the shipbreaking process and an investigation reveals that the commercial operator did not have adequate liability insurance or SLC; both parties (the original shipowner and shipbreaking facility) would be held jointly and severally responsible for compensation claims.

Where no insurance is available, or if the ship was never insured for breaking, the SLC model would promote legal action through the courts in the country of the ship's flag or home State. If that is the case, an appropriate third party, such as a worker's advocate would be authorised to file and handle a compensation claim.

Table 9.1 Checklist for compliance with the Hong Kong Convention, 2009 and the IMO Guidelines for the Development of a Shiprecycling Plan, 2004 (Guidelines)

No	Checklist	Hong Kong Convention (HKC) article/ regulation/the IMO Guidelines for the Development of the Ship Recycling Plan (Guidelines)	Required Standards under the Hong Kong Convention (HKC) for considering concession on premium to be paid by a shipbreaking yard
1	Worker registration and personal protective equipment (PPE)	(R 22)	As per the HKC, the registration of workers is one of the important requirements. Providing PPE is also an important requirement of the HKC
2	On-site pollution and safety control equipment	(R 22) (S 4 of the *Guidelines*)	Before issuing SLC, it is a regulatory requirement to check the on-site management capacity of a shipbreaking yard. As a standard shipbreaking yard, the Turkish shipbreaking industry maintains a 200 sqm storage building, roofed and unique sealed floor plus drainage. It is built for storage of asbestos/6tons, bilge water/50t, sludge/12t, waste oil/214t and further dangerous solid waste/55 m^3 for controlling on-site oil pollution and wastes are transported to waste management facility
3	Emergency preparedness. On-site equipment (variable)	(R21 of the HKC) (S 3 of the *Guidelines*)	Frequent accidents require appropriate emergency responses
4	Prevention of adverse effects of human health (gas-free entry, spill prevention)	(R 19) (S 4 of the *Guidelines*)	Free a ship's chamber from any unseen gas is necessary to prevent adverse effects on human health. In addition, an on-site inspection team is required to check any spill prevention
5	Preparation of various plans (Emergency Health and Safety management, ship recycling action plans)	(R 18) (S 5 of the *Guidelines*)	Proper plans in an emergency and a proper ship recycling plan can reduce shipbreaking accidents on a large scale
6	Incident reporting	(R 23)	The reporting requirement is a vital issue in case of a shipbreaking accident
7	Training of workers	(R 22) (S 3.3 of the *Guidelines*)	Following the regulation of the HKC, minimum 4 one-day training requirement is needed. The Turkish ship recycling industry maintains the evidence of suitable workers' training

(continued)

Table 9.1 (continued)

No	Checklist	Hong Kong Convention (HKC) article/regulation/the IMO Guidelines for the Development of the Ship Recycling Plan (Guidelines)	Required Standards under the Hong Kong Convention (HKC) for considering concession on premium to be paid by a shipbreaking yard
8	Establish management systems to protect workers and the environment	(R 17) (S 4.2 of the *Guidelines*)	Discharging the waste into seawater has been the main problem in the sound management of a ship's waste. Therefore, proper drainage, collection and disposal of the waste are essential requirements under the HKC since these will have reduced environmental and health consequences
9	Safe and environmentally sound management of hazardous materials	(R 20) (S 4.2 and 4.3.4 of the *Guidelines*)	A standard shipbreaking yard uses specialists to remove and clean hazardous materials before starting the shipbreaking process
10	Reporting the start of shipbreaking	(R 24)	A shipbreaking yard is required to show the evidence of compliance with notification requirements
11	Reporting completion	(R 25)	Same as above
12	a. Upgrade facilities to Dry Dock b. Monitoring Laboratories c. Thermal Treatment Facility d. Health care system	(Ss 3–5 of the *Guidelines* broadly)	Maintaining proper monitoring laboratories, thermal treatment facilities, and Healthcare systems are essential guidelines adopted within the Hong Kong convention guidelines

Source World Bank Report (2010), the *Hong Kong Convention*, and the IMO *Guidelines for the Development of the Ship Recycling Plan*[5]

Financial support for such a litigation could be given from the annual or one-off SLC administrative fee paid to the IMO (See Appendix A).

An important aspect of the SLC is its ability to trace and hold accountable the most recent insurance policy associated with a ship. This process is critical for three main reasons. First, it encourages sellers and buyers to explicitly consider SLC obligations and shipbreaking insurance at the time of transfer of ownership, as sellers will seek to avoid potential exposure for their previous policy. Second, it encourages compliance with the SLC system because it is cheaper and easier for all shipowners (either

[5] The Table was developed following report published by the World Bank in 2010; See details of the report Maria Sarraf et al., 'Ship Breaking and Recycling Industry in Bangladesh and Pakistan,' (Report No. 58275-SAS, World Bank, 2010) 46. *(World Bank Report 2010)*. The Maritime Environment Protection Committee, *IMO Guidelines for the Development of the Ship Recycling Plan*, IMO Doc MEPC/Circ.419, 12 November 2004.

shipbreaking yards, cash buyers, or even open registry countries that own ships for a short period) to insure and certify the ship rather than facing litigation (see Chaps. 3 and 6). In this scheme, every entity that has an interest in a ship, even a fleeting owner, has a binary choice: either (a) obtain insurance so that injured workers can pursue compensation via third-party-run claims or (b) risk a suit in their own domestic courts in the absence of insurance. Third, the system serves a continuous connection between the ship's current and initial owner with reference to its initial SLC.

The continuous connection helps address the problem of reflagging, in the sense that the ultimate power is expected to assume the insurance and certification obligations and notify the International Maritime Organisation (IMO) of the proposed sale. This traceability incurs that the injured can proceed 'downstream,' i.e., find the last valid insurance and receive compensation from the insurer of the shipbreaking facility, who would then add the insurance provider of the shipowner to pay compensation.

In terms of legal justification, holding prior owners accountable is grounded in their financial gains from the use and sale of a ship, their operational involvement, and their duty to comply with both national and international maritime regulations. According to the *UN Guiding Principles,* companies are responsible for any negative human rights outcomes that cause, contribute to, or are connected to through their operations or business relationships.[6] This framework emphasises that liability stems from association rather than direct control, thereby extending the scope of responsibility to former owners under the SLC framework.

Direct Claim

The proposed SLC framework aims at paying adequate amount of compensation to victim workers without unnecessary delay. In this context, 'avoiding unnecessary delay' refers to the legal and procedural mechanisms that facilitate timely access to justice and expedite decisions regarding compensation.[7] Chapters 7 and 8 highlight two primary avenues for the payment of compensation. They are direct claims and litigation. While each method has its own merits, the SLC framework advocates for dual-tract approach. This is to ensure that no claim is left unresolved due to procedural shortcomings or jurisdictional ambiguities.

In relation to direct claims, workers or their legal representatives—such as a Worker's Advocate—should be empowered to file claims directly with the insurance provider of the shipbreaking company. If the insurer fails to respond (without formally

[6] John Ruggie, *Guiding Principles for the Implementation of the United Nations 'Protect, Respect and Remedy Framework,* Report of the Special Representative of the Secretary-General on the issue of human rights and transnational corporations and other business enterprises, UN Doc A/HRC/17/31 (March 2011), art 17(a).

[7] International Law Commission, *Draft Principle on the Allocation of Loss in Transboundary Harm Arising Out of Hazardous Activities, with Commentaries*, UNGA, Fifty-eighth Session, UN Doc no. A/61/10 (2006).

rejecting the claim), the claimant should be able to seek judicial intervention. In supporting this, under the proposed SLC, it is important for shipbreaking nations to enact domestic laws that establish a legal right for workers to take actions when insurers or shipbreaking companies fail to respond. In addition, it is required for the courts to allow issuing asset-freezing orders if there is a credible litigation that includes the elements of fraud or breach of contract.

In case an insurer denies a direct claim, the proposed legislation should enable victims to sue the shipbreaking facility in the jurisdiction where the incident occurred. This is to ensure that legal recourse remains available even when direct claims are rejected.

Given the lack of formal contractual ties between workers and insurers, or even between workers and shipbreaking facilities—the framework recommends a judicial review process.[8] This process would allow courts to reassess denied claims under SLC system, offering a safeguard against unjust outcomes. Because there is no contractual relationship between the insurer of a shipbreaking yard and the worker and possibly no employment relationship between the workers and the shipbreaking yard, the review mechanism would empower the local courts to review the decision of an unsuccessful claim made under the SLC.

Importantly, while governments are not expected to fund compensation directly, they are responsible for creating a legal infrastructure that compels insurers and shipbreaking companies to honour valid claims without unnecessary delays.

Strict and Joint Liability

Besides compensation, the SLC framework proposes a robust liability regime inspired by precedents in oil spills, hazardous waste, and mining. It recommends strict liability to hold parties accountable regardless of fault and joint liability to make both shipowners and shipbreaking facility accountable through their corresponding insurance policies. Because of the inherent risks in shipbreaking, insurance coverage must be comprehensive. A joint liability model where shipowners cover commercial

[8] There are maybe five reasons why a claim might be unsuccessful:

- damage not caused by an insurable event – 'the insurance policy will only cover damage caused by an insurable event (that is no damage that was preexisting or caused by some other event)'.
- nondisclosure–'the shipbreaking yard has not disclosed information when they applied for or renewed the policy or the worker did not disclose something'.
- 'operation of a condition or exclusion clause–the worker or the shipbreaking yard has failed to comply with an insurer's requirement or the policy does not cover the loss'.
- 'fraud - the insurer believes the worker or the shipbreaking yard have acted fraudulently in some way'.
- 'policy cancellation': See for detail at Legal Aid Queensland, Understanding the Reason for an Insurance Claim Refusal (Web Page) .Understanding the reason for an insurance claim refusal - Legal Aid Queensland

operation and shipbreaking facility covers operational hazards of shipbreaking would ensure sufficient financial protection. Sustaining the system would largely depend on shipowners' long-term premium contributions.

The shipbreaking facility's insurance policy would serve as the first point of contact for victims, which would connect the claim to the shipowner's insurer, increasing the likelihood of successful compensation. This linkage is vital for streamlining the process and reducing bureaucratic hurdles. However, the linkage should not allow insurers to increase premiums arbitrarily. In controlling arbitrarily rise of premiums by insurers, the framework introduces baseline metrics with maximum recorded fatalities, injuries, and illnesses and average ship weight. These baseline metrics (provided in section "Enforcement Measures" below) would limit premium hikes and encourage safer practices. If a shipbreaking facility maintains a clean safety record, its premiums and administrative fees would drop. Conversely, repeated incidents would trigger higher premiums and potential intervention by the International Maritime Organisation (IMO).

Prompt compensation and exclusion of unnecessary legal entanglements are necessary to make the SLC work efficiently. To that end, the SLC framework proposes to eliminate the need to prove fault by a victim worker. This would prevent shipbreaking companies from deflecting blame onto victims and ensure that insurers cannot deny claims except in rare cases like fraud. In substance, strict liability would guarantee that affected workers receive compensation without being burdened by complex legal procedure. Strict liability is required to avoid, for example, circumstances in which a non-compliant shipbreaking company may seek to escape the liability by arguing that the damage resulted from the fault of the victim. With strict liability, a shipbreaking company cannot seek to escape liability in this way.

The same meaning is relevant to shipbreaking for strict liability in the context of insurance coverage, meaning that, except in very limited circumstances, such as a fraudulent claim, insurers must not try to escape compensation payments for the harm caused to a shipbreaking worker.

Limitation of Liability and Insurance for Financial Security

Within the proposed SLC framework, the insurance premiums function as financial guarantees for compensation. The SLC establishes capped liability for both commercial shipping and shipbreaking operations, based on criteria outlined in section "Enforcement Measures" below. This liability limit proves crucial as it enables insurers to restrict their financial exposure to predetermined amounts per claim. Additionally, restricting the liability of insured parties prevents unreasonable escalation of premium costs and SLC administrative charges. The liability cap fulfils three fundamental objectives: (1) establishing clear liability parameters for both commercial shipping and shipbreaking activities, (2) defining the boundaries of insurance provider obligations, and (3) clarifying the liability thresholds for workers as beneficiaries.

While shipowners face limited liability during commercial operations, questions emerge regarding the practicality of requiring commercial vessel owners to maintain insurance premiums throughout the ship's operational lifetime until breaking. From a shipbreaking perspective, given that this represents compensation insurance with inherent risks management implications, this book suggests allowing shipowners to transfer insurance costs and SLC administrative fees to those utilising ships for personal and commercial activities.

As discussed before, shipbreaking facilities, serving as ships' final owners, must secure separate shipbreaking insurance and new SLC documentation, independent from previous owners' coverage arrangements. This means each ship acquisition by shipbreaking facility would require establishing fresh insurance policies. The subsequent insurance structure is to enable continuous monitoring of operational standards, with dismantling insurance premiums reflecting facilities' advancement toward maintaining appropriate standards.

The baselines in section "Establishing the Baselines for the Shipbreaking Insurance and SLC Administrative Fee" below establish maximum premium rates through independent assessors designated by insurance companies, who may grant premium reductions following on-site evaluations. The standards outlined in Table 9.1, which specify regulatory requirements under the *Hong Kong Convention*, serve as evaluation tools for determining such reductions. Since shipbreaking facilities must obtain new insurance and SLC documentation for each subsequent ship purchase, future insurers will reassess existing standards when considering concessions. This process would ideally result in progressive standard improvements driven by repeated insurance industry inspections for future ship acquisitions. These inspection documents also generate valuable data concerning shipbreaking facility standards.

Similarly, insurance premiums for commercial ships (excluding shipbreaking facilities) correspond to the quantity and characteristics of hazardous materials documented in inventory of hazardous materials (IHM) reports within ship's structures. Increased amount of hazardous material concentrations would be a criteria to increase shipowner premiums to maximum levels specified in section "Enforcement Measures" baselines. Conversely, reduced hazardous materials levels would lower premium costs. For instance, shipowners maintaining hazardous materials inventories certified by internationally recognised organisations and conducting regular surveys per the *Hong Kiong Convention* requirements could reduce premiums to 50% of maximum limits due decreased shipbreaking risk. Likewise, shipbreaking facilities maintaining quality standards, such as proper worker registration, could achieve approximately 8–10% reductions from maximum baseline limits discussed in section "Enforcement Measures".

The insurance sector operates globally and commonly within maritime commerce, with regulatory frameworks primarily based on utmost good faith principles regarding information disclosure.[9] According to this principle, an applicant has a mandatory duty to disclose all material facts relevant to the acceptance and rating of the risk.

---

[9] *Insurance Contracts Act 1984* (UK), s 13.

Following insurance contract execution, shipbreaking facility standards should become clearly apparent. However, merely providing information to insurers may prove insufficient. Shipbreaking represents an industry characterised by numerous technical aspects, complex organisational structures, and consequently substantial additional risks beyond standard shipping operations. Due to these unique characteristics and hazards, an important requirement would be to introduce independent verification procedures conducted by specialised third-party entities to evaluate and approve shipbreaking operations on insurers' behalf. Currently, classification societies certify shipbreaking facilities across South Asia, but this new requirement would expand demand for specialised verifier categories.

Independent verifiers offer multiple advantages, including addressing existing certification model deficiencies within shipbreaking facilities. As examined in Chap. 3, most shipbreaking facilities receive certification from classification societies lacking independence from shipowners; international organisations, including the United Nations and the European Union, do not recognise their role. Should the SLC take effect, an independent surveyor, such as Grieg Green, would intervene through the insurance company.[10] This independent verification process would establish opportunities for private entities to collaborate with the IMO, strengthening global shipbreaking oversight through private–public partnerships.

Insured Object

Under the proposed SLC framework, shipbreaking insurance is a precondition for the SLC and includes liability for both shipowners and shipbreaking yards for death, injuries and work-related diseases suffered by workers. Since workers are the ultimate sufferers, with no funds, and hence no one to champion their injury and/or death,[11] the SLC framework emphasises the issue of injustice to them.

From the perspective of a financial instrument, although the framework is similar to the ship recycling licence proposed under the *EU Ship Recycling Regulation*,[12] the proposed SLC framework is different. Unlike the *EU Ship Recycling Regulation* licence framework (see Chap. 6), the proposed SLC aims to remedy work-related deaths, injuries and diseases on the basis of rectificatory justice theory. Notably, a consequence of the proposed SLC framework is that the insurance industry will likely monitor rates of deaths, injuries, and work-related diseases (based on claims) for shipbreaking yards, and the IMO will likely use the data maintained by the insurance industries to evaluate improvements in the occupational health and safety standards of the shipbreaking yards. Under the proposed SLC framework, there is

[10] GRIEG GREEN, 'Ship Recycling' (Webpage) https://grieggreen.com/project/ship_recycling/

[11] Saiful Karim, *Shipbreaking in Developing Countries: A Requiem for Environmental Justice from the Perspectives of Bangladesh* (Taylor and Francis Group, 2018) 125–126.

[12] See section "Analysis of the Proposals Within the EU to Impose Financial Liability on EU Shipowners" of Chap. 6.

scope for the IMO to take a larger regulatory and compliance role and, for example, to determine that a shipbreaking yard has failed to take adequate steps to improve standards and thus to decide that a shipbreaking yard should not be issued a further SLC until standards improve. This interventionist approach is vital for encouraging non-compliant shipbreaking yards to improve their standards.

Serious Economic Loss

The proposed SLC is aimed at mitigating economic harm suffered by workers at shipbreaking sector. Keeping the aim in mind, the SLC would therefore cover claims for loss of income from personal injury, and loss of future income, as representing the ways and means of supporting a family member or deceased worker or injured worker. The SLC would widely support recovery for 'economic loss, pain, and suffering, permanent disability, loss of quality of life, loss of amenities, or consortium'. Directly associated material losses such as loss of earnings and earning capacity, and medical expenses including costs for achieving full rehabilitation would also need to be covered under the proposed SLC. Nonmaterial damage, such as for the loss of loaved ones, pain, and suffering, and the affront to sensibilities with an intrusion on the person, home or private life, would also be compatible.[13]

When calculating compensation for loss of profit, practical parameters have to be set. The premiums should neither be too high or too low, nor payments of compensation to workers should be too high or too low. The suggested SLC system will impose only a fair cost of monetary burden to the maritime industry. That having been said, an acceptable amount or related liability is required, however the cost must be linear, so that the larger the size of a ship, the more related liability is required compared to smaller ships. This mechanism ensures that the ratio of the licence cost of larger ships is greater than that of smaller ships. In particular, the framework proposes calculation of the annual SLC administrative fee and the annual insurance premium on the basis of the weight of a ship sold for breaking rather than based on the number of ships broken each year at all shipbreaking facilities worldwide.

The proposed SLC framework is inclusive of all ships that are subject to the scheme regardless of age, size, or type of a ship, the quantity of wastes generated on board or internal waste facilities. Older vessels with higher risk of onboard hazardous materials present greater risks to workers and thus are a major point of focus within the proposed SLC framework. Because of higher risks, their insurance premiums should be higher than younger ships. The next section explains this in detail.

[13] V.S Mishra, 'Emerging Right to Compensation in Indian Environmental Law' (2001) 23 *Delhi Law Review* 58–79; International Law Commission, *Draft Articles on State Responsibility for Internationally Wrongful Acts*, (Yearbook 2001) 2 (Part Two) 98–105, art 36 (b).

Establishing the Baselines for the Shipbreaking Insurance and SLC Administrative Fee

For a shipbreaking worker compensation scheme to function properly (i.e., to pay an adequate amount of compensation to shipbreaking workers), there must be an effective methodology for determining the annual SLC administrative charge and the annual premium to be paid for a ship. The following factors are considered the critical baselines for determining the premium to be paid for a particular ship:

Insurance for all ships;
the average amount of light displacement tonnage (LDT) recycled in the last five years globally;
the aggregate number of deaths and injuries over the last five years in global shipbreaking yards; and
the compensation benchmark set under the ILO's *Employment Injury Benefits* Convention, 1964.

Using the above baselines, the proposed SLC framework uses a simple formula to calculate the premium for shipbreaking insurance, and the SLC fee is as follows:

$$\frac{\left\{\frac{\left(\begin{array}{c}\text{last 5 years}'\text{ aggregate number of global deaths \& injuries}\\ \times\text{compensation benchmark}\end{array}\right)}{\text{average amount of LDTs broken(last 5 years)}}\right\}}{2}$$

The proposed SLC recommends the formula to determine an overall SLC charge for a ship and a shipbreaking yard, which would be proportionated as a 30% SLC administrative fee and 70% for annual insurance premium payment. Considering further below, the proposed SLC framework also proposes the appointment of an independent verifier by an insurance company, who uses the formula to calculate the maximum SLC charge for a ship.

However, the amount is not absolute. Under the proposed SLC framework, after the maximum SLC charge for a ship is fixed, an independent verifier representing the insurer can give a concession to the insurance premium upon examining the amount and nature of hazardous materials reported in a ship's IHM. The idea is to monitor whether a ship follows the *Hong Kong Convention*'s guidelines on IHM, meaning that the quality of an IHM would be the basis for an independent verifier to decide on a premium concession. This would not affect the SLC fee, which will not change. For an effective application of the system, unless an internationally recognised institution issues the IHM, the independent verifier should not accept the IHM as the basis for providing such a concession on the premium.[14] The IMO can issue a list of such institutions and update the list regularly to assist in following the SLC requirements.

The above formula also determines an overall SLC charge for a shipbreaking yard, with an independent verifier appointed by an interested insurance company determining the maximum charge. Then, under the proposed SLC framework, the independent verifier examines the existing facilities maintained by a shipbreaking yard and calculates the amount of concession from the insurance premium. But this would not affect the SLC administrative fee. Accordingly, if a shipbreaking yard follows all the requirements listed in Table 9.1, it will pay no premium except the primary SLC administrative fee (30% of the SLC charge).

The next few sections explain the basis for the baselines and their contribution to determining an adequate amount of compensation via the formula in Section F of this Part.

Shipyard to Shipbreaking Yard Approach

A 'cradle-to-grave' approach requiring shipowners to maintain an SLC (and, thus, shipbreaking insurance) across a ship's life cycle would be an additional requirement to the *Hong Kong Convention.*[15] It is an important objective leading to impose 'life of ship' (LoS) planning over the operational life of a ship. Such provisions for the ship's eventual recycling would become an administrative feature of commercial operation of every ship in the form of a requirement to maintain an SLC. The SLC is thus required to be maintained from the time the ship leaves the shipyard until it is entirely torn down into its constituent bits and pieces.

Adopting a comprehensive approach that spans from ship construction to breaking offers a pragmatic solution to the challenge of associating the issuance of a SLC with a fixed point in a ship's operational life. Importantly, international maritime law does not prescribe a definitive age at which commercial ships must be retied. This regulatory gap complicates efforts to establish a uniform age limit for a ship's retirement, particularly given the diversity of ship types governed by the *Hong Kong Convention.* Empirical data underscores this variability. According to IHS World Fleet statistics, ships exceeding 100 gross tonnage generally enter the shipbreaking market at an average age of 33 years.[16] In contrast, research conducted by Ecorys, DNV. GL and Erasmus University indicates a broader age range for shipbreaking, spanning from

[14] *Bangladesh Environmental Lawyers Association (BELA) v Janata Steel Corporation*, [Writ Petition No. 8466 of 2019] High Court Division (26 February 2020) (*Janata Steel*).

[15] World Bank Report, Ibid 59.

[16] IHS Markit, 'World Fleet Statistics 2018: A Composition of the World Fleet Development' (Web Page, 31 December 2018) https://ihsmarkit.com/industry/maritime.html.

10 to 29 years.[17] These findings highlight the impracticality of anchoring the SLC requirement to a singular age threshold.

The proposed SLC framework is intended to function as a complementary mechanism to the *Hong Kong Convention*. To that end, it must accommodate the extensive array of ship types encompassed within the Convention's scope. Article 2(7) of the *Hong Kong Convention* defines 'ship' expansively, including all marine-operating ships—ranging from submersibles and floating platforms to floating storage units (FSUs) and floating production storage and offloading units (FPSOs), as well as ships that have been stripped of operational equipment or being towed'. Article 3 delineates exclusions, specifying that the Convention does not apply to military ships, government-operated ships engaged in non-commercial service [art 3(2)] or to 'ships under 500 gross tonnage that operate exclusively within the territorial waters of their flag State [art 3(3)].

While the SLC framework is designed to be age-neutral in its general application, it must also acknowledge the correlation between age of a ship and internal contamination. Older ships, with no precleaning requirement tend to accumulate greater volumes of hazardous materials, thereby elevating occupational health and safety risks for shipbreaking workers. In light of this, it is proposed that vessels exceeding 30 years of age be subject to an enhanced certification process. This would entail a modified SLC, incorporating increased administrative fees and a higher insurance premium to reflect the increased risks profile associated with breaking aged ships.

The Supply of Ships for Breaking

The insurance premium and SLC administrative fee depend on the average tonnage of ships broken each year globally. As indicated in Table 9.2, the average annual gross tonnage of ships that entered the demolition market for the period of 2014–2018 was 23.5 million tonnes. South Asian shipbreaking nations account for an average of 80% of the total tonnage per year, including 91.78% of the tonnage in 2018. On these data, most of the global fleet is broken in shipbreaking yards in South Asia, in workplaces that present significant occupational health and safety concerns to workers and in employment relationships that are insecure and short-term and that often lack any direct contractual relationship between the worker and the owner/operator of the shipbreaking yard.

The demand for ships in the South Asian shipbreaking industry depends on the steel price and the demand for steel scrap in Bangladesh, India, and Pakistan, and market forecasts for the Asian subcontinent indicate a strong ongoing demand for ships to be broken. The data sourced from the United Nations Conference on Trade

[17] ECORYS-DNV-GL-Erasmus University of Rotterdam, Financial Instrument to Facilitate Safe and Sound Ship Recycling' (Research Report, The EU Commission Directorate-General for Environment, June 2016) 34. *(ECORYS-DNV-GL Study, 2016).*

Table 9.2 Country-specific amount of shipbreaking between 2014 and 2018

Countries	2014	2015	2016	2017	2018	Average
Bangladesh	4,346,296	8,050,930	9,530,264	6,869,287	8,687,384	
India	6,966,362	5,167,041	9,477,130	6,938,028	4,719,968	
Pakistan	3,909,134	4,519,769	5,480,340	3,795,033	3,968,452	
Total	15,221,792	17,737,740	24,487,734	17,602,348	17,375,807	
Percentage	67.9%	76%	84.4%	76.8%	91.78%	80%
China	5,281,169	4,414,908	3,331,546	3,445,145	359,073	
Percentage in China	23.54%	18.9%	11.44%	15.03%	9.1%	
World total	22,431,039	23,339,989	29,134,953	22,915,519	189,304,082	23.5 million

Source The United Nations Conference on Trade and Development[18]

and Development[19] reveal that the steel price will continue to increase. The recent sale price of old ships also provides evidence of such high sale prices; for example, in 2021, a Bangladeshi shipbreaking yard purchased a ship paying approximately USD 600 per LDT.[20] Allied Shipbrokers, a Greek shipping company, noted that the offered price for ships is on the rise, citing the increasing demand for steel scrap as the reason.[21] In the maritime industry, gross tonnage (GT) from the sellers' perspective is typically used to measure the size of a ship. However, in the global shipbreaking market, light displacement tonnage (LDT) is used to measure the weight of a ship.[22]

Average Rates of Death, Injury, and Disease

The most critical baseline is the aggregate deaths, injuries, and diseases of workers in global shipbreaking yards. Thousands of workers have lost their lives, and many more have been severely injured from shipbreaking.[23] The South Asian shipbreaking industry accounts for the vast majority of these deaths and injuries. According to

---

[18] United Nations Conference on Trade and Development, 'Ship Scrapping by Country of Demolition' *Annual Report* (Webpage) https://unctadstat.unctad.org/wds/TableViewer/tableView.aspx?ReportId=89492.

[19] Ibid.

[20] Bestoasis, 'Global Ship Recycling Market' (Week 33 - Ship Recycling Report- Best Oasis Limited, 6 to 13 August 2021) https://www.best-oasis.com/reports/week-33-ship-recycling-report-best-oasis-limited

[21] Kirstein Leinnekopper, 'Ship Recycling Market Waking Up after Disappointing Summer' *Recycling International* (Web Page, 9 October 2019) https://recyclinginternational.com/ferrous-metals/ship-recycling-market-waking-up-after-disappointing-summer/27942/

[22] *ECORYS-DNV-GL Study, 2016* (n 18) 70.

[23] See section "Opposite View" of Chap. 3; Greenpeace, 'End of Life Ships: The Human Cost of Breaking Ships' (Research Report,2005) *(Greenpeace Report)*; Young Power in Social Action,

several sources, one worker dies in South Asian shipbreaking yards weekly, and at least one worker suffers an injury every day.[24] The sources do not include unreported deaths and casualties because of work-related diseases; however, considering these sources, approximately 50 workers are likely to die from work-related diseases (and the number may be significantly greater), and approximately 200 workers suffer serious injuries each year in global shipbreaking yards, meaning that the total rate of casualties is approximately 250 per year.[25]

Application of the ILO's Employment Injury Benefit Convention 1964 as an International Standard

An international benchmark is required to fix the annual premium and compensation payment. An established principle is that compensation frameworks should link the amount of compensation payable to the profits generated by an enterprise.[26] The amount of compensation payable, however, should not punish (i.e., be punitive) or award more than the actual loss suffered.[27]

Keeping adequate compensation in mind, the proposed SLC framework brings shipowners within a civil liability framework in the shipbreaking industry in accordance with the equity-based principle that an industry must provide workers with respectful and dignified treatment.[28] The SLC framework—by creating a requirement that all ships maintain an SLC across their operating life—also makes the chain of business relationships transparent and relates shipowners to shipbreaking yards. This accords with the principle that, for a global industry, a multinational enterprise should seek ways to 'prevent or mitigate adverse human rights impacts' in circumstances where a multinational enterprise does not itself contribute to adverse human rights impacts, but these impacts are 'nevertheless directly linked to its operations, products or services by its business relationship with another entity'.[29]

'Shipbreaking in Bangladesh: Worker Rights Violation' (Web Page) https://shipbreakingbd.info/worker-rights-violation/

[24] Ibid; Young Power in Social Action, Death Trap? A-List of Dead Workers from the Year of 2005 to 2012 (September 2012) Death Trap | Shipbreaking in Bangladesh (shipbreakingbd.info) ; Karim (n 18) 20; NGO Shipbreaking Platform, *Annual Report 2009* (Annual Report, 2009) to *Annual Report 2018* (Annual Report, 2018).

[25] Ibid.

[26] Law Commission of India, Proposal to Constitute Environmental Courts, (Research Report No. 186, September 2003) 31.

[27] Berhard Graefrath, 'Responsibility and Damages Caused: Relationship between Responsibilities and Damages', in Recueil des Cours (ed) *Collected Courses of the Hague Academy of International Law*, (Vol 185, 1985) 9–150, 100–102.

[28] *MC Mehta v Union of India*, Supreme Court of India (1987) SCR (1) 819 (the Oleum gas leak case).

[29] *OECD Guidelines for Multinational Enterprises- Recommendations for Responsible Business Conduct,* 31–33.

Even rudimentary human rights due diligence by shipping companies would reveal the potential for end-of-life ships to be ultimately sold into the South Asian shipbreaking industry and then for the breaking of that ship to result in deaths, injuries and work-related diseases.[30] Therefore, in the global industry context of the maritime industry (and its linkage of commercial shipping with shipbreaking in South Asia), it is preferable for the proposed SLC to rely on an existing international benchmark and, specifically, for the framework to rely on the international standards of the International Labour Organisation's (ILO) *Employment Injury Benefits Convention 1964*. Among other things, the *Employment Injury Benefits Convention* provides that, in determining compensation, the competent authority of a Member State should consider the following:

- benefit for occupational accidents and diseases;
- requirements for the payment of medical care and rehabilitation services for workers; and
- maintenance of income for injured workers and their dependents during temporary or permanent disability periods or in case of death'.[31]

The *Employment Injury Benefits Convention* of *1964* states that yearly medical care and sickness benefits for temporary and permanent disability must be set at 60% of the reference salary.[32] In addition, it is essential to pay a flat-rate benefit: at least 60% of the wage of the unskilled worker. The reference salary is the annual minimum wage determined by each state.[33] In the case of permanent incapacity, a lump sum can replace these benefits, and in the event of death, the benefit must be 50% of the reference salary for a widow with two or more children.[34] The resulting pensions must be for life in the form of periodic payments, and for a dependent of the dead worker, it must be at least for the next 18 years or until a minor child becomes an adult.[35]

Using these parameters, Table 9.3 compares the minimum amounts of compensation of the nations where shipbreaking yards are based with those of the major ship selling nations, including Germany, Greece, and Russia. Table 9.3 provides a comparative outlook and determines an international standard for calculating the compensation and premium.

Table 9.2 also shows that, on average, the compensation available in major ship-selling nations is much greater than that in South Asia's shipbreaking nations. The formula mentioned at the beginning of this part uses this more generous amount

---

[30] Ibid.

[31] See ss 9–12, 18–20 of *the Employment Injury Benefits Convention.*

[32] Ibid, Ch 2.

[33] Arts 19 and 20 determine payments according to either the previous earnings of the workers or an ordinary adult male labourer: at Ibid.

[34] Ibid; Ariel Pino, Employment Injury Schemes-The ILO Perspective, International Labour Organisation office for the Caribbean, file:///C:/Users/277587 K/Documents/Employment%20Injury%20Schemes%20-%20the%20ILO%20Perspective.pdf.

[35] *Employment Injury Benefits Convention, 1964,* arts 13, 14, 19 and 20.

Table 9.3 Comparative rate of employment injury benefits between shipbreaking and ship selling nations in terms of the minimum wage for unskilled workers

Countries	Category of worker	Reference salary/Minimum wage per day (USD)	Reference salary/ Minimum wage per month (USD)	Reference salary/ Minimum wage per year (USD) (column 5)		Compensation Amount		
			Incaapacity-60% of the average wage as periodical payment/ pension (USD) + 60% flat rate benefit (column 7)			Death- Pension 50% of the average in the event of death of the breadwinner (USD) (column 8)		
1	2	3	4	5	6 *Average Salary (USD)*	7 *In case of incapacity*[36]	8 *Death case*	9 Total-7 + 8
Shipbreaking countries								
India	unskilled	5.61[37]	145.86	1750.32	1583.04	949.82 + 949.82 = 1899.64	791	2690.64
Pakistan	unskilled	6.11	152.70[38]	1832.40	1583.04			
Bangladesh	unskilled	3.74	97.20	1166.40	1583.04			
Ship selling countries								

(continued)

36 Ibid.

37 India has different level of minimum wages for unskilled workers in different industries, but from April 2020 per day 420 rupees is used as the standard for workers in mining and related industries whereas for the workers engaged in telecommunication the amount is 629 rupees per day: at Office of the Chief Labour Commissioner, 'Ministry of Labour and Employment, Government of India' (Report no.1/VDA(2)/2020-LS-II, 08 May 2020).

38 Pakistan follows the Minimum wages ordinance (Pakistan) for the payment of minimum wages to all unskilled workers which applies to all industrial establishments' employees except of Federal or Provincial Governments' employees: at Wage Indicator.org, *Work and Wages* (Web Page) Fair Work wages in Pakistan - About Basic wage and Payment of Bonus Act - WageIndicator.org I entered the search term 'minimum wage of Pakistan'.

Table 9.3 (continued)

Countries	Category of worker	Reference salary/Minimum wage per day (USD)	Reference salary/ Minimum wage per month (USD)	Reference salary/ Minimum wage per year (USD) (column 5)		Compensation Amount		
Germany	unskilled		1831.60	21,979.2	12,452	7471.2 + 7471.2 = 14,942.62	6226	21,168.62
Greece	unskilled		880.76	10,569.12				
Russia	unskilled		326	3912				
Japan	unskilled		1439.78	12,277.36				
Singapore	unskilled		915	10,980				
South Korea	unskilled		1250	15,000				

Note Table 9.2 was prepared via the following sources: Country Comparison, 'India vs Pakistan', *Country Economy.com* (Web Page) https://countryeconomy.com/countries/compare/india/pakistan?; Country Comparison, 'The Minimum Wage Goes Up in Bangladesh', *Country Economy.com* https://countryeconomy.com/national-minimum-wage/bangladesh; D. Elagina, 'Monthly Minimum Wage in Russia and Its Major Cities in 2020' (Web Page, June 2020); 'John Stotz, 'Average and Minimum Salary in Singapore' *Check in Price* (Web Page, 25 January 2020 https://checkinprice.com/average-minimum-salary-in-singapore/

as an example in the next part to calculate the premium and SLC administrative fee.

Under Arts 9 and 10 of the *Employment Injury Benefits Convention*, an injured worker can receive adequate medical care and allied benefits. The benefits include (a) general practitioner and specialist inpatient and outpatient care, including domiciliary visits; (b) dental and nursing care at home or in the hospital or other medical institution; (c) maintenance in the hospital; (d) dental, pharmaceutical, optical, and other medical or surgical supplies, including prosthetic appliances kept in repair and renewed as necessary; and (e) emergency treatment at the workplace.

Compensation Amount under the Proposed Baselines

The purpose of Table 9.3 mentioned below is to propose amounts (and types) of compensation for killed, injured or ill workers in the shipbreaking industry, who would be the intended beneficiaries of the proposed SLC. Following the above benchmark of the *Employment Injury Benefits Convention* and the average wage of major ship-selling nations, if a worker becomes permanently disabled or sick, he or she will receive approximately USD 15,000 per year, and the payment will continue until his or her death or until his or her last minor child becomes an adult (see Column 7 of Table 9.3). If a worker dies, his or her next of kin would receive USD 6226 per year until his or her youngest child reaches adulthood (see Column 8 of Table 9.3).

On the other hand, following the national average wage of major shipbreaking nations, the amount would be much lower. For example, if a worker becomes permanently disabled or sick, he or she will receive approximately USD 1900 per year, and the payment will continue until his or her death or if his or her last minor child becomes an adult (see Column 7 of Table 9.3). If a worker dies, his or her next of kin would receive just USD 800 per year until his or her youngest child reaches adulthood (see Column 8 of Table 9.3).

In terms of the two rates of compensation, as is considered below, the SLC prefers the rates of major ship-selling nations to those of major shipbreaking nations to provide the greatest benefit to workers. As the national wage is the basis of the international standard introduced under the *Employment Injury Benefit Convention* to provide compensation, which is much lower in shipbreaking nations than in ship selling nations, recommending the rate of shipbreaking nations would provide a back door exit to shipowners and shipbreaking yards. Shipowners and shipbreaking yards should not escape their responsibilities by paying such a low compensation amount.

The SLC also recognises the notion of adequacy. Accordingly, in addition to the standard system for determining compensation mentioned above, a clear mechanism for dispute resolution must be included. For example, subsequent to a dispute on the compensation amount, compensation can be fixed by mutual understanding between parties following a due process of law, but this would need to be administered carefully to take into account the weaker bargaining position of workers and their families.[39] Therefore, in this context, an arbitration system may be a useful platform. Using arbitration under the existing law of shipbreaking nations would provide recourse if the parties cannot agree on some aspects of a claim.

Compensation Amount of the Major Ship Selling Nations

As indicated in Chap. 2, since shipbreaking is the value chain of major shipping nations and statutory compensation amounts are well below the international standard in South Asia, the proposed SLC framework should preferably apply major ship selling nations' standard compensation amounts as opposed to those of major shipbreaking nations. A question may arise, however, as to whether a worker in a developing country should receive such a high standard of compensation.

An underlying reason to argue for the higher standard is to consider the loss to the global maritime industry from not being able to break ships in South Asia. Global maritime industry should be able to break their ships in South Asian shipbreaking industry. However, it should be done by providing a compensation rate on the basis of the wage rate of major ship-selling nations and the ILO's *Employment Injury Benefit Convention*, is more reasonable than losing the profit that shipowners receive from selling ships to South Asian shipbreaking countries. As was considered in Chaps. 3 and 5, shipbreaking in major shipping nations, including Germany, Greece, Japan, Singapore, Russia, South Korea, and the United Arab Emirates, is not profitable for their maritime industry because their shipowners would not receive the same high sale profit as they receive by selling ships to South Asia's shipbreaking industry.[40] One of the reasons is the modest demand for steel scraps and reusable materials for old ships in developed countries.

Another argument for preferring the compensation rate of major ship-selling nations to that of major shipbreaking nations is the global character of the proposed SLC mechanism. The amount of compensation should reflect the standard maintained in developed countries, and in doing so, the SLC would establish an acceptable standard by basing the annual compensation on the ILO benchmark following average compensation paid to major ship selling nations. Moreover, given that the objective of the SLC is to provide adequate compensation to workers, the standard will assist in that direction.[41] It would also create an obvious incentive for the insurance industry to monitor and seek improvements in workplace conditions. However, it is also crucial to recognise the difficulties associated with this preference for two main reasons.

---

[39] International Law Commission, *Draft Principle on the Allocation of Loss in Transboundary Harm Arising Out of Hazardous Activities, with Commentaries*, UNGA, Fifty-eighth Session, UN Doc no. A/61/10 (2006).

[40] NGO Shipbreaking Platform, Annual Reports (n 25).

[41] International Law Commission (n 47) 78.

First, preferring the compensation rate of major ship selling nations to that of major shipbreaking nations may have unintended consequences, such as making shipbreaking insurance prohibitively expensive or encouraging workers to injure themselves. Second, the proposed SLC framework is also mindful that it is against the guiding principle of the post-incident compensation scheme. It does not corroborate the 'Respecting National Sovereignty' principle, which refers to giving preference to national laws and institutions in deciding a compensation scheme unless they do fall below the international standards of the ILO's *Employment Injury Benefit Convention.*[42]

Alternatively, to resolve the above difficulties, the SLC may instead follow the rate of compensation available in the major shipbreaking nations (see Table 9.3), being the host state of shipbreaking yards where workers face casualties, in accordance with the framework of international standards of the ILO's *Employment Injury Benefit Convention*. By analogy, in terms of providing post-incident compensation to workers in the readymade garment industry (RMG) based in Bangladesh, the international community has followed the same scheme, despite recognising that they are the supply chain of global brands, which are based on developed nations.[43] Although, in comparison with developed countries, the rate that follows the developing countries' standard is very low, the positive side is that it is less questionable under the established principle of compensation and is in line with the international standards of the ILO's *Employment Injury Benefit Convention.*[44]

The *Employment Injury Benefit Convention* determines compensation payments according to arts 19 and 20; these refer to either the previous earnings of the affected worker or an 'ordinary adult male labourer'. In line with the ILO's *Employment Injury Benefit Convention*, workers are eligible to claim compensation for lost wages following their domestic rate, for the entire period of impairment, or in the case of a deceased worker for up to the period of a dependent's eligibility to obtain a job. As seen in Table 9.2, following the international standards of the ILO's *Employment Injury Benefit Convention*, which provides compensation on the basis of the national wage of a host state, the possible amount of compensation would be much lower in South Asian shipbreaking countries than in major ship selling nations, but it would not make shipbreaking insurance too expensive for commercial operation of a ship or instigate workers to make false claims by injuring themselves. Moreover, it would not go beyond the established principle of 'Respecting National Sovereignty' referred to above.

---

42 Rebecca Prentice, 'Just Compensation? The Price of Death and Injury after the Rana Plaza Garment Factory Collapse' in *The Politics and Ethics of the Just Price* (Emerald Publishing, vol 39, 2019) https://www.emerald.com/books/edited-volume/15167/chapter-abstract/86360462/Just-Compensation-The-Price-of-Death-and-Injury?redirectedFrom=fulltext.

43 Ibid.

44 See details about the principles: Ibid 3.

An Estimate of the Annual SLC Administrative Fee and Insurance Premium

Using the formula stated in section "Establishing the Baselines for the Shipbreaking Insurance and SLC Administrative Fee" above and the major ship selling nations' rate of compensation explained in Table 9.3, a shipowner or a shipbreaking company would pay approximately:

$$\frac{\frac{250\,(\text{last5years'aggregatenumberofglobaldeathsandinjuries} - \text{seeSectionCabove}) \times \text{USD}14,943\,(\text{compensationbenchmarkinmajorshipsellingnations} - \text{seeTable 9.3})}{23,500,000\,(\text{average LDTsbrokeninlastfiveyears}-\text{seeTable 9.2})}}{2}$$

$$= 0.080\,\text{USDperLDTfortheSLC}$$

Conversely, when the compensation rates of major shipbreaking nations are used, the amount would be only USD 250 × 2000/USD 23,500,000/2 = 0.0106 per LDT. These two alternatives are determined via the formula (see Section "Enforcement Measures" above) and consider the average number of casualties at 250 (see Section B above), average total ILO benchmark compensation for major ship selling nations (approximately USD 14,943) (see Table 9.3 mentioned in Section C), and average LDT (23,500,000) broken every year (see Table 9.2).

The above amount includes both the premium for shipbreaking insurance and the SLC fee. As the amount would include a 30% fee for the SLC and the remaining 70% for paying an insurance premium, for a cargo ship weighing 20,000 LDT,[45] a shipbreaking facility owner would pay a maximum (20,000 × 0.080) or USD 1600 for the shipbreaking liability insurance and the SLC. A shipowner also has to pay the same amount per year until the end of the life of the ship. The amount is just an indicative value when the above baselines are used. Conversely, considering the second estimate mentioned above, a shipbreaking facility would have to pay only approximately (20,000 × 0.0106) or USD 212 for shipbreaking liability insurance and the SLC, whereas for a ship's commercial operation, the USD 212 amount would be an annual payment across its life span.

Because of the potential risks, for the SLC fee and the insurance premium for a shipbreaking yard, charging a lesser fee from a shipbreaking yard, which is fully compliant with the *Hong Kong Convention* requirements, than from a shipbreaking yard, which is not compliant with the *Hong Kong Convention* requirements, is recommended. It may even be a minimum fee if a shipbreaking yard can show evidence of the highest level of compliance with the *Hong Kong Convention*. Table 9.2 provides an example of a checklist that could be used as a model for how fee concessions

---

[45] The average highest LDT contained by each ship broken in Bangladesh is 20000: at Mohammad Sujauddin et al., 'Characterisation of Shipbreaking Industry in Bangladesh' (2015) (17) *Journal of Material Cycles and Waste Management,* 72–83.

could be provided to shipbreaking yards. This is to encourage the improvement of standards of shipbreaking, with the intention that charging lower fees and premiums would encourage non-compliant shipbreaking yards to be compliant with the *Hong Kong Convention* standards.

Before justifying the SLC in the context of providing compensation and preventing accidents, the next section explores the enforcement measures of the proposed SLC system.

Enforcement Measures

Minimum Premium Amount

The unwillingness of shipowners to take on extra financial burden is likely to be a significant challenge for the proposed SLC. According to the proposed SLC, however, compared with the amount shipowners earn from the commercial operation of their ships, the amount prescribed under the formula is reasonable. For example, data published by Hellenic Shipping, an online daily newspaper for international shipping, show that in June 2020, the average daily earnings of a Cape-Size ship, the largest cargo ship in the world, reached USD 4250/day, and between January 2019 and June 2020, earnings were approximately USD 15,000 per day (see Fig. 9.4).[46]

Periodical Inspection of a Shipbreaking Yard by the Insurer

Another challenge for the SLC would be to police shipbreaking yards. As discussed previously, the proposed SLC framework recommends that there be periodic inspections of shipbreaking yards by an independent verifier, appointed by the insurer to ensure their independence from shipbreaking companies. A good option would be to appoint reputable international organisations with experience in this verification process.

---

[46] Dry Bulk Market, 'Capsize Earnings Leap USD 4250 per Day- Largest Daily Jump since 2013', *Hellenic Shipping News Worldwide* (online at 19 June 2020) https://www.hellenicshippingnews.com/capesize-earnings-leap-usd-4250-per-day-largest-daily-jump-since-2013/

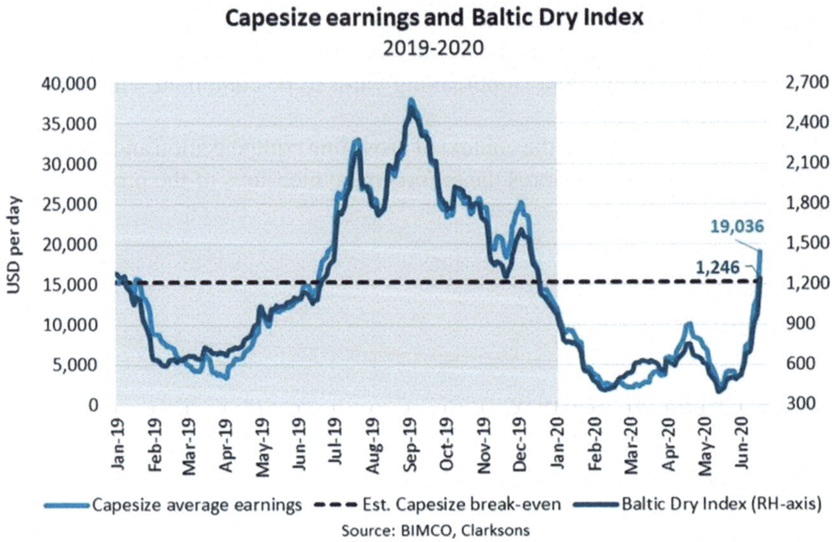

Fig. 9.4 Daily earnings of a CapeSize vessel (*Source* Hellenic Shipping News Worldwide[47])

Policing the Commercial Life of a Ship

In relation to policing commercial operations of a ship, the SLC framework can use the existing port state control (PSC) mechanism.[48] By introducing PSC under the proposed SLC, one of the lessons learned from the case study of the *Load Lines Certificate* (see Chap. 7) can be applied. Each port State already utilises its existing PSC system to check whether a ship maintains an updated *load line certificate* for its international safety, security and environmental standards, and these administrative arrangements could be adapted to include compliance with the SLC requirements.

The port state control system is a mechanism introduced by the Paris Memorandum of Understanding, consisting of 27 participating maritime administrations. The basic principle is to make shipowners responsible for complying with the requirements laid out in international maritime conventions.[49] According to the PSC system, unless shipowners follow the international standards required for their ships, a port authority can deny port entry and arrest the ship for an indefinite time until the problems identified are resolved.[50] The proposed SLC recommends applying the same

---

[47] Ibid.

[48] Ho-Sam Bang and Duck-Jong Jang, Recent Developments in Regional Memorandums of Understanding on Port State Control (2012) 43 (2) *Ocean Development and International Law* 170–187.

[49] Paris MoU, on Port State Control, 'Organisation' (Web Page) parismou.org/about-us/organisation .

[50] See *Paris Memorandum of Understanding on Port State Control*, adopted 26 January 1982, IMO Res A.1052(27), entered into force 1 July 1982, ss 3(4), 3(6) and 3(8).

system for maintaining and ensuring the proper maintenance of shipbreaking liability insurance and SLC by a commercial ship. This independent inspection under the PSC system would also ensure transparency during the commercial life of a ship.[51]

As most major ship selling nations are already involved in the PSC system, another advantage of this approach is the reduced administrative costs achieved through sharing each PSC's existing administrative set up. Notably, the *Hong Kong Convention* also empowers State parties to detain, warn, dismiss, or exclude a ship if a ship entering a port of a Member State does not follow the requirements of the *Hong Kong Convention*.[52] However, the *Hong Kong Convention* does not explicitly mention the PSC or any other system to enforce this requirement. The proposal to use the PSC system is to fill this gap.

Role of the Insurance Provider in Respecting the Claims of Compensation and Enforcement

Insurance providers would have the duty to respect each claim for compensation made and to conduct an impartial investigation into each claim. In addition to managing and investigating claims, insurance companies assess the risk presented by a proposed insure (i.e., a shipbreaking yard for shipbreaking insurance) before issuing an insurance policy, continue periodic investigations, and monitor the level of risk and other factors. As the cradle to the grave approach proposed under the *Hong Kong Convention* requires a survey of each ship, the insurance provider would assess the risk for potential shipowner insurances following such a survey.

The mechanism would be acceptable to insurance providers since introducing an insurance mechanism from early life would reduce their risk. This would also lead to regular inspection and suggested repairs so that the risks related to breaking a ship are reduced, leading to less pressure on insurance companies.

Consequences of Breach

The objective of the SLC is to facilitate swift and efficient access to compensation if a valid claim is made. The proposed SLC framework is a model based on global governance and rectificatory justice theory. Failure to comply with the requirements of maintaining the SLC and shipbreaking insurance should be followed by no further sale of ships for breaking to a shipbreaking yard. The proposed SLC should also explicitly mention that non-compliant shipbreaking yards might be blocked and barred from purchasing more ships. This denial of an SLC and blacklisting of a shipbreaking facility would be a strategy to assist shipowners in making informed

---

[51] Ibid.

[52] The *Hong Kong Convention*, art 9.

decisions about the final destination of a ship and being informed about the risks ahead of selling ships to those blacklisted shipbreaking yards. Alternatively, if a shipowner continues selling a ship to blacklisted shipbreaking yards, the IMO may impose heavy fines on the shipowner. Shipbreaking nations should also ban blacklisted shipbreaking yards locally and impose heavy fines for continuing shipbreaking. The fines can be used to pay the Worker's Advocate or NGO for their involvement with the claim process of the affected workers.

The insurance- and certification-based regulatory model is rooted in the principles of corporate social responsibility (see Chap. 7). This model is a basis for solving many other global problems, including waste trade and sound management (see Chap. 8). The initiative dominated by insurance and certification would remove elements viewed as counters business profits, such as litigation.

Conclusion

The SLC framework proposed in this chapter, aims to provide a systemic approach to ensure an international standard of compensation for shipbreaking workers facing work-related deaths, injuries, or diseases. By introducing the proposed SLC framework, the IMO would be responsible for supervising the flag change of a ship and the facility standard of a shipbreaking yard. This mechanism is similar to the IMO passing an international mechanism to control the overloading of a ship or to pay compensation to a victim of an oil spill incident (see Chap. 7, section "Plimsoll Line Incident and Importance of a Load Lines Certificate").

Under the proposed framework, the SLC and insurance would attract a maximum of USD 0.080 per LDT from a shipowner and shipbreaking yard each year upon registration. This is a minimal amount compared with the annual operating income of a ship and a shipbreaking yard for a system that would provide a good amount of compensation to a shipbreaking worker (approximately USD 15,000 for a permanently disabled worker and USD 6226 to a deceased worker's family annually). The framework also recognises that the relevant insurance industry determines the actual SLC and insurance premium after considering the risk involved in breaking each ship.

The global shipbreaking industry would meet the challenge concerning the periodical inspection of a ship and shipbreaking yard by introducing the framework. The insurance industry would monitor a ship and shipbreaking yard to assess the premium each year on the basis of the baselines discussed in this chapter. Thus, the SLC and insurance premium would be higher for a ship with more waste than others would, and a shipbreaking yard would pay the maximum premium if the yard owner cannot ensure full compliance with the *Hong Kong Convention*, as demonstrated in Table 12. An important development of the framework is to address the liability of shipowners, including cash buyers and shipbreaking yards. Under the proposed framework, neither a long-term nor a short-term shipowner can transfer a ship without notifying the IMO. Moreover, for breaches of insurance contracts, another critical challenge that the SLC could meet is to empower shipbreaking workers by providing a means to fund lawyers (e.g., Worker Advocates) from the SLC administrative fee to fight on behalf of the individual worker.

Notably, a direct implication of the proposed SLC is that the insurance industry globally monitors substandard shipbreaking yards, and the IMO uses their data to assume their progress rate. An indirect consequence would be that if the IMO finds that a shipbreaking yard is not taking any steps to improve its standard, then the IMO might decide to block them and issue no further SLC. This interventionist approach is vital for motivating non-compliant shipbreaking yards to improve their standards.

Chapter 10 undertakes an evaluation of the SLC as rectificatory global justice theory and its potential to change the non-compliant behaviour of the maritime and shipbreaking industry toward its safety standards.

Bibliography

Articles/Books/Reports

Mishra, V.S., 'Emerging Right to Compensation in Indian Environmental Law' (2001) 23 *Delhi Law Review*, 58–79

Sujauddin, Mohammad et al, 'Characterisation of Shipbreaking Industry in Bangladesh' (2015) (17) *Journal of Material Cycles and Waste Management*, 72

Graefrath, Berhard, 'Responsibility and Damages Caused: Relationship between Responsibilities and Damages', in Recueil des Cours (ed) *Collected Courses of the Hague Academy of International Law* (Vol 185, 1985)

Karim, Saiful, *Shipbreaking in Developing Countries: A Requiem for Environmental Justice from the Perspectives of Bangladesh* (Taylor and Francis Group, 2018)

Walther, Reto, 'UN Guiding Principles on Business and Human Rights and Effective Remedies-A State-Based Nonjudicial Grievance Mechanism for Switzerland' (Bachelor Thesis, Zurich University of Applied Sciences- School of Management and Law,15 May 2014)

Bestoasis, 'Global Ship Recycling Market' (Week 33 - Ship Recycling Report- Best Oasis Limited, 6 to 13 August 2021) https://www.best-oasis.com/reports/week-33-ship-recycling-report-best-oasis-limited

ECORYS-DNV-GL-Erasmus University of Rotterdam, Financial Instrument to Facilitate Safe and Sound Ship Recycling' (Research Report, The EU Commission Directorate-General for Environment, June 2016)

Greenpeace, 'End of Life Ships: The Human Cost of Breaking Ships' (Research Report, 2005)

Law Commission of India, Proposal to Constitute Environmental Courts (Research Report No. 186, September 2003)

Office of the Chief Labour Commissioner, 'Ministry of Labour and Employment, Government of India' (Report no.1/VDA(2)/2020-LS-II, 08 May 2020)

Prentice, Rebecca, 'Workers' Right to Compensation after Garment Factory Disasters: Making Rights a Reality', *University of Sussex* (Research Report, C&A Foundation, 2018)

Ruggie, John, *Guiding Principles for the Implementation of the United Nations 'Protect, Respect and Remedy Framework,* Report of the Special Representative of the Secretary-General on the issue of human rights and transnational corporations and other business enterprises, UN Doc A/HRC/17/31 (March 2011)

Sarraf, Maria et al, 'Ship Breaking and Recycling Industry in Bangladesh and Pakistan' (Report No. 58275-SAS, World Bank, 2010)

United Nations Conference on Trade and Development, 'Ship Scrapping by Country of Demolition' *Annual Report* (Webpage) https://unctadstat.unctad.org/wds/TableViewer/tableView.aspx?ReportId=89492

Cases

Bangladesh Environmental Lawyers Association (BELA) v Janata Steel Corporation, [Writ Petition No. 8466 of 2019] High Court Division (26 February 2020)
MC Mehta v Union of India, Supreme Court of India (1987) SCR (1) 819

Legislations

Insurance Contracts Act 1984 (UK)
Minimum Wages Ordinance, 1961 (Pakistan)

Treaties

Employment Injury Benefits Convention, 1964 (amended in 1980), adopted on 17 June 1964, ILO Convention no. 121, entered into force 28 July 1967 (*Employment Injury Benefits Convention)*
International Law Commission, *Draft Articles on State Responsibility for Internationally Wrongful Acts*, (Yearbook 2001) 2 (Part Two)
International Law Commission, *Draft Principle on the Allocation of Loss in Transboundary Harm Arising Out of Hazardous Activities, with Commentaries*, UNGA, Fifty-eighth Session, UN Doc no. A/61/10 (2006)
OECD, *OECD Guidelines for Multinational Enterprises- Recommendations for Responsible Business Conduct* (Report 8 June 2023, OECD) https://doi.org/10.1787/81f92357-en
Paris Memorandum of Understanding on Port State Control, adopted 26 January 1982, IMO Res A.1052(27), entered into force 1 July 1982
The Hong Kong International Convention for the Safe and Environmentally Sound Recycling of Ships, opened for Signature 1 September 2009, IMO Doc. SR/CONF45 (not yet in force)
The Maritime Environment Protection Committee, *IMO Guidelines for the Development of the Ship Recycling Plan*, IMO Doc MEPC/Circ.419, 12 November 2004
United Nations Convention on the Law of the Seas, adopted on 10 December 1982, 1982 UNTS 397, entered into force on 1 November 1994

Others

Dry Bulk Market, 'Capsize Earnings Leap USD 4250 per Day- Largest Daily Jump since 2013', *Hellenic Shipping News Worldwide* (online at 19 June 2020) https://www.hellenicshippingnews.com/capesize-earnings-leap-usd-4250-per-day-largest-daily-jump-since-2013/
GRIEG GREEN, 'Ship Recycling' (We Page) https://grieggreen.com/project/ship_recycling/
IHS Markit, 'World Fleet Statistics 2018: A Composition of the World Fleet Development' (Web Page, 31 December 2018) https://ihsmarkit.com/industry/maritime.html

International Maritime Organisation, 'Registration of Ships and Fraudulent Registration Matters' (Webpage) Registration of ships and fraudulent registration matters (imo.org)

International Maritime Organisation, Registration of Ships and Fraudulent Registration (Web Page) https://www.imo.org/en/OurWork/Legal/Pages/Registration-of-ships-and-fraudulent-registration-matters.aspx

Legal Aid Queensland, Understanding the Reason for an Insurance Claim Refusal (Web Page) Understanding the reason for an insurance claim refusal - Legal Aid Queensland

Leinnekopper, Kirstein, 'Ship Recycling Market Waking Up after Disappointing Summer' *Recycling International* (Web Page, 9 October 2019) https://recyclinginternational.com/ferrous-metals/ship-recycling-market-waking-up-after-disappointing-summer/27942/

Paris MoU, on Port State Control, 'Organisation' (Web Page) parismou.org/about-us/organisation.

Pino, Ariel, Employment Injury Schemes-The ILO Perspective, International Labour Organisation office for the Caribbean, file:///C:/Users/277587K/Documents/Employment%20Injury%20Schemes%20-%20the%20ILO%20Perspective.pdf

Shah, Captain Anwar, 'Port State Control and Memorandum of Understanding' (Blog Post, 1 September 2016) http://captainanwarshah.blogspot.com/2015/09/port-state-control-and-memorandum-of.html

Wage Indicator.org, *Work and Wages* (Web Page) Fair Work wages in Pakistan - About Basic wage and Payment of Bonus Act - WageIndicator.org

Young Power in Social Action, 'Shipbreaking in Bangladesh: Worker Rights Violation' (Web Page) https://shipbreakingbd.info/worker-rights-violation/

Young Power in Social Action, Death Trap? A-List of Dead Workers from the Year of 2005 to 2012 (September 2012) Death Trap | Shipbreaking in Bangladesh (shipbreakingbd.info)

Chapter 10
Concluding Remarks

Abstract The book has proposed a civil liability regime specific for the shipbreaking sector based on the theory of rectificatory global justice. The regime is referred to as shipbreaking liability certificate or SLC. The proposed SLC is intended to set up a global system to provide compensation to workers if they are killed, injured, or suffered a work-related disease arising from shipbreaking-related activities. Alongside compensation, an indirect effect of the SLC would be to change current industry practice. The SLC scheme explained in Chap. 9 of the book may be applicable regionally or globally where the shipbreaking practices are used.

Keywords National and international regulations · Business chain · Shipbreaking workers · Open registry countries · Financial liability · Legal void

Introduction

The current national and international legal regimes offer no way to address the financial liability of shipowners. Because of this legal void, even though all the actors in the business chain including the shipping industry, cash buyers, and open registry countries make huge profits,[1] not one of them is held to account for the routine death, injury, and illness experienced by shipbreaking workers.[2]

These routine death, injury, and illness have raised the issue of injustice at shipbreaking sector, which leads to draw on the theory of rectificatory justice that aims at striking a balance between business profit and human consequences.[3] The emphasis of rectificatory justice is remedying an injustice, which is particularly important for governance of the shipbreaking industry. This is because, rectificatory justice provides a way of thinking about how to rectify the injustice suffered by victim

[1] Chapter 3 has first evaluated the business interest of the maritime industry and found that annual income of the industry is around USD 2350 million.

[2] See Chap. 5 of the book.

[3] Peter Singer, 'Famine, Affluence and Morality' (1972) 1 *Philosophy and Public Affairs* 229, 229–233.

M. Z. Ali, *Worker Injustices in the South Asian Shipbreaking Industry*, International Law in Asia, https://doi.org/10.1007/978-981-95-8325-6_10

workers at shipbreaking industry. In doing so, the conceptualisation of rectificatory justice is to identify and remedy an injustice in the shipbreaking industry; i.e., the want of adequate and prompt compensation for workers who face shipbreaking related deaths, injuries, and diseases.[4] Alternatively, since it is difficult to completely stop the suffering of workers in the shipbreaking industry in the short term, the application of the rectificatory justice theory in the SLC would at least introduce a remedy system, so as to make sure that the workers in the shipbreaking sector would not be wronged.[5]

Rectificatory justice theory seeks to identify one strong and a weak party in a business relationship and in rectifying the injustice it looks for a balance between their profit and obligations. The dominant sides of the shipbreaking industry are the maritime industry and their business profit, involvement of which within the shipbreaking industry show a clear case of injustice, because they do not recognise the interests of shipbreaking workers.[6] Regarding this, the postcolonial theory (postcolonialism) is relevant as it questions whether the laws have vested overwhelming power with no accountability in controlling agency located in the west.[7] Two other arguments suggest that applying the postcolonial theory is appropriate to shipbreaking sector. The first is that the shipbreaking regulations have been enacted well after the end of colonialism, but they very much serve the interest of international shipowners predominantly based in the Western world who seem to have more focus on their bottom line than the resource constraints of the emerging world. Second, the laws do not take into account that the developing countries have inadequate resources to upgrade the safety and environmental standards of their shipbreaking activity.

The proposition that international institutions are structurally biased toward the development world is another cause to use postcolonialism.[8] This biasness is reflected in the *Hong Kong International Convention for the Safe and Environmentally Sound Recycling of Ships* (*Hong Kong Convention*).[9] While *Hong Kong Convention* is the only instrument available in this field, it was designed to promote a business model enabling ships from major shipping countries to sell ships with hazardous materials to shipbreaking companies in South Asia and to circumvent financial responsibility

[4] Amartya Sen, 'Rawls versus Bentham: An Axiomatic Examination of the Pure Distribution Problem' (1974) 4 *Theory and Decision* 301, 302–309 https://doi-org.dbgw.lis.curtin.edu.au/10.1007/BF00136651.

[5] Amartya Sen, *The Idea of Justice* (Allen Lane, 2009) 7.

[6] Corinna Mieth, 'Global Injustice: Individual Duties and Non-Ideal Institutional Circumstances' (2012) 12(1) *Civitas-Revista de Ciencias Sociais* 47, 47–50.

[7] Christopher George Weeramanty, *Universalising International Law* (Martinus Nijhoff Publishers, 2004) 85.

[8] Thomas Pogge, 'World Poverty and Human Rights' (2005) 19(1) *Ethics and International Affairs* 1–7.

[9] *The Hong Kong International Convention for the Safe and Environmentally Sound Recycling of Ships*, opened for Signature 1 September 2009, IMO Doc. SR/CONF45 (entered into force 26 June 2025) Annex ('*Regulation for Safe and Environmentally Sound Recycling of Ships*).

for cleaning of hazardous substances from ships and for the compensation of work-related death, injury, and disease.[10]

The argument of global injustice, grounded in postcolonial legal theory, offers a distinctive lens through which the structural inequalities embedded in the global maritime economy can be examined. Central to the critique is the observation that the shipbreaking sector is an essential but a hazardous part of maritime logistics, which operates without imposing legal accountability on international shipowners for occupational fatalities, injuries, illnesses, or environmental degradation.[11] By invoking principles of rectificatory global justice, the proposed SLC framework seeks to establish a civil liability mechanism that would obligate shipowners to compensate for harm incurred by workers in the shipbreaking process. This includes recognition of deaths, injuries, and chronic health conditions arising from unsafe shipbreaking practices.[12]

Prior to formalising such a framework, it is imperative to investigate the human rights dimensions of shipbreaking through the dual prisms of global injustice and postcolonial critique.[13] A review of international documentation-including European Union case studies, analyses of oil transport logistics and broader shipping industry practices support the contention that a transnational regulatory architecture is both necessary and feasible.[14] The viability of such a framework, however, hinges on its ability to enforce shared responsibility across all stakeholders engaged in shipbreaking, particularly in South Asia where the industry is mostly concentrated.[15]

Further inquiry into the economic implications of raising operational standards in the sector reveals a critical tension: enhancing safety and environmental protocols may inadvertently escalate costs, and thereby disincentivising shipowners from engaging South Asian facilities.[16] This would catalyse a geographic shift in shipbreaking activities toward regions with laxer regulations and lower overheads, undermining reform efforts.[17]

The central issue for South Asian shipbreaking industries lies in reconciling competitive pricing with ethical labour practices. Their market dominance has historically been sustained by offering premium purchase princes to shipowners, financed

---

[10] Md Saiful Karim, 'Recycling of Ships' in *Prevention of Pollution of the Maritime Environment from Vessels: Potential Limit of the International Maritime Organisation*' (Springer, 2015) 98–100.

[11] Stephen M. Gardiner, 'Ethics and Global Climate Change' (April 2004) 114(4) *University of Chicago Press Journals* 580, 555–600; Alpana Roy, 'Postcolonial Theory and Law: A Critical Introduction' (2008) 29 *Adelaide Law Review* 315, 317.

[12] See Chap. 9 of the book.

[13] See Chap. 3 of the book.

[14] Ibid.

[15] See Chap. 3 of the book.

[16] George Cairns, 'A Critical Scenario Analysis of end-of-life Ship Disposal: The Bottom of the Pyramid as Opportunity and Graveyard' (2014) 10(3) *Journal of Critical Perspectives on International Business* 172, 172–175.

[17] Yaa Agyare-Dwomoh, A Green Compliant Ship Recycling Facility in South Africa, Frost and Sullivan Africa (online) https://frost-sullivan-africa.prezly.com/a-green-compliant-ship-recycling-facility-in-south-africa.

through minimal investment in worker safety and environmental safeguards. Data suggests that approximately 82% of total shipbreaking expenditure is allocated to acquiring ships,[18] leaving negligible resources for compliance with health, safety, and environmental norms.[19] This economic model, perpetuates a 'race to the bottom scenario', wherein shipowners are incentivised to sell to shipbreaking facilities that maintain substandard conditions—characterised by beaching techniques, importing ships without pre-cleaning, and breaking ships with bare hands—to offer high purchase prices to shipowners.[20] The consequences are severe: frequent worker casualties, chronic occupational diseases, and ecological damage with enduring effects on coastal and estuarine ecosystems.[21] Despite these harms, affected workers and communities lack the legal capacity or institutional support to seek redress. The absence of formal employment contracts, identity documentation, and registration systems renders shipbreaking workers invisible within legal frameworks. This systemic exclusion underpinned the major inquiry, namely:

> What legal and liability framework is required to make the international maritime industry accountable for the harms to human life and health (workers' deaths, physical injuries, and work-related diseases) in shipbreaking countries?

Need to Strike a Balance Between Business Profit and Human Consequences

An examination of the national and international legal frameworks has demonstrated a legal failure to strike a balance between high business profit offered to the shipping industry and human cost in the shipbreaking industry.

The regulatory frameworks undertaken by India, Bangladesh, and Pakistan,[22] tend to be dictated by each country's need for steel, obtained from broken ships, and for the local employment the industry generates. These factors require each nation to maintain a significant market share in the global shipbreaking business. The three South Asian shipbreaking countries thus follow weak regulatory policies out of fear they might lose their market share of the shipbreaking business.[23] Their weak regulatory policies are therefore favourable to retaining the shipbreaking industry but are not enough to create safe workplaces and compensate workers for work-related deaths, injuries, and diseases.

The regulatory frameworks at the international level have even more problems.[24] In contrast to most global industries, which have both prevention and compensation

[18] See Chap. 3 of the book.

[19] See Chap. 4 of the book.

[20] See Chap. 4 of the book.

[21] See Chap. 3 of the book.

[22] See Chap. 4 of the book.

[23] Ibid.

[24] See Chap. 5 of the book.

systems,[25] the international legal framework for shipbreaking only concentrates on a weak preventive system that has done little to improve workplace health and safety in South Asian shipbreaking yards and which provides no compensation scheme for workers.

The weakness in the legal settings represents a global injustice. The injustice argument stems from two additional reasons. First, the *Hong Kong Convention* does not consider the specific needs of developing countries. The *Hong Kong Convention* requires shipbreaking countries to make their own investment to improve occupational health and safety standards in shipbreaking yards in their jurisdictions.[26] As other authors have pointed out, shipbreaking in South Asia is a matter of global injustice as this requirement shifts the responsibility for workplace health and safety and worker compensation exclusively to developing countries.[27] In this way, the *Hong Kong Convention* is unjust in that it creates a substantial benefit for the global shipping industry at the expense of developing countries and their environments and workers.[28] Second, whilst shipbreaking reportedly engenders a heavy cost to workers in developing countries, the *Hong Kong Convention* does not prioritize compensation for work-related injuries, deaths, or diseases to workers.[29]

The critical examination of the existing regulatory options for the shipbreaking industry reinforces the need to strike a more just balance between the benefits that the South Asian shipbreaking industry provides to the global shipping industry and loss to the workers in the downstream shipbreaking activities is the best option. The proposed SLC focuses on the balancing approach. Further, the implementation of the SLC scheme focuses on changing the industry practice. The central claim is that the shipbreaking industry requires such a global civil liability mechanism not only to compensate shipbreaking workers who suffer work-related fatalities, injuries, or diseases, but also to change the industry practice by tightening the change of ownership from cradle to grave of all ships.[30] This would also require ensuring responsibility of everybody in the business chain by keeping the business profitable for all parties.

---

[25] Mining and Waste Trade as discussed in Chap. 7 of the book.

[26] K. Jain, J.F. Pruyn and J. Hopman, 'Critical Analysis of the Hong Kong International Convention on Ship Recycling' (2013) 7 (10) *International Journal of Environment, Ecological, Geological and Mining Engineering* 683, 686.

[27] Karim (n 22) 16–19.

[28] Saurabh Bhattachargee, 'From Basel to Hong Kong: International Environment Regulation of Ship-Recycling Takes One Step Forward and Two Steps Back,' 2009 (2) *Trade Law and Development* 193, 214–215; Michael Galley, *Shipbreaking: Hazards and Liabilities* (Springer International Publishing, 2014) 155.

[29] Ingvild Jenssem et al., 'Impact Report 2018–2019' (Research Report, NGO Shipbreaking Platform, 2020) https://shipbreakingplatform.org/wp-content/uploads/2020/06/NGOSBP-Bi-Annual-Report-18-19.pdf; NGO Shipbreaking Platform, 'Two Fatal Accidents at Indian Yards Under EU Scrutiny' (Press Release, 10th September 2019) https://shipbreakingplatform.org/fatal-accidents-at-indian-yards-under-eu-scrutiny/.

[30] Chapter 9.

Lessons Learned from the Case Studies for an Effective Balance Between Profit and Loss

Financial and Criminal Liability Approaches of the European Union

An examination of the regulatory mechanisms of the European Union (EU) shows that although the EU supports imposing responsibility on shipowners, the EU mechanisms have not gone far enough.[31] They fall short of promoting an ethical and sustainable shipbreaking practice in South Asia and thereby supporting an appropriate balance between business profits and workers' welfare.

The main problem is that the *EU Ship Recycling Regulation*, being the principal legal mechanism in the EU, does not regulate the reflagging practice strictly.[32] A EU-based owner can thus change flag from its original EU jurisdiction to a non-EU jurisdiction and, in this way, can send ships to the South Asian shipbreaking industry.

The EU has received several proposals from a number of institutions, such as Erasmus University of Rotterdam, to address the problem of reflagging by the introduction of a financial mechanism. The main idea behind these proposals is to impose financial liability on EU shipowners if ships from the EU go to South Asia by changing flags.[33] Imposing financial liability is crucial for a legal intervention in the system for effective checks and balance, but considered further below, these proposals do not introduce a system to compensate workers who suffer deaths, injuries, or work-related diseases whilst breaking the reflagged EU ships in South Asia.[34]

A proper financial mechanism, on the contrary, must function to allocate the business profit to those who face the loss. From the perspective of rectificatory justice, the main entity to benefit from the system should be the shipbreaking workers. The system should benefit and empower the workers, so that they can claim compensation as of right, but this approach is missing from the financial mechanisms proposed by several institutions to the EU.

The proposals submitted to the EU fall short of imposing financial liability on shipowners in the true sense. Instead of proposing to compensate the victims, the proposals set mechanisms to raise funds from EU shipowners throughout the life span of a ship and to pay them back from the fund at the end-of-life of their ships if they can show evidence of recycling their ships in a EU listed shipbreaking yard. This proposed payback system in fact has recognised that the EU shipowners may lose a

---

[31] Chapter 6.

[32] Reflagging refers to changing of flag of a ship in consequence of changing the ownership of a ship; *Regulation (EU) No. 1257/2013 of the European Parliament and of the Council of 20 November 2013 on Ship Recycling and Amending Regulation (EC) No. 1013/2016 and Directive 2009/16/EC, 2013*, OJ (L 330) 1 (*EU Ship Recycling Regulation)*.

[33] See Chap. 6 of the book.

[34] See Chap. 6 of the book.

significant amount of selling price if they sell their ships to a EU listed shipbreaking yard.

The central idea is therefore to provide financial incentive to EU shipowners for selling ships to EU listed shipbreaking yards by returning them from the accumulated funds—the cost equivalent to the price gap for selling a ship to a EU listed shipbreaking yard and a non-EU listed shipbreaking yard. The proposal is based on the statistics that a non-EU listed shipbreaking yard would pay a higher price for purchasing ships since they do not need to comply with the greater health and safety requirements of the *EU Ship Recycling Regulation*. None of the South Asian shipbreaking yards could, however, gain a place in the shipbreaking yards' list published by the EU in 2021.[35] This payment option to shipowners is, however, an incorrect approach to regulating EU shipowners. Having said that, it is true that the proposed financial mechanisms in the EU present a lesson for the global shipbreaking industry. Importantly, the EU financial mechanisms underpin the argument for a global shipbreaking licence and insurance, which can address the problem in the shipbreaking industry in a global context.

Criminal liability on shipowners is the other EU approach discussed in Chap. 6. Under the EU *Ship Recycling Regulation*, sending ships to shipbreaking yards that use beaching practice is a criminal offence.[36] A recent decision of a District Court of Rotterdam in *Seatrade*, is one of the most recent examples of this approach.[37] In this case, the Court ordered a Dutch shipping company, Seatrade to pay a heavy fine of EUR 750,000 for their intention to break four ships at India and Bangladesh's shipbreaking yards. The Court also directed that sending ships to India and Bangladesh as waste is a serious criminal offence that warrants imprisonment of the directors, however, considering it is an offence committed for the first time, the Court waived the prison sentence and alternatively imposed a 12 months' suspension on their directorship positions in any company.[38] However, the criminal liability approach is not practical in the global context of the business.[39] This is because, the Court has imposed heavy fines on the EU shipowners for sending ships to South Asia, which may have a deterrent effect on EU shipowners and in consequence, South Asian shipbreaking may suffer business loss if EU shipowners stop the sale of ships to South Asia's shipbreaking industry.

The analysis of the EU approaches demonstrate that the EU has not perceived shipbreaking as a means by which South Asian countries can pursue their economic development by sourcing iron ore and providing livelihood to poor workers. In contrast, the EU approaches purport to improve the situation as regards shipbreaking but do not

---

[35] See Chap. 6 of the book.

[36] See Chap. 6 of the book.

[37] *State v Seatrade* [Rotterdam District Court, three-judge economic division for criminal cases], Public Prosecutor Office 10/994550-15, 15 March 2018 reported in (2018) Rechtspraak.nl 1, ECLI:NL:RBROT:2018:2108.

[38] See Chap. 6, section "Imposition of Criminal Liability by the District Court of Rotterdam" of the book.

[39] See Chap. 3 of the book.

actually do so. The EU approaches also demonstrate that the developed economies have used shipbreaking to externalise their wastes, as an end-of-life activity of the maritime industry's business. From the perspective of developing countries, that dependency must not lead to exploiting their workers and environment.[40]

From the analysis of the domestic, international, and EU-based regulatory frameworks it is clear that there are limited mechanisms to compensate the shipbreaking workers who suffer deaths, injuries, or diseases. Because of the legal gap, common law actions in tort are the only current means by which a civil court can find shipowners responsible for harms suffered by workers and obliged to pay compensation as damages. By using the duty of care principle before the home State court of shipowners, workers can engage in a highly contested and lengthy tort action–however, in practice, such an action is not feasible to seek redress for workers in the shipbreaking industry in South Asia except in rare cases (e.g., where a third party supports the costs of the litigation).

Tort Liability Approach in the UK

A positive aspect of *Maran Shipping* is,[41] unlike the criminal fine in *Seatrade*, the Court of Appeal found a UK shipowner primarily responsible for the payment of compensation to the wife of a shipbreaking worker who fell to his death whilst breaking a ship of a UK owner, Maran (UK) Shipping Limited. Subject to a final decision on compensation payment, the Court also found that the shipowner had a duty of care because the owner received a high sale price and created scope for a substandard shipbreaking yard to exploit the worker and environment. As Lord Justice Bean (concurring) stated: 'the Defendant obtained the highest possible price for the Vessel and sought to wash their hands of responsibility for anything, however foreseeable, which happened after that'.[42]

The Court established the duty of the shipowners because the shipowner created the danger for the shipbreaking worker mainly for profit and with full knowledge about the outcome.[43] However, the problem with such tort action is its length and the lack of real outcome from the proceedings. As happened in *Maran Shipping*, the plaintiff is yet to receive any compensation payment declared by the Court, after four years of a lengthy and highly contested case. The Court of Appeal of the England and Wales only had to decide whether a duty of care existed, but it is the High Court of Justice, being the Court of original jurisdiction will decide the final issue of compensation after trial.

---

[40] See Chap. 2 of the book.

[41] *Hamida Begum (on behalf of MD Khalil Mollah) v Maran (UK) Limited* [2021] EWCA Civ 326. (*'Maran Shipping'*): at Chap. 2.

[42] Ibid. [141].

[43] Ibid. [116].

However, the prolonged time and still an undecided issue of compensation demonstrate the difficulty of obtaining compensation under tort law. In tort cases, it is also essential to establish jurisdiction, but establishing jurisdiction is difficult with respect to shipbreaking related death, injury, and disease, because of the involvement of many inter-State parties, including the operating owner of a ship, cash buyers, open registry country, and shipbreaking yards.

Because of the issues, although tort law remains relevant to the question of compensatory damages, a cause of action in tort does not offer a reasonable solution to plaintiff workers. The claim may fail, unless a plaintiff worker can prove that he or she was injured or suffered a disease (or, for a family member bringing the claim, that the relative faced death) while breaking a ship owned by a particular shipowner, and that the original shipowner had tight control over the total process of selling a ship.

Hence, other post-incident legal reforms in the shipping industry that aim at creating a civil liability scheme to ensure responsibility of all parties involved in the business and pay compensation to the injured parties provide adequate guidance in in proposing the SLC framework.

Civil Liability Approach in the Shipping Industry in Oil Spill Incidents

With the aim of paying adequate compensation in the event of maritime oil spill incidents, the International Maritime Organization (IMO) adopted the *Convention on Civil Liability for Oil Pollution Damage* (1969 *Civil Liability Convention*) in 1969 and the *Convention on the Establishment of An International Fund for Compensation for Oil Pollution Damage* (1971 *Fund Convention*) in 1971.[44] The goal of the regime is to share responsibility and compensate victims of oil spill incidents that occur during the course of transport of oil. From 1969 to 2006, these two Conventions went through several changes to make the shipowners accountable and address the actual loss suffered by the injured parties.[45] Forming these policies would not have

[44] *International Convention on Civil Liability for Oil Pollution Damage,* opened for signature 29 November 1969, [1969] UNTS 319 (entered into force 19 June 1975) *(1969 Civil Liability Convention)*; the Convention was replaced by the *1992 Protocol to the International Convention on Civil Liability for Oil Pollution Damage,* opened for signature 27 November 1992, [1992] UKTS 86 (entered into force 30 May 1996) *(1992 Civil Liability Convention)*; *International Convention on the Establishment of An International Fund for Compensation for Oil Pollution Damage*, opened for signature 18 December 1971, [1971] ILM 284 (entered into force 16 October 1978) *(1971 Fund Convention)*. This *1971 Fund Convention* was superseded by the *Protocol of 1992* to the *International Convention on the Establishment of An International Fund for Compensation for Oil Pollution Damage*, opened for signature 27 November 1992, [1992] UKTS 87 (entered into force 24 May 2002) *(1992 Fund Convention)*.

[45] Steven Edward Farnworth, 'Liability for Pollution Damage from Offshore Oil Spills: the CLC and Fund Conventions, The EU's Environmental Liability Directive and their Implications for New Zealand Law' (PhD Thesis, University of Waikato, 2017) 329.

been possible unless the shipping and oil industries had accepted their responsibilities - shared responsibility and associated duties for the harms suffered to humans and environment.[46]

By applying the shared responsibility approach of the oil and shipping industries, the IMO achieved an effective policy to address a global problem of oil spillage. There are several key features to this approach. First, the approach resolves the issue of establishing who bears liability. Under the 1969 *Civil Liability Convention*, a ship of a State Party is responsible to pay a limited amount of compensation for polluting the coastal environment and causing economic loss to another State Party in the event of a maritime oil spill. Nevertheless, as the limitation of the compensation amount had proved to be inadequate in the case of larger ships, the IMO introduced the 1971 *Fund Convention* that required the oil industries to undertake liability and supplement the financial limit set under the 1969 *Civil Liability Convention.*

Second, the approach resolved the issue in relation to the scope of liability. According to the 1969 *Civil Liability Convention*, liability is strict. The Convention based the liability on size, rather than value of a ship. Every ship has to maintain insurance for inter-state oil transfer and an injured party can claim directly from the insurance for any economic loss.

Maintaining the global nature of the 1969 *Civil Liability Convention* and the 1971 *Fund Convention* was another very important development of law in this area. These Conventions originally gave the power to the national courts of the host States to define and quantify the damage. As a result, national courts awarded unexpected and very large amounts of compensation. In a number of cases, the national courts declared compensation based on some theoretical models, as with Soviet Methodica in the *Antonio Gramsci* case, which referred to calculating liability by estimating the amount of water contaminated by an oil spill incident.[47] In order to maintain the global nature of the regime, the IMO adopted two amendments in 1992 that converted the earlier 1969 *Civil Liability Convention* and 1971 *Fund Convention* into the 1992 *Civil Liability* and 1992 *Fund Conventions*–and introduced post-spill pollution damage studies to quantify compensation claims. Overall, the main idea was to calculate actual remediable harm caused by an oil spill incident rather than any speculative or punitive damages.[48]

Under the 1992 *Civil Liability Convention*, shipowner means a party registered as the ship's owner, or if the ship is not registered, the party who owns the ship.[49] Whether the shipowner is strictly involved in the operation of the ship is not relevant

[46] See Chap. 7 of the book.

[47] *International Maritime Organization Official Records of the International Conference on Liability and Compensation for Damage in Connection with the Carriages of Certain Substances by Sea, 1984* and *the International Conference on the Revision of the 1969 Civil Liability Convention and the 1971 Fund Convention*, 1992 Vol 2 (IMO, London, 1993) LEG/CONF.6/C.2/SR.3 AT 348–349.

[48] Steven Edward Farnworth, 'Liability for Pollution Damage from Offshore Oil Spills: the CLC and Fund Conventions, The EU's Environmental Liability Directive and their Implications for New Zealand Law' (PhD Thesis, University of Waikato, 2017) 330–331.

[49] *1992 Civil Liability Convention*, art 1 (3).

under the Convention–owner refers to whoever is controlling the ship or who has a passive interest in the ship.[50]

Two important lessons learned from the above oil transportation regime are that: the global shipbreaking industry can implement a civil liability framework with an insurance to act as financial security for any human loss; and forming such a global framework for compensation requires industry support. From the perspective of shipbreaking, the maritime industry, as an influential part of the shipbreaking industry, must take the responsibility to trigger such a legal framework, respecting their corporate liability for the human face of the problem. However, oil transportation and ship transfer are two different perspectives. In the case of shipbreaking, a number of parties get involved, including cash buyers and open registry countries, due to the change of ownership. So direct adoption of the features of the oil transportation mechanisms is not enough for shipbreaking which leads to learn lessons from the certification system of the *International Load Line Convention 1930 and 1966* (*Load Lines Convention*) to track a ship's ownership changes.

Certification System for Tightening the Change of Ownership

The *Load Lines Convention* operates to ensure the safety of ocean-going ships, irrespective of who owns the ship.[51] Every ship must maintain the *Load Lines Certificate* for sailing on international waters and for confirming whether the ship complies with international maritime standards. Drawing analogy with the *Load Lines Convention*, under the proposed SLC it is a requirement for every ship to maintain a shipbreaking liability certificate from cradle to grave. A shipbreaking liability certificate issued by the IMO can thus tighten the change of ownership.[52] However, since the IMO has no onsite inspection system, it may not be possible for the IMO to implement the certificate for shipbreaking yards.

Shipbreaking yards require an additional financial mechanism to push for changes to the unsafe shipbreaking practices, such as beaching, and conventional shipbreaking practices, and to facilitate the payment of compensation.[53] For these particular aspects, lessons learnt from the Piper Alpha incident, an offshore oil rig explosion that killed 167 workers is important. The Piper Alpha incident presents an important

---

[50] Peter Wetterstein, 'Environmental Impairment Liability after the Erika and Prestige Accidents', (2004) 46 *Scandinavian Study of Law* 230, 243.

[51] *International Load Line Convention 1930*, opened for signature 5 July 1930, UNTS 858 (entered into force 1 January 1931) superseded by *1966 International Convention on Load Lines* opened for signature 05 April 1966, 640 UNTS 133 (entered into force 21 July 1968). *(Loadlines Convention*); It is one of the widely ratified of all the IMO conventions: at Phillip Alman et al., 'The International Load Lines Convention: Crossroad to the Future' (October 1992) 29(4) *Marine Technology* 233, 234.

[52] See Chap. 7 of the book.

[53] See Chap. 1 of the book.

lesson with respect to the insurance industry's risk assessment and its influence in changing such unsafe industry practices.[54]

Insurance System for a Risk Assessment and Change to the Unsafe Shipbreaking Practices

Piper Alpha illustrated that the insurance industry's strict enforcement of relevant guidelines can change industry practice. In fact, 'high risk leads to high premiums for insurance' was the principle that forced the offshore industries to implement existing regulatory guidelines for offshore complexes. This risk-based insurance approach is equally relevant to putting pressure on the shipbreaking yards. In other words, this approach would allow insurance to react in line with potential risks in breaking ships. For instance, if the injured workers in the shipbreaking industry have insurance coverage and they start making claims, the insurance will react to this risk, making it more expensive to cover shipbreaking risks and bring about change in the shipbreaking industry.

Based on this example from the Piper Alpha incident, an introduction of a compulsory shipbreaking liability insurance for each shipowner and shipbreaking yard is vital, so that insurance companies can conduct risk assessments followed by onsite inspections of a ship and shipbreaking yard. Further, such pressure from insurance company is important because unless insurers put pressure on the shipowners to comply with the existing regulatory and voluntary standards, the shipbreaking industry would remain non-compliant and risky for workers.

Overall, learning from the post-incident legal forms, it is viable to advocate for a multi-faceted approach using the above regulatory and insurance measures. The approach is to provide a remedy for the victims of shipbreaking accidents and improve workplace health and safety. Importantly, rather than replacing the *Hong Kong Convention*, it is necessary to argue for an additional mechanism to it because the *Hong Kong Convention* is still relevant in regulating the industry.

Indeed, the *Hong Kong Convention* has become a customary principle of law for shipbreaking and its regulatory approach because major shipbreaking nations in South Asia have been using the *Hong Kong Convention* as a model for developing their national laws on shipbreaking. Further, it is not clear whether the highly acclaimed *Hong Kong Convention* is going to address the desired changes and promote improved standards in the South Asian shipbreaking industry. It is also not clear whether the *Hong Kong Convention* will succeed in stopping future shipbreaking incidents and pollution. Considering the uncertainties about the success of the *Hong Kong Convention*, lessons drawn for a supplementary mechanism from the *Basel* and *Kiev Protocols* would prove to be vital.[55]

---

[54] See Chap. 7 of the book.

[55] *Basel Protocol on Liability and Compensation for Damage Resulting from the transboundary Movements of Hazardous Wastes and Their Disposali*, opened for signature 10 December 1999, UN

The international community introduced the *Basel Protocol on Liability and Compensation for Damage Resulting from the transboundary Movements of Hazardous Wastes and Their Disposal* (*Basel Protocol*) and *Protocol on Civil Liability and Compensation for Damage Caused by the Transboundary Effects of Industrial Accidents on Transboundary Waters* (*Kiev Protocol*) to supplement their corresponding conventions after two inter-State incidents involving the waste trade and mining industries.[56]

A unique feature of the *Basel Protocol* is that the instrument transfers liability to the person in control of the wastes and resolves the gap in its pre-existing *Convention on the Control of Transboundary Movements of Hazardous Wastes and their Disposal* (*Basel Convention*).[57] The *Basel Protocol* also allows the victims to claim compensation directly from the insurers and has a provision to allow workers to claim compensation before a court. Insurance is thus mandatory for each inter-State transfer of wastes. The *Kiev Protocol* also resolves the gap in its pre-existing conventions: *Convention on the Protection and Use of Transboundary Watercourses, and International Lakes* and *Convention on the Transboundary Effects of Industrial Accidents* (*Helsinki Conventions*) and provides important lessons for introducing the strict liability of the most beneficial party for paying compensation to the injured parties.

Lessons learned from these *Basel* and *Kiev Protocols* revealed that as a globally accepted legal approach, the IMO may introduce a protocol or regulation to supplement the legal gaps in the *Hong Kong Convention* that does not address the issue of compensation payment to injured workers, those suffering from work-related diseases, or to the families of deceased workers. Such a supplementary liability and compensation framework is vital when an industry is highly dangerous and global in nature involving a number of international private parties.

Doc. UNEP/CHW.1/WG/1/9/2 (not yet in force). *(Basel Protocol)*; *the Protocol on Civil Liability and Compensation for Damage Caused by the Transboundary Effects of Industrial Accidents on Transboundary Waters to the 1992 Convention on the Protection and Use of Transboundary Watercourses and Use of Transboundary Watercourses and International Lakes and to the 1992 Convention on the Transboundary Effects of Industrial Accidents,* opened for signature 21 May 2003, UN Doc. ECE/MP.WAT/11-ECE/CP.TEIA/9 (not yet in force). *(Kiev Protocol)*

[56] *The Convention on the Protection and Use of Transboundary Watercourses, and International Lakes*, signed 17 March 1992, 1936 UNTS 269 (entered into force 6 October 1996); *the Convention on the Transboundary Effects of Industrial Accidents*, signed 18 March 1992, 2105 UNTS 457 (entered into force 18 April 2000). *(the 1992 Helsinki Conventions)*

[57] *The Basel Convention on the Control of Trans-boundary Movements of Hazardous Wastes and their Disposal*, opened for signature 22 March 1989, 1673 UNTS 126 (entered into force 5 May 1992). (*The Basel Convention*)

Translating the Lessons into the Shipbreaking Liability Certificate (SLC)

The lessons learned from the case studies have contributed to the development of the proposed SLC framework that aims to reform the industry practice with a focus on compensation to the workers who suffer workplace death, injury, or work-related disease.

The SLC framework considers the characteristics of the shipbreaking business and the factors that promote the industry in South Asia. The SLC includes the annual volume of ships for breaking, the rate of deaths and injuries, and the international standard of compensation, to determine the SLC charge that includes 30% for SLC administrative fee and the remaining 70% for the shipbreaking liability insurance premium.[58] Moreover, the proposal is to introduce the certificate system for each shipowner as a mechanism to tighten the change of ownership. It also includes mandatory shipbreaking insurance for each ship both for commercial operation and shipbreaking operations. Chapter 9 has explained the administration, operation, and enforcement of the SLC in detail. The IMO is to administer the proposed SLC following the two mechanisms stated below.

First, with respect to the commercial operation of ships, every ship has to maintain the SLC both for sailing on international waters and for breaking. Being an umbrella institution, the IMO or someone acting on its behalf would administer the two SLCs. This would be useful to bring transparency in inter-State transfer of ships. The proposed SLC for a shipbreaking yard would mean that a shipbreaking yard willing to purchase a ship must have IMO confirmation to determine whether a ship has been maintaining a SLC for sailing on international waters.

The underlying concept behind this process is to monitor a ship's inter-State sale process. A cost-free IMO verification process would assist a shipbreaking yard in this process. As discussed in Chap. 1, as a sale agreement between a shipowner and shipbreaking yard starts the process of shipbreaking, the proposed SLC recommends that the sale agreement must include a declaration that the ship has an updated SLC and that the IMO has verified the SLC. Without a confirmation from the IMO, a shipowner, including a cash buyer, cannot transfer a ship. After sale, the parties must inform the IMO about change of ownership so that the IMO has information about the last sale of a ship. In the same vein, before final sale of a ship to a shipbreaking yard, a shipowner must obtain verification from the IMO that the shipbreaking yard has the ship-specific SLC issued by the IMO or someone acting on its behalf.[59]

Second, mandatory shipbreaking insurance as a pre-requisite to obtaining the SLC for both shipowner and a shipbreaking yard can be a timely approach. Besides a guarantee to pay compensation, this insurance mechanism would assist in bringing about accountability for shipowners. Historically, insurance has played a key role in regulating an internationally recognised business, especially if it is risky to human

[58] See Chap. 9 of the book.

[59] Ibid.

health. For example, both the oil and the shipping industries are committed under the *Civil Liability Convention 1992* and the *Fund Convention 1992* to insure each inter-State transfer of oil, which is a key component to tracking each shipowner and oil industry involved in an inter-State oil transfer. Similarly, a compulsory shipbreaking insurance for all ships may, not only cover the risk of deaths and injuries of workers from shipbreaking but also track all shipowners, including a cash buyer involved in selling a ship.[60]

The proposed SLC has two parts in relation to its expenditure.[61] The first 30% of the total cost is for the administrative cost to run the SLC system by the IMO–for example, the IMO may use the amount to maintain a database for all ships, their owners, and insurers. The remaining 70% is to pay the insurance premium. An international maritime insurer can open the insurance and maintain it.[62]

A simple formula using the industry's perspectives, such as weight of a ship, average deaths and injury rates, and an international compensation standard is essential in case of shipbreaking. Based on this formula, the net forecast amount to obtain a shipbreaking liability certificate for a ship weighing 20,000 LDTs would be around USD 1600 annually for a shipowner. If a worker becomes permanently disabled or sick, he or she will receive around USD 5000 per year, and the payment will continue until his or her death or until his or her last minor child becomes an adult (see Column 7 of Table 14). The family of a worker who has died will receive USD 6226 per year, until his or her youngest child reaches adulthood (see Column 8 of Table 14). A lump sum amount would also be acceptable if it is not below the standard amount. Alternatively, insurance companies and the court system can determine the amount of compensation payout for the workers.[63]

The SLC model has the potential not only to be a good system to change overall industry practice by making all shipowners accountable for the deaths, injuries, and diseases in the shipbreaking industry, but it also includes a good compensatory mechanism for paying an adequate compensation payment. As discussed in Chap. 9, the mechanism would bridge the gap between the two scenarios. On one hand, it would bring about transparency and change industry practice in the international shipbreaking market, and on the other hand, it would provide an international standard of compensation to the victim workers.

The SLC, being a civil liability and compensation framework can bring about the necessary change in the industry practice by making all parties responsible in the business process. The shipping industry does bear responsibility for the deaths, injuries and work-related diseases and drive change in the ongoing unsafe industry practices. The next part explains the desired outcomes of the SLC.

---

[60] Ibid.

[61] Ibid.

[62] Ibid.

[63] Chapter 9.

Evaluation of the SLC Framework

One of the important contributions of the proposed SLC framework is to educate shipping industries about their role in the end-of-life consequences of a ship. Many shipping companies and international States with major shipping companies may not have enough knowledge of a ship's destination, since a ship reaches a shipbreaking yard after reflagging and renaming. Such a mechanism would educate the parties as well as introduce financial obligations.

SLC with insurance would ensure an adequate level of pre-cleaning of internal materials. Compulsory insurance and SLC would ensure that pre-cleaning has a link to the insurance premium and costs would be higher if the ships are not pre-cleaned. Alternatively, because pre-cleaning would reduce the in-built waste of a ship, and so the premium level, it would provide a choice to the shipping companies to select between higher premiums and pre-cleaning.

The proposed SLC recommends for a high amount of premium for shipbreaking yards that use the beaching method following a checklist approach (Table 12). As discussed in Chap. 3, the beaching practice used in the South Asian shipbreaking industry is dangerous for workers and environment compared with the dry docking method used in the standard shipbreaking yards, and thus the mechanism and the amount of premium should distinguish between beaching and dry dock methods. Under the proposed SLC, a shipbreaking yard using dry dock method must not have to pay the same amount as for using the beaching method. The introduction of a high premium for substandard shipbreaking yards (e.g., beaching yards) may eventually incentivise the shipbreaking yards to adopt the dry dock method.

The SLC administrative fee and premium should not create a financial burden on the maritime industry. The proposed SLC thus follows a 'weight based' approach. This means the SLC fee and compensation would depend on the Light Displacement Tonnage rather than the number of ships broken each year.[64] This approach is practical because to determine an acceptable level of liability, it is necessary to have the cost linear, with bigger ships having more liability than smaller ships. This means that the ratio of the administrative fee and premium cost of bigger ships would be more than the smaller ships. The proposed SLC also follows the 'less rate of deaths and injuries, less insurance premium' approach. Put another way, the fewer the casualties, the lower the insurance premium. A reasonable expectation of this approach is to keep the insurance premium as low as possible, the shipowners and shipbreaking businesses will take genuine step to prevent casualties.

The proposed SLC may encourage improving the facilities of a shipbreaking yard anywhere in the world. This is because, under the proposed SLC framework, the insurer needs to consider the available facilities of a shipbreaking yard to determine the concession from the maximum premium calculated following the baselines (see section 'Enforcement Measures' of Chap. 9) for a shipbreaking yard before

[64] Light Displacement Tonnage means 'the weight of a ship with all its permanent equipment excluding the weight of cargoes, persons, fuel, dunnage and ballast': at *Dictionary.com* (online at 23 April 2020).

purchasing a ship-specific SLC. A shipbreaking yard with all *Hong Kong Convention* facilities would need not to pay a premium except the SLC administrative fee (30% of the total SLC charge). This would incentivise the compliant shipbreaking yards.

By accepting the proposed SLC, the international shipping industry may see shipbreaking as a means of improving the economy of the developing country, rather than only as an end for the maritime industry. The employment and economic impacts for the shipbreaking industry will depend on the volume of ships (calculated in LDT) broken in South Asia.

Accordingly, if, because of the SLC framework, the health and safety standards in shipbreaking yards improve, this will not have an adverse impact on the shipbreaking business. Moreover, because of the financial security, the shipbreaking industry would acquire skilled workers. On the other hand, if the substandard shipbreaking yards do not invest in improving their standards to become compliant with the IMO guidelines, then the IMO should discourage the ship's purchase and use of the shipbreaking yard by not issuing the SLC.

An underlying objective of the SLC is to gradually change the industry practices and to monitor the changes taking place. The insurance premium should take into consideration the improvement of standards in the shipbreaking industry, and the SLC is to monitor the change of ownership from cradle to grave of ships. It is emphasised that for shipbreaking to survive in South Asia, there needs to be a major shift from the current practices and the SLC can assist in bringing about the necessary change.

Future Research Direction

From the perspective of the shipbreaking industry's global nature, future research would look for adequate government and industry support and aid to run a pilot study on the operation of the SLC. Future research also needs to focus on regulatory frameworks in other countries, such as in China and Turkey, to examine how their domestic legal frameworks address the legal gap in the compensatory framework and see how the SLC framework would contribute to these countries.

Future research could also investigate the willingness of the IMO Member States to introduce an international agreement following the SLC model. This could be similar to the *Kiev* and *Basel Protocols* to compensate loss of victims from transboundary harms of waste trade and industrial activities.

Another direction to future research would be to examine the importance of unionisation for making changes in the industry practice. This could be useful to persuade the ILO to introduce the proposed SLC framework in case of the IMO's reluctance to that direction. Future researchers could also investigate the reinsurance market in relation to the proposed shipbreaking insurance in the shipbreaking industry. This would give more information about the possibility of introducing the shipbreaking insurance. Moreover, future researchers could also test the views of the industries, such as the maritime insurer, on the SLC framework.

Concluding Comments

The proposed SLC mechanism is something that is achievable in a truly effective and practicable manner with the support from the global shipping industry. Efforts to ensure policymaking and implementation of the SLC must in the first place come from the shipping companies and their States, who hold majority membership in the IMO. However, it is true that the EU, with its community-based financial liability scheme, can make a useful contribution in that direction. Nevertheless, instead of giving benefit to the shipowners, the EU, being the biggest unit of major shipping nations, should take leadership to establish a remedy system as proposed in this book. The legal framework for the proposed SLC would thus originate from the IMO followed by the EU's support.

The assessment and review of the proposed SLC mechanism by the international community in general, and by the shipping industry in particular, should be based upon an integrated understanding of the above noted underlying values and policy objectives. Their coherency also is vital both for furthering the international principles of law by exposing the questionable business model of shipbreaking, and for bolstering support for applying the rectificatory justice theory that would in a true sense rectify the global injustice happening in the South Asian shipbreaking industry.

In conclusion, arguably, the implementation of the proposed SLC would be the missing thread that would enable ships to complete their sailing from cradle-to-grave upholding justice to shipbreaking workers and environment.

Bibliography

Articles/Books/Reports

Adshead, Julie, 'The Application and Development of the Polluter-Pays Principle Across Jurisdictions in Liability for Marine Oil Pollution: The Tales of the 'Erika' and the 'Prestige' (2018) 30 *Journal of Environmental Law* 425

Anghie, Antony, 'Francisco de Vitoria and the Colonial Origins of International Law' (1996) 5 (3) *Society and Legal Studies* 321

Ahmed, Ishtiaque, 'Ungovernable Ships At The End of Lives and The Response of The Hong Kong Convention: A Critical Appraisal of the Treaty on Shipbreaking from the Perspective of South Asian Shipbreaking Nations' (2020) 18 *Santa Clara Journal of International Law* 124

Ahmed, Ishtiaque, 'Unravelling Socio-Economic and Ecological Distribution Conflicts in Shipbreaking in Bangladesh for Addressing Negative Externalities in Law and Policy Making,' 2020 (29) 2, *Minnesota Journal of International Law* 159

Ahmed, Rukhsar and Kamran Siddiqui, 'Shipbreaking Industry in Pakistan-Problems and Prospects' (September 2013) 3 (9) *International Journal of Management, IT and Engineering* 140

Alman, Phillip et al., 'The International Load Lines Convention: Crossroad to the Future' (October 1992) 29(4) *Marine Technology* 233

Bhattachargee, Saurabh, 'From Basel to Hong Kong: International Environment Regulation of Ship-Recycling Takes One Step Forward and Two Steps Back,' 2009 (2) *Trade Law and Development* 193

Cairns, George, 'A Critical Scenario Analysis of end-of-life Ship Disposal: The Bottom of the Pyramid as Opportunity and Graveyard' (2014) 10(3) *Journal of Critical Perspectives on International Business* 172

Gardiner, Stephen M., 'Ethics and Global Climate Change' (April 2004) 114(4) *University of Chicago Press Journals* 580, 555–600

Roy, Alpana, 'Postcolonial Theory and Law: A Critical Introduction' (2008) 29 *Adelaide Law Review* 315

Jain, K., J.F. Pruyn and J. Hopman, 'Critical Analysis of the Hong Kong International Convention on Ship Recycling' (2013) 7 (10) *International Journal of Environment, Ecological, Geological and Mining Engineering* 683

Mieth, Corinna, 'Global Injustice: Individual Duties and Non-Ideal Institutional Circumstances' (2012) 12(1) *Civitas-Revista de Ciencias Sociais* 47

Pogge, Thomas, 'World Poverty and Human Rights' (2005) 19(1) *Ethics and International Affairs* 1

Sen, Amartya, 'Rawls versus Bentham: An Axiomatic Examination of the Pure Distribution Problem' (1974) 4 *Theory and Decision* 301, 302–309 https://doi-org.dbgw.lis.curtin.edu.au/10.1007/BF00136651

Singer, Peter, 'Famine, Affluence and Morality' (1972) 1 *Philosophy and Public Affairs* 229, 229–233

Wetterstein, Peter, 'Environmental Impairment Liability after the Erika and Prestige Accidents', (2004) 46 *Scandinavian Study of Law* 230

Christopher George Weeramanty, *Universalising International Law* (Martinus Nijhoff Publishers, 2004) 85

Farnworth, Steven Edward, 'Liability for Pollution Damage from Offshore Oil Spills: the CLC and Fund Conventions, The EU's Environmental Liability Directive and their Implications for New Zealand Law' (PhD Thesis, University of Waikato, 2017)

Galley, Michael, *Shipbreaking: Hazards and Liabilities* (Springer International Publishing, 2014)

Karim, Md Saiful, 'Recycling of Ships' in *Prevention of Pollution of the Maritime Environment from Vessels: Potential Limit of the International Maritime Organisation*' (Springer, 2015)

Karim, Saiful, *Shipbreaking in Developing Countries: A Requiem for Environmental Justice from the Perspectives of Bangladesh* (Taylor and Francis Group, 2018)

Sen, Amartya, *The Idea of Justice* (Allen Lane, 2009) 7

Jenssem, Ingvild et al, 'Impact Report 2018–2019' (Research Report, NGO Shipbreaking Platform, 2020) https://shipbreakingplatform.org/wp-content/uploads/2020/06/NGOSBP-Bi-Annual-Report-18-19.pdf

Cases

State v Seatrade [Rotterdam District Court, three-judge economic division for criminal cases], Public Prosecutor Office 10/994550–15, 15 March 2018 reported in (2018) Rechtspraak.nl 1, ECLI:NL:RBROT:2018:2108 .

Hamida Begum (on behalf of MD Khalil Mollah) v Maran (UK) Limited [2021] EWCA Civ 326. (*'Maran Shipping'*)

Treaties

1992 Protocol to the International Convention on Civil Liability for Oil Pollution Damage, opened for signature 27 November 1992, [1992] UKTS 86 (entered into force 30 May 1996)

Basel Convention on the Control of Trans-boundary Movements of Hazardous Wastes and their Disposal, opened for signature 22 March 1989, 1673 UNTS 126 (entered into force 5 May 1992)

Basel Protocol on Liability and Compensation for Damage Resulting from the transboundary Movements of Hazardous Wastes and Their Disposal, opened for signature 10 December 1999, UN Doc. UNEP/CHW.1/WG/1/9/2 (not yet in force)

Convention on the Protection and Use of Transboundary Watercourses, and International Lakes, signed 17 March 1992, 1936 UNTS 269 (entered into force 6 October 1996); *the Convention on the Transboundary Effects of Industrial Accidents*, signed 18 March 1992, 2105 UNTS 457 (entered into force 18 April 2000)

International Conference on the Revision of the 1969 Civil Liability Convention and the 1971 Fund Convention, 1992 Vol 2 (IMO, London, 1993) LEG/CONF.6/C.2/SR.3 AT 348–349

International Convention on Civil Liability for Oil Pollution Damage, opened for signature 29 November 1969, [1969] UNTS 319 (entered into force 19 June 1975)

International Convention on the Establishment of An International Fund for Compensation for Oil Pollution Damage, opened for signature 18 December 1971, [1971] ILM 284 (entered into force 16 October 1978)

International Load Line Convention 1930, opened for signature 5 July 1930, UNTS 858 (entered into force 1 January 1931) superseded by *1966 International Convention on Load Lines* opened for signature 05 April 1966 , 640 UNTS 133 (entered into force 21 July 1968)

International Maritime Organization Official Records of the International Conference on Liability and Compensation for Damage in Connection with the Carriages of Certain Substances by Sea, 1984

Protocol of 1992 to the *International Convention on the Establishment of An International Fund for Compensation for Oil Pollution Damage*, opened for signature 27 November 1992, [1992] UKTS 87 (entered into force 24 May 2002)

Protocol on Civil Liability and Compensation for Damage Caused by the Transboundary Effects of Industrial Accidents on Transboundary Waters to the 1992 Convention on the Protection and Use of Transboundary Watercourses and Use of Transboundary Watercourses and International Lakes and to the 1992 Convention on the Transboundary Effects of Industrial Accidents, opened for signature 21 May 2003, UN Doc. ECE/MP.WAT/11-ECE/CP.TEIA/9 (not yet in force)

Regulation (EU) No. 1257/2013 of the European Parliament and of the Council of 20 November 2013 on Ship Recycling and Amending Regulation (EC) No. 1013/2016 and Directive 2009/16/ EC, 2013, OJ (L 330) 1

The Hong Kong International Convention for the Safe and Environmentally Sound Recycling of Ships, opened for Signature 1 September 2009, IMO Doc. SR/CONF45 (not yet in force) Annex (*'Regulation for Safe and Environmentally Sound Recycling of Ships)*

Others

Agyare-Dwomoh, Yaa, A Green Compliant Ship Recycling Facility in South Africa, Frost and Sullivan Africa (online) https://frost-sullivan-africa.prezly.com/a-green-compliant-ship-recycling-facility-in-south-africa

NGO Shipbreaking Platform, 'Two Fatal Accidents at Indian Yards Under EU Scrutiny' (Press Release, 10th September 2019) https://shipbreakingplatform.org/fatal-accidents-at-indian-yards-under-eu-scrutiny/

Appendix
A–Insurance Claim Procedure

1. *The Grievance Procedure*

An injured or diseased worker or a family member of a deceased worker or a NGO on behalf of the worker or their family may file a claim. The most efficient way would be to allow for a defined independent entity, such as a Worker's Advocate as mentioned earlier, to represent the workers in making compensation claims. If necessary, the Worker's Advocate or other entity could also organise sessions to provide legal advice and representation. The SLC administrative fee may provide financial support to such entity for their legal fee.

Involvement of a defined independent entity would empower the victim. In the absence of collective representations and functioning worker-management dialogue,[1] representation by the entity may be a valuable means of improving access to justice for the workers.

Following a claim, the insurance provider or the shipbreaking yard may have the right to add the shipowner's insurer of the particular ship to the insurance claim and proceed with the payment jointly followed by medical examinations or such other steps, as are necessary steps. Co-payment or deductibles between the two insurers or guarantors are required to provide maximum protection to victims, but failure from the insured to pay deductibles or co-payments cannot be an excuse to delay any such claims. If necessary, the relevant shipowners and shipbreaking yards can later indemnify the amount of the insurances.

2. *Filing a Claim*

The proposed SLC may set up a toll-free 'Worker Helpline' to provide workers with an independent reporting channel to anonymise concerns about a shipbreaking yard to the insurance provider. In addition, the insurance provider of a shipbreaking yard would be required to open a website for the purpose of introducing an online platform to workers for filing a compensation claim. Under the proposed SLC, wearing

[1] International Metalworkers Foundation, 'Status of Shipbreaking Workers in India- A Survey' (Project Report, IMF-FNV Project in India, 2004–2007) 2.

M. Z. Ali, *Worker Injustices in the South Asian Shipbreaking Industry*, International Law in Asia, https://doi.org/10.1007/978-981-95-8325-6

a tag that includes the 'Worker Helpline' number and website address should be a compulsory requirement.

The helpline and website should have an individualised channel for assisting the compensation claim. A better option would be to have a body such as a NGO to assist and support workers in making the claims before a defined independent entity such as a Worker's Advocate starts representing the workers in making compensation claims. The IMO can provide financial assistances to the NGO out of annual SLC administrative fees for ensuring the independence from insurers.

3. *Fact-Finding*

Following a claim, the duty would lie on the insurance provider of the shipbreaking yard to add the shipowner's insurance provider in the claim process and to notify the concerned shipbreaking yard owner immediately. The notification would allow shipbreaking yards to comment on the claim's authenticity. Equally, considering comments and the victim's claim, the insurance providers are to conduct a preliminary investigation and test the claim's veracity before proceeding to the final investigation. At this stage, the insurance provider of a shipbreaking yard can pay compensation to the victim, which can be set-off later from the final compensation amount after finalisation of the investigation process. The insurance providers would then pay the compensation from the insurances jointly. The process may empower the workers to seek relief quickly, as they are often otherwise unable to proceed with disputes due to impediments such as finances, distance, and weak labour status. The same procedure will be applied after a court's direction if a victim has to go to court at any stage. The IMO should consider these factors seriously.

The manufacturer's authorised representative in the EU is Springer Nature Customer Service Centre GmbH, Europaplatz 3, 69115 Heidelberg, Germany. If you have any concerns regarding our products, please contact ProductSafety@springernature.com

Printed and bound by CPI Group (UK) Ltd, Croydon, CR0 4YY
21/09/2026
02219986-0010